Communications
in Computer and Information Science   792

Commenced Publication in 2007
Founding and Former Series Editors:
Alfredo Cuzzocrea, Xiaoyong Du, Orhun Kara, Ting Liu, Dominik Ślęzak,
and Xiaokang Yang

More information about this series at http://www.springer.com/series/7899

Sokratis K. Katsikas · Vasilios Zorkadis (Eds.)

E-Democracy – Privacy-Preserving, Secure, Intelligent E-Government Services

7th International Conference, E-Democracy 2017
Athens, Greece, December 14–15, 2017
Proceedings

 Springer

Editors
Sokratis K. Katsikas 🆔
Norwegian University of Science
   and Technology
Gjøvik
Norway

Vasilios Zorkadis 🆔
Data Protection Authority
Athens
Greece

ISSN 1865-0929   ISSN 1865-0937 (electronic)
Communications in Computer and Information Science
ISBN 978-3-319-71116-4   ISBN 978-3-319-71117-1   (eBook)
https://doi.org/10.1007/978-3-319-71117-1

Library of Congress Control Number: 2017959603

Printed on acid-free paper

This Springer imprint is published by Springer Nature
The registered company is Springer International Publishing AG
The registered company address is: Gewerbestrasse 11, 6330 Cham, Switzerland

Preface

This book contains the proceedings of the 7th International Conference on eDemocracy (e-Democracy 2017), held in Athens, Greece, December 14–15, 2017. The conference continues from previous events that have always been held in Athens, the cradle of democracy, initially every three years starting in 2003 and every two years since 2009.

ICT innovations such as big data, Internet of Things, cloud computing as well as intelligent systems employed in e-Government services raise issues relating to security, privacy, and data protection. Governments want to integrate more services and enhance participation, but they have to convince the users that they can be trusted. At the same time, e-government services need to improve their efficiency and to do so they need to re-engineer their back office processes, to support them with intelligent systems, but also improve openness, collaboration, and citizen participation. This last point can be hugely enhanced by offering citizens participation in devolved decision-making and e-voting facilities for elections. Such services are often quoted as being dependent on political will, but are the systems and services ready? Are they privacy-friendly and secure to withstand attacks and malicious or even terrorist activities in cyberspace? Are they trustworthy to be embraced by the citizens in a digital world that is moving fast and becoming more intelligent? And finally, where should be drawn the "golden line" between anonymity and confidentiality, and accountability and certification?

These were the questions and the focus of the 7th occasion of the International Conference on e-Democracy. The conference was organized by the Scientific Council for the Information Society, in co-operation with the Hellenic Data Protection Authority. It was intended, as in previous occasions, to provide a forum for presenting and debating the latest developments in the field, from a technical, political, legal, and regulatory point of view. The conference attracted 44 high-quality submissions, each of which was assigned to four referees for review; the review process resulted in accepting 18 papers to be included in the conference proceedings.

e-Democracy 2017 brought together academic researchers, industry developers, and policy makers. We thank the attendees for coming to Athens to participate and debate the new emerging advances in the field of e-democracy.

We would like to express our thanks to all those who assisted us in organizing the event and putting together the program. We are very grateful to the Program Committee members for their timely and rigorous reviews of the papers. Thanks are also due to the Organizing Committee for the event. Last but by no means least, we would like to thank all the authors who submitted their work to the conference and contributed to an interesting set of conference proceedings.

December 2017

Sokratis K. Katsikas
Vasilios Zorkadis

Organization

Conference Honorary Chair

Alexander B. Sideridis — Agricultural University of Athens, Greece

Steering Committee

Co-chairs

Sokratis K. Katsikas — Norwegian University of Science and Technology, Gjøvik, Norway and University of Piraeus, Greece

Vasilis Zorkadis — Scientific Council for the Information Society, Greece

Secretary

Philippos Mitletton — Scientific Council for the Information Society, Greece

Treasurer

George Loukeris — Scientific Council for the Information Society, Greece

Members

Constantina Costopoulou	Agricultural University of Athens, Greece
Constantine Yialouris	Agricultural University of Athens, Greece
Elias Pimenidis	University of the West of England, UK
Euripidis N. Loukis	University of the Aegean, Greece
Zoi Kardasiadou	European Data Protection Supervisor, EU
Irene Vassilaki	Scientific Council for the Information Society, Greece
Lazaros Iliadis	Democritus University of Thrace, Greece
Spyros Voulgaris	Vrije Universiteit, The Netherlands
Charalampos Patrikakis	Technological Educational Institute of Piraeus, Greece

Technical Program Committee

Co-chairs

Sokratis K. Katsikas   Norwegian University of Science and Technology,
     Gjøvik, Norway and University of Piraeus, Greece
Vasilis Zorkadis   Scientific Council for the Information Society, Greece

Members

Zacharoula Andreopoulou	Aristotle University of Thessaloniki, Greece
Panagiotis Andriotis	University of the West of England, UK
Leonidas Anthopoulos	University of Applied Science (TEI) of Larissa, Greece
Maria Bottis	Ionian University, Greece
Athena Bourka	ENISA, EU
Elias Carayannis	George Washington University, USA
David Chadwick	University of Kent, UK
Nathan Clarke	University of Plymouth, UK
Tina Costopoulou	Agricultural University of Athens, Greece
Ernesto Damiani	EBTIC/Khalifa University, UAE
Sabrina De Capitani di Vimercati	Università degli Studi di Milano, Italy
Prokopios Drogkaris	ENISA, EU
Carmen Fernández-Gago	University of Malaga, Spain
Sara Foresti	Università degli Studi di Milano, Italy
Steven Furnell	University of Plymouth, UK
Jürgen Fuß	University of Applied Sciences Upper Austria, Austria
Dimitris Geneiatakis	Aristotle University of Thessaloniki, Greece
Christos Georgiadis	University of Macedonia, Greece
Dimitris Gouscos	University of Athens, Greece
Evangelos Grigoroudis	Technical University of Crete, Greece
Stefanos Gritzalis	University of the Aegean, Greece
M.P. Gupta	Indian Institute of Technology Delhi (IIT Delhi), India
Marit Hansen	Unabhängiges Landeszentrum für Datenschutz Schleswig-Holstein, Germany
Lazaros Iliadis	Democritus University of Thrace, Greece
Christos Kalloniatis	University of the Aegean, Greece
Ioanna Kantzavelou	Technological Educational Institute of Athens, Greece
Zoe Kardasiadou	EDPS, EU
Sotiris Karetsos	Agricultural University of Athens, Greece
Maria Karyda	University of the Aegean, Greece
Spyros Kokolakis	University of the Aegean, Greece
Nicholas Kolokotronis	University of Peloponnese, Greece
Panayiotis Kotzanikolaou	University of Piraeus, Greece
Stewart Kowalski	Norwegian University of Science and Technology, Norway

Costas Lambrinoudakis	University of Piraeus, Greece
Georgios Lappas	Technological Educational Institute (T.E.I.) of Western Macedonia, Greece
Kostas Limniotis	Hellenic Data Protection Authority, Greece
Antonio Lioy	Politecnico di Torino, Italy
Javier Lopez	University of Malaga, Spain
Nikos Lorentzos	Agricultural University of Athens, Greece
Euripidis Loukis	University of the Aegean, Greece
Emmanouil Magkos	Ionian University, Greece
Vojtech Merunka	Czech Technical University in Prague, Czech University of Life Sciences in Prague, Czech Republic
Lilian Mitrou	University of the Aegean, Greece
Martin Molhanec	Czech Technical University in Prague, Czech Republic
Haralambos Mouratidis	University of Brighton, UK
Maria Ntaliani	Agricultural University of Athens, Greece
Christoforos Ntantogian	University of Piraeus, Greece
Martin Olivier	University of Pretoria, South Africa
Rolf Oppliger	eSECURITY Technologies, Switzerland
Peter Parycek	Danube University Krems, Austria
Andreas Pashalidis	BSI, Germany
Charalampos Patrikakis	Piraeus University of Applied Sciences, Greece
Alois Paulin	Vienna University of Technology, Austria
Günther Pernul	Universität Regensburg, Germany
Elias Pimenidis	University of the West of England, UK
Nikolaos Polatidis	University of Brighton, UK
Vassilis Prevelakis	Technical University Braunschweig, Germany
Panagiotis Rizomiliotis	University of the Aegean, Greece
Pierangela Samarati	Università degli Studi di Milano, Italy
Vittorio Scarano	University of Salerno, Italy
Alexander Sideridis	Agricultural University of Athens, Greece
Miguel Soriano	Universitat Politècnica de Catalunya, Spain
Theodoros Spyridopoulos	University of the West of England, UK
Antonis Stasis	Hellenic Ministry of Interior and Administrative Reconstruction, Greece
Stephanie Teufel	University of Fribourg, Switzerland
Aggeliki Tsohou	Ionian University, Greece
Vasileios Vlachos	Technological Educational Institute of Larissa, Greece
Spyros Voulgaris	VU University Amsterdam, The Netherlands
Edgar Weippl	SBA Research, Austria
Christos Xenakis	University of Piraeus, Greece
Constantine Yialouris	Agricultural University of Athens, Greece
Thomas Zacharias	University of Edinburgh, UK
Jianying Zhou	Singapore University of Technology and Design, Singapore

Additional Reviewers

Vasiliki Diamantopoulou	University of Brighton, UK
Sebastian Groll	Nexis Secure, Germany
Dimitrios Kogias	Piraeus University of Applied Sciences, Greece
Stefanos Malliaros	University of Piraeus, Greece
Christian Richthammer	Universität Regensburg, Germany
Maria Sideri	University of the Aegean, Greece
Manfred Vielberth	Universität Regensburg, Germany

Contents

E-Democracy

e-Participation Provision and Demand Analysis for Greek Municipalities

Constantina Costopoulou[1](✉), Filotheos Ntalianis[2], Maria Ntaliani[1], Sotiris Karetsos[1], and Evagelia Gkoutzioupa[1]

[1] Informatics Laboratory, Department of Agricultural Economics and Rural Development, Agricultural University of Athens, 75 Iera Odos, 118 55 Athens, Greece
`{tina,ntaliani,karetsos}@aua.gr, evagelia.gkoutz@gmail.com`
[2] Department of Business Administration, University of Piraeus, Karaoli & Dimitriou 80, 185 34 Piraeus, Greece
`filotheos@unipi.gr`

Abstract. Municipalities have acknowledged that improving citizens' access to online information and services, and engaging them in policy and decision-making enhance local democracy. Electronic participation can empower citizens who are interested in government decision-making and public issues. The objective of this article is to investigate the supply side and the demand side of electronic participation in Greek municipalities. Using content analysis for 325 Greek municipal portals we depict the supply of electronic participation for 2017, by employing the Citizen Web Empowerment Index. A comparison of the index for 2015 and 2017 is presented. Electronic participation demand is estimated using a sample of 212 citizens. The main findings show that municipal electronic participation provision progress is slow paced, although citizens express interest for involvement in local government issues. Municipalities should focus on well-designed electronic participation tools and services, taking into account citizens' needs to engage them in public affairs.

Keywords: Electronic participation · Electronic democracy · Citizens · Municipalities · Greece

1 Introduction

Empowering citizens through enhancing the collaboration among governments and the public, improving access to information and services, and engaging them in policy and decision-making through Information and Communication Technology (ICT) is considered as electronic participation (e-participation) [1, 2]. E-participation creates democratic and instrumental values [3]. It is related to fostering civic engagement and open, participatory governance focusing on citizens' needs, enabling opportunities for consultation and dialogue between citizens and governments, and making societies more inclusive [1].

E-participation is not merely a one-way, but rather a two-way transaction that requires not only the involvement of public agencies but also the engagement of citizens

© Springer International Publishing AG 2017
S.K. Katsikas and V. Zorkadis (Eds.): E-Democracy 2017, CCIS 792, pp. 3–14, 2017.
https://doi.org/10.1007/978-3-319-71117-1_1

[4]. Nowadays, citizens have expressed an increasing interest in participating in local community issues. Thus, governments try to improve the efficiency and effectiveness of public services, using new tools at local level. Nonetheless, research shows that there has not been achieved widespread support for citizen participation through electronic government (e-government) at local level, for instance electronic deliberation [5]. Municipalities can play a significant role in enhancing e-participation.

In literature, e-participation research focuses mainly on the fields of e-participation services, functionality, supply, effects, and evaluation. Surprisingly, only a small number of studies addresses the demand side of e-participation. Various authors support that till today although literature on the supply side of e-government services is increasing only few studies take into account citizens' requirements [3, 6–9].

In this light, the following research questions will be addressed in this article:

- *What is the status of e-participation services provided by municipalities?*
- *What types of e-participation services would be desired by citizens?*

The empirical research on Greek municipalities described in this article attempts to give answers to the questions through two surveys, namely e-participation provision and demand. The structure of the paper is as follows: after this introduction, a background of e-participation and Greek local government is given. Next, we provide an analysis of the supply side of e-participation of 325 Greek municipalities. A content analysis of their portals has been undertaken based on the Citizen Web Empowerment Index (CWEI). Then, we depict the demand side of e-participation by Greek citizens using a sample of 212 citizens. The article ends with the findings of this study and a discussion on the research questions.

2   Background

This section gives a brief overview of the e-participation concept, the level of e-participation and the local government structure in Greece. E-participation is still an evolving concept [1]. It is defined as the use of ICT to broaden and deepen political participation by enabling citizens to connect with one another and with their elected representatives [10]. Factors influencing the e-participation development include: international drivers of change, demographic characteristics, level of ICT development, level of democracy, types of participation, decision-making and legal framework, institutional and political resistance, digital divide, security and trust, privacy concerns and autonomy, attention to the demand side and evaluation [11].

ICT could facilitate citizen participation in public affairs. Basic tools (email, online chatting, online discussion forums), Web 2.0 tools (blogs, Facebook, online social networking, Twitter), mechanisms (electronic voting, reputation systems), and tracking and analysis techniques (data mining, simulations, data visualization) can contribute to better engaging citizens to contact government, express themselves, participate in discussions, and propose public issues.

The United Nations (UN) measure e-participation according to a three-stage model based on the E-Participation Index (EPI) that includes: (i) *e-information* – provision of information on the Internet, (ii) *e-consultation* – organizing public consultations online, and (iii) *e-decision-making* – involving citizens directly in decision processes. The goal of the EPI index is to assess the availability of e-participation tools on national government portals for each of the above uses at a particular time instance. The comparative ranking of countries can just be used as an indicative of the broad trends in promoting citizen engagement [1, 12].

In 2014, according to the UN measurement on e-participation development, Greece holds the 17th position with EPI 0.80 (with max value 1), receiving 77.8% (out of 100) for e-information, 86.4% for e-consultation and 22.2% for e-decision making stages (UN, 2014). In the same survey for 2016, United Kingdom holds the first place with EPI equal to 1, and Australia and Japan hold the second place with EPI 0.98. Greece is placed 65th with EPI 0.61, analyzed in 58.8% for e-information, 78.9% for e-consultation and 28.6% for e-decision making stages [1]. Comparing the EPI for 2014 and 2016 for Greece, a significant decrease can be noticed. This is reflected for all three stages percentages.

Focusing on the Greek case, the administrative division supports three levels of local government. The first level includes 325 municipalities, which consists of municipal units, and these are composed of communities; the second level consists of 13 regions; and the third level consists of 7 decentralized administrations. The decentralized administrations are supervised by the general secretary appointed by the Greek Government. The regions and municipalities are fully self-governed.

In 1998, the administrative system changed with the implementation of "Kapodistrias plan". Before and after the "Kapodistrias" reform, the difference between municipalities and communities was merely a matter of size. Municipalities were big and urban whereas communities were small, single villages. From 441 municipalities and 5,382 communities (a total of 5,775), the reform reduced to 900 municipalities and 133 communities (a total of 1,033) [13]. As of 1 January 2011, in accordance with the "Kallikratis programme", the administrative system of Greece was drastically overhauled. The "Kallikratis programme" reduced even further the number of municipalities to just 325.

3 e-Participation Provision

3.1 CWEI 2017

Previous work of the authors [14, 15] has focused on measuring in 2015 e-participation in Greek municipalities by using "Citizens Web Empowerment Index" (CWEI), proposed by [16]. CWEI has been chosen because it can directly be implemented and has already been used in literature for measuring citizen participation in municipalities. The EPI index presented in Sect. 2 cannot be used for the case of municipalities, since it is a comparative index for measuring e-participation among countries. CWEI is a multidimensional indicator as it is composed of four sub-indicators, namely e-information, Web 2.0 tools and services, e-consultation and e-decision making process. The objective of these sub-indicators, is the measurement of various aspects of citizens' participation via their municipal portal. These sub-indicators are described as follows [17]:

- E-information: considers the presence of general information on the municipal portal referring to the city and its policies.
- Web 2.0 tools and services: refers to the existence of social networking tools, Web TV and open government data strategy.
- E-consultation: refers to various elements relative to the way of receiving information through the municipal portal.
- E-decision making process: assesses evidence that municipality considers the opinion of citizens and others in decision-making processes.

Each sub-indicator is calculated on the basis of the presence of certain elements characterizing the structure of the portal under study. The maximum CWEI value is 100, whereas each sub-indicator has a different theoretical value:

$$CWEI = e\text{-}information + web\,2.0\,tools\,and\,services + e\text{-}consultation + e\text{-}decision\,making$$

In order to compare the level of e-participation provision between 2015 and 2017, a new measurement was conducted in 2017. Out of 325 municipalities, 321 were examined according to the CWEI index, since four of them either do not have a portal or their portal is under construction (the municipalities of Zacharo, Oropediou–Lasithi, the island of Serifos, and Fourni islands). The measurement of CWEI took place from March till April 2017. The characteristics of the index have been evaluated by three experts. The evaluation of municipalities' portals is based on quantitative content analysis according to the criteria of the CWEI index that are analyzed as follows.

Regarding the "e-information" sub-indicator the following results have been found:

- *Government structure:* only 5% provides no information on the municipality organizational structure; 6% has a few; 24% has average; 56% much; and 9% very much.
- *Segmentation or life events*: 20% has none; 17% a few; 36% has average; 21% much; and 6% very much.
- *Contact details:* 1% has none information for communicating with the municipality administration and employees; 12% a few; 23% average; 30% much; and 34% very much.
- *Policies and procedures:* 9% has none data on policies and procedures followed and relevant legislation; 32% a few; 32% average; 19% much; and 8% very much.
- *Budget:* 49% has none information on the municipality budget; 9% a few; 11% average; 15% much; and 16% very much.
- *City Council minutes:* 50% has available information on memoirs of the City Council meetings; 24% a few; 10% average; 12% much; and 4% very much.
- *Newsletter and/or Web magazine:* 78 municipalities (25%) have only newsletter and 26 (8%) only Web magazine. 198 municipalities (62%) have neither of the two and only 16 (5%) have both.

Concerning the "Web 2.0 tools and services" sub-indicator, the following results have been found:

- *Blog, Forum:* 8 (3%) municipalities have only a separate blog; 37 (11%) municipalities have only a forum; 274 (86%) have neither of them and none municipality has both.

Chat: 4 municipalities have chat.

- *Social network presence:* 177 Facebook, 5 Flickr, 89 Youtube, none Skype, 86 Twitter, 6 Instagram, 10 LinkedIn, 5 Pinterest, 3 issuu, 1 others and 134 have none of them. It is noted that in this measurement each municipality could select more than one social network.
- *Mobile services:* 70% has no applications for mobile devices; 26% has only RSS; 2% has only mobile applications; and 2% has RSS and mobile applications.
- *Web TV:* 1% (3 municipalities) have a Web TV to communicate information.
- *Open data strategy:* 3% has no information for the municipality's strategy and time schedule; 21% has a few; 29% average; 26% much; and 21% very much.

It has to be noted that the "Web strategy evaluation" characteristic in "Web 2.0 tools and services" sub-indicator of CWEI, has not been taken into account because it could not be applied in this study. Referring to the "e-consultation" sub-indicator the following results have been found:

- *Online polls and surveys*: 82% of the municipalities have none, 3% have only polls and 15% has both polls and surveys.
- *Online complaints:* 73% of the municipalities have online forms for enabling citizens in submitting their complaints.
- *Reputation systems:* 94% has no reputation systems.
- *Mayor's direct online relation with citizens:* 52% has services for establishing the Mayor's direct online relation with citizens.

Concerning the "e-decision making process" sub-indicator the following results have been found:

- *Evidence for citizen opinion consideration:* 88% has not at all such evidence; 6% has a few; 4% average; 1% much; and 1% very much.
- *Evidence for complaint consideration:* 88% has not at all such evidence; 6% has a few; 4% average; 1% much; and 1% very much.

3.2　Comparison CWEI 2015 and 2017

By adopting the CWEI index for the evaluation of municipal portals, in this section we present the comparison for the years of 2015 and 2017. It has to be noted that, for compatibility reasons only 318 portals were considered for the comparison, since the CWEI measurement requires the inclusion of the same municipal portals. For the estimation of the average CWEI, its four sub-indicators were initially calculated. SPSS software has been used for the statistical analysis.

In 2015, the average e-information value was 63.61, the Web 2.0 tools and services was 22.27, the e-consultation was 29.09 and the e-decision making process 11.64 (Fig. 1).

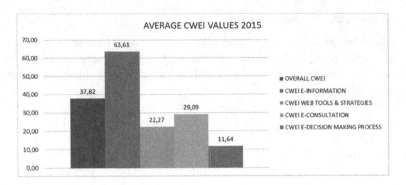

Fig. 1. CWEI 2015

In 2017, the average e-information value was 72.10, the Web 2.0 tools and services was 29.40, the e-consultation was 32.94 and the e-decision making process 11.79 (Fig. 2).

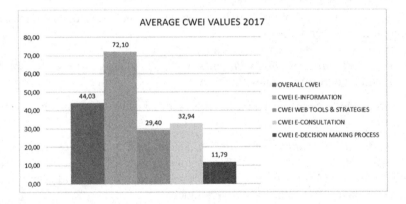

Fig. 2. CWEI 2017

The average value of CWEI was 37.82 in 2015 and 44.03 in 2017. Table 1 shows the average CWEI sub-indicator values for the assessment of 2015 and 2017. Overall, a small increase of the sub-indicators can be noticed between the years 2015 and 2017. We observe that the higher value stands for the "e-information" sub-indicator for both 2015 and 2017. This is explained since "e-information" comprises the first level of e-participation maturity, referring to the online provision of public information and access to information upon demand to citizens. E-information is the first level for e-participation that governments try to achieve. Municipalities are trying to provide structured and updated information on their websites for achieving the e-information level more than one decade. The sub-indicators of "Web 2.0 tools and services" and "e-consultation" show a slight increase. Furthermore, the "e-decision making process" indicator has the lowest value compared to the other sub-indicators without any change from 2015.

Table 1. CWEI assessment 2015 & 2017

Average CWEI sub-indicator values	2015	2017
E-information	63.61	72.10
Web 2.0 tools and services	22.27	29.40
E-consultation	29.09	32.94
E-decision making process	11.64	11.79

4 e-Participation Demand

To answer the second research question for citizens' participation demand a question-naire survey was conducted between March and April 2017, during which the e-partic-ipation supply survey was also conducted. The sample includes 212 citizens that have visited their municipal portal. Before answering the questionnaire, participants were invited to visit once again their municipal portal. The first version of the questionnaire was designed and initially distributed to ten citizens in order to check and revise it. Then, the revised questionnaire was distributed in the regions of Attica and Thessaly in elec-tronic form (collected electronically) and in print (collected via interviews). The ques-tionnaire was divided into three parts, regarding:

- *Demographics:* gender, age, educational level, skills (PC, smartphone, and Internet);
- *Citizen information and transactions with the municipality:* ways and frequency citi-zens are informed and transact with their municipality; and,
- *e-Participation in the municipality:* the extent to which citizens are aware of the services offered by their municipalities, their views on them and the future use they intend to make.

Five-point Likert scales were employed for all items (1 = none, 2 = few, 3 = average, 4 = much, 5 = very much). The average response rate was 94.3% and a total of 200 valid responses were returned.

4.1 Demographics

The demographics of the sample are presented in detail in Table 2. In summary, out of 200 valid respondents, 59% were female and 41% were male. Half of the respondents were 17–25 years old (50%), the age range of 26–35 years was 18.5%, 36–45 years old was 6.5%, 46–55 years old was 12.5% and finally aged over 56 was about 12.5% of the sample. Concerning the educational level, 64.5% of respondents had a higher education degree, 19% had completed secondary education, 15.5% hold a postgraduate or a PhD degree and only 1% had completed primary education. Regarding their knowledge on using a PC, 44.5% was very good, 35% good, 14% average, 5% little and 1.5% none. Regarding their knowledge on using a smart phone, 55.5% was very good, 34.5% good, 7.5% average, 2.5% little and 0% none. Regarding their knowledge on using the Internet, 51.5% was very good, 34% good, 10.5% average, 2.5% little and 1.5% none.

Table 2. Demographics

Profile of Respondents	Frequency	Percentage (%)
Gender		
Male	82	41
Female	118	59
Age (yrs.)		
17–25	100	50
26–35	37	18.5
36–45	13	6.5
46–55	25	12.5
56+	25	12.5
Educational Level		
Primary	2	1
Secondary	38	19
University	129	64.5
Postgraduate	31	15.5
Ability to Use PC		
None	3	1.5
Little	10	5
Average	28	14
Good	70	35
Very good	89	44.5
Ability to Use Smartphone		
None	0	0
Little	5	2.5
Average	15	7.5
Good	69	34.5
Very good	111	55.5
Ability to User Internet		
None	3	1.5
Little	5	2.5
Average	21	10.5
Good	68	34
Very good	103	51.5

4.2 Citizen Information and Transactions with the Municipality

The "citizen information and transactions with the municipality" part of the question-naire investigated the use of different ways by citizens to interact with their municipality. 59% of the sample never visits municipality agencies, and 50% never telephone them. They rarely access the municipality portal via a PC (35%) to get information or transact. The majority has never interacted through a smartphone using a mobile app or SMS (53%), or through social networking (35%).

4.3 e-Participation in the Municipality

Regarding awareness of e-participation services that are provided by the municipality, 36% are aware, 48.5% are not aware, and 15.5% did not answer. 63.5% do not either agree or disagree that the provided municipal e-participation services are easy to use. 62.5% agree that they can easily be acquainted with the use of municipal e-participation services and 66% agree that they can easily be trained on using them.

Regarding citizens' views on using e-participation services, 54.5% agree that such services save time and make citizens more productive, 63.5% agree that such services are useful, 45% agree that their participation is more effective, 49.5% agree that the services help in enhancing more often participation/communication. Finally, 38% do not either agree or disagree on the statement that the usage of e-participation services is more transparent than using the traditional ones.

Citizens have expressed their interest on using municipal e-services for receiving e-information as follows: average interest for the municipality budget (29.5%), and much interest for cultural events/voluntary actions (39%), municipality news (32.5%), and municipality results (e.g. elections) (27.5%).

Concerning "Web 2.0 tools and services", citizens have expressed much interest for communicating with other citizens (26.5%) and expressing their opinions (38%).

Regarding "e-consultation" much interest has been shown for participating in voting (32.5%), for submitting complaints (35.6%), and much communicating with the Mayor (26.5%). Concerning e-decision making process much interest has been shown for decisions of the City Council (29.5%).

Citizens are neutral (43.5%) on the statement that people that affect their behavior and are important to them believe that they should use municipal e-participation service. Also, citizens neither agree nor disagree (39.5%) on the statement that they use municipal e-participation services because many people do. Citizens agree that they have the resources (e.g. computer, Internet) to use their municipality's e-participation services (43%) and that they have the adequate knowledge to use such services (46.5%).

Concerning citizens' intention to use municipal e-participation services in the near future, 62.5% replied that they will through the municipal portal, 42.5% through a smart phone, and 47.5% through social media. They also intend to use in the future the municipal portal (75%), their smartphone (52%) and social media (57.5%) for participating through municipal services. In general, 60% of the participants stated that they would like to use their smartphone for using municipal e-participation services.

5 Conclusions

This article tries to contribute to our knowledge about e-participation supply and demand in Greek municipalities. The research is subject to certain limitations. Regarding the research on the supply side of e-participation more coders should be used in future evaluation of municipal portals. Regarding the demand side of e-participation, the research should include a larger sample of citizens from more municipalities that would represent the whole country, so as to give more concrete results.

Despite the above limitations, the article can give insights for the posed research questions:

What is the status of e-participation services provided by municipalities?

The case study results show that the overall e-participation progress in 2017 can be considered as slow paced comparing to 2015 status. These results reflect the progress of municipal portals and are not related with the results regarding the national portals depicted by the EPI index. Specifically, the average CWEI presents an increase of about 16% in the two years. According to the sub-indicator values, e-information has the highest value. This is achieved by the advanced maturity level of portals for information provision. The sub-indicator of Web 2.0 tools and services remains at a low level. This is explained by the average usage of social media networking tools (186 municipalities only use them), as well as lack of mobile apps (only 12 municipalities) and Web TV (only three municipalities). Regarding e-consultation sub-indicator presents a limited increase. Particularly, 233 municipalities support online complaints and 166 support mayor's direct online contact with citizens. However, online polls and reputation systems present very low values. Finally, the e-decision making process sub-indicator presents no change from 2015. It is worth noting that the value of the average CWEI from the analysis of the portals of 104 Italian cities was 37.30 in 2012 and 40.24 in 2013 [18]. Greek and Italian surveys show that the path towards high maturity of e-participation is still long.

What types of e-participation services would be desired by citizens?

The results of the demand side of e-participation survey indicate most interesting services for citizens are: cultural events, municipality news and results, communicating with other citizens, expressing opinions, voting, submitting complaints, communicating with the Mayor and getting informed on decisions of the City Council. Citizens feel ready in terms of digital skills and technology acquired to use the aforementioned services. However, they need to have well designed tools and services to motivate them to engage in e-participation. High level functionality of these services will provide convenient and efficient ways for citizens' empowerment and attract them to use e-participation services more [2].

The research results can provide insights for the improvement of e-participation current status in municipalities. Since e-participation initiatives are relatively new and there cannot be a single e-participation model suitable for all countries [19], Greek municipalities have to determine a clear strategy for providing high maturity e-participation. This strategy should be focused on the CWEI sub-indicators, using a systematic method for selecting future services that are meaningful to citizens. The empirical research showed that special attention should be given to "Web 2.0 tools and services" and the "e-decision making process" sub-indicators. Regarding the "Web 2.0 tools and services" sub-indicator, despite the fact that Greek Internet users are highly involved in social media networking and mobile use, municipalities still ignore their significant role to citizens' engagement in e-participation. Summarizing, municipalities should incorporate social media tools and mobile services in their portals for local public affairs. Furthermore, municipalities should focus on providing evidence of citizen consideration in the "e-decision making process". As citizens are willing to express themselves, vote, complain or get informed, municipalities have to take into account citizens' requirements and indicate in their websites the impact of public demand. According to the type of services demanded by citizens, municipalities have to give emphasis to the development of services regarding municipality results, communication with the Mayor, municipality budget and participating in surveys. Social media should be considered as an alternative means for participating in public events and issues.

It is expected that this research will encourage public servants, local governments, researchers and policy makers to better understand the state of the art, as well as which e-participation tools should be used and which services should be developed in the future for enhancing citizens' e-participation adoption.

References

1. UN: E-government Survey 2016 (2016). http://workspace.unpan.org/sites/Internet/Documents/UNPAN96407.pdf
2. Zheng, Y.: Explaining citizens' e-participation usage: functionality of e-participation applications. Adm. Soc. **49**(3), 423–442 (2017)
3. Lee, J., Kim, S.: Citizens' e-participation on agenda setting in local governance: do individual social capital and e-participation management matter? Public Manag. Rev. (2017). https://doi.org/10.1080/14719037.2017.1340507
4. Wirtz, B.W., Weyerer, J.C., Rösch, M.: Citizen and open government: an empirical analysis of antecedents of open government data. Int. J. Pub. Adm. (2017). https://doi.org/10.1080/01900692.2016.1263659
5. Mossberger, K., Wu, Y., Jimenez, B.S.: Developments and challenges in e-participation in major US cities. In: Routledge Handbook on Information Technology in Government, p. 219 (2017)
6. Gauld, R., Goldfinch, S., Horsburgh, S.: Do they want it? Do they use it? The 'Demand-Side' of e-Government in Australia and New Zealand. Gov. Inf. Q. **27**(2), 177–186 (2010)
7. Gil-García, J.R.: Enacting Electronic Government Success: An Integrative Study of Government-Wide Portals, Organizational Capabilities, and Institutions. Springer, New York (2012). https://doi.org/10.1007/978-1-4614-2015-6
8. Reddick, C.G., Norris, D.F.: E-participation in local governments: an examination of political-managerial support and impacts. Transform. Gov. People Process Policy **7**(4), 453–476 (2013)
9. Reddick, C.G., Norris, D.F.: E-participation in local governments: an empirical examination of impacts. In: Proceedings of the 14th Annual International Conference on Digital Government Research, pp. 198–204. ACM (2013)
10. Macintosh, A.: Characterizing e-participation in policy-making. In: The Proceedings of the Thirty-Seventh Annual Hawaii International Conference on System Sciences (HICSS-37), 5–8 January 2004, Big Island (2004)
11. Vidiasova, L., Trutnev, D., Vidiasov, E.: E-participation development factors: the results of an expert survey. In: Proceedings of the 18th Annual International Conference on Digital Government Research, pp. 572–573. ACM (2017)
12. UN: United Nations E-Government Survey (2014). http://unpan3.un.org/egovkb/Portals/egovkb/Documents/un/2014-Survey/E-Gov_Complete_Survey-2014.pdf
13. Wikipedia: Kapodistrias reform (2015). https://en.wikipedia.org/wiki/Kapodistrias_reform
14. Ntaliani, M., Costopoulou, C., Karetsos, S., Molhanec, M.: Citizen e-Empowerment in Greek and Czech municipalities. In: Katsikas, S.K., Sideridis, A.B. (eds.) e-Democracy 2015. CCIS, vol. 570, pp. 124–133. Springer, Cham (2015). https://doi.org/10.1007/978-3-319-27164-4_9

15. Ntaliani, M., Costopoulou, C., Karetsos, S.: Investigating the mobile side of e-Participation. Int. J. Electron. Gov. (2018, to be published)
16. Bellio, E., Buccoliero, L.: Citizen web empowerment across Italian cities: a benchmarking approach. In: Citizen E-participation in Urban Governance: Crowdsourcing and Collaborative Creativity: Crowdsourcing and Collaborative Creativity, p. 284 (2013)
17. Buccoliero, L., Bellio, E.: Citizens web empowerment in European municipalities. J. e-Gov. **33**(4), 225–236 (2010)
18. Bellio, E., Buccoliero, L.: Digital cities web marketing strategies in Italy: the path towards citizen empowerment. In: Obaidat, M.S., Filipe, J. (eds.) ICETE 2013. CCIS, vol. 456, pp. 142–159. Springer, Heidelberg (2014). https://doi.org/10.1007/978-3-662-44788-8_9
19. Filatova, O., Balabanova, S., Golubev, V., Ibragimov, I.: E-participation in EEU countries: a case study of government websites. In: Proceedings of the International Conference on Electronic Governance and Open Society: Challenges in Eurasia, pp. 145–151. ACM (2017)

Zonal Constructed Language and Education Support of e-Democracy – The Interslavic Experience

Maria Kocór[1], Lina Yordanova[2], Jan van Steenbergen[3], and Vojtěch Merunka[4,5(✉)]

[1] Faculty of Pedagogy, Rzeszów University, Rzeszów, Poland
mariakoc@vp.pl
[2] Faculty of Economics, Trakia University, Stara Zagora, Bulgaria
linayor@gmail.com
[3] Independent researcher, IJmuiden, Netherlands
ijzeren.jan@gmail.com
[4] Department of Information Engineering, Czech University of Life Sciences in Prague,
Prague, Czechia
vmerunka@gmail.com
[5] Department of Software Engineering, Czech Technical University in Prague, Prague, Czechia

Abstract. This article brings the idea of improving the quality of information systems to support democracy and public administration in Slavic countries between Western Europe and Russia through the use of a zonal constructed language that can successfully replace English and improve the overall quality of ICT used for e-Democracy assignments. The connection with education, from which everything begins, is also emphasised. This article describes the results of public research in the form of surveys and the first practical experiences of the authors. The idea of improving computer translations between national languages is also mentioned. It is assumed that language, education and e-democracy create a developing triad. Finally, this article describes the future development of this idea.

Keywords: e-Democracy education · Zonal constructed language · Language of human-computer interaction · Receptive multilingualism · Computer-based translation · International knowledge transfer · Slavic countries

1 Introduction

E-democracy is a political dialogue in which citizens, and communities in general, engage in the political process using computer-based technology. It refers to the practical use of information systems to support democratic processes, and encompasses activities that increase citizen involvement, such as virtual town meetings, open meetings, cyber campaigns, feedback polls, public surveys and community forums such as e-voting, etc. In general, it is all about supporting communication and participation of people in various political, cultural and spiritual activities in the modern world, as defined in the higher levels of the Maslow's hierarchy of human needs (Maslow 1943).

© Springer International Publishing AG 2017
S.K. Katsikas and V. Zorkadis (Eds.): E-Democracy 2017, CCIS 792, pp. 15–30, 2017.
https://doi.org/10.1007/978-3-319-71117-1_2

Information systems, like every system, consist of components and the links between them. These components are not only computer software and hardware, but also people who determine the quality of the outcome.

To communicate within Europe, people learn English. Yet, a lot of people still do not speak English sufficiently well. An alternative for using English might be *receptive multilingualism*. Speakers of two different, but related languages both speak their own language and are still able to understand each other to a certain extent. Receptive multilingualism is possible when languages are mutually intelligible. The Scandinavian languages, for instance, have a high degree of mutual intelligibility, and receptive multilingualism is widely used in Scandinavia. The advantages of this communication are that the speakers only need to focus on understanding the other language and that they can express themselves in their native language.

Effective multilingual behaviour to support civic participation in e-democracy requires proper education. After all, language is the basic tool for education, but without education it can hardly be promoted, applied and developed. The same goes for e-democracy, which requires both younger and older generations to be educated into citizens who consciously use ICT for development policies.

In this article, we will attempt to demonstrate the interdependence between zonal constructed languages like Interslavic, e-democracy and education in the light of the views and experiences of authors from different countries and scientific institutions.

2   Motivation

The *Report on e-democracy by the European Parliament from 16 February 2017* (Report 2017) emphasises the need for simplification of institutional language and procedures and for the organisation of multimedia content that explains the keys to the main decision-making processes, in order to promote understanding and participation. Also, it notes that in order to ensure equal accessibility of e-democracy tools for all citizens, high-quality multilingual translation is important when information is to be disseminated and read by all citizens. In other words, comprehensibility of the used language is essential for working e-democracy, and obviously, not all citizens can be expected to master professional legal English.

Similarly, the *OECD report of 2003 on e-Democracy* (OECD 2003) speaks about the need for using ICT to increase citizens' participation by means of a comprehensible language, not by promoting English as the only language of ICT. Likewise, the conclusions of the *International e-Democracy Conference in Athens* (Katsikas and Sideridis 2015) confirm that the interest in the use of ICT in public life (and, vice versa, technophobia against ICT), including social networks and community life, is directly dependent on the use of a language that the domestic population can understand.

Next, there is enormous pressure on the standardisation of legislation, implementing regulations and technical standards in the world, most of all within the EU. Without this standardisation, the idea of e-democracy is impossible. However, small nations are unable to translate everything in time and thus end up maintaining the status quo in their small, little known national languages. The consequence is that democracy is jeopardised through the loss of participation in public life and an overall loss of contact with the modern world, which to ordinary people merely means a different world dominated by English and computers.

For all the reasons stated above it is clear that the use of a comprehensible language to the public is a crucial factor in the success of all e-democracy processes and technologies. The role of education cannot be underestimated here, because the state of education - its purposes, its contents, its level, its methods and means, the competences of teachers - is tantamount to both the willingness of people to learn the language in question, the level of their language skills and the political maturity needed for the application of modern information technology for development. In other words, e-democracy requires a solid motivational and linguistic base, both of which are determined by language and education.

3   The Linguistic Landscape in Central and Eastern Europe

A particular opportunity for improving e-democracy by means of receptive multilingualism can be found in the Slavic zone between Western Europe and Russia. This region is largely covered by small countries with populations between 2 and 10 million inhabitants. None of these nations has any colonial past, and their impact in the bigger European picture is minor. Yet, it should not be forgotten that the Slavic nations together represent 1/3 of the total population of geographic Europe.

The Slavs have much more in common than linguistic kinship, ancient history and folklore. Less than thirty years ago, they all lived in closed, largely passive societies ruled by communist regimes, a few years later they all found themselves in a post-communist vacuum, each of them struggling to find its own place in a rapidly changing world. In today's global village, national borders are losing their importance and isolation is no longer an option. To face the challenges of modern times, partnership within the same geopolitical realm is inevitable, especially since the emergence of a mental gap between life and culture of the own nation, and the "western" outer world is very dangerous and can easily be abused politically.

Most Slavic languages are official in one small or middle-sized country only. In other countries, active knowledge of these languages is highly uncommon and remains mostly the domain of mixed families and language professionals. The only exceptions here are populations that for a longer period of time have been exposed to some dominant language: Czech in Czechoslovakia, Serbo-Croatian in Yugoslavia and Russian in the Soviet Union. This lack of linguistic cohesion puts these nations under considerable pressure in the modern globalised world, and significantly complicates the processes of e-democracy and advancing European integration.

3.1   The Role of English

Due to its status as a global lingua franca, English is a common tool for the exchange of knowledge between these nations, even though the United Kingdom is currently separating itself from Europe. However, a vast majority of people are excluded from this process. Most Slavic speakers are either monolingual, or their knowledge of foreign languages is extremely limited. In Poland, the Czech Republic, Slovakia and Bulgaria knowledge of English is restricted to 20–30% of the population (Euro-barometer 2006). In addition, the level of this knowledge is often low, insufficient for even the most basic communication. In Poland, for example, only 12.7% of the individuals who know a foreign language are actually proficient in it (Eurostat 2015). The general tendency is that the further East one travels, the harder it becomes to have a conversation in any other language than the local one. In the Russian Federation, English is spoken by less than 5.5% of the population (All-Russian Census 2010).

In addition, English is a very specific language, with its own culture, semantics, syntax, etc. This is why, for example, computer translations via Google Translate between Czech and Polish or Croatian are totally unusable, often even absurd and ridiculous. English is simply not suitable as a pivot language between Slavic (and not only Slavic) languages.

3.2   Russian as a Lingua Franca

It has been argued that Russian could reclaim its role as a lingua franca for Central and Eastern Europe. Russia, after all, is by far the largest Slavic nation, accounting for roughly half of all Slavic mother tongue speakers, and spoken fluently by a vast majority in Ukraine, Belarus and the Baltic states. It is the only Slavic country with a long and unbroken tradition of statehood, and has always played a key role as a regional superpower. Besides, isn't Russian the language of many brilliant minds, with an incredibly rich literature and broad usage in science?

The truth is, however, that Russian has irreversibly failed to ever become a Slavic lingua franca. For a long time, it has been overused as a tool for political domination, and people in other countries still tend to perceive it as the language of the oppressor. A genuine lingua franca cannot be imposed with brutal force, but must be chosen freely (Donskis 2014).

Another problem is the Russian language itself. Had it been sufficiently simple and understandable to other Slavs, resistance against it could probably be overcome with time. But Russian has specific phonetics, a very complicated grammar, a particular Cyrillic alphabet and a lot of vocabulary that lacks universal Slavic qualities—all things that place it far from the imaginary linguistic centre of Slavic.

3.3   Receptive Multilingualism

A lingua franca is not the only possible means of communication between people who do not speak each other's language, and this brings us to the issue of receptive, or passive, multilingualism. In short, this means that each side speaks their own language, while trying to actively understand the language of the other side.

Compared to other languages families, the Slavic languages have a relatively high degree of mutual intelligibility. More than anything else, this is due to the fact that their common ancestor Proto-Slavic started developing into separate branches and individual languages at a relatively late point in history. In the 10th century there still was a reasonable degree of linguistic unity with no more than some dialectical differentiation. Even in the 19th century Pan-Slavists voiced the opinion that all Slavic languages were dialects of a single Slavic language, an assumption they based on the example of other languages with highly divergent dialects, such as Greek, Arabic, English and German. If all dialects of these languages could be united under a single language, they argued, why couldn't the same thing be achieved for Slavs? (Majar 1865).

During the last two decades, research has been conducted on Slavic intercomprehension. Pioneer in the field is the Slavist Lew Zybatow, who initiated and led the project EuroComSlav, aimed at enhancing intercomprehension by showing the learner how much he already knows without actually knowing that he knows. This is achieved by means of "seven sieves", the most important of which are: international vocabulary, common inherited vocabulary, and recognising correspondences between languages in sound, spelling and pronunciation (Zybatow 2002).

Another recent project exploring receptive multilingualism among Slavs is the Mutual intelligibility of closely related languages (MICReLa) project of the University of Groningen. One of the outcomes of this research is that receptive multilingualism functions among Czechs and Slovaks in much the same way as among Scandinavians, and although the same cannot be said about combinations like Slovak/Croatian, Slovak/Polish or Croatian/Slovene, receptive multilingualism is possible here as well, albeit with some practice. Other combinations, however, tend to be more problematic, especially when Bulgarian is involved (Golubovic and Gooskens 2015).

Although MICReLa focuses on the six Slavic languages spoken in the European Union, we may assume that the same conclusions can be applied to the remaining Slavic languages as well. Thus, a Pole will understand Ukrainian or Belarussian reasonably well if it is spoken slowly and clearly. As soon as languages are more remote, however, communication is not so simple anymore. In contacts between, for example, a Russian and a Slovene, or a Czech and a Bulgarian, it is unlikely that resorting to gestures or some other intermediary language can be avoided. As Heinz (2009) demonstrates, Slavic intercomprehension is especially problematic when it comes to auditive transfer, because prosody and the absence of orthographical differences are minor advantages compared to problems of a phonological nature, such as incorrect identification of phonemes and word boundaries, as well as misinterpretations on a morphological and lexical level, caused by deceptive cognates and wrong associations.

Another issue is the difference in scripts. The border between the Latin and Cyrillic alphabets runs right through the middle of Slavic territory, coinciding more or less with the border between Roman Catholicism and Orthodoxy. At the left side of this border (especially in Poland, the Czech Republic and Slovakia), knowledge of the Cyrillic alphabet is rather uncommon. One might expect that most people who speak a language that uses a non-Latin alphabet must have enough knowledge of the Latin alphabet, but a recent study reveals that a lot of young people in the former Soviet Union have serious problems understanding Slavic texts written in a Latin alphabet.

In other words, receptive multilingualism is possible, but only on a limited scale. The direct consequence of this fact, in combination with widespread monolingualism and the lack of a widely known and accepted lingua franca, is that many Slavic people are practically cut off from the world outside their own country, which forces them into isolation and makes active participation virtually impossible. This is especially dangerous in countries where pluralism leaves much to be desired, and access to neutral, reliable information is scarce.

4   The Interslavic Experiment

What significantly stands in the way of mutual intelligibility is the fact that every Slavic language has idiosyncrasies (specific phonological alterations, changes in grammar, shifts in the meanings of words, borrowings from neighbouring, non-Slavic languages, etc.) that make it harder to understand for speakers of other languages. However, these hindrances can be overcome. One peculiarity of the Slavic languages is that the sound changes that distinguish the modern languages from their common ancestor Proto-Slavic are highly predictable. Other connecting elements are the presence of large amounts of international vocabulary in all Slavic languages, a similar grammatical structure, and a considerable number of common inherited words Zybatow (2002) provides a list of 1500 words labelled as Pan-Slavic).

The seven sieves of the EuroComSlav project are aimed at *recognising* elements in other Slavic languages. However, the same principles can also be taken one step further, namely by applying them *actively*. This can be achieved by consciously avoiding the aforementioned idiosyncrasies, using words and grammatical elements that are broadly understandable in the Slavic world, and presenting them in a spoken and/or written form that makes them easily recognisable. This idea has culminated in the creation of an Interslavic language, the main premise of which is that it should be understandable to all Slavs, no matter which nation they belong to.

The idea of such a language is far from new. In the 16th century the Croatian priest Šime Budinić published his translations of works by Peter Canisius into a complex literary language he called "Slovignsky", in which he mixed Serbo-Croatian, Church Slavonic, Czech and Polish, using both Latin and Cyrillic. In the years 1659–1666 another Croatian priest, Juraj Križanić, was the first to actually describe the language itself, which he also used for his magnum opus *Politika*. At the height of Pan-Slavism in the 19th century several language projects were published in the process of creating a literary standard for South Slavic, all of them essentially modernisations of the Old Church Slavonic language, and during the 20th century various authors have attempted to create a simplified "Slavic Esperanto" (Meyer 2014, p. 158).

The Interslavic Project was initiated in 2006 under the name *Slovianski*. Initially, different possible language forms were being experimented with, all based on the modern Slavic languages. In 2009 it was decided that only the most naturalistic version, initiated and developed by Jan van Steenbergen, would be continued. In 2011 a close collaboration was started with another project, *Neoslavonic* by Vojtěch Merunka, which had been published one year earlier. Unlike *Slovianski*, *Neoslavonic* was geared towards modernising and simplifying Old Church Slavonic, although surprisingly both approaches gave almost identical results. During subsequent years, differences between both "dialects" have gradually vanished, allowing them to evolve into a single language called *Interslavic* instead (van Steenbergen 2016).

Interslavic is a so-called *zonal constructed language*, a language created to facilitate communication between speakers of a group of closely related languages. Languages of this type are fundamentally different from languages intended for global communication, such as Esperanto. The latter are typically characterised by simplicity and regularity, whereas in zonal languages the main focus lies on familiarity and immediate passive understanding. That does not mean that a zonal language cannot be simple, only that the type and level of simplicity are always conditioned by the speakers of the particular language family it serves. From that point of view, the process of creating Interslavic bears similarities to the codification of languages like Rumantsch Grischun, Bahasa Indonesia or Modern Hebrew.

Orthography, grammar, syntax and vocabulary of Interslavic are determined by two major design criteria. The first is that all six major sub-branches of Slavic (Russian, Ukrainian/Belarussian, Polish, Czech/Slovak, Serbo-Croatian/Slovene and Bulgarian/Macedonian) are weighed equally in establishing the largest common denominator. The second is that Interslavic never borrows directly from any Slavic language, but applies a consistent system of regular derivation from reconstructed proto-forms instead. This is necessary to ensure etymological coherence and to prevent the language from becoming a hodgepodge of elements from different languages.

A typical feature of Interslavic is that its components can easily be applied to any of the ethnic Slavic languages, which has the advantage that every element one learns can be put to use immediately. As a result, the learning process differs significantly from the way other languages are learned: it is a matter of gradually learning how to transform one's own native language into Interslavic. The more one learns, the closer one comes to the core of Interslavic: the scientific extrapolation of the language at the very centre of the Slavic languages.

It is important to note that Interslavic does not only allow a writer or speaker to make himself understandable to speakers of any Slavic language. Thanks to the seven sieves, it will also help him in getting a better passive understanding of other Slavic languages. And although Interslavic is primarily intended to be used by Slavs in contacts with other Slavs, the same educational value can work equally well for non-Slavs, as at will allow them to get a basic understanding of all Slavic languages at once, and also considerably facilitate their access to the Slavic-speaking world.

4.1 CISLa 2017

Since its inception, Interslavic has been much discussed in the press and on the Internet, both within its circle of currently ca. 2,000 users and interested bystanders and elsewhere. Extensive use in various contexts and feedback from all Slavic countries have made it clear that the primary purpose of Interslavic, to be understood by Slavs of any nationality without prior study, has been achieved. Until recently, however, this could be said only about written Interslavic, as experiences with spoken Interslavic were scarce and mostly limited to individual contacts.

On 1–2 June 2017 the first Conference on the Interslavic language (CISLa 2017) took place in the Czech town of Staré Město near Uherské Hradiště. There were 64 active participants from 12 different countries, including representatives of several organisations and institutions and experts in the fields of interlinguistics, Slavistics, pedagogy and history. Among the items discussed were: language problems in civil participation, e-democracy, knowledge transfer, and the potential role of zonal constructed languages in education, tourism, digital economy and the development of civil societies in a globalised world.

The conference was a milestone, because for the first time in history Interslavic was used during an official, public event. Most presentations and discussions were either held in Interslavic or translated consecutively into Interslavic, which turned out to be sufficient for all Slavic participants – including Poles and Bulgarians – to understand almost everything. A remarkable and rather unexpected side effect was also that a few participants who had never learned Interslavic, suddenly started speaking it during the conference. This shows how easily passive multilingualism, with the right tools, can be transformed into active multilingualism. The success of the conference also demonstrates clearly that the Interslavic language makes it possible to organise Slavic multinational activities, such as scientific conferences, cultural happenings, sports events and even beauty pageants with the help of a single interpreter.

5   The Issue of Computer Translation

The Slavic languages are so-called fusional (or inflecting) languages, which means that most information about the grammatical category of a word and its role in the sentence is contained in endings (declension and conjugation). Other examples of fusional languages are Indo-European languages like Sanskrit, Greek (both classical and modern), Latin, Lithuanian, Latvian and Albanian, Semitic languages like Hebrew, Arabic and Aramaic, and many other languages throughout the world. Because of these endings, the Slavic languages do not depend on the position of words for expressing grammatical categories, e.g. word order is rather flexible.

English is completely different in this respect. Whether a word is a noun, adjective, verb, subject, object or something else is determined entirely by its position within the sentence. Because English has very few declension and conjugation suffixes, a fixed word is needed to recognise grammatical categories.

This relative simplicity of English is the basis of the *Google Translate algorithm*, which is based on simple search and replacement of the longest sequences of words (Google 2016; Sutskever 2014). The Google database has a very huge number of parallel texts, many of which originating from institutions of European Union:

(a) If we want to translate something from one language to another, the algorithm searches if the whole sentence has already been translated, and
(b) if not, it searches for the longest fragments and then glues them together.
(c) Finally, even if it does not find any fragment, it is looking for a transitive path and mostly finds the translation way through English.

It is obvious that this algorithm gives the worst results in translating the fusional languages of Central and Eastern Europe, because these languages have free word order and in addition, there are not enough parallel texts in the Google database. This is the cause of unusable, bizarre and ridiculous translations that have been made through English. The solution to this problem lies in the following:

(a) A different translation algorithm that takes into account free word order and does not interpret a sentence as a linear sequence of words, but as a multi-dimensional structure of words. This algorithm, with the Interslavic zonal constructed language as the pivot language, was described at the Conference on Advanced Information Systems Engineering (CAiSE) last year in Ljubljana (Molhanec et al. 2016).

(b) Using a constructed zonal language that is much closer to the languages of a given area than English. A properly chosen zonal language is understandable even without the need for any learning, and due to its proximity to national languages, computer translations would be of much better quality.

6 International Survey on the Internet

Our international survey on the passive intelligibility of Interslavic has been conducted in all Slavic countries from November 2015 to January 2016. This survey is still available at the website of the Slavic Union (www.slovane.org). The results were taken in RSForms! for Joomla and processed in Matlab R2015b for MacOS.

The survey consisted of 5 pages and took a few minutes to respond. Information about the survey was spread through advertising on the social networks Facebook and VKontakte. The target group was formed by the entire Slavic population in the age between 16 and 80 years, who identified themselves as having knowledge of any natural Slavic language.

Our statistical hypothesis was whether the Slavic population would passively understand the language at a level corresponding to that of a slightly advanced speaker. Concretely this means the ability to understand written text and to recognise at least 5 of 7 missing words in the cloze test. The cloze test is a task where a certain number of words (in this case 7 words) are omitted from a professional text and replaced by a gap. This gap is normally a horizontal line with the average length of all deleted words in the written version of the test, or a beep of uniform length in the spoken version. The participants' task was fill in the 'gaps' with the right words. The cloze test was inspired by the MICReLa research group, based at the University of Groningen, University of Erlangen, Syddansk University in Odense, University of Copenhagen, University of Ljubljana, and Constantine the Philosopher University in Nitra, who developed a similar online language game to investigate passive intelligibility of professional texts in various national languages of the Europe, compared to the desirability of English (MICReLa 2016).

Until May 2017, we received 1,700 valid responses in total. Female respondents were outnumbered by male respondents in the ratio of about 5:1, but gender differences were minimal and far below the value of statistical error. Our respondents from different Slavic nations answered with different willingness and frequency—for example, there were more respondents from a small country like Slovenia than from Russia. For that reason, we recalculated (using weighted averages) our results according to the size of the real population in particular Slavic countries, in order to get a statistically correct representation of the whole Slavic population. We also obtained 51 responses from people whose native language is not Slavic, but who understand some Slavic language because of their surroundings (school, friends …).

Our hypothesis was confirmed with a sufficient degree of probability, namely 0.816. We used the test "guess missing words in a professional text". The mean values of all respondents are in the interval between 79% and 93%. (These results are in rescaled values, where 100% equals 7 correct words from 7 missing words in total, 86% equals 6 correct words from 7 words in total, 71% equals 5 correct words from 7 words in total, 57% equals 4 correct words from 7 words in total, and so on.) Only 18% of the respondents (315 out of 1,700) answered below the expected 5 correct words from a total of 7 unknown words. Our hypothesis turned out valid for respondents with a non-Slavic mother tongue, who learned a Slavic language later, too. The total mean value was 84%, i.e. nearly 6 correct words from 7 unknown words in total. Some of the partial results of this survey are also very interesting:

(1) There is no dependence on age and gender. Differences in results are below the statistical error, which is about 2%.

(2) Among Slavic nations, the best results were achieved by Ruthenians, Czechs, Slovaks, Poles and Belarusians (between 87% and 93%). The lowest results were achieved by all South-Slavic nations (between 79% and 81%).

(3) In contrast to the previous result, the group of South Slavic nations gave Interslavic a higher aesthetic evaluation (value around 60%) than the other Slavic nations (value around 55%).

(4) All Slavic nations expressed slightly worse values in their self-assessment than their actual intelligibility results (for example, the total mean value of real intelligibility is 84%, but the total mean value of self-assessment is only 70% in comparable rescaled values).

(5) There is a clear dependence on education. Slavic people who completed higher education have 88% of mean intelligibility, Slavic people without any university experience have only mean 73% of the average (secondary education only) and 72% of the average (primary education only).

(6) Self-assessment showed that members of smaller nations understand the similar languages of their neighbours better than members of the bigger nations. The biggest asymmetry was between Belarusians, Ukrainians, and Russians. Ukrainians understand Russian at the level of 80% and Belarusians understand Russian at the level of 71%, but Russians understand Ukrainian at a level of only 46% and Belarusian at a level of 39%. A similar difference is also visible between the smaller Slovenian nation and the bigger Croatian nation.

(7) People were surprised how much information they were able to understand. Yet, especially younger people still preferred English, even though their English skills were very poor and they would understand much more using Interslavic.

In conclusion, we can say that passive understanding of Interslavic without any prior learning meets the conditions that roughly match the local language-skill requirements for immigrants to obtain citizenship in most European countries. Also, we dare say that Interslavic inscriptions on products, in public transport and in offices (e.g., town halls, local government bodies, bus and railway stations, airports ...) would be better for many people than the current inscriptions in English.

7   Survey in Bulgaria

In the first half of 2017, it was conducted to find out how well Bulgarians are able to understand the Interslavic zonal constructed language written in Latin alphabet, without any previous training. Of course, texts written in Cyrillic are considered to be much more understandable, as Cyrillic is the alphabet used in Bulgaria.

The hypothesis subject to proof was the following: the Interslavic language can be used by Bulgarians to support international communication and knowledge transfer with only little effort.

The survey was set up as a software application in Google forms, and contained 20 professional questions of different types, separated into two main groups. The first group of questions were linguistic questions with answers based on experience, intelligence and logic of the respondents. The second group of questions aimed to reveal people's language culture and their personal opinion about the Interslavic language. The motto of the survey, "This is a language of Slavophiles", was very welcomed.

The survey was filled out by students and colleagues of Trakia University, as well as several friends and relatives not working in our university or the educational sphere. The number of the respondents was up to 70. Nevertheless, the data were processed further in-depth, and the results presented here are very positive and promising.

The answers to the first group of questions revealed that about 85–93% of the respondents had successfully translated the words and short paragraphs. 94% correctly recognised forms of the verbs "to have" and "to be" in various persons and tenses; 81% correctly found other verbs. 69% knew that if we change word order in a sentence, there is no loss of meaning. Only 50.8% recognised that there are noun cases in this language and guessed the right case endings, but 85% of the respondents learned them quickly.

The number of incorrect answers ranged from 7% (older students and colleagues) to 50% of mainly young people (first-grade students).

The following conclusions can be drawn after analysis of the survey results:

(1) The Slavic Latin script is definitely a big difficulty for the young Bulgarians. They made mistakes and returned unexpected, funny answers.
(2) Another problem was with Bulgarian Cyrillic, which has a character for semivowel ъ, while other Slavic languages using this semivowel do not have such character in their Latin alphabets.
(3) Unlike other Slavic languages, Interslavic included, the Bulgarian language does not have noun cases. This was confusing to some respondents.
(4) The Interslavic language is understandable for Bulgarians even when written in the Latin alphabet. Cyrillic, however, would give a much more favourable result.
(5) 67% of the respondents want to study this language in the future.

The authors of the survey believe that the results prove the hypothesis about the Interslavic language being sufficiently understandable without any prior training, notwithstanding its grammar based on cases and its Latin orthography.

8 Polish Initiatives and Experiences

Cooperation between institutions of higher education in Poland, the Czech Republic, Slovakia and other Slavic countries has been the source of numerous good experiences, casting a very positive light on the phenomenon of receptive multilingualism among Slavs. Many Polish scholars have used Polish or Interslavic in their communication with their contacts abroad, without any trouble in their mutual understanding. This cooperation has borne fruit in the form of Poles participating in numerous Czech and Slovak conferences and classes within the framework of the Erasmus programme. During these occasions, everyone spoke his own language. This worked better than English, which not everybody could speak fluently. Other positive experiences include a field trip by a guest from Ostrava, editorial cooperation and co-authorship of many scientific works with scholars from Banská Bystrica, Nitra, etc. These contacts are continuously being maintained and developed via the Internet.

During the first half of 2017, a poll has been conducted among 250 pedagogy students of the University of Rzeszów regarding their knowledge about the Interslavic language and the necessity of teaching it. A question about the need for implementing Interslavic was answered positively by most respondents, however, what they lacked was broader knowledge about it. The students were also asked about their contacts with other Slavic countries, and although the opinions were divided here, those who had had more frequent contacts expressed themselves very positively about their scientific, cultural, touristic and other experiences. The respondents recognise the need for promoting and learning Interslavic, which in itself is an excellent argument for further, broader research to confirm these conclusions.

These linguistically and educationally constructive experiences have been a major reason for participating in the CISLa 2017 conference and the Days of Polish and Croatian culture in June 2017, and strengthen us in our belief that the Interslavic language deserves to be promoted, taught and used.

Without intense contacts and a continuous exchange of experiences between the countries involved in promotional activities, however, there is no way of convincing people of the advantages of the Interslavic language. These positive experiences may not always be directly related to e-democracy, but they seem to be an important link that connects language, education and e-democracy.

9 Suggestions for Further Research

All these considerations and experiences should be a stimulus for broader research on the willingness of citizens in different Slavic countries to use the Interslavic language, as well as its potential role in the rise of cyberdemocracy. Of particular importance is also more research on the possibilities of implementing Interslavic in education.

In the search for reciprocal connections between language, education and e-democ-racy, the theoretical model at Fig. 1 can be proposed. This proposed model can serve as the basis for empirical research in the various countries where the project is initiated. It requires further argumentation and detail, as it displays the mutual relationship between three complex processes that simultaneously constitute the basic values of the informa-tion society. What can e-democracy do for e-democracy, what can language do for language, and what can education do for education, if these three elements do not work together, supporting each other and encouraging each other's constant improvement and development? This thought deserves discussion on a global level, because it might reveal an authentic need of the homo interneticus (Walat 2016), who is still insufficiently adapted to the conditions imposed on him by media and politics.

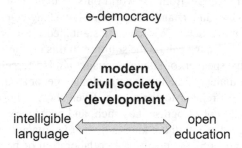

Fig. 1. Modern civil society development triad [authors].

At the CISLa 2017 conference in Staré Město, M. Kocór voiced the idea of a common research project, which, based on the new arguments and considerations mentioned in this article, could be expanded with the relation between the Inter-slavic language, e-democracy and participation at various levels of education in the Slavic countries. Especially in those Slavic countries where knowledge of English is low, research on the openness of citizens towards a more comprehensible Slavic language (see V. Merunka's research) in the context of improving e-democracy and the need for corresponding education is warranted. In this context, it is crucial to investigate what the needs and experiences of citizens are when it comes to using and comprehending the Interslavic language, and what they expect from education in terms of language, media and informatics.

The expected outcome of this outlined project is that at different school levels educa-tional models will be proposed and introduced, both directed at a common language for the Slavic countries and the e-democratic development of their citizens. Subsequently, these models will require evaluation, and proposals can be made for improvement. After all, e-democracy should not merely concentrate on motivating people and forming an understandable language, but also on a critical, creative and responsive attitude from those engaged in the process.

10 Conclusion

Although the Slavic countries of Central and Eastern Europe constitute roughly one third of the entire continent, their populations are under heavy pressure in a world in which borders gradually lose their meaning and traditional values need re-evaluation. Democracy and civil societies are still a relatively young phenomenon in the region, with political instability constantly lurking behind the corner. Under such conditions, building, developing and protecting e-democracy is paramount in helping these societies reach socio-political maturity and preventing them from missing the boat.

A major factor that stands in the way of full participation is language. Knowledge of English and other foreign languages is at a persistently low level in the region, which effectively cuts off many people from the world outside their own countries. Research demonstrates that a passive understanding of other Slavic languages can play a positive role, but on a rather limited scale. We have substantiated reasons to believe that the Interslavic constructed language can be the solution to this problem.

Our experience is that speakers of Slavic languages tend to perceive Interslavic either as an ancient or remote dialect of their own native language, or as an unidentified neighbouring language closely related to their own. Even those who are sceptical about constructed languages do not recognise it as such, and people are often surprised how much they can understand of it without knowing what language it is.

The Interslavic language is the result of a collaboration of people involved in the improvement of information systems for civilians who are not necessarily ICT experts with good knowledge of English. The people-friendly Interslavic language can help us to overcome the technophobia that complicates the deployment of e-democracy applications in practice, while simultaneously saving costs, because instead of creating 15 different Slavic language versions, we need only one version.

Our research performed under the populations of various countries on their ability to comprehend Interslavic, allows us to draw far-reaching conclusions regarding its usefulness and the possibility for people to use it easily and effectively without much preparation. Therefore, its practical implementation on a broader scale in economy, trade, tourism and culture, but also in e-democracy and at various levels of education deserves our urgent support. And meanwhile, the interdependence between language, education and e-democracy also merits further discussion and research.

Beside e-democracy applications, other possibilities for its use are in business, international transport (information texts and labels in trains, buses, planes), marketing (product manuals and descriptions), tourism (info leaflets, news) and social events. For example, Interslavic could serve as a practical auxiliary language for multinational Slavic groups in touristic destinations, historical and cultural places and exhibitions, companies and religious communities. It can also play a positive role in science, research and education. Based on our experiences described above, excellent results can be achieved through scientific and didactical travels, common projects, grants, exchange of students and scholars, and other forms of cooperation.

Acknowledgement. The authors would like to express the support of the Czech research grant project SGS17/197/OHK4/3T/14 of the Czech Technical University in Prague and the Bulgarian research grant project 1/2017 of the Trakia University in Stara Zagora.

References

All-Russian Census: Composition by Nationality and Language Ability, Citizenship (2010). http://www.gks.ru/free_doc/new_site/perepis2010/croc/Documents/Vol4/pub-04-05.pdf

Donskis, L.: The Failed Lingua Franca of Eastern Europe? In: New Eastern Europe, No. 2(VI), pp. 63–72 (2014). ISSN: 2083-7372

Eurobarometer 243: European and their Languages, February 2006. http://ec.europa.eu/commfrontoffice/publicopinion/archives/ebs/ebs_243_en.pdf

Eurostat: Foreign language skills statistics, October 2015. http://ec.europa.eu/eurostat/statistics-explained/index.php/Foreign_language_skills_statistics#Further_Eurostat_information

Golubović, J., Gooskens, C.: Mutual intelligibility between West and South Slavic languages. Russ. Linguist. **39**, 351 (2015). https://doi.org/10.1007/s11185-015-9150-9

Google's Neural Machine Translation System: Bridging the Gap between Human and Machine Translation. Technical report (2016)

Heinz, C.: Understanding what you've never learned? - Chances and limitations of spontaneous auditive transfer between Slavic languages. WU Online Papers in International Business Communication/Series One: Intercultural Communication and Language Learning, 5. Department für Fremdsprachliche Wirtschaftskommunikation, WU Vienna University of Economics and Business, Vienna (2009)

Katsikas, S.K., Sideridis, A.B.: e-Democracy – citizen rights in the world of the new computing paradigms. CCIS, vol. 570. Springer, Cham (2015). https://doi.org/10.1007/978-3-319-27164-7

Maslow, A.H.: A theory of human motivation. Psychol. Rev. **50**(4), 370–396 (1943). https://doi.org/10.1037/h0054346. [psychclassics.yorku.ca]

Meyer, A.-M.: Wiederbelebung einer Utopie. Probleme und Perspektiven slavischer Plansprachen im Zeitalter des Internets. In: Bamberger Beiträge zur Linguistik 6. Univ. of Bamberg Press, Bamberg (2014). ISBN 978-3-86309-233-7

Majar, M.: Uzajemni pravopis slavjanski (English: Mutual Slavic Orthography) (1865). [available in Google Books]

MICReLa Research Group: Mutual intelligibility of closely related languages, the language game (2016). http://www.let.rug.nl/gooskens/project/

Molhanec, M., Merunka, V., Heršak, E.: Ontology-based translation of the fusion free word order languages - neoslavonic example. In: Pergl, R., Molhanec, M., Babkin, E., Fosso Wamba, S. (eds.) EOMAS 2016. LNBIP, vol. 272, pp. 139–153. Springer, Cham (2016). https://doi.org/10.1007/978-3-319-49454-8_10

OECD: Promise and Problems of e-Democracy - Challenges of Online Citizen Engagement. OECD Publications, Paris (2003). ISBN 92-64-01948-0

The report on E-democracy in the European Union: potential and challenges from 16 February 2017, Committee on Constitutional Affairs, European Commission. http://www.europarl.europa.eu

Rezultaty i memorandum iz prvoj naučnoj konferencije o medžuslovjanskom jezyku - CISLa 2017 (English: Results and memorandum from the first scientific conference on the Interslavic language, CISLa 2017). http://cisla.slavic-union.org/

van Steenbergen, J.: Constructed Slavic languages in the 21th century. In: Grundlagenstudien aus Kybernetik und Geisteswissenschaft, nr. 57:2, Akademia Libroservo, pp. 102–113 (2016). ISSN 0723-4899

Sutskever, I., Vinyals, O., Le, Q.V.: Sequence to sequence learning with neural networks. In: Advances in Neural Information Processing Systems (2014)

Walat, W.: Homo interneticus – wyzwanie dla współczesnej edukacji. In: Edukacja–Technika – Informatyka, no. 4/18, UR, Rzeszów (2016). ISSN 2080-9069

Zybatow, L.N.: EuroComSlav and EuroComTranslat – the Answers to the Challenges of the EU-Enlargement (2002)

Privacy

Using Personalization Technologies for Political Purposes: Privacy Implications

Paola Mavriki[✉] and Maria Karyda

Department of Information and Communication Systems Engineering, University of the Aegean,
83200 Karlovassi, Samos, Greece
icsdm14079@icsd.aegean.gr, mka@aegean.gr

Abstract. A growing body of literature has recently focused on the adoption of personalization methods and tools traditionally used in e-commerce, in the area of political marketing and communication. However, the impact of adopting personalization applications for political purposes has not been studied yet. This paper contributes to filling this gap, by analyzing privacy threats stemming from the use of personalization tools for political purposes and identifying their impact on individuals and society. This paper also identifies issues that need further research, as big data, individual targeting, the development of behavioral science and sophisticated personalization techniques are reshaping political communication and pose new privacy risks.

Keywords: Political marketing · Personalization technologies · Privacy

1 Introduction

Web 2.0 technology has changed the way people all over the world interact and communicate [13], while networking and instant messaging have shaped the Web 2.0 in a place where people largely use their real identities to communicate with their family, friends and colleagues [48]. Whether publishing their status on Social Networking Services, creating, sharing or browsing websites, communicating or conducting commercial transactions, users entrust service providers with large amounts of personal data. This data can be used to assist users in their internet experience, by providing them personalized services [53].

Personalization tools have been recently used for purposes such as shaping public's political opinion, mobilization through protest networks, personalized propaganda by extremist groups etc. [4, 5, 11, 23, 46]. Election candidates, political parties, lobbyist and interest groups that seek to drive public opinion, advance their own ideologies, win elections or pass legislation and referenda in response to the needs and wants of selected people and groups, are also turning to marketing principles and procedures [42] and adopt techniques and tools that have proven effective in commerce [34]. Business intelligence and analytics tools are used for opinion mining, social network analysis, to support online political participation, e-democracy, political blogs and forums analysis, e-government service delivery, and process transparency and accountability. Moreover,

© Springer International Publishing AG 2017
S.K. Katsikas and V. Zorkadis (Eds.): E-Democracy 2017, CCIS 792, pp. 33–46, 2017.
https://doi.org/10.1007/978-3-319-71117-1_3

semantic information directory and ontological development are employed to deliver customized e-government services [9].

The impact of commercial marketing on individual privacy has been extensively studied [1, 17, 19, 52, 56]. On the contrary, studies that identify and evaluate privacy threats stemming from personalization technologies in the case of political marketing are scarce, while several researchers express their concerns [6, 16, 48, 58]. Academic literature has explored the use of personalization techniques and tools for political purposes [5, 21, 23], but to the best of our knowledge, there is no work focusing on privacy issues involved with.

At the same time, the accessibility of big data, individual targeting and the development of behavioral science, are remodeling political communication and affect many aspects of personal life including privacy. Also, as personalization technologies are evolving rapidly, new frameworks for understanding new risks and consequences are needed. This work aims to identify privacy risks and their implications, arising from repurposed for political marketing personalization techniques and tools.

The remaining paper is structured as follows: in the following Section, we analyze basic personalization methods, tools and their applications, continuing in Sect. 3 with the analysis of associated privacy risks. Section 4 analyzes privacy implications related to the use of personalization technologies for political objectives. In Sect. 5, we discuss the various contexts of political marketing studies and argue that new privacy risks arise from new technologies. We conclude with a discussion on open issues and further research.

2   Background: Personalization Methods, Tools and Applications

Any use of any information about the user to alter the presented content could be considered as personalizing interaction and it can be applied to any system [26]. Web personalization refers to personalization processes in the Web and it is considered as the process of individualized matching to consumer preferences through automated processes in the web environment [43]. Research in web personalization mostly adopts a technological point of view addressing issues such as user profiling, recommender systems, data collection and processing etc. Thus, customization and adaptation are often used as synonyms to personalization, due to different views and approaches adopted in literature [15, 49]. "Adaptive Web systems" are systems that tailor their appearance and behavior to each individual user or user group [7] through techniques as collaborative, content-based and knowledge-based recommendation for example [8].

Personal data can be gathered in an explicit way - if the user provides demographics, preferences, ratings, or other information explicitly to the system, or in an implicit way – if the system infers preferences from data collected, for instance, via a registration process or via the use of software that monitors user activity. Explicit personalization functionalities on websites include, Email Newsletters, One-to-one Collaborative Filtering, Homepage Customization, Mobile Editions and Apps, My Page, RSS Feeds, SMS Alerts and Widgets-applications, while the collection of implicit user information can be performed through Geo-targeted functionalities, Multiple Metrics or Social Collaborative Filtering [47].

Amoroso and Reinig [15] classify the technologies used in personalization management systems into four broad categories: user behavior tracking technologies, personalization database technologies, personalized user interface technologies and personalized just-in-time applications in mobile commerce capitalizing on a user's current location, activity, and surrounding environment.

The collection process of web browsing history related data (location, interests, purchases, employment status, sexual orientation, financial challenges, medical conditions etc.) is a valuable tool for profiling purposes [40, 41]. Web tracking is mostly performed by monitoring IP addresses and cookies, using techniques such as JavaScript, super cookies, fingerprinting, or DPI (Deep Packet Inspection) [62].

Recently, "big data" has become one of the most promoted marketing rally points: the value of big data market was estimated to US$50.1 billion in 2015 [3]. Big data analysis techniques (e.g. statistics, data mining, neural networks, social network analysis, signal processing, pattern recognition, optimization methods and visualization approaches) can process high volume data from multiple sources. This enables linking user attribute data from different sources and aggregating them into a single user profile. Moreover, user information from different sources can be correlated to validate or invalidate the information discovered from one source [24]. Recent research explores uses of big data for election predictions [3] as there has been a growing interest in mining online political sentiment to predict the outcome of elections [51].

Adaptive User Interfaces adapt themselves automatically at run time to context changes and offer an alternative to the traditional "one-size-fits-all". They support personalized access to information, by adaptively altering the appearance of links on every browsed page using methods such as direct guidance, adaptive ordering, link hiding or removal and adaptive link annotation [7]. Moreover, the potentials of personalization have increased dramatically since the introduction of social networking programming interfaces [48].

Geolocation technology has become a basic substructure for location positioning services and location-aware applications running on smartphones such as iPhone and Android devices. Geolocation data can be collected in several ways such as web browsing via IP addresses, mobile phones, GPS devices, radio frequency identification (RFID), credit/debit card transactions, tags in photographs and postings (such as geotags or check-ins using applications such as Foursquare) on social network sites such as Facebook and Twitter [61]. Knowledge of the geographical location of a mobile device is utilized by Location-based services (LSB) application for providing services based on that information, such as finding friends on social networks, map assistance by location points of interest etc. [14, 59].

3   Privacy Risks Associated with Personalization Technology

The concept of privacy varies according to context and environment. For many, privacy is a complex issue, difficult to define and restrict within limits due to multiple interests at stake and many actors involved [45, 52, 57]. Alan F. Westin, defined 50 years ago the modern right to privacy, as the right 'to determine how much of their personal information is disclosed and to whom, how it should be maintained and how disseminated' [57]. Solove [45] identifies four basic groups of harmful activities related to privacy: information collection, information processing, information dissemination and invasion. Information collection can be harmful if the data is processed (stored, combined, manipulated, searched and used).

Each of the phases of personalization process (data collection, user model creation, and adaptation) involves various challenges on privacy [48]. Through the general progression from information collection, to processing and dissemination, the data is moving further away from the control of the individual.

Advertisers are nowadays able to track and to sell to an individual in real-time, through digital ad exchanges. Real-time bidding is available for targeting consumers whether they are visiting a website, watching an online video or using their mobile phone [10]. Also, several advertising data providers buy identifying information, retrieve the user's dossier from an offline consumer database, and use it to target advertising [32]. Moreover, open APIs technologies and a growing number of social applications are utilized by SNSs to solicit, collect and open up user data for advertisers and others that have to gain from users' valuable data [6].

The range of data collection is increasing as new technologies capture and infer more and more information. Face recognition technologies for example, are becoming increasingly powerful in automatically identifying people's identities in video feeds or photo collections. They can be used to infer a wide range of knowledge about people's behavior. As the data is gathered and analyzed automatically, the control that people have on this information is highly limited [48]. New privacy risks stem from new types of data collection and analysis such as the new technologies for tracking location on mobile devices used in location based personalization [17].

According to Castelluccia and Narayanan [62], one of the biggest privacy risks involved in information collection by tracking, is global surveillance. This surveillance can be performed by government, for security or political reasons or by companies for commercial reasons, and it can lead to self-censorship and inhibition. Because of its inhibitory effects, surveillance is a tool of social control, enhancing the power of social norms which work more effectively when people are being observed by others in the community. Surveillance can also adversely impact freedom, creativity and self-development [45]. Data collection by tracking can be performed without the individual web users being aware, the exact purposes for the collection of the data are not clear and the limitations are undefined [40, 41]. Potential harms include error, abuse, lack of transparency and accountability. Summarizing, the harm to users from data collection by web tracking could be physical, psychological, economic or emotional distress [32].

At the user modeling stage, privacy risks originate from new technologies for analyzing the data. Profiling with big data techniques is considered a significant threat to user privacy [24] as technologies such as collaborative filtering and machine learning allow new predictions to be inferred from data [17]. Information processing involves various ways of connecting data together and linking it to the people to whom it pertains.

According to Solove [45], the forms of information processing are aggregation, identification, insecurity, secondary use and exclusion. Aggregation, meaning gathering information about a person, leads to a portrait of a person and it can cause dignitary harms, because of how it unsettles expectations. Aggregation can also increase the power that others have over individuals [45]. Personalization based on information aggregation is becoming widespread in industry and also as a research field in academia [48].

Kosinsky [28] shows in his study about Facebook's "likes", that it is possible to reveal vital information about people. He shows that, based on an average of 68 Facebook "likes" by a user, it is possible to predict a user's skin color (with 95% accuracy), his/her sexual orientation (88% accuracy) and political affiliation (85%). Moreover, intelligence, religious affiliation, alcohol, cigarette and drug use, ethnicity, religious and political views and even happiness, could all be determined. From the data it was even possible to deduce whether someone's parents were divorced [17, 23, 28].

It is often argued that most of the tracking is harmless because traces are anonymous but these traces can be deanonymised and linked to an identity via different methods. Narayanan has proposed recently a taxonomy of several ways in which a pseudonymous browsing history might become identified [62].

Discovering a user's identity once in a pseudonymous system is sufficient to also identify past and future interactions with the user [32]. Identification can inhibit one's ability to be anonymous or pseudonymous. Anonymity and pseudonymity protect people from bias based on their identities and enable people to vote, speak and associate more freely by protecting them from the danger of reprisal [45].

Present conditions for sharing through social applications include a lack of control over one's own information, a lack of transparency as to what information is being collected and how this information is being used. This way, privacy, data security, contextual integrity, user autonomy and freedom could be undermined [6]. People might not give out data if they know about a potential secondary use, such as spam or other forms of intrusive advertising. The potential for secondary use generates also fear and uncertainty over how one's information will be used in the future, creating a sense of powerlessness and vulnerability. New risks, at the adaptation phase, originate from distributing the adapted and personalized content, and are linked with threats such as breach of confidentiality, disclosure (revelation of truthful information about a person that impacts the way others judge the person's character), exposure, increased accessibility, blackmail, appropriation and distortion [45].

Researchers have extensively studied the problem of protecting privacy in Location-Based services (LBSs), where the service delivered depends on the user's location. Especially GeoSNs (Geo-Social Networks) allow users to post their locations so other users can access to it. The dissemination of location information among users can be a concern. Furthermore, user tagging could allow GeoSNs participants to report location information about other individuals who have a small degree of control or no control over the published data. Due to the release of spatiotemporal information, GeoSNs expose users to several privacy threats.

Generally, in LBSs, two major categories of threats are involved: the release of location information (when the user's identity is known) and re-identification through location referring to an adversary's ability to reduce a user's degree of anonymity by considering location information. For instance, by knowing that an anonymous GeoSNs user was in a given place at a given time, an adversary could exclude several candidate individuals and possibly identify the user. The same knowledge can also reveal information such as health problems, affiliations, and habits. If the user considers his involvement in the GeoSN to be sensitive, re-identification is a privacy violation.

Moreover, publishing a user's location can let an adversary infer that the user isn't at a certain place at a given time. In most GeoSNs, an adversary might be able to observe multiple users' presence in the same place; some users consider such co-location to be sensitive. Also, the location information an adversary can acquire by observing multiple users, might reveal sensitive information about the relationship among those users. In GeoSNs, user tagging might enable others to discover such relationships even without directly observing the users being involved [55].

4 Repurposing Personalization Techniques for Political Marketing

4.1 Case Study: The Trump Campaign

The 2016 presidential campaign of Donald Trump nominee for President of the United States was formally launched on June 16, 2015, at Trump Tower in New York City. There were three principal components to Trump's digital campaign operation: the marketing agency Giles-Parscale, the microtargeting firm Cambridge Analytica, and the Republican Party's digital team [23, 36]. Until June 2016, Trump's digital campaign was represented by a rudimentary website created for $1,500 by Brad Parscale, a marketing entrepreneur [23]. Brad Parscale, with almost no political experience, made the decision to spend much of his budget on Facebook, which he had used in commercial contexts to target audiences [36].

In June 2016, was announced that Donald Trump had hired Cambridge Analytica a Big Data company [23]. Cambridge Analytica, also new to the world of presidential campaigning, had worked on the Brexit campaign as well as the primary campaign of Senator Ted Cruz [36].

According to [23], while other campaigners have so far relied on demographics, Cambridge Analytica was using psychometrics. As Alexander Nix the company CEO declared, campaigning was based on a combination of three elements: behavioral science using the OCEAN Model, Big Data analysis and ad targeting. By Cambridge Analytica's account, the campaign targeted 13.5 million persuadable voters in sixteen battleground states, discovering the hidden Trump voters, especially in the Midwest, whom the polls had ignored. They also targeted Clinton supporters, especially "white liberals, young women and African Americans" [36].

"Pretty much every message that Trump put out was data-driven," and "we were able to form a model to predict the personality of every single adult in the United States of America." the company CEO Alexander Nix declared during a presentation of the company on The Concordia Summit Economic Forum on September 19, 2016, just over a month before the US elections.

According to Nix, the Cambridge Analytica buys personal data from a range of different sources like land registries, automotive data, shopping data, bonus cards, club memberships, what magazines you read, what churches you attend; "in the US, almost all personal data is for sale". Cambridge Analytica aggregated this data with the electoral rolls of the Republican Party and online data, and calculated a Big Five personality profile. This way, digital footprints became real people and the voters were targeted with an appropriate political message, a different one for everyone.

The Trump digital campaign also used "dark" sponsored Facebook posts that can only be seen by users with specific profiles; which included for example videos aimed at African-Americans in which Hillary Clinton referred to black men as predators.

On the day of the third presidential debate between Trump and Clinton, Trump's team tested 175,000 different ad variations for his arguments, in order to find the right versions above all, via Facebook. For targeting the recipients in the optimal psychological way, the messages differed for the most part only in microscopic details: different headings, colors, captions, with a photo or video. "This fine-tuning reaches all the way down to the smallest groups" Nix explained in an interview with Grassegger and Krogerus "We can address villages or apartment blocks in a targeted way. Even individuals".

The Cambridge Analytica is incorporated in the US, where laws regarding the release of personal data are laxer than in European Union countries. From July 2016, Trump's canvassers were provided with an app with which they could identify the political views and personality types of the inhabitants of a house. Trump's people only rang at the doors of houses that the app rated as receptive to his messages. The canvassers came prepared with guidelines for conversations tailored to the personality type of the resident. In turn, the canvassers fed the reactions into the app and the new data flowed back to the dashboards of the Trump campaign. Groundgame, an app for election canvassing that integrates voter data with "geospatial visualization technology," was also used by campaigners for Trump and Brexit. Cambridge Analytica, divided the US population into 32 personality types, and focused on just 17 states [23].

Cambridge Analytica's psychographic-profiling method, gathered much attention and criticism, even from Republican campaign consultants [36]. However, in a statement after the German publication of the article of Grassegger and Krogerus, a Cambridge Analytica spokesperson declared that "Cambridge Analytica does not use data from Facebook. Psychographics was hardly used at all. Cambridge Analytica did not engage in efforts to discourage any Americans from casting their vote in the presidential election. Its efforts were solely directed towards increasing the number of voters in the election" [23].

Finally, the campaign also benefited from the Republican Party's data operation, which since 2012 had invested heavily in list-building and other technological tools [36].

4.2 Implications

Personalization techniques and tools, which marketers are using for improving their marketing on the web [54], remodeled the political communication into an increasingly personalized, private transaction. Hence, the public sphere is fundamentally reshaped by making it less and less public as these approaches can be used to both profile and interact individually with voters outside the public sphere. For instance, a Facebook ad targeted at a particular voter, which nobody else can see it [50].

According to Tufekci [50], the big datasets along with advances in computational techniques, allow political campaigns the modeling of an individual voter preferences and attributes at a high level of precision, often without asking the voter a single direct question. The results of such models may match the quality of the answers that were only extractable via direct questions and far exceed the scope of information that could be gathered about a voter via traditional methods.

For now, there is no evidence that psychometric methods have influenced the outcome of the 2016 US presidential election. Cambridge Analytica was unwilling to provide any proof of the effectiveness of its campaign [23].

Donald Trump's campaign however, was not the first which adopted political marketing's personalization techniques and tools. One way of mobilizing Obama's supporters during the'08 electoral campaign for instance, was through a free application for the Apple iPhone which used supporters' geographic location to identify relevant local political activities in which the supporter could immediately engage [11]. Also, the G20 met in London on 2 April 2009, attracted a complex protest ecology involving multiple actors. Many organizations have used networks for communication and mobilization of protesters with many bridges among them such as travelling Twitter streams or common organizational sponsorships. PPF (Put People First) protest campaign's website offered 23 personalized technological engagement mechanisms [4].

Nowadays, it is routinely argued that "winning parliamentary or presidential elections without marketing is almost impossible" [18]. According to Campus [18], pre-campaign market research helps to figure out "what type of leadership is most in demand by those segments of the electorate that are also potential constituencies". Once their image is "packaged" according to the demands of voters, politicians are "sold" on the (electoral) market by means of advertisement; empirical research on political advertisement has demonstrated its strong impact on voters' perceptions of the candidates [18].

Authors agree that political campaigns are investing more and more in digital advertising using social networks data [4, 50]. Twitter has also become a legitimate communication channel in the political area [39]. Over one hundred thousand tweets dating from August 13 to September 19, 2009, containing the names of the six parties represented in the German parliament, were collected and analyzed using sentiment analysis software. Tumasjan et al. [51] concluded that the number of tweets/mentions of a party is directly proportional to the probability of winning the elections. Yet, as scholars agree, Internet has an undeniable impact on the ways and means through which the public engages with politics. According to Pearson and O'Connell in [21] note, 'in 2009, Twitter was a novelty in politics but in 2012, it's a necessity'. It can be expected that sentiment analysis will be part of every campaign in the future [39].

Willson in her study [58], refers to a different aspect of the potential implications of personalization which may have long-term effects not only on the individuals but also at the level of the society. Among others, she mentions implications such as the reduction in exposure to diversity through increased personalization, concerns over the surveillance potential of data bodies and data histories with state and corporate decisions impacting on groups and individuals, based on data sets and analysis/risk management strategies, manipulation of results in ways that might impact on particular populations, demographics or individuals financially, socially or politically.

On the other hand, the act and process of engaging with a campaign may well have multiple benefits for a citizen's civic skills (such as political sophistication), social capital and overall participation.

However, despite the hopes of reformers, political elites do not employ new communication channels with the aim of citizen empowerment or greater democratic deliberation [5]. The goal of the candidate investment in media tools, remains winning elections. Another aspect of using personalization technologies for political purposes is related to the often controlled by private platforms databases and the equipment and expertise required to effectively use this data. This environment favors incumbents who already are in the possession of valuable data, also entrenched and moneyed candidates within parties, as well as the data–rich among existing parties [50]. Political branding has gained increased attention within marketing and political science journals, highlighting the growing consensus that parties and politicians can usefully be conceptualized as brands [33]. The "selling" of politicians will become more expansive and improved, if more expensive [50].

5   Discussion

Understanding the human behavior is a key element for marketers to influence customers and competitors and generate profits. Over the last thirty years, since Kotler and Levy (1969) first suggested this transferability of thinking, many basic marketing ideas have been accepted in the social area [25].

Initially, political marketing was used more or less interchangeably with propaganda. The purpose of the related activities however, was the same: mass persuasion. According to Scammel [44], the new "marketing" label reflects a quest for a more neutral term as propaganda being discredited, and partly the observation that professionals from the commercial marketing industry, especially advertising, were increasingly involved in political persuasion [34].

In opposition to the commercial marketing of goods and services, the focus of political marketing is to "market" ideas, values or candidates of a political party. By political marketing, a campaigning organization communicates messages, interacts with and responds to supporters, delivers to all stakeholders public information, advice and leadership. Additionally, it develops credibility and trust with supporters, provides training, information resources, and campaign material for candidates, agents, marketers, and/or other party activists [2].

The political marketing is studied extensively in various contexts. Lees-Marshment [29] refers to a permanent campaign which includes the behavior at the beginning to the end of an electoral cycle (not just the election campaign) and involves the leadership, MPs (and candidates), membership, staff, symbols, constitution, activities such as party conferences and policies [27].

Some authors [12, 33], refer to political branding which has gained increased attention within marketing and political science journals, highlighting the growing consensus that parties and politicians can usefully be conceptualized as brands. Lilleker [30] studies the public political communication as a marketing tool and refers to "cyber-parties" which are evolving. Understanding political preferences is important for presenting tailored information and personalizing the user's experience [22]. According to Rahat and Sheafer [37], the central problem in the studies of political personalization is the mixing of different types of political personalization.

The concept of personalization is used by various scholars in different contexts with different meanings. The point, however, that all researchers agree with is the fact that the Internet has fundamentally changed the way campaigns strategize and communicate with their constituents.

Politicians, governments, various organizations, even extremists, are adopting the last few years the more and more sophisticated tools that personalization technologies offer for "marketing" their idea and beliefs. Political Campaign Software Products such as Ecanvasser[1], Wild Apricot[2], CiviCRM[3], RakletCUBallot[4], Click & Pledge[5], Camtrack[6], NGP VAN[7] etc., are available for political marketing services.

Cambridge Analytica website offers two categories of services: a commercial (Data-driven marketing) and a political one (Data-driven campaigns). "By knowing your electorate better, we achieve greater influence while lowering overall costs" they refer related to the support of political campaigns.

ISIS, also used between April to June 2014, an app "The Dawn of Glad Tidings", which imitated the functions of the app named Thunderclap that has been used for political campaigns in the US [35]. Bennett and Segerberg study [4], show the use of several personalization methods by protest organizations campaign websites (e.g. Put People First, Climate Camp, Meltdown) during the G20 met in London on 2 April, 2009. Also the Obama 2008 and 2012 electoral campaigns were analyzed by several researchers [5, 16, 21], showing that the political e-marketing adopted successfully the personalization tools of commercial e-marketing.

The Brexit campaign is also parallelized with the 2016 US presidential election [23, 38]. The "Leave.EU" campaign supported by Nigel Farage, commissioned the same company (Cambridge Analytica) for supporting its online campaign. Also, there has been a growing interest recently in mining online political sentiment for predicting the outcome of elections [51].

New privacy risks arise from new technologies such as tracking location, analyzing data or collaborative filtering and machine learning, which allow new predictions to be inferred from data. Furthermore, since one new trend is the social-based personalization, the development of data-mining software based on large data ware-housing applications

---

[1] https://www.ecanvasser.com/.
[2] https://www.capterra.com/p/110128/Wild-Apricot/.
[3] https://www.capterra.com/p/79192/CiviCRM/.
[4] https://www.capterra.com/p/148555/Raklet/.
[5] https://www.capterra.com/p/54088/Click-Pledge/.
[6] https://www.capterra.com/p/155984/Camtrack/.
[7] https://www.capterra.com/p/148396/NGP-VAN/.

raise new questions related to new privacy risks. The Web 2 era, induced globally in the political area new dynamic parameters that seems to have a potential effect on political decisions and beliefs.

The availability of big data, the shift to individual targeting, the rise of behavioral science in the service of persuasion and the growth of new power brokers on the Internet who controls the data and algorithms, will affect many aspects of life in this century. Overall, as Tufekci refers: "the impact is not so much like increasing the power of a magnifying glass as it is like re-purposing the glass by putting two or more together to make fundamentally new tools, like the microscope or the telescope, turning unseen objects into objects of scientific inquiry and manipulation" [50].

6 Conclusions

In this work, we show that personalization tools and techniques are used increasingly for political purposes and we analyze the privacy risks and related harmful activities involved in the stages of the personalization process.

This research has identified that the use of personalization tools in the political area results in two broad categories of privacy implications: (a) Implications with direct impact on individuals. These implications arise from activities in all phases of personalization processes, including the information collection, the information processing and adaptation; (b) Implications related to society. For example, tracking techniques used by governments for global surveillance could evolve in social control tools. Another example is that user involvement can be bought leading to a manipulation of the results in ways that might impact financially, socially or politically [20].

To the best our knowledge, this is the first study focusing on privacy issues involved in personalization technologies repurposed for political marketing. In this paper, we also highlight the need for further research related to new privacy risks linked to the use of new personalization technologies in the political area.

It seems that privacy issues intertwine with electoral outcomes but future research is needed to clarify the mechanisms of these processes. Personalization tools become more and more sophisticated and, in combination with the new dynamic information environment, shape new contexts for privacy protection which need a deeper understanding. The implications of using big data for example, in combination to machine learning techniques are affecting already many aspects of life including privacy in ways which need further research.

Scholars agree that text mining, user profiling and localization, sentiment analysis, social sensing are only some of the means used to accomplish a deep analysis of the traces that people continually leave on social media [31, 60]. The scale and the complexity of collaborative filtering used by recommender systems also raise questions regarding new privacy risks.

Political e-marketing is a relatively new research field and there are not enough studies yet related to the impact on individuals and society, of using the personal information gathered by personalization techniques in the context of election campaigns and beliefs dissemination. Conclusively, there is a clear need to reconsider or extend political area related frameworks, to clarify the factors involved and to identify security and privacy implications.

References

1. Awad, N.F., Krishnan, M.S.: The personalization privacy paradox: an empirical evaluation of information transparency and the willingness to be profiled online for personalization. MIS Q. **30**, 13–28 (2006)
2. Baines, P.R., et al.: "Market" classification and political campaigning: some strategic implications. J. Polit. Mark. **2**(2), 47–66 (2003)
3. Baruh, L., Popescu, M.: Big data analytics and the limits of privacy self-management. New Med. Soc. **19**(4), 579–596 (2017)
4. Bennett, W.L., Segerberg, A.: Digital media and the personalization of collective action: Social technology and the organization of protests against the global economic crisis. Inf. Commun. Soc. **14**(6), 770–799 (2011)
5. Bimber, B.: Digital media in the Obama campaigns of 2008 and 2012: adaptation to the personalized political communication environment. J. Inf. Technol. Polit. **11**(2), 130–150 (2014)
6. Bodle, R.: Regimes of sharing: open APIs, interoperability, and Facebook. Inf. Commun. Soc. **14**(3), 320–337 (2011)
7. Brusilovsky, P., Millán, E.: User models for adaptive hypermedia and adaptive educational systems. In: Brusilovsky, P., Kobsa, A., Nejdl, W. (eds.) The Adaptive Web. LNCS, vol. 4321, pp. 3–53. Springer, Heidelberg (2007). https://doi.org/10.1007/978-3-540-72079-9_1
8. Burke, R.: Hybrid recommender systems: Survey and experiments. User Model. User-Adapt. Inter. **12**(4), 331–370 (2002)
9. Chen, H., et al.: Business intelligence and analytics: from big data to big impact. MIS Q. **36**(4), 1165–1188 (2012)
10. Chester, J.: Cookie wars: How new data profiling and targeting techniques threaten citizens and consumers in the "big data" era. In: Gutwirth, S., Leenes, R., De Hert, P., Poullet, Y. (eds.) European Data Protection: In Good Health?, pp. 53–77. Springer, Dordrecht (2012). https://doi.org/10.1007/978-94-007-2903-2_4
11. Cogburn, D.L., Espinoza-Vasquez, F.K.: From networked nominee to networked nation: examining the impact of Web 2.0 and social media on political participation and civic engagement in the 2008 Obama campaign. J. Polit. **10**(1–2), 189–213 (2011)
12. Cwalina, W., Falkowski, A.: Political branding: political candidates positioning based on inter-object associative affinity index. J. Polit. Mark. **14**(1–2), 152–174 (2015)
13. Darwish, A., Lakhtaria, K.I.: The impact of the new Web 2.0 technologies in communication, development, and revolutions of societies. J. Adv. Inf. Technol. **2**(4), 204–216 (2011)
14. Doshi, P., et al.: Location based services and integration of Google maps in android. Int. J. Eng. Comput. Sci. **3**, 5072–5077 (2014)
15. Fan, H., Poole, M.S.: What is personalization? Perspectives on the design and implementation of personalization in information systems. J. Organ. Comput. Electron. Commer. **16**(3–4), 179–202 (2006)
16. Garcia, W.S.: Politics, journalism and Web 2.0 in the 2008 US presidential elections (2009)
17. Garcia-Rivadulla, S.: Personalization vs. privacy: an inevitable trade-off? IFLA J. **42**(3), 227–238 (2016)
18. Garzia, D.: The personalization of politics in Western democracies: causes and consequences on leader–follower relationships. Leadersh. Q. **22**(4), 697–709 (2011)

19. Gasparetti, F.: Personalization and context-awareness in social local search: state-of-the-art and future research challenges. Pervasive Mob. Comput. **38**(Part 2), 446–473 (2017)
20. Gerlitz, C. et al.: Hit, link, like and share. Organising the social and the fabric of the web. In: Digital Methods Winter Conference Proceedings, pp. 1–29 (2011)
21. Gerodimos, R., Justinussen, J.: Obama's 2012 Facebook campaign: political communication in the age of the like button. J. Inf. Technol. Polit. **12**(2), 113–132 (2015)
22. Golbeck, J., Hansen, D.: Computing political preference among twitter followers. In: Proceedings of the SIGCHI Conference on Human Factors in Computing Systems, pp. 1105–1108. ACM (2011)
23. Grassegger, H., Krogerus, M.: The data that turned the world upside down (2017). Luettavissa: http://motherboard.vice.com/read/big-data-cambridge-analytica-brexit-trump. Luettu. 28 2017
24. Habegger, B., Hasan, O., Brunie, L., Bennani, N., Kosch, H., Damiani, E.: Personalization vs. privacy in big data analysis. Int. J. Big Data 25–35 (2014)
25. Hastings, G., Saren, M.: The critical contribution of social marketing: theory and application. Mark. Theor. **3**(3), 305–322 (2003)
26. Karat, J., et al.: Personalizing interaction. In: Karat, C.-M., Blom, J.O., Karat, J. (eds.) Designing Personalized User Experiences in eCommerce, pp. 7–17. Springer, Dordrecht (2004). https://doi.org/10.1007/1-4020-2148-8_2
27. Kolovos, I., Harris, P.: Political marketing and political communication: the relationship revisited (2005)
28. Kosinski, M., et al.: Manifestations of user personality in website choice and behaviour on online social networks. Mach. Learn. **95**(3), 357–380 (2014)
29. Lees-Marshment, J.: The marriage of politics and marketing. Polit. Stud. **49**(4), 692–713 (2001)
30. Lilleker, D.G.: Interactivity and branding: public political communication as a marketing tool. J. Polit. Mark. **14**(1–2), 111–128 (2015)
31. Liu, B., Zhang, L.: A survey of opinion mining and sentiment analysis. In: Aggarwal, C., Zhai, C. (eds.) Mining Text Data, pp. 415–463. Springer, Boston (2012). https://doi.org/10.1007/978-1-4614-3223-4_13
32. Mayer, J.R., Mitchell, J.C.: Third-party web tracking: policy and technology. In: 2012 IEEE Symposium on Security and Privacy (SP), pp. 413–427. IEEE (2012)
33. Needham, C., Smith, G.: Introduction: political branding. J. Polit. Mark. **14**(1–2), 1–6 (2015)
34. Nor, C.S.M., et al.: Political marketing vs. commercial marketing: something in common for gains. Eur. J. Mark. **28**(3), 20–31 (2006)
35. Pellerin C.: Communicating terror: an analysis of ISIS communication. http://www.sciencespo.fr/psia/sites/sciencespo.fr.psia/files/PELLERINClara_KSP_Paper_Award.pdf. Accessed 10 Sept 2017
36. Persily, N.: Can democracy survive the internet? J. Democr. **28**(2), 63–76 (2017)
37. Rahat, G., Sheafer, T.: The personalization(s) of politics: Israel, 1949–2003. Polit. Commun. **24**(1), 65–80 (2007)
38. Ramswell, P.Q.: Derision, division–decision: parallels between Brexit and the 2016 US presidential election. Eur. Polit. Sci. **16**(2), 217–232 (2017)
39. Ringsquandl, M., Petkovic, D.: Analyzing political sentiment on twitter. In: AAAI Spring Symposium: Analyzing Microtext, pp. 40–47 (2013)
40. Roosendaal, A.: Facebook Tracks and Traces Everyone: Like This! Social Science Research Network, Rochester (2010)

41. Roosendaal, A.: We are all connected to Facebook ... by Facebook! In: Gutwirth, S., Leenes, R., De Hert, P., Poullet, Y. (eds.) European Data Protection: In Good Health?, pp. 3–19. Springer, Dordrecht (2012). https://doi.org/10.1007/978-94-007-2903-2_1
42. Safiullah, M., et al.: Social media as an upcoming tool for political marketing effectiveness. Asia Pac. Manag. Rev. **22**(1), 10–15 (2017)
43. Salonen, V., Karjaluoto, H.: Web personalization: the state of the art and future avenues for research and practice. Telemat. Inform. **33**(4), 1088–1104 (2016)
44. Scammell, M.: Political marketing: lessons for political science. Polit. Stud. **47**(4), 718–739 (1999)
45. Solove, D.J.: A Taxonomy of Privacy. Social Science Research Network, Rochester (2005)
46. Sorj, B.: Internet, public sphere and political marketing: between the promotion of communication and moralist solipsism. Humanit. Technol. Rev. **27**, 45–68 (2008)
47. Thurman, N., Schifferes, S.: The future of personalization at news websites: lessons from a longitudinal study. Journal. Stud. **13**(5–6), 775–790 (2012)
48. Toch, E., et al.: Personalization and privacy: a survey of privacy risks and remedies in personalization-based systems. User Model. User-Adapt. Inter. **22**(1), 203–220 (2012)
49. Treiblmaier, H. et al.: Evaluating personalization and customization from an ethical point of view: an empirical study. In: Proceedings of the 37th Annual Hawaii International Conference on System Sciences, 10 pp. IEEE (2004)
50. Tufekci, Z.: Engineering the public: big data, surveillance and computational politics. First Monday **19**(7), 7 July 2014. http://dx.doi.org/10.5210/fm.v19i7.4901, http://firstmonday.org/ojs/index.php/fm/article/view/4901/4097
51. Tumasjan, A., et al.: Predicting elections with twitter: what 140 characters reveal about political sentiment. ICWSM **10**(1), 178–185 (2010)
52. Van De Garde-Perik, E., et al.: Investigating privacy attitudes and behavior in relation to personalization. Soc. Sci. Comput. Rev. **26**(1), 20–43 (2008)
53. Vemou, K., Karyda, M.: Evaluating privacy practices in Web 2.0 services. In: MCIS, p. 7 (2015)
54. Vesanen, J.: What is personalization? A conceptual framework. Eur. J. Mark. **41**(5/6), 409–418 (2007)
55. Vicente, C.R., et al.: Location-related privacy in geo-social networks. IEEE Internet Comput. **15**(3), 20–27 (2011)
56. Wang, Y., Kobsa, A.: Respecting users' individual privacy constraints in web personalization. In: Conati, C., McCoy, K., Paliouras, G. (eds.) UM 2007. LNCS, vol. 4511, pp. 157–166. Springer, Heidelberg (2007). https://doi.org/10.1007/978-3-540-73078-1_19
57. Westin, A.F.: Social and political dimensions of privacy. J. Soc. Issues **59**(2), 431–453 (2003)
58. Willson, M.: The politics of social filtering. Convergence **20**(2), 218–232 (2014)
59. Yun, H., et al.: Understanding the use of location-based service applications: do privacy concerns matter? J. Electron. Commer. Res. **14**(3), 215 (2013)
60. Zeng, D., et al.: Social media analytics and intelligence. IEEE Intell. Syst. **25**(6), 13–16 (2010)
61. Geolocation: Risks, issues and strategies, ISACA (2011). http://www.isaca.org/Groups/Professional. Accessed 7 Sept 2017
62. Privacy considerations of online behavioral tracking — ENISA. https://www.enisa.europa.eu/publications/privacy-considerations-of-online-behavioural-tracking. Accessed 2 Sept 2017

Transparency-Enabling Systems for Open Governance: Their Impact on Citizens' Trust and the Role of Information Privacy

Aristomenis Gritzalis[1,2], Aggeliki Tsohou[3(✉)], and Costas Lambrinoudakis[1]

[1] Department of Digital Systems, University of Piraeus,
80 Karaoli and Dimitriou Str., 18534 Piraeus, Greece
agritz@ssl-unipi.gr, clam@unipi.gr
[2] School of Social and Political Sciences, University of Edinburgh, 15a George Square,
Edinburgh, EH8 9LD, UK
[3] Department of Informatics, Ionian University, 7 Tsirigoti Square, 49100 Corfu, Greece
atsohou@ionio.gr

Abstract. Several governments and citizens embrace information systems that are designed to enable transparency of public expenses and discourage corruption in the public sector. The objective of this paper is to examine the capacity and value of information systems designed to enhance transparency, from a citizens'/ users' perspective. Our purpose is to address research questions associated with the actual impact of transparency-enabling systems and openness on citizens' trust, as well as on uncertainty towards governmental policies and actions. We also explored the impact of privacy requirements and personal data protection regulations on the system and citizens' willingness to access public data. To the best of our knowledge, these are largely unexplored issues in the related literature. Our study involves the design of a web survey and the execution of an empirical study with citizens who have used such a system in Greece. In particular, we focused on the Greek system 'Diavgeia', which is the national transparency and anti-corruption system.

Keywords: Information systems · Transparency · Anti-corruption · Privacy · Trust

1 Introduction

There are multiple perspectives on examining the impact of information technology (IT) and its consequences to the social and technical world (Orlikowski and Iacono 2001). Researchers have studied the ways in which IT can increase productivity and alter social relations, how it becomes embedded in organizational structures, which technical and non-technical attributes enable IT acceptance and diffusion, etc. A significant stream of research explores how IT becomes the tool to intentionally bring change and innovation, such as increasing productivity, altering work practices and processes, enhancing privacy, enforcing rules, and others.

The role of IT is fundamental for addressing multiple challenges faced by modern societies. The EU and the U.S.A. (Obama 2009) consistently support a paradigm shift

© Springer International Publishing AG 2017
S.K. Katsikas and V. Zorkadis (Eds.): E-Democracy 2017, CCIS 792, pp. 47–63, 2017.
https://doi.org/10.1007/978-3-319-71117-1_4

of public management towards open government. The new paradigm urges for opening public data and services, creating new public services and opening government processes and decisions to foster citizen participation and engagement. Transparency for the financial and administrative actions of governments is considered a core mechanism for reducing corruption in the public sector (Brautigam 1992; O'Hara 2012; Jaeger and Bertot 2010b). Although the capacity of IT for enabling transparency is evident, it is challenging to design, implement, diffuse and institutionalise such systems because they are associated with wide-scale changes (Jaeger and Bertot 2010a). The adoption of open government systems is associated with changes such as altering work processes in public organizations, requiring interoperability with existing systems, distorting the power balance among stakeholders, managing users' resistance, and many others.

In this paper, we focus on a specific type of information system that can support open government, namely transparency-enabling systems. IT has the capacity to reshape political demands, such as transparency (Eynon 2007), to affect the way citizens act and think, and to enable trust in institutions (Srivastava and Teo 2005). The circumstances within which IT can strengthen democracy are not fully clear, yet IT-enabled transparency seems to be approached not just as a necessary measure against malfunction in the democratic process, but as an independent ethical obligation, that is an end in itself. Transparency has been defined as the opening of procedures that are not immediately visible to those not directly involved, aiming to display how well an institution works (Moser 2001). This definition not only indicates what the word means, but also brings out a purpose behind it: institutional functionality in service of the public good, increasing of trust and mitigation of uncertainty. Some indicative transparency-enabling systems include the website enforcing the Federal Funding Accountability and Transparency Act (usaspending.gov) in the United States, the Public Services and Procurement system in Canada (tpsgc-pwgsc.gc.ca), and the Openaid in Sweden (Openaid.se) that reports data on aid funds. Given that few scholars have investigated the implementation of transparency and anti-corruption systems for open government (Dawes and Helbig 2010; Jaeger and Bertot 2010a, b; Kim et al. 2009; Scholl and Luna-Reyes 2011), the research area remains unexplored.

The relationship between IT-mediated transparency and citizens' trust could enlighten the future of e-governance and the role of technology in the democratic process. Transparency is a major weapon against corruption and offers institutions the possibility to gain citizens' trust in times of crisis, wide uncertainty and deep confusion (Meijer 2009). Therefore, transparency-enabling information systems seem to have the capacity to become a political and institutional defense mechanism, for developed and developing countries (Rahul De' 2005) alike. However, researchers have expressed concerns that more openness is not the equivalent of more trust (Licht 2011; Grimmelikhuijsen et al. 2013; Meijer 2009). Others point out that transparency and politicians' accountability to citizens do not necessarily mean more honesty and less corruption; on the contrary other things like accountability make a much more significant effect in this direction (V-Dem Weekly Graphs 2016). Other scholars have been emphatically negative towards the results and importance of transparency, claiming that regarding it as problem solving is illusory and disorientating (Tsoukas 1997; Strathern 2000). Furthermore, transparency tools have also been criticized by personal data protection experts and authorities due to potential privacy concerns (Tzermias et al. 2014; European Commission: Article 29 Data Protection Working Party 2015). Transparency may also trigger a counterproductive political and media witch-hunt and there are indications that isolated transparency measures are linked to policy and presentational blame-avoidance strategies (Hood 2007).

Transparency therefore is perceived on the one hand as a way to reduce uncertainty in public governance, while on the other hand there are several counterarguments. The objective of this paper is to examine IT-enabled transparency from the citizens' perspective, and address three largely unexplored research questions: (a) Does more governmental openness lead to more citizens' trust in institutions and less uncertainty, (b) Do individual privacy rights affect the citizens' willingness to access public data, and (c) Does the structure and inclusiveness of a transparency system/portal affect citizens' trust in public authorities. The study includes an empirical investigation using an online survey. For our empirical research we used the case of 'Diavgeia', which is the national transparency and anti-corruption system of Greece since 2010. This system is enforced through national legislation which states that all decisions resulting in public expenditures should be publicly announced in this online platform, otherwise they are invalid. 'Diavgeia' is the largest network of individuals and collective entities that can be found in the Greek public sector. Thousands of acts are daily uploaded in it, in a way that has been regarded as exceptionally innovative and with great accuracy. Because of this system, the everyday activities of every public institution are brought to light for whoever is interested in them. Interested parties include journalists, academics, open data specialists, individual citizens, non-governmental organisations, and others. 'Diavgeia' has been selected and presented as a Best Practice at the 6th European Quality Conference (2011), and has also been presented as a major successful open government reform at the Open Government Partnership OGP, an international platform of 69 Countries committed to making their governments more open, accountable, and responsive to citizens.

The rest of the paper is structured as follows. The next section presents a thematic analysis of the existing work related to transparency and anti-corruption systems. Section 3 presents our research methodology and design, emphasizing on the survey instrument development. Section 4 presents the analysis of the findings and Sect. 5 the discussion of the research implications. Section 6 concludes the paper.

2 Analysis of Existing Work on Transparency and Anti-corruption Systems

2.1 Facilitating Factors and Obstacles

Researchers have investigated the implementation of transparency and anti-corruption systems, including the facilitating factors and the possible obstacles. In the following paragraphs, we describe in brief the existing literature on four systems, namely OPEN, the Bhoomi Project, the Czech Public e-Procurement Information System and a system for land records and parcel information for the state of New York. The aforementioned have been selected as indicative examples of Transparency and Anti-Corruption

Systems, since they focus on different application domains and have been implemented in geographically dispersed areas.

Kim and Cho (2005) examined a system named OPEN, used by the Seoul Metropolitan Government in order to reduce administrative delays and mishandlings of civil affairs. The system resulted in successful and transparent online monitoring of the status of citizens' applications until they were finalised. The facilitating factors for the successful implementation of OPEN were powerful leadership, small sized and simple IT, and customer-oriented IT. Kim and Cho (2005) identified four obstacles in the system implementation. Initially, the existence of two directing bodies (bureaus) led to conflicts and collisions. Further, additional workload emerged for civil officials, since the preexisting system was still running. Technical support was not available due to financial shortcomings, resulting in instability and low speed. Finally, civil officials manifested strong resistance due to the undermining of their authority and the additional workload.

Thomas (2009) and Otta et al. (2015) studied the Bhoomi Project, which is an e-governance system in an Indian state for the digitization of land records. The system's success was allocated to hard-working leadership, minimization of staff resistance by harnessing political support, and extensive training coupled with a participatory style. Nevertheless, the system's implementation faced various obstacles, such as the existence of forged documents, the lack of funds, the illiteracy of some users, the lack of cross-departmental computerisation, as well as many infrastructural bottlenecks.

Chvalkovská and Skuhrovec (2010) examined the Czech Public e-Procurement information system. They integrated a Transparency Index within the e-Procurement system, which demonstrated the drawbacks of the tools in use towards increasing transparency. Among the obstacles that they faced were the difficulty to extract aggregate data from the system, the inability of the public to effectively exercise control over procurements and the lack of statistical features that would facilitate this control. Without addressing those issues, the researchers claimed that although the system provides access to the public procurement data, public control and transparency are practically non-existent.

Dawes and Helbig (2010) dealt with the use of land records and parcel information of the state of New York. They studied how the various public agencies and private organizations use these records and concluded that the data are not of satisfactory quality since there are many handling flaws, such as lack of feedback mechanisms between data users and data collectors. As facilitating factors, the researchers recommended the creation of formal feedback mechanisms that would connect users and sources with the development of new skills, so that the staff would be able to support public information access and use. Additionally, they proposed the creation of new roles in order to coordinate agency-level and government-wide programs with user support services. Jaeger and Bertot (2010b) investigated the case of the platform introduced by the Obama administration aiming to increase transparency and access to government information. Among the challenges the authors identified are the inclusion of members of the public with limited access to the internet or with limited IT skills, and the use of non-governmental channels to disseminate government information. Further, an important challenge they underlined is that after the platform was in use for some time, it became difficult to manage all the available data. The study highlighted that as the volume of information uploaded to the platform increases, the users have difficulties in finding the content they are looking for; thus transparency can actually be limited, despite the guaranteed availability of the information.

2.2 The Role of Involved Stakeholders

Another aspect of transparency information systems that has been studied by researchers is the role of the involved stakeholders. Rahul De' (2005) also examined the Bhoomi Project, from the perspective of the conflicts between stakeholders. De' (2005) argued that in order to enable the system it is necessary to go beyond its functionality and focus on stakeholders' conflicts of interest and resistance. For this purpose he developed a framework that classifies stakeholders, based on the benefits they acquire from the system: there is a demand-side and a supply-side. The demand side benefits from transparency, effectiveness and efficiency, meaning that the system fosters its professional interests. Therefore, this side has an interest in the implementation of such a transparency-enabling information system. The supply side is not involved in the system's implementation, but supports it as well since it facilitates new, modern public services and moderates corruption.

2.3 Privacy Concerns and Data Protection Considerations

This subject is quite significant for our research objective, especially because it deals with the contradictory aspects of two desirable societal principles: transparency and information privacy. This contradiction seemingly breeds a challenge for designing and implementing transparency-enabling systems. Tzermias et al. (2014) examined the privacy risks that emerge from the use of transparency systems and illustrated a serious compromise for citizens' privacy due to the disclosure of personal information in public data sources. The unveiling of such information would enable the drawing of the full profile of an individual, that is to produce a detailed description of the person (e.g. father's name, full address, profession, civil status etc.). Tzermias et al. (2014) used data administered by the Greek system 'Diavgeia', which makes their study uniquely relevant to ours. They examined various repositories in the system and investigated the possibility of privacy violation incidents through 'Diavgeia'. They assessed the data in consideration to privacy risks such as identity theft, fraud, and stalking; Eventually, various vulnerabilities were discovered that enable the collection of personal data; such vulnerabilities open the way for a variety of privacy violation incidents, namely impersonation attacks, identity thefts, confidence trickster attacks and so on. Although information privacy is not equivalent to personal data protection, there is a direct link between them. A large amount of personal information can be found in 'Diavgeia', which puts individual privacy rights in the spotlight. Furthermore, Tzermias et al. (2014) proposed countermeasures to prevent information leaks that could violate information privacy. More specifically, they recommended *Rate-limiting* techniques to throttle the number of requests originating from a specific user or host, *CAPTCHA* methods for preventing brute force attacks, data sanitization techniques, accountability mechanisms, and others. As an additional note, other personal data protection concerns should also be considered, such as the potential usage of the personal data that 'Diavgeia' processes for purposes that exceed the original intentions, like the development of open data action plans.

2.4   Enabling Trust and Reducing Uncertainty

An interesting question surrounding the implementation of transparency and anti-corruption systems is whether they enable citizens' trust and mitigate societal uncertainty towards the *modus operandi* of public institutions; that is the way in which they operate. Referring to uncertainty in this context, we mainly point to the citizens' distrust towards the moral code and the efficiency of public officials' operations – more and more frequently these two tend to coalesce in the public sphere, forming an inclusive notion of citizens' "uncertainty". That said, it is clear that there is a rather long distance between (dis)trust and (un)certainty; the two, though, are well-linked.

Grimmelikhuijsen et al. (2013) conducted a cross-country comparative experiment to study the effect of transparency on trust in government. The paper examined transparency in decision-making, in policy content and policy outcomes, while classifying transparent information based on their inclusiveness, usability and quality. According to the experiment, they argued that trustworthiness requires performance evaluation, benevolence and honesty. It was also revealed that the role of national culture has a major influence over the concept of transparency and, as a conclusion, more openness does not necessarily increase trust in government. Licht (2011) investigated the effect of transparency in decision making, as well as governments' legitimacy and credibility. The results of the study highlighted that transparent decision-making tends to weaken trust in the healthcare sector, whereas no empirical support was found supporting that transparency enables increased legitimacy. O'Hara (2012) studied the UK government's transparency programme in crime and criminal justice and the fostering of trust through three theories; social capital theories, rational choice theories and deliberative democracy theories. Through their analysis they discovered that although transparency of information is crucial, it is not sufficient on its own to foster citizens' trust. Publishing data is not enough; several changes are needed at an institutional and procedural level in order for the published information to be meaningful for the citizens and enhance their trust.

3   Research Design

3.1   Methodology

The current research aims to explore IT-enabled transparency from the citizens' perspective; in this frame, our study focuses on public perceptions of IT-enabled transparency with regards to a number of aspects. Our case is the 'Diavgeia' system and thus we explore the Greek citizens' perceptions of 'Diavgeia' and its potential relation with trust in public authorities. Given that the population is too large for probabilistic sampling, we chose to apply the availability sampling technique was chosen and applied, which relies on all available, easily reached participants (Babbie 2011). A web survey instrument was developed in order to allow individuals to participate anytime and from anywhere. The research questionnaire was designed with the intention to reveal citizens' views. The purpose is not to validate an existing or already developed theory, but to explore the citizens' understanding, thus we established face validity for the instrument (Bryman 2008). The survey was publicly announced on social media and other diffusion channels (e.g., communities and forums) and was completed by 130 people.

3.2   The Five Sections of the Empirical Investigation

The survey includes 38 questions separated in five thematic sections, and a three-point likert scale was employed. Through the questionnaire we attempted to evoke insights regarding the queries that emerged from the literature analysis, including the effectiveness of transparency systems and the presumably corollary trust to the authorities. Hereupon, the five sections of the survey are elaborated; the survey instrument itself can be found as an appendix.

The Citizen in Front of an Open Door
In the first section, our objective is to illustrate the citizens' stance towards openness. Moreover, a brief outline of the respondents' experiences with 'Diavgeia' is delineated. It is attempted to discover their degree of awareness about the system's functions, its legal background, and the nature of public data they can access through it. 'Diavgeia' could be considered as the gargantuan door of Greek bureaucracy; it leads to a labyrinth of laws, resolutions, political decisions, administrative actions, legal agreements, contracts and many others. This door is always open to every single citizen, the potentially interested in its services and (meta)data.

'Diavgeia' and Its Consequences
The second thematic section aims to explore how citizens feel about the 'Diavgeia' system's significance, its progress and effectiveness so far. The respondents are asked about the public authorities' accessibility and accountability during the 6-year time that 'Diavgeia' has been running, in contrast to the prior period. This section also aims to investigate how trust in government relates to citizens' confidence and satisfaction towards this system. Additionally, we explore the connection between the system's efficiency and the frequency of its usage, the role of third parties/stakeholders in assessing public data, as well as the citizens' trust in them.

'Diavgeia' as an Information System
The third part of the survey aims to reveal the system's user-friendliness, functionality and operational complexity, exploring how these characteristics can interfere with citizens' intention to use it. This section also focuses on how these characteristics can affect citizens' satisfaction with the public officials who designed and operate it.

'Diavgeia' as a Tool for Trust and Empowerment
The fourth part of the survey instrument relates to the way citizens understand 'Diavgeia' as a mechanism for controlling or scrutinizing the activities of public authorities. This part aims to highlight the level of citizen empowerment that derives from this system according to its users, while gathering their perceptions of its efficacy and potential development.

Privacy vs. Transparency
The last section of the survey focuses on the privacy concerns that seem to be conflicting with the system's transparency benefits. This section aims to investigate how citizens perceive the potential privacy attenuation to the detriment of the public officials or citizens that are involved in public activities/expenditures; e.g., being appointed in a public body. Nonetheless, it is supposed that citizens and public officers would not expect to remain safely anonymous while being in favour of public transparency.

4   Results of the Empirical Investigation

4.1   Citizens' Perceptions of Openness

The results of this section relate to the role of governmental openness when it comes to decisions and policies, as a prerequisite for citizens' trust. A significant percentage of the participants (73.08%) considers openness of public authorities to be a critical requirement attached to their satisfaction. This eminently high percentage of those who demand openness in order to be satisfied indicates that transparency systems – and 'Diavgeia' in particular – are indeed necessary to fulfill the specific desire of unobstructed access to governmental and administrative actions. Equally, the participants respond that openness is not just a prerequisite for satisfaction; more so, 75.15% of them regards it as a catalyst for confidence towards central and local government.

Another issue that is under investigation in this survey relates to the citizens' understanding of their so called 'right to know'. The findings indicate that there is a strong public feeling concerning this issue: 78.46% of the participants believes that it has the right to access every kind of information of public interest. Interestingly though, when the respondents were asked to compare this right of theirs against the public servants' right to privacy, quite a few changed their attitude as the sample is divided in three almost equal parts; only 35.38% of the respondents remained positive, while 34.92% disagreed and 31.75% was unsure.

4.2   Citizen's Perceptions of 'Diavgeia' and Its Value

Within the survey, the respondents' awareness of 'Diavgeia''s functions and characteristics was also explored. Although a 86.15% argues that it has used the 'Diavgeia' system at some time in the past and 54.62% declares to be confident with regards to its functions, the findings indicate that almost half of the participants are confused in relation to specific functions. Only 33.07% of the respondents is familiar with the benefits of 'Diavgeia' and 40.77% is aware of the legal establishment and status of the system. On the other hand, 61.54% claims that it is familiar with the system's practical objective and 65.38% declares that 'Diavgeia' has the potential to eliminate corruption if it becomes legally and politically stronger. The respondents also state that the frequency by which they use the system is depends (66.15%) on their ease to do so.

With respect to the issue of trust towards the system, 58.46% states that it is confident that 'Diavgeia' is a reliable source of information and legal facts, and 62.31% are convinced that the authorities are kept more accountable because of the systems' existence and enforcement. The respondents also seem to agree in their majority (54.62%) that 'Diavgeia' has the potential to eliminate maladministration in the public sector. A principal objective of the system was to tackle over-spending in the public sector by obliging accessibility to all public expenses. It seems that the citizens feel uncertain (42.31%) whether 'Diavgeia' is successful in tackling overspending, but at the same time has been successful in mitigating irrational public expenditures (47.69%). When the participants are asked whether they trust the government more than before the launching of 'Diavgeia', only 33.08% reply positively; this leads to the conclusion that transparency systems do enhance trust towards public authorities, but are not sufficient on their own to create it. This conclusion derives from the survey's findings, which indicate that citizens are convinced of the systems' credibility and efficiency in holding authorities accountable, but still their trust has not been established.

Given that transparency tools offer information to the citizens, it is inevitable to consider if they feel capable of using them for making observations about political activities. The majority (52.31%) of our respondents claims that it feels capable of drawing conclusions based on information of 'Diavgeia', which indicates that the system is indeed perceived as useful and has the potential to serve its purpose. Another utility of such systems is that they are expected to make governments more accessible to the citizens; however, our findings indicate that this is not the case with 'Diavgeia', since the majority (46.92%) of the respondents feels uncertain about the degree of government's accessibility and only 33.85% agrees that this has been achieved. Further, citizens (52.31%) feel that 'Diavgeia' has the potential to improve the relationship between the citizenry and the government, as it provides (59.23%) a sense of control which derives directly from the system's launching.

4.3 Citizens' Perception of Own Role

It is expected that in a democratic society every citizen has an important role on the public affairs. Those who participated in our research agree that the system on its own cannot bring merits without the citizens' active involvement; 73.85% responded positively that the relevance and benefits of 'Diavgeia' depend on the level of citizens' participation and frequency of use. The respondents also embrace the role of 'Diavgeia' as a means of altering the citizens' attitude towards government, with a 54.62% believing that the system's data could significantly improve their stance. Citizens indeed feel that they hold enough power to influence their government (48.46%) and that 'Diavgeia' empowers them further (47.69%).

4.4 Citizens' Perception of the Role of Media

It could be argued that transparency systems are unnecessary because the media and other third parties could make the same kind of information available to the public. The results of our survey contradict this opinion, given that the majority (45.38%) is doubtful about whether such third parties are trustworthy.

4.5 Synopsis of Results

The survey includes 38 questions, yet the questions presented below are the ones that triggered significant statistical responses, therefore may have significant implications (Table 1).

Table 1. Citizens' opinion on transparency tools: the case of Diavgeia.

Survey question	The respondents are
Is openness a prerequisite for your satisfaction with the authorities?	Positive: 73.08%
Is openness a catalyst for your confidence in the central and local government?	Positive: 75.15%
Is it a citizen's right to have access to every kind of data of public interest?	Positive: 78.46%
Would you accept the override of individual privacy rights of all kinds of public servants in the interest of 'the citizen's right to know'?	Positive: 35.38%
Are you confident that you know what kinds of functions are provided in 'Diavgeia'?	Positive: 54.62%
Are you familiar with how 'Diavgeia' could be useful to a potential user?	Positive: 33.07%
Are you aware of 'Diavgeia''s legal status?	Positive: 40.77%
Have you ever used 'Diavgeia'?	Positive: 86.15%
Are you confident that 'Diavgeia' is a reliable source of information and legal facts?	Positive: 58.46%
Are the authorities more accountable because of the data accessible through 'Diavgeia'?	Positive: 62.31%
Do you trust the state government more than before the launching of 'Diavgeia''?	Positive: 33.08%
Is your local government more trustworthy after 'Diavgeia''s launching?	Positive: 37.30%
Do you feel capable of assessing 'Diavgeia''s data and drawing conclusions about political/administrative actions?	Positive: 52.31%
Has the government become more accessible after 'Diavgeia''s enactment as a law?	Uncertain: 46.92%
Would you agree with the view that 'Diavgeia' could potentially eliminate maladministration in the public sector?	Positive: 54.62%
Does 'Diavgeia' have an effect on extensive and high public spending?	Uncertain: 42.31%
Does 'Diavgeia' impact on irrational public spending?	Positive: 47.69%
Do you think that 'Diavgeia''s data could improve your attitude towards a government?	Positive: 54.62%
Do you believe that the relevance and benefits of 'Diavgeia' depend on citizens' participation and frequency of access?'	Positive: 73.85%
Would you trust third parties (experts or media professionals) to evaluate open public data of political/legal interest?	Uncertain: 45.38%
Does the usage frequency of 'Diavgeia' rely on users' ease with its way of working?	Positive: 66.15%
Do you believe that 'Diavgeia''s framework improves the government-citizen relationship?	Positive: 52.31%
Have citizens obtained more control due to the enactment of 'Diavgeia'?	Positive: 59.23%
Does 'Diavgeia' make you feel empowered?	Positive: 47.69%

5   Discussion

The purpose of this paper is to examine the impact of transparency-enabling systems on citizens' trust, and their way of thinking about governmental authorities and actions. The research findings of our survey highlight a plethora of opinions about the value of transparency-enabling systems. Citizens seem to eagerly ask for openness in the actions of public authorities, and perceive this openness as a prerequisite for trust and confidence in the government. On the other hand, they seem not to fully take advantage of the system's capacity, as they are not sufficiently familiar with its usefulness and legal status. These findings are in line with concerns raised by previous researchers (O'Hara 2012; Jaeger and Bertot 2010b) and relate to the challenges that hamper the functionality of transparency-enabling systems to unfold completely. One of the main issues that our empirical research reveals regards the contradiction between transparency and information privacy, which will be discussed further in this section.

Literature analysis provided us with the motivation to empirically explore how information privacy issues might come to conflict with citizens' desire for openness and transparency. The results indicate that the citizens are indeed strongly in favour of openness and transparency, as they believe it is their right to have access to every kind of data of public interest (78.46%). On the other hand, they also have mixed feelings about sacrificing individual privacy rights over informational rights. Overcoming this issue is quite challenging and the way to achieve it requires a heavy workload on behalf of political and social scientists; should the privacy rights be set aside when they are confronted with other principal rights, such as democracy, accountability and public welfare? To what extent accountability and accessibility determine public welfare? Such a challenge can potentially be manifested in different ways, depending on the public domain in question. For instance, O'Hara (2012) examined the transparency of public processes with regards to the openness of data concerning crime and criminal justice. Allowing this kind of data to be published might impact on the well-being of crime victims; e.g., public data might reveal the location of a crime, and such information is sufficient to identify the victim. Moreover, even without the chance to draw inferences for individuals based on their personal information, transparency might push people not to report crimes they might have encountered, so that their name would never be publicly associated with such incidents. Having considered the above, it is evident that the releasing of governmental information cannot be a 'blind' process; on the contrary, all data should be carefully scrutinised to discourage any inferences that might be drawn either from a single piece of information or from a combination of different data. Diamantopoulou et al. (2017a, b) recommend the use of a Privacy Level Agreement (PLA) between citizens and governmental bodies (i.e. Public Administrations) aiming to enhance transparency, thus making these bodies more trustworthy. The use of this PLA focuses on accountability and only imposes to public bodies the collection of what is absolutely necessary for each e-service. Janssen and van den Hoven (2015) focus on this particular challenge as well as on how big data analytics might enable transparency in governmental actions through the analysis of public data. At the same time, big data analytics may violate individual privacy due to a number of correlations that could then be made for individuals. Information quality, data handling processes, human behavior and legislation are all elements that are important for shaping the desired balance between transparency and privacy.

In order to further elaborate on this issue, in this research we examined the privacy policy of the 'Diavgeia' platform. First, we took into consideration the information privacy framework of ISO 29100 (2011). According to the international privacy framework, any information system that processes personally identifiable information should satisfy eleven principles, including Consent and Choice, Purpose legitimacy and specification, Data minimization, Accuracy and Quality, Information Security, and others. It is therefore the obligation of the system's owner to ensure that these information privacy principles are fulfilled. Furthermore, the completion of privacy policies should be evaluated in relation to the relevant personal data protection legislation at a national as well as EU level. Although an analysis of this personal data protection regulation is outside the scope of this paper, the related privacy requirements for 'Diavgeia' are today specified by the Law 2472/1997. The information privacy policy of the system clarifies that all information published in it should always be used in accordance to this law, and only for purposes of increasing transparency and controlling governmental activities. It also states that any information published in the platform may be used, re-used or communicated, either for free and non-commercial, or any commercial purposes. The system's owner makes all the possible efforts to ensure data quality (Accuracy and Quality principle), proper function of the system against malfunctions, malware, etc., (Information Security principle) and notifies the users regarding any of their personal data that is collected when using the system (Consent and Choice). Through our evaluation of the platform's information privacy policy we can conclude that it is well designed in compliance to personal data protection national legislation.

Nonetheless, our argument is that transparency-enabling systems are a unique case of information privacy concerns, especially because of the duel that comes with them; transparency on the one side and information privacy on the other. For example, the information privacy policy of 'Diavgeia' states that all the content of the platform should be published "as it is", including all relevant information such as names, photos, and other representations. It also states that the system's owner does not hold any responsibility for potential implications to users of the platform. Even if this statement might be regarded to be in compliance with the personal data protection legislation, it should be highlighted that further privacy considerations should be taken, tailored to the domain of public data that is about to be exposed every time.

6   Conclusions

Transparency-enabling systems and anti-corruption software appears to have a significant capacity to improve governmental policies, reduce unnecessary expenditures and enable citizens' trust towards the public administrative bodies. However, research studies indicate that their implementation is not always easy and fruitful, as many obstacles might hinder their capacities. Further, it is implied in the literature that personal data protection concerns may be in conflict with the transparency benefits resulting by such systems. Given that these issues are largely unexplored, this study examines IT-mediated transparency from the citizens' perspective with an empirical investigation employing a survey in Greece. Our empirical case is the national transparency platform 'Diavgeia' in Greece.

The first objective of this study relates to whether governmental openness leads to increased citizens' trust in institutions, as well as reduced uncertainty regarding both the efficiency and the integrity of public authorities. The empirical data demonstrates a significantly positive response; governmental openness is believed to be a trust-enhancing factor. Our second objective refers to the connection of privacy regulations and citizens' willingness to access public data. The investigation shows that the citizens remain unsure about this issue: on the one hand they feel that it is an undeniable right of theirs to access all sorts of public data, yet on the other hand they are not confident to demand the publication of data that would put personal privacy at risk. Finally, with respect to the third objective of this study, we understand that the structure and user-friendliness of 'Diavgeia' are significantly important for the citizens willing to use it, access the information it provides and draw conclusions from it. Overall, this study leads us to the deduction that transparency and anti-corruption software is perceived as highly valuable by the citizenry, but there are quite a few obstacles that hinder the use of these data sources. One of these issues relates to information privacy concerns that emerge due to data openness, as discussed earlier in this study by analyzing the privacy policy of 'Diavgeia' with regards to widely accepted information privacy principles.

Appendix I: Demographics

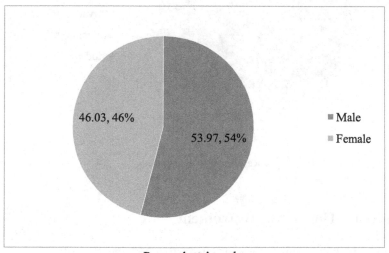

Respondents' gender

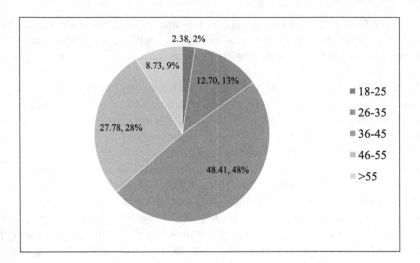

Respondents' age

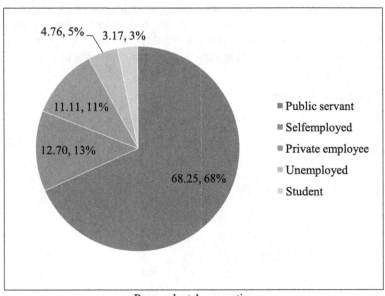

Respondents' occupation

Appendix II: The Survey Instrument

1. Is openness a prerequisite for your satisfaction with the authorities?
2. Is it a citizen's right to have access to every kind of data of public interest?
3. Are you confident that you know what kinds of functions are provided in 'Diavgeia'?

4. Are you familiar with how 'Diavgeia' could be useful to a potential user?
5. Are you aware of 'Diavgeia''s legal status?
6. Are you confident that 'Diavgeia' is a reliable source of information and legal facts?
7. Have you ever used 'Diavgeia'?
8. Do you feel capable of assessing 'Diavgeia''s data and drawing conclusions about political/administrative actions?
9. Should the citizens' capability of evaluating public data determine the degree of openness and transparency?
10. Has the government become more accessible after 'Diavgeia''s enactment as a law?
11. Are the authorities more accountable because of the data that are accessible through 'Diavgeia'?
12. Would you agree with the view that 'Diavgeia' could potentially eliminate maladministration in the public sector?
13. Does 'Diavgeia' have an effect on extensive and high public spending?
14. Does 'Diavgeia' impact on irrational public spending?
15. Do you believe that 'Diavgeia' prevents corruption?
16. Is corruption in the public sector mitigated because of 'Diavgeia'?
17. Do you trust the central government more than before the launching of 'Diavgeia'?
18. Is your local government more trustworthy after 'Diavgeia''s launching?
19. Do you believe that the relevance and benefits of 'Diavgeia' depend on citizens' participation and frequency of access?
20. Would you trust third parties (experts or media professionals) to evaluate open public data of political/legal interest?
21. Could Media or NGOs adequately replace citizens in assessing open public data?
22. Does the usage frequency of 'Diavgeia' rely on users' ease with its way of working?
23. Would you say that 'Diavgeia''s functionality impacts on citizens' interest in using it?
24. Do you believe that 'Diavgeia''s framework improves the government-citizens relationship?
25. Could 'Diavgeia''s structure and user-friendliness affect the user's opinion of its importance?
26. Have citizens obtained more control due to the enactment of 'Diavgeia'?
27. In your opinion, does the government pay attention to 'Diavgeia'?
28. Do you think that 'Diavgeia''s data could improve your attitude towards a government?
29. Would you claim that a legally and politically stronger 'Diavgeia' could potentially eliminate corruption?
30. Would a more inclusive and strict 'Diavgeia' boost government's trustworthiness?
31. Does 'Diavgeia' make you feel empowered?
32. Do you think that citizens have a say in what government does?
33. Would you agree with the view that public officials care about your thoughts?
34. Does it matter, in your opinion, that private data of every kind of public employees/servants can be found online?
35. Would you consider yourself familiar with the risks of publishing personal information online?
36. Would you accept the override of individual privacy rights of all kinds of public servants in the interest of 'the citizen's right to know'?

37. Would the weakening of a public servant's privacy make you trust him more?
38. Is openness a catalyst for your confidence in the central and local government?

References

Babbie, E.: Introduction to Social Research. Kritiki publications, Athens (2011)

Brautigam, D.: Governance, economy, and foreign aid. Stud. Comparative Int. Dev. **27**(3), 3–25 (1992)

Bryman, A.: Social Research Methods, 3rd edn. Oxford University Press, Oxford (2008)

Chvalkovská, J., Skuhrovec, J.: Measuring transparency in public spending: case of Czech public e-procurement information system, IES Working Paper, No. 11/2010 (2010)

Dawes, S.S., Helbig, N.: Information strategies for open government: challenges and prospects for deriving public value from government transparency. In: Wimmer, M.A. et al. (Eds.) Electronic Government. EGOV 2010, LNCS. vol. 6228, pp. 50–60 (2010)

De', R.: E-Government systems in developing countries: stakeholders and conflict. In: Proceedings of the 4th International Conference, EGOV 2005. Copenhagen, Denmark, pp. 26–37, August 2005

de Fine Licht, J.: Do we really want to know? The potentially negative effect of transparency in decision making on perceived legitimacy. Scand. Polit. Stud. **34**, 183–201 (2011)

Diamantopoulou, V., Angelopoulos, K., Flake, J., Praitano, A., Ruiz, J.F., Jürjens, J., Pavlidis, M., Bonutto, A., Castillo Sanz, D., Mouratidis, H., García Robles, J., Tozzi, A.E.: Privacy data management and awareness for public administrations: a case study from the healthcare domain. In: Schweighofer, E., Leitold, H., Mitrakas, A., Rannenberg, K. (eds.) Proceedings of the 5th ENISA Annual Privacy Forum, pp. 219–236, June 2017, Vienna, Austria, Springer LNCS (2017a)

Diamantopoulou, V., Pavlidis, M., Mouratidis, H.: Privacy level agreements for public administration information systems. In: Franh, X., Ralyté, J., Matulevičius, R., Salinesi, C., Wieringa, R. (eds.) Proceedings of the CAiSE Forum 29th International Conference on Advanced Information Systems Engineering, pp. 97–104, June 2017, Essen, Germany. CEUR LNCS (2017b)

Directive 95/46/EC of the European Parliament and of the Council of 24 October 1995 on the protection of individuals with regard to the processing of personal data and on the free movement of such data. http://eur-lex.europa.eu/LexUriServ/LexUriServ.do?uri=CELEX: 31995L0046:en:HTML

European Commission: Article 29 Data Protection Working Party: Press release on the independence of data protection authorities (2015). http://ec.europa.eu/justice/data-protection/article-29/press-material/press-release/art29_press_material/2015/20150618_wp29_press_release_on_the_independence_of_data_protection_authorities.pdf

Eynon, R.: Breaking Barriers to eGovernment: Overcoming obstacles to improving European public services. DG Information Society and Media. European Commission 90 (2007)

Grimmelikhuijsen, S., Porumbescu, G., Hong, B., Im, T.: The Effect of transparency on trust in government: a cross-national comparative experiment. Public Adm. Rev. **73**, 575–586 (2013)

Hood, C.: What happens when transparency meets blame avoidance?. Public Manag. Rev. **9**(2), 191–210 (2007)

Jaeger, P.T., Bertot, J.C.: Designing, implementing, and evaluating user centered and citizen-centered e-government. Int. J. Electron. Gov. Res. **6**(2), 1–17 (2010a)

Jaeger, P.T., Bertot, J.C.: Transparency and technological change: ensuring equal and sustained public access to government information. Gov. Inf. Q. **27**, 371–376 (2010b)

Janssen, M., van den Hoven, J.: Big and Open Linked Data (BOLD) in government: a challenge to transparency and privacy? Gov. Inf. Q. **32**, 363–368 (2015)

Kim, S., Cho, K.: Achieving administrative transparency through information systems: a case study in the seoul metropolitan government. In: Wimmer, M.A., Traunmüller, R., Grönlund, Å., Andersen, K.V. (eds.) Electronic Government. EGOV 2005. LNCS, vol. 3591, 113–123 Springer, Heidelberg (2005). https://doi.org/10.1007/11545156_11

Kim, S., Kim, H.J., Lee, H.: An institutional analysis of an e-government system for anti-corruption: the case of OPEN. Gov. Info. Quart. **26**(1), 42–50 (2009)

Law 2472/1997 on the Protection of Individuals with regard to the Processing of Personal Data (as amended). https://www.dpa.gr

Meijer, A.: Understanding modern transparency. Int. Rev. Adm. Sci. **75**(2), 255–269 (2009)

Moser, C.: How open is "open as possible"? three different approaches to transparency and openness in regulating access to EU documents. HIS Polit. Sci. Ser. **80** (2001)

Obama, B.: Transparency and Open Government. Memorandum for the heads of executive departments and agencies (2009)

Otta, S., Ray, S., Nanda, C.: E-Governance: a special focus to Bhoomi project. J. Eng. Comput. Appl. Sci. (JECAS) **4**(4) (2015)

O'Hara, K.: Transparency, open data and trust in government: shaping the infosphere. In: Proceedings Web Science (2012)

Orlikowski, W., Iacono, S.: Research commentary: desperately seeking the "IT" in IT research—a call to theorizing the IT artifact. Inf. Syst. Res. **12**(2), 121–134 (2001)

Scholl, H., Luna-Reyes, L.: Uncovering dynamics of open government, transparency, participation, and collaboration. In: Proceedings of the 44th Hawaii International Conference on System Sciences (HICSS), January 2011, pp. 1–11 (2011)

Srivastava, S.C., Teo, T.: Citizen trust development for e-government adoption: case of Singapore. In: PACIS 2005 Proceedings, p. 59 (2005)

Strathern, M.: The tyranny of transparency. Br. Edu. Res. J. **26**(3), 309–321 (2000)

Thomas, P.: Bhoomi, Gyan Ganga, e-governance and the right to information: ICTs and development in India. Telematics Inf. **26**(1), 20–31 (2009)

Tsoukas, H.: The tyranny of light: the temptations and the paradoxes of the information society. Futures **29**(9), 827–843 (1997)

Tzermias, Z., Prevelakis, V., Ioannidis, S.: Privacy risks from public data sources. In: Cuppens-Boulahia, N., Cuppens, F., Jajodia, S., Abou El Kalam, A., Sans, T. (eds.) SEC 2014. IAICT, vol. 428, pp. 156–168. Springer, Heidelberg (2014). https://doi.org/10.1007/978-3-642-55415-5_13

V-Dem Institute: The relationship between liberal democracy and corruption (2016). https://www.v-dem.net/en/news/relationship-between-liberal-democracy-and-corruption/

Default OSN Privacy Settings: Privacy Risks

Alexandra Michota[1] and Sokratis Katsikas[1,2(✉)]

[1] Systems Security Laboratory, Department of Digital Systems,
School of Information and Communication Technologies, University of Piraeus,
150 Androutsou St., 18532 Piraeus, Greece
amichota@unipi.gr,
[2] Center for Cyber and Information Security, Norwegian University of Science
and Technology, P.O. Box 191, 2802 Gjøvik, Norway
sokratis.katsikas@ntnu.no, ska@unipi.gr

Abstract. Empirical privacy evaluation in OSNs may provide a better under standing of the effectiveness and the efficiency of the default privacy controls and those customized by the users. Proper user perception of the privacy risk could restrict possible privacy violation issues by enabling user participation in actively managing privacy. In this paper we assess the current state of play of OSN privacy risks. To this end, a new data classification model is first proposed. Based on this, a method for assessing the privacy risks associated with data assets is proposed, which is applied to the case where the default privacy controls are assumed. Recommendations on how the resulting risks can be mitigated are given, which reduce the risk.

Keywords: Privacy risk · Asset · Data classification · Risk treatment

1 Introduction

Privacy expectations may be influenced by the users' sharing activity with the Online Social Network (OSN) audiences; by each OSN user's privacy preferences; and by the terms of and agreements with the OSN provider. The challenge of sustaining high privacy levels in OSNs is of great importance in an era when data oversharing has exploded. Privacy risk scores daily increase due to the fact that OSN users are publishing willingly their Personally Identifiable Information (PII) treasure, although in most cases they fail to use the privacy features in a manner consistent with their intentions. This is not only attributed to the providers' neglect of designing usable privacy setting interfaces, but also to back-end privacy breaches and vague privacy policy guidelines [1].

The aim of this paper is to propose a simple and easy-to-use method for identifying and analyzing privacy risks in OSNs and then to suggest corrective action plans for them. Privacy risk is defined as the "potential loss of control over personal information" [2]. In this study, privacy risk is defined as the potential for PII exposure when the privacy levels do not meet or exceed the agreed audience visibility that could result in embarrassment of the data subject. We focus on the privacy risks incurred when a user leaves the default privacy settings unchanged.

© Springer International Publishing AG 2017
S.K. Katsikas and V. Zorkadis (Eds.): E-Democracy 2017, CCIS 792, pp. 64–78, 2017.
https://doi.org/10.1007/978-3-319-71117-1_5

The method we used in this study was based on the recommendations of the ISO 31000:2009 standard for Risk Management [3]. The proposed Privacy Risk Assessment Method involves the identification of the assets, and the assessment of likelihood and impact of a privacy violation incident. To complete the picture, the risk mitigation strategy that should be followed for treating the identified risks is also provided [4]. The method is described herein as it applies to the case of the most popular OSN, namely Facebook; however, its application to other OSNs is more or less straightforward.

To this end, the sharing data are categorized and classified in a common base data model, according to their potential for privacy invasion when sharing them in OSNs. Furthermore, with a view towards creating a common risk register for OSN privacy, we considered the ten most popular Facebook actions [5] and we identified the accordant privacy risks in case of an incident. Then, a visualized risk scoring matrix was designed, aiming to provide awareness to the data subjects that willingly share their PII treasure via their daily social networking interactions.

The remainder of this paper is structured as follows: the related work is presented in Sect. 2. In Sect. 3 we introduce a data classification model to be used for identifying and classifying critical PII. Section 4 describes the proposed method for assessing privacy risks and its application to the case of Facebook. Section 5 summarizes our conclusions and outlines directions for future work.

2 Related Work

The types of risks vary depending on the nature of affected assets; as different types of information are published in online communities, it would be very useful to classify all this data. In [6] a general taxonomy for social networking data is presented. Then, based on the nature of the data and the reason why this is shared, a different approach is investigated in [7]; herein, a classification of different types of OSNs and different data contained in OSNs is provided. A Privacy Framework that classifies user's data, associates privacy concerns with data, classifies viewers of data, determines privacy levels and defines tracking levels is presented in [8]; the cases of Myspace, Facebook and LinkedIn are examined. Beyond the new taxonomy of data types that is proposed in [9], a metric to assess their privacy relevance is developed for the topmost leading social networks namely Facebook, Google+, Twitter, LinkedIn and Instagram. Serious concerns about which types of PII is processed highlight the need of creating customized groups for this content; in this study, the data taxonomy we recommend is an extension of the classification that was presented in [10].

Privacy grading systems aim to provide detailed information for enhancing users' awareness [11]. A framework to compute a privacy score of an OSN user is proposed in [12]. Several studies over the relationship between the social network graph topology and the achievable privacy in OSNs were presented in [13] but much works has still to be done. In [14] a new model and a privacy scoring formula are proposed that aim to calculate the amount of PII that may be exposed to Facebook Apps. Moreover, a useful tool in order to detect and report unintended information loss in OSNs that also quantifies the privacy risk attributed to friend relationships in Facebook was presented in [15]. In [16], an innovative suggestion inserted the Privacy Index and the Privacy Quotient to measure a user's privacy exposure in an OSN and to measure the privacy of the user's profile.

A quantitative analysis approach is necessary in order to assess privacy impact for OSNs and that is what was provided in [17]. However, the risk identification seems not to be enough to avoid possible emerging threats that may be concealed in OSN interactions. Privacy policy visualization tools have been proposed presenting the users' privacy issue in a manner more comprehensible that this has used before [6–9] but they have been proved insufficient as they do not cover every aspect of privacy in online social networks. Based on the predicates of a privacy policy model, a privacy policy visualization model for Facebook was presented in [18]; this aimed to help both the data providers and the data collectors to better understand the content of designed policies. Three different approaches that highlight the need for usable privacy and security field are presented in [19]. The effects of visualization on security and privacy were investigated in [20] and showed that visualization may influence positively the users who can better comprehend the applied safeguarding measures for their PII and make them trust the providers. However, due to the fact that the mobile applications are becoming more and more popular, the need for enhancing users' awareness over possible privacy risks that may arise when installing applications in their mobile devices is apparent. A privacy meter that visualizes such risks through mobile applications on Android devices was presented in [21] and seems to make the privacy management easier for the users. Beyond other OSNs, Facebook aims just to make the users keep in mind to choose an audience before they share their content with it. Facebook checkup is a tool that was added in Facebook in 2014 and consists of an audience selector that enables users to review their privacy practices and settings [29]. Although privacy strength estimators seem to provide acceptable privacy guidelines by helping the users to keep their accounts protected [30], research on the OSN privacy more often than not remains at the level of identifying and analyzing privacy problems, rather than proposing solutions.

In a privacy evaluation framework, the most difficult procedure is to select the proper metrics in order to meet the objectives of the evaluation. A wide variety of privacy metrics has been proposed in the literature to rank the level of protection offered by OSNs. Although OSN users seem to personalize their privacy of the PII they are sharing via their OSN accounts, privacy assurance cannot be guaranteed in various cases [22], as the privacy control mechanisms seem not to reflect their real privacy intentions. Not only the lack of privacy risk awareness but also the misconception that the privacy controls they set are sufficient to prevent unauthorized access and misuse of their shared PII may cause serious privacy leakage.

3   Data Classification

Our proposed classification builds upon [10] and extends the taxonomy proposed by Årnes et al. for the personal data processed by Facebook; it also aims to amend deficiencies highlighted in existing taxonomies [6, 7, 9] that have been proposed for

OSN data. First, an overall data analysis and review of the common data categories as they are defined in each OSN was performed. Then, a user-oriented approach was followed, by analyzing data that is used in the 10 most popular OSN activities.

Based on the deficiencies we identified in the aforementioned taxonomies, this classification was built around three core pillars:

a. **User-friendly terminology.** Vague terms and inaccurate naming of classes may create wrong perception to the users regarding the content of each class. The ultimate goal of the proposed classification was the users to be familiar with class names used in this classification. For instance, OSN users can easily understand a term such as "meta tags" comparing to "metadata" used by Årnes, as the tag feature is one of the most popular functions of Facebook and prepares the users for the data types expected to be included in such a category.
b. **High granularity.** Existing taxonomies present lack of granularity in data categories definition and this creates difficulties in verifying what data may be included in these categories.
c. **Completeness.** Previous taxonomies do not cover all available OSN data types, such as missing data related to "Third Party Data" and "Communication Data".

The data categories we defined are the following:

- **Registration Data** is the data that a new user should give to an OSN provider in order to become a member of an OSN and use it.
- **Enriched Profile Data** includes data types that are not mandatory to be complete for retaining an OSN user account but it is recommended the related data sets to be filled in for enhancing users' OSN activities. This category contains a. text-based data, b. multimedia and c. data that is shared in OSN pages, e.g. contact information, familial information, education information, employment information, visual information etc.
- **Social Graph Data** is the data that describes users' social interaction or declares her ratings/interests such as connection relationship, public endorsement of pages, group membership etc.
- **Publish Sharing** category includes all the data that an OSN user shares on her own pages or what other OSN users share on her pages; OSN user may have control over the content once she shares it or not;
- **Meta-Tags** is the data that is added by others by using labels over sharing content and discloses which users are interlinked with this content. More specifically, this category includes status tagging, photo tagging, geo tagging, hashtagging [22].
- **Third Party Data** includes the data types that are used when an OSN user enjoys the Facebook integrated third party services like applications, games etc.
- **Financial Data** is any type of purchase data such as credit card information.
- **Connection Data** is the data that shows the activities that are associated with users' Facebook accounts.
- **Communication Data** includes the data that is used to provide communication between two OSN users.

Table 1 depicts our proposed data classification for the case of Facebook. The second column aggregates all the data derived from Facebook data analysis; and the last column presents the data categories we classified, identifying them with a Data ID, from D1 to D9. Subcategories are also defined for the cases that sensitive[1] information is included in the main categories; a prefix "S" derived from the term sensitive precedes the Data ID was used for these subcategories in order to be distinguished. Due to the fact that the D2 category also includes political and religious PII, we classified these in subcategory SD2.

Table 1. Proposed data classification for Facebook

Proposed data classification	Facebook data items	Data ID
Registration data	Display name, Verified email, Birthday, Gender, Verified mobile phone, Password	D1
Enriched profile data 1. Text-based 2. Multimedia 3. Pages	1. Work, Education, Professional skills, Places you have lived, Contact info (phone, address, other OSN profiles, website, email), Basic info (birthday, gender, nameday, interested in, languages, religious views, political views) Other names, Relationship, Family members, About you, Favorite quotes 2. Photos, Videos 3. Pages	D2, SD2
Social graph data	Connections, Groups, Likes, Followings, Events	D3
Publish sharing	Status/Post (that can be enriched by adding photos, tag, url, what you are up to, check-in)	D4
Meta tags	Tagged photos/videos and Facial data for tag suggestions status/comments mentions, check-in	D5
Third party data	Facebook-integrated Games, Applications, and Websites you and your friends use	D6
Financial data	Billing information (Name of banking institution, credit card number)	D7
Connection data	Log files, Cookies, IP address, Browser type, Device type, GPS location, Time zone	D8
–	–	–
Communication data	Messenger, Poke, Call	D9

It is worthwhile to mention that although the Name belongs to the contact information category, in this study we will not include it in this area. The reason why this content item is excluded from the scoring matrix is due to the searchability feature that is incorporated in each OSN that makes the name public by default. The provision of their name is the critical element when an individual decides to sign up in an OSN.

---

[1] Article 9 (1), (2): http://ec.europa.eu/justice/data-protection/reform/files/regulation_oj_en.pdf.

4   Assessment of Privacy Risks

As mentioned in Sect. 1, the method proposed in this study is based on the ISO 31000:2009 standard. The scope of this risk-based privacy review involves evaluating the privacy levels that are offered by default in OSNs in conjunction with the different types of data that are shared to theses online communities by examining popular OSN actions, starting from the creation of an OSN account until its deletion.

The approach follows four steps:

- risk identification based on possible privacy issues.
- assessment of impact.
- assessment of likelihood
- assessment of privacy-related risks

In this paper, we first identify the privacy related risks that are met often in OSNs; these are presented and analyzed in Sect. 4.1. Section 4.2 describes the impact and the likelihood assessment for this study. Impact evaluation was based on two factors, first, the nature of the data that is used in OSNs (see Table 4) and second, the type of incident that may occur (see Table 3) and we considered three levels, namely low, moderate and major; likelihood evaluation was based on the default visibility levels that are offered in Facebook (see Table 5) and we considered three levels, namely low, moderate and high. Last but not least, by applying the results of Sect. 4.2, we evaluated the privacy risks (see Table 6) that are presented in Sect. 4.3.

4.1   Risk Identification

As seen in Table 2, we identified the asset risks for the most common social networking activities and we considered the corresponding privacy issues that may arise during them. We assumed that when an OSN user performs a social networking action, at least one data category as defined in Table 1 is affected. For the D2 and D7 data categories that include sensitive data, we considered OSN activities including users' sensitive information as affected assets. The privacy issues identified in association with each OSN action were taken as indicative examples. It should also be noted that this study is not an exhaustive analysis that aggregates the total number of risks that may be concealed in OSNs; it rather presents part of them and highlights the likely repercussions that privacy violations may have to users' PII.

Despite the fact that OSN users may feel protected when they apply strict privacy settings, it is highly possible that privacy breaches may occur. As seen in Table 2, risks were identified in the most frequent OSN actions, from the stage of account creation as described in AR1 when examining the case that transparent policy terms and conditions are not provided to the user, until its deletion, as described in AR10 when examining the case of fake reports. In the latter case, in the case of Facebook, after clicking "Report", two options are offered to the user, namely "Report content shared" or "Report this account." Then the user is requested to explain the reasons why she reports an account and suggestions for resolving this problem appear in a new window. Based on the complaint the user described the options that are recommended include

Table 2. Asset risk matrix

OSN action	Data category	Privacy issue	Asset risk	Risk ID
Create a FB Account	D1	Non transparent policy terms and conditions	Use and disclosure of PII with OSN users' direct consent without providing an alternative	AR1
Update your religion and political views	SD2	Collection of data not required for the specified purpose	Misuse of sensitive PII	AR2
Like a page	D3	Selling of your public endorsement	Unauthorized access of PII to unknown audiences and excessive processing for use	AR3
Update a status by adding mood, location and photo	D4	Excessive collection due to the sharing & merging of datasets	Privacy requirements of the data are not satisfied for the PII combination sharing; PII disclosure occurs	AR4
Tagged in a photo	D5	No proper implementation of privacy control mechanisms	Unintentional PII disclosure to unknown audiences	AR5
Play a game by installing the suggested app	D6	Sharing of data with third parties	Excessive disclosure of PII	AR6
Pay for a page ad	SD7	Operator - side data leakage	Breach of official secrecy during processing of sensitive data	AR7
Remember the device you last logged in	D8	Non anonymity due to identifiers' collection and storage	Disclosure of your location data/user's physical presence	AR8
Send a private message	D9	Tracking your communication	Unauthorized use and access to private discussions	AR9
Deleted content	D4	Fake reports	PII loss	AR10

"Unfollow", "Unfriend", "Block", and "Submit to Facebook for Review." Until Facebook evaluates the related reports, the user's PII remains visible in her profile.

Missing legal grounds for the processing of users' sensitive data create serious risks. According to AR2, the update of users' political and religious opinions would be preferable to be avoided.

The public endorsement in OSN pages seems to help advertisers to satisfy their commercial goals. It is not a coincidence that targeted suggestions for pages with content similar to that an OSN user is reading on the internet are created, due to the keyword scanning mechanisms that are used by OSNs. AR3 focuses on the excessive and unauthorized access to the users' PII.

In the case of Facebook, "Nearby friends" is a new feature that was added recently on the top of users' friend list that provides information about users' location and is available through the Facebook mobile application. However, the most popular feature for users' location declaration remains the "check-in". When we tried to combine different content types in a sharing post, we ended up that according to AR4, the most important risk is highlighted because the privacy limitations of the data are not satisfied for the whole dataset.

Even when one is not willing to share one's PII to one's OSN profile, data disclosure may be achieved from one's friends OSN activities, and as a result private things about one may become visible to unknown audiences. In most cases, a user's PII is discovered by content that is added by others, such as tagged data [22]. AR5 describes a similar case with unintentional PII disclosure due to a possible conflict during the implementation of different privacy options between the user who tags the content and the tagged user.

In order to play a game in Facebook, the users are requested to install the suggested app. Users' PII is given to third parties through these applications. According to [23], when a user accepts the installation of such an app, she gives her permission for accessing her public information, her profile information; she accepts receiving related emails to the registered email address; she is granting access to her posts in News Feed, to her family and relationship information, to her photos and videos, to her friends' information. AR6 focuses on the excessive collection of users' PII and on the data economy that is not respected during the processing of PII.

When a user buys a page advertisement, the service providers collect and process her PII for the financial transaction. User's payment information includes her credit/debit card number, expiration date, security code, authentication data, billing, shipping and contact information [24]. AR7, the risk that arises in this case, is a possible breach of privacy during processing of sensitive data, assuming that the relevant operator is responsible for the data leakage.

AR8 describes a feature that provides users with direct and quick access to their accounts by giving them the choice of remembering the device they last logged in. However, the collection of identifiers creates risks, as anonymity is not ensured. As seen in AR8, users' location data as well as their physical presence are disclosed.

Facebook messenger is now also available as an independent application for access via mobile devices. However, the content of private messages known as inboxes seems not to be invisible for all Facebook stakeholders. Data mining when links are contained to these messages is a usual phenomenon. As described in AR9, the unauthorized use and access to sensitive discussions creates threats for the PII protection when communications are monitored.

Facebook reporting helps the users to protect the social network from any digital threats that can harm the users' privacy. The OSN Service Provider (OSNSP) team is available to face incidents and problems such as pornography, hate speech, threats, graphic violence, bullying and spam. After a report has been submitted to the OSNSP team, it is reviewed, and its conformance to the Facebook policies and statements is examined; then, it is decided whether the reported content will be removed or not. Furthermore, notices are received by the users who have shared these content types; actions after reporting include revocation of users' ability; disablement of certain profile features for the user; cancelation of a Facebook account; reporting to law enforcement. Sometimes users' sharing content is deleted due to a number of fake reports. AR10 describes such a case, and as a result PII loss is possible [25].

4.2   Impact and Likelihood Assessment

According to [26], the Privacy Risk equals the likelihood of an incident occurring times its impact.

The level of impact from a privacy-related incident e.g. privacy breaches due to data leakage is the magnitude of harm that results from the consequences of unauthorized disclosure modification, destruction, or loss of PII. The likelihood of a privacy-related incident's occurrence is a risk factor that is estimated by analyzing the probability that a given threat is capable of exploiting a given vulnerability.

The nature of the data was used for assessing the impact and the current default privacy controls were used for assessing the likelihood; the stricter the default privacy levels are, the lower the likelihood of PII disclosure is and the more accessible the PII is to bigger audiences, the more possible the PII disclosure is.

For the purpose of our approach, we consider four levels of impact, namely Low, Moderate, Major and Critical, as shown in Table 3 below. As stated above, the level of impact is correlated to the repercussions that a possible data breach may have to the PII of the data subjects involved. For instance, loss of tangible PII assets, be they sensitive PII or not is considered to have major impact for the privacy risks we have defined in our study, as there is no possibility of individual access and participation of data subjects to recover their PII. However, in case of unauthorized access and disclosure of PII, data subjects may apply stronger privacy restrictions, in order to mitigate such a type of risk; as a result the impact will be assessed as low.

Table 3. Impact levels

Potential impacts	Impact levels	
	PII	Sensitive PII
Access/Disclosure	Low	Major
Modification	Moderate	Major
Misuse	Moderate	Major
Loss/Destruction	Major	Major

As seen in Table 4, a classification of the data categories we defined in Table 1 according to their nature is presented. Whether this PII is sensitive or not was based on the recommendation presented in [27].

Table 4. PII asset categorization

Data assets	Data ID
PII	D1, D3, D4, D5, D6, D8, D9, D2
Sensitive PII	D7, D2

The assessment of likelihood is based on the default visibility levels namely "Public", "Friends of friends", "Friends", "Only me" that was considered per data category. Three levels are defined, namely Low, Moderate and High. High likelihood means that many people are allowed to see the OSN sharing content; this corresponds to the "public" option (Table 5).

Table 5. Likelihood levels

Default visibility levels	Likelihood levels	
Public/everyone	High	Users' content is visible to everyone
Friends, Friends of Friends	Moderate	Users' content visibility is restricted to specific audiences
Only Me	Low	Users' content is visible only to the content owner

Having assessed the impact in case of a data breach and the likelihood of this happening, the evaluation of risk is possible; the assumption of the worst-case scenario with highest possible impact on the data subjects was made.

4.3 Risk Assessment

By applying the results of Sect. 4.2, the following Table 6 results:

Table 6. Privacy risks in Facebook

Risk ID	Affected PII assets	Asset value	Default visibility level	Impact	Likelihood	Risk
AR1	D1	P	F/P	Moderate	Moderate/High	Minimum/High
AR2	D2	S	F	Major	Moderate	High
AR3	D3	P	P	Moderate	High	High
AR4	D4	P	F	Moderate	Moderate	Minimum
AR5	D5	P	FoF	Moderate	Moderate	Minimum
AR6	D6	P	F	Moderate	Moderate	Minimum
AR7	D7	S	M	Major	Low	Minimum
AR8	D8	P	M	Moderate	Low	Low
AR9	D9	P	M	Moderate	Low	Low
AR10	D2, D4	P, S	F	Major	High	Critical

For the Asset Value, we used "P" for Personal information and "S" for Sensitive information. For the visibility level, we considered the four choices that are offered by Facebook. "Only me" (M) is the strictest privacy level that declares that no one can see the sharing PII apart from the content owner. The "Public" (P) choice corresponds to the minimum privacy level and declares that the sharing content is visible to everyone. The intermediate levels are the "Friends" (F) and "Friends of friends" (FoF) privacy choices.

As seen in Table 6, two levels were considered for the default visibility level of D1 because a combination of PII is used for the users' registration. More specifically, while the majority of the information that should be provided for the registration process is visible to users' friends, the display name and the registration email address are visible to everyone on Facebook. Furthermore, on May 2014, Facebook changed the default post privacy setting from "Public" to "Friends".

The last column in Table 6 shows the risk level of the privacy-related incident scenarios. The risk is measured on a three-value qualitative scale and is calculated according to the rules shown in Fig. 1. The meaning of each value of risk is explained in Table 7.

LIKELIHOOD	PRIVACY RISK RANKING MATRIX		
HIGH	Minimum Risk	High Risk	Critical Risk
MODERATE	Low Risk	Minimum Risk	High Risk
LOW	Low Risk	Low Risk	Minimum Risk
IMPACT	LOW	MODERATE	MAJOR

Fig. 1. Privacy risk matrix

Table 7. Risk levels

Privacy risk	
Risk level	Meaning
Low	Satisfactory privacy levels can ensure PII protection
Minimum	Privacy levels cannot ensure PII Protection
High	Unsatisfactory privacy levels for the PII protection; corrective action plans should be designed
Critical	Unacceptable privacy levels for the PII protection; catastrophic consequences without recovery chance

4.4 Risk Management

The majority of the risk assessment results show that the privacy levels need improvements; thus, risk management activities should be undertaken in order to address the identified privacy risks. Risk treatment options include modification, retention, avoidance and sharing.

As seen in Table 8, we recommend a risk treatment action for asset risks we identified in Table 2. For the asset risks' treatment, the active participation of the user is necessary.

Table 8. Risk treatment

Risk treatment option	OSN user action
Risk modification	Customization of visibility levels
Risk retention	Direct consent
Risk avoidance	No PII sharing
Risk sharing	Individual PII insurance

Risk modification is the risk mitigation that can be achieved by reducing either the incident's likelihood or its impact. In this study, due to the fact that risk impact was defined based on the PII sensitivity, it is not possible to reduce impact; thus, we selected to reduce the risk likelihood by amending the visibility level.

The majority of the default settings in Facebook tends to make the users' content visible to the public audience [28]. Thus, as seen in Table 9, when a user customizes her privacy settings by selecting limited audiences, she can decrease the privacy score without letting her PII exposed to everyone. This grading component is a dynamic field as it can easily change by the user's initiative. Figure 2 depicts the new risk scores as decreased after customizing the visibility level.

Table 9. Mitigated risks in Facebook

Risk ID	Affected PII assets	Asset value	Default visibility level	Customized visibility level	Impact	Likelihood	Risk
AR1	D1	P	F/P	F	Moderate	**Moderate**	**Minimum**
AR2	D2	S	F	F	Major	Moderate	High
AR3	D3	P	P	F	Moderate	**Moderate**	**Minimum**
AR4	D4	P	F	F	Moderate	Moderate	Minimum
AR5	D5	P	FoF	F	Moderate	Moderate	Minimum
AR6	D6	P	F	F	Moderate	Moderate	Minimum
AR7	D7	S	M	M	Major	Low	Minimum
AR8	D8	P	M	M	Moderate	Low	Low
AR9	D9	P	M	M	Moderate	Low	Low
AR10	D2, D4	P, S	F	M	Major	**Low**	**Minimum**

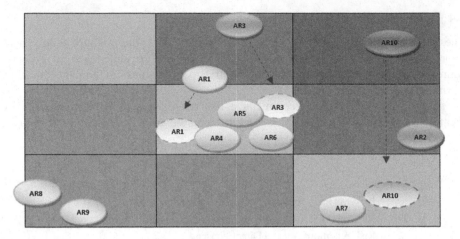

Fig. 2. Asset risk visualization

Benchmarking of best practices also recommend monitoring of changes that would impact individuals' privacy as well as monitoring of the effectiveness of implemented privacy controls.

Risk retention is the handling of risks that cannot be avoided. Additional controls should be implemented in case that risk levels are higher than those assessed, based on the risk acceptance criteria. The risk acceptance criteria include: a cost-benefit analysis that compares the estimated benefit with the estimated risk; different risk management techniques for the different risk levels; provision for future additional treatment, when it is necessary. When the level of risk does not meet the risk acceptance criteria, the establishment of a retention program that could cover possible privacy gaps through corrective action plans is required. The main goal of this treatment option is the maintenance of consistency with retention practices. As seen in Table 8, when we cannot avoid a risk, guidelines that make the stakeholders aware of the best practice techniques for the retained risks are recommended.

Risk avoidance means elimination of risk. This can be achieved in two different ways; either the likelihood or the impact of the risk to be set to zero. As seen in Table 8, we recommend no sharing of sensitive PII in Facebook or the implementation of "Only me" visibility option for such content types.

When sharing the risk with another party or parties, insurance arrangements are performed; insurance partners are used in order to spread responsibility and liability. A risk can be shared either in whole or partially.

5   Conclusions

The main purpose of this study was to show that when OSN accounts are managed fairly, efficiently and effectively, the risk of privacy breaches may be managed. The research objectives were to assess whether the current framework of privacy controls offered for OSN PII management is appropriate and consistent with users' needs. The results of this examination provide detailed and simple information that allows a non-technical or non-privacy aware person to understand how their PII and privacy might be invaded.

The need for enhancements in the current default privacy controls provided by Facebook became evident, as high and critical privacy risks were identified. In view of the reluctancy of the service provider to increase the default privacy levels, users should take the initiative to increase the privacy levels on their sharing PII by following the provided recommendations.

The method proposed in this paper can be applied to other OSNs as well. It is our intention to pursue this direction of research in the future, so as to develop a comprehensive understanding of the privacy risks of default privacy settings in all popular OSNs, to be subsequently used for recommending appropriate mitigation action to their users.

Acknowledgement. The authors acknowledge, with special thanks, the support of the Research Center of the University of Piraeus to presenting this work.

References

1. Koops, B.: The trouble with European data protection law. Int. Data Priv. Law **4**(4), 250–261 (2014)
2. Featherman, M., Pavlou, P.: Predicting e-services adoption: a perceived risk facets perspective. Int. J. Hum. Comput. Stud. **59**(4), 451–474 (2003)
3. ISO 31000:2009 Risk management - Principles and guidelines, ISO (2009)
4. Betterley, R.S.: Cyber/Privacy Insurance Market Survey –2014: "Maybe Next Year" Turns Into "I Need It Now". International Risk Management Institute, Inc. (IRMI) (2014)
5. Most popular activities of Facebook users worldwide as of 1st quarter 2016. The Statista Portal (2016). http://www.statista.com/statistics/420714/top-facebook-activities-worldwide/. Accessed 7 July 2017
6. Schneier, B.: A taxonomy of social networking data. IEEE Secur. Priv. **8**(4), 88 (2010)
7. Beye, M., Jeckmans, A., Erkin, Z., Hartel, P., Lagendijk, R., Tang, Q.: Privacy in online social networks. In: Abraham, A. (ed.) Computational Social Networks: Security and Privacy. Springer, London (2012). https://doi.org/10.1007/978-3-642-27901-0_1
8. Ho, A., Maiga, A., Aimeur, E.: Privacy protection issues in social networking sites. In: ACS/IEEE International Conference on Computer Systems and Applications (AICCSA), Los Alamitos (2009)
9. Richthammer, C., Netter, M., Riesner, M., Sänger, J., Pernul, G.: Taxonomy of social network data types. EURASIP J. Inf. Secur. **11**, 1–17 (2014)
10. Årnes, A., Skorstad, J., Michelsen, L.: Social Network Services and Privacy. Datatilsynet, Oslo (2011)
11. Racz, N., Weippl, E., Seufert, A.: A frame of reference for research of integrated governance, risk and compliance (GRC). In: De Decker, B., Schaumüller-Bichl, I. (eds.) CMS 2010. LNCS, vol. 6109, pp. 106–117. Springer, Heidelberg (2010). https://doi.org/10.1007/978-3-642-13241-4_11
12. Liu, K., Terzi, E.: A framework for computing the privacy scores of users in online social networks. ACM Trans. Knowl. Discov. Data **5**(1), 1–30 (2010)

13. Cutillo, L., Molva, R., Onen, M.: Analysis of privacy in online social networks from the graph theory perspective. In: 2011 IEEE Global Telecommunications Conference (GLOBECOM 2011), Kathmandu, Nepal (2011)
14. Symeonids, I., Beato, F., Tsormpatzoudi, P., Preneel, B.: Collateral damage of Facebook apps: an enhanced privacy scoring model. In: IACR Cryptology ePrint Archive, IACR (2015)
15. Becker, J., Chen, H.: Measuring privacy risk in online social networks (2009). http://web.cs. ucdavis.edu/~hchen/paper/w2sp2009.pdf. Accessed 11 July 2017
16. Ananthula, S., Abuzaghleh, O., Alla, N., Prabha, S.: Measuring privacy in online social networks. Int. J. Secur. Priv. Trust Manage. (IJSPTM) **4**(2), 1–9 (2015)
17. Wang, Y., Nepali, R.: Privacy impact assessment for online social networks. In: International Conference on Collaboration Technologies and Systems (CTS), Atlanta, Georgia, USA (2015)
18. Ghazinour, K., Majedi, M., Barker, K.: A model for privacy policy visualization. In: 33rd Annual IEEE International Computer Software and Applications Conference (COMPSAC 2009), Seattle, WA, USA (2009)
19. Birge, C.: Enhancing research into usable privacy and security. In: 27th ACM International Conference on Design of Communication, Bloomington, Indiana, USA (2009)
20. Becker, J., Heddier, M., Öksuz, A.: The Effect of providing visualizations in privacy policies on trust in data privacy and security. In: 47th Hawaii International Conference on System Sciences (HICSS), Waikoloa, HI, USA (2014)
21. Kang, J., Kim, H., Cheong, Y.G., Huh, J.H.: Visualizing privacy risks of mobile applications through a privacy meter. In: Lopez, J., Wu, Y. (eds.) ISPEC 2015. LNCS, vol. 9065, pp. 548–558. Springer, Cham (2015). https://doi.org/10.1007/978-3-319-17533-1_37
22. Michota, A.K., Katsikas, S.K.: Tagged data breaches in online social networks. In: Katsikas, S.K., Sideridis, A.B. (eds.) e-Democracy 2015. CCIS, vol. 570, pp. 95–106. Springer, Cham (2015). https://doi.org/10.1007/978-3-319-27164-4_7
23. Wüest, S.: The Risks of Social Networking. Symantec (2006)
24. Facebook Data Policy (2017). https://www.facebook.com/policy.php. Accessed 11 July 2017
25. Open Web Application Security Project (OWASP) (2017). https://www.owasp.org/index. php/Main_Page. Accessed 11 July 2017
26. Brooks, S., Garcia, M., Lefkovitz, N., Lightman, S., Nadeau, E.: An introduction to privacy engineering and risk management in federal systems. National Institute of Standards and Technology, Gaithersburg, MD, USA (2017)
27. Directive 95/46/EC of the European Parliament and of the Council of 24 October 1995 on the protection of individuals with regard to the processing of personal data and on the free movement of such data, Brussels: European Commission (1995)
28. Michota, A., Katsikas, S.: The evolution of privacy-by-default in social networks. In: 18th Panhellenic Conference in Informatics (PCI 2014), Athens, Greece (2014)
29. Facebook. What's the Privacy Checkup and how can I find it? (2015). Retrieved May 2015. https://www.facebook.com/help/443357099140264
30. NIST SP 800-63-1. Electronic authentication guidelines. From National Institute of Standards and Technology (2011)

"I Have Learned that I Must Think Twice Before…". An Educational Intervention for Enhancing Students' Privacy Awareness in Facebook

Maria Sideri[1], Angeliki Kitsiou[1], Eleni Tzortzaki[2], Christos Kalloniatis[1(✉)], and Stefanos Gritzalis[2]

[1] Privacy Engineering and Social Informatics Laboratory, Department of Cultural Technology and Communication, University of the Aegean, 81100 Lesvos, Greece
{msid,a.kitsiou,chkallon}@aegean.gr
[2] Information and Communication Systems Security Laboratory, Department of Information and Communications Systems Engineering, University of the Aegean, 83200 Samos, Greece
{etzortzaki,sgritz}@aegean.gr

Abstract. Social Network Sites have doubtless become part of our lives, facilitating communication and interaction between social actors. Within this frame users disclose personal information for several reasons while at the same time they express privacy concerns. "Privacy Paradox" reveals that despite privacy concerns, users, most of the times, fail to protect their privacy within SNSs, putting thus themselves and other users to risk. In this respect, several researches have shown that users' privacy awareness increase is of major importance, focusing on the crucial role of education towards this. This research aims to explore the effects of a long-term University-based educational intervention for enhancing students' digital knowledge and skills in order to protect their privacy in SNSs efficiently. The educational intervention centered on a semester course of a Greek University, provides encouraging findings regarding students' privacy awareness enhancement.

Keywords: Social network sites · Facebook · Privacy concerns · Privacy awareness · Educational intervention · Semester course

1 Introduction

Social Network Sites (SNSs) are currently the most dynamically developing personal networking tool [1]. Their descriptive nature creates intimate feelings, which encourage information flow within them [2]. In this frame, users voluntarily provide personal information and/ or carelessly consent to its collection, while at the same time they raise anxieties about their privacy and the security of their information. The interrelation between privacy on SNSs and information disclosure *"is characterized by a constant tension between confidentiality and transparency"* [3] (p. 642). The Privacy Paradox [4] eventually results from a conflict situation between people's fear and anxiety of being observable, supervised and vulnerable because of personal information disclosed and their disclosure behavior in SNSs. To address that, beyond legislation and providers'

© Springer International Publishing AG 2017
S.K. Katsikas and V. Zorkadis (Eds.): E-Democracy 2017, CCIS 792, pp. 79–94, 2017.
https://doi.org/10.1007/978-3-319-71117-1_6

techniques for privacy protection, users' privacy awareness increase and protective behavior adoption has been underlined of major importance. Privacy literacy is thus crucial in order for online privacy to be strengthened [5]. In this frame, educational interventions providing knowledge and skills on privacy management are expected to have a positive effect on users' behavior, altering existing disclosure practices.

This paper refers to an innovative educational intervention to enhance Greek University students' awareness providing insight to possible alteration of their privacy concerns and privacy management in Facebook. The intervention took place during the semester course entitled "Social Media: Identity, Communities and Application Fields", offered by the Department of Cultural Technology and Communication of the University of the Aegean. The paper is organized as follows. In Sect. 2, related work which focuses on digital literacy and educational interventions for enhancing users' knowledge and skills is presented. Section 3 refers to methodology applied, presenting research question and explicating study's design and the research stages followed. Section 4 presents the results of the research and discusses findings, while Sect. 5 concludes the paper and raises future research directions.

2 Related Work on Previous Educational Interventions

Researchers trying to interpret human behavior in SNSs investigate the factors that affect users to disclose personal information despite their stated privacy concerns. In this frame, information control, awareness level and risk perception are important to understand people's failure to transform their concerns into privacy protective behavior [6]. Digital literacy has been shown to have a positive effect on the protection of online privacy [7] aiming to enhance users' awareness about the extent of their knowledge [8] and to help them to accurately assess online risks [9] especially those arising from information disclosure. Trepte et al. [10] argue that online privacy literacy may be defined as a combination of declarative knowledge (knowledge about technical aspects of information protection, related with laws and directives) and procedural knowledge (ability to use strategies for individual privacy regulation and information protection). In this frame, educational campaigns are of major importance since they are expected to improve users' knowledge and provide skills to combat cyber threats and consequently reduce the possibilities of being attacked [11].

Digital literacy is indicated as basic life –skill that should be included in the education system from an early age [12]. Within this context, Taneja et al. [13] underline the obligation of schools, colleges and public libraries to develop educational interventions *"to reinforce individuals' beliefs related to information resource safety, information resource vulnerability, privacy concern, threat severity, privacy intrusion… and intrinsic cost associated with the use of privacy controls"* (p. 172). Especially, in the frame of education, at all levels, educators and teachers should launch educational programs in order for young people to modify the way they perceive their social context [14] and to raise their awareness [15].

Although the issue of online safety has been implemented in education, the results coming up from educational programs need further attention. Even though there is a huge number of researches focusing on variables affecting users' awareness, researches focusing on the role and impact of school education on privacy attitudes and behavior on SNSs are relatively recent and focus mostly on school students, Vanderhoven et al. [15] argue that the attention given by school education to privacy attitudes and safe behavior is rather incidental, since these issues are not integrated in a course or in the curriculum. Furthermore, most of the developed educational packages about safety and security mostly focus on Internet risks in general [16], do not tackle with SNSs' specific risks and are not theoretically grounded [17] since few of them have been evaluated empirically [16]. This leads to a lack of educational lines that should be taken into consideration when designing such programs [18].

Referring to the outcomes of the educational packages that have been evaluated, Vanderhoven et al. [17] and Mishna et al. [19] argue that in cases when raising awareness and knowledge increase were observed, they were not followed though by risky behavior decrease which constitutes the ultimate goal of the intervention. This is consistent with the argument that media literacy education increases knowledge about the specific topic of the course, although changes in attitude and behavior usually may not come up [20]. The inconsistency between expected and observed goals leads to the acknowledgment that there is little information about the characteristics that educational interventions should have in order to be effective both on users' awareness and behavior, as well as about the circumstances required for intervention's successful completion [21].

Within this frame, Vanderhoven's et al. [16] study aimed to "*propose a list of validated theoretical design principles for future development of educational materials about risks on SNSs*" (p. 459). The research was addressed to teenagers of secondary education to measure possible change regarding awareness, attitude and behavior within SNSs focusing on three different categories of SNS risks; content, contact and commercial. The findings show a positive impact of the given courses on awareness. The course on content risks had a positive effect on awareness of both content and contact risks. The same was observed with reference to the course on contact risks, while the course on commercial risks had a positive effect on awareness of these risks only. Nevertheless, no impact on students' attitudes and a limited only impact on their behavior were revealed. Students that had attended the course on content risks had changed privacy settings and the content of their profile, the ones that had attended the course on contact risks had changed privacy settings and their personal information, while the ones having attended the course on commercial risks had changed privacy settings and account settings as well. Thus, the goal of behavior change was merely achieved [16, 17]. The authors attribute the non-impact on attitude and the limited impact on behavior to courses' duration (only an hour) and to peers influence as well, explaining that impact may be revealed later in time [17].

ConRed program [18] also focused on users' awareness enhancement aiming to reveal users' perceptions about the degree of control they exert over information they share, to introduce familiarity with safety and personal information protection mechanisms on Internet and social networks and to reduce risks as cyber-bullying, harassment and addiction to the Internet. The program was designed according to the principles of normative social behavior theory and was organized around the areas of (a) Internet and social networks; (b) benefits of Internet use and instrumental skills and (c) risks and advice on usage. It was addressed to the whole education community under scope (students, teachers and families) and its results were positive referring to students' involvement reduce in cases of cyber-bullying, excessive use of Internet and the risk of addiction. The outcomes also revealed a greater awareness of the students with reference to learning and using strategies in order to increase their control over the information released as well as to keep uploaded information private.

3   Methodology

3.1   Question Raised

Though most students use SNSs daily, they are in their majority unaware of possible risks or ignore the results coming up from information disclosure and don't show up privacy protective behavior even in the cases they realize that their personal information may be accessed and used by others. Since online privacy literacy is crucial for users' privacy awareness increase [5], attention should be paid to educational interventions in the context either of formal or informal education. As far as formal education in Greece is concerned, primary and secondary education have already focused on the online safety issue, including the topic of security in the current curricula of Informatics [22, 23]. Though the adopted educational approach focuses on security issues regarding Internet usage in general, without addressing specifically the issue of privacy risks in SNSs, while in cases where educational interventions are oriented to these risks do not have long enough duration, as they are usually provided in one or two hours lessons.

In this regard, building up on previous literature and going beyond the short-term courses of Greek school education that focus on Internet risks, a major research question is raised concerning the effects of a long-term University-based educational intervention for enhancing students' privacy literacy regarding SNSs. To address that, our research aims at providing insight to possible alteration of Greek students' privacy concerns and privacy management in Facebook (FB), which derive from an innovative educational intervention during the semester course entitled "Social Media: Identity, Communities and Application Fields", offered by the Department of Cultural Technology and Communication of the University of the Aegean. This research extends previous researches addressed to school students (not in Greece) trying to investigate the outcomes of a new type of intervention that includes experimental learning activities being addressed to people that are expected to evaluate privacy significantly.

3.2   Study Design

Our study focused on the undergraduate curricula of the Department of Cultural Technology and Communication, since it provides interdisciplinary knowledge and skills regarding three disciplines: IT, Communication and Culture. The syllabus of the course "Social Media: Identity, Communities and Application Fields" included the required sections, in which our intervention could be structured and applied. The group of students attending this course with the probable exception of those that have attended a special non-formal education course on social media is expected to have knowledge of general scope with reference to social media risks resulting mostly by usage experience. This is also reinforced by the fact that the course on "Data Security in the Information Society" is offered in the last semester of the graduate program.

The course "Social Media: Identity, Communities and Application Fields" is provided in three stages. In the first, students are theoretically introduced to online social networking as a social phenomenon. In the second, issues such as the online presentation of digital self, the function of the online communities, the sense of belonging in an online group, the reputation and recognition in SNSs, possible costs as result of online behavior, privacy protection and privacy paradox as well are presented. Stage 3 addresses issues regarding the impact of social media on social life, referring to behaviors such as cyber-bulling or cyber-sex, social media usage in the fields of education, culture, employment, economy, politics, communities of fans or social movements as well as social media's effect in shaping public opinion. In the frame of our intervention, the topics of stage 2 and 3 were discussed in class, after the elaboration of the respective experiential learning activities.

In each of the three stages of our intervention, main instructions regarding both personal strategies and technical mechanisms were provided in order to enhance students' knowledge and technical skills for the protection of their personal information. To assure external validity, two collaborating researchers verified that the course was offered accordingly to the syllabus, with special emphasis on the collaborative learning activities. To evaluate the effects of this long-term educational intervention, a two-phase experimental study was conducted. The students enrolled in this course were asked to state voluntarily, in face-to-face structured interviews, their perceptions regarding privacy issues in FB, in two distinct phases; Phase I at the beginning of the course and Phase II after the completion of the lectures. Basic prerequisite for participating in the study was having a FB account. From the fifty-four (54) enrolled students, twenty-three (23) of them volunteered to participate in our experimental research procedures.

3.3   Phase I-Instrumentation and Procedure

During the first week of the course, data were gathered in order to initially explore students' attitudes and representations regarding a series of privacy issues on FB. A structured interview schedule was developed and standardized, following a fixed format which was centered on FB usage and students' social capital outcomes within it, privacy settings management and disclosing information, privacy concerns, privacy risks, students' awareness and their strategies for privacy protection. Specifically, Phase I-interview schedule included the following five sections of close-ended questions on a 5-Point Likert scale:

1. *Facebook Usage.* This section was designed to explore students' motivation to create a FB account and the management of their FB profile (sub-section 1), as well as their perceived social capital outcomes deriving from FB usage (sub-section 2). The items of the latter were adopted from [24] Internet Social Capital Scale.

2. *FB Profile and Privacy Settings management.* This section of questions, aiming to explore students' usage of FB profile settings and FB privacy settings, included items

with reference to privacy settings' activation when creating the profile, privacy settings' change and profile's visibility.

3. FB Self-disclosure. This section comprises of two sub-sections also, concerning personal information that students disclose directly on their profile and information they disclose on posts or other activities.

4. FB Privacy concerns. The first sub-section includes items concerning the extent of worries to issues such as companies' access to students' personal information, personalized advertisements or phishing, while the second explores concerns regarding disclosure of sensitive personal information to unwanted or unknown audience.

5. FB Privacy risks, awareness and protection strategies. This section divided into three sub-sections aiming to explore students' perceptions regarding privacy risks, their privacy awareness, as well as the privacy strategies they follow in FB.

Additionally, a set of three items to address students' socio-demographic character-istics was included in the last part of the instrument.

3.4   Phase II-Instrumentation and Control Procedure

After the completion of the course's lectures, the same interviewing procedure was followed in order to explore the impact of the semester course on the students. Phase II-interview schedule consisted of five sections of close-ended questions, on 5-Point Likert Scale, including repeated measurements from Phase I-interview. The Phase II-interview aimed to investigate possible changes regarding students' privacy perceptions, self-disclosure behaviors and privacy management in FB, such as the adoption of stricter privacy strategies by the end of the course in comparison to the ones they previously adopted. The sections focus on:

1. Facebook Usage. This section of dichotomous questions was designed to verify students' knowledge sources regarding FB usage.

2. FB Self-disclosure, FB Profile and Privacy Settings management. The six sub-sections of dichotomous questions aimed to examine the possible alteration of students' disclosed information and their privacy settings management. Sub-sections 1 and 2 focus on the addition or removal, respectively, of personal information while the third one includes items regarding possible changes in provided information, within the last three months. Sub-sections 4 and 5 explore possible alteration regarding the restriction or the extension of students' profile visibility, while sub-section 6 refers to alteration of students' privacy settings during the last three months and to the reasons they motivated them to change the settings.

3. FB Privacy concerns. In this section, which includes repeated measurements from Phase I- interview schedule, students were asked once more to rate their privacy concerns in order to explore if these concerns were increased or diminished after the completion of our educational intervention.

4. FB Privacy behavior and protection strategies. This section, including items most of which derived from Phase-I interview, was developed for controlling if students altered their privacy behaviors and their protection strategies after the completion of the course.

5. Educational Intervention Evaluation. This section aimed to explore the outcomes deriving from our educational intervention. Students were asked to rate the perceived theoretical and technical knowledge on a 5-Point Likert scale.

To set-up our intervention efficiently a pre-test was administrated to three students, including both the structured interviews of Phase I and Phase II and the teaching material of the course. This procedure intended to address the issues of data collection and instruments reliability, as well as to identify the range of students' embedded knowledge, deriving from the educational material taught. To conduct the students' interviews advantageously and to increase their reliability, the interview schedule in both Phases was followed in the exact same order, in the exact same way for each one, without following up on the interviewees' answers in.

4   Results and Discussion

To evaluate the outcomes of our educational intervention regarding students' privacy awareness and behavior, Phase I and Phase II records were analyzed using quantitive and qualitive speech analysis and were compared.

4.1   Facebook Usage

Findings of Phase I indicate that most of the students (48%) had created a FB profile at the age of 15 or 16 years old, 26% at the age of 12–14 years old, while 22% at the age of 17–22 years old. FB intensity usage measures are very high, since most of the students spend at least three hours per day on FB, including some who are connected all day, while only 17% spends up to one hour.

Most of the students (91%) stated that they created a FB profile in order to maintain and extend their relationships, as well as to have fun. These findings are consistent with previous research [25] regarding students' motives for participating in FB. However, it is extremely noteworthy that findings regarding students' perceived social capital benefits within FB highlight some contradictories. Most of the students (57%) declared that relationships in FB are not real, while a great proportion of them (52%) were uncertain regarding the FB positive impact on the improvement of their relationships. This indicates that the correlation between students' motivations for participation in FB and their anticipated social capital benefits needs to be further explored, since it may be affected by other variables, such as privacy concerns.

As far as students' technical knowledge for the creation of their profile and FB functions is concerned, most of them (61%) stated that they had learned by themselves how to utilize it, while to 35% a friend's help was provided. Only 4% of the students were advised by family on how to create their profile and act within FB. This finding indicates that parents should be more involved in these procedures, since students engage with FB in adolescent. Findings of Phase I are supported by the findings of Phase II, whereby the same ratio of the students affirmed that they had discovered FB functions mainly by themselves or through help offered by a friend. Furthermore, in Phase II, students admitted not having the required knowledge regarding all FB functions, while 83% of them declared that their previous formal education had not contributed to the enhancement of this knowledge.

4.2 FB Profile and Privacy Settings Management

Findings of Phase I show that most of the students (74%) had their profile visible to all, while the rest of them, in equally ratios (8.5%), provided visibility to friends, selected friends or friends and their friends. An important shift concerning students' FB Profile management is recorded according to the findings of Phase II. Specifically, 65% of those who had their profile visible to public, restricted it to friends only, 18% to friends and their friends, and 13% to selected friends. An almost identical shift is indicated regarding students' FB privacy settings management, comparing findings of Phase I and Phase II. At Phase I, only 35% of the students had activated Privacy Settings when creating their Profile, 3% had not, while 52% stated either that they had not noticed the privacy settings or did not understand what they were supposed to do. Not using privacy settings [26] has been recorded as risky behavior. In Phase II, 57% of those who had not activated privacy settings declared that they had changed them within the last three months, a period coincident with the semester course, justifying this change in the context of obtaining more privacy protection within FB, as well as because of the attention they paid to the security notices that came up.

The above findings are encouraging showing the positive effect of our educational intervention regarding the adoption of certain practices by students in order to protect their privacy and emphatically support previous work [15] as far as the necessity of education targeted on this issue is concerned.

4.3 FB Self-disclosure

Findings of Phase I indicate that the majority of students had used their actual personal information in their FB profiles. Specifically, according to the following Table 1, they used:

Table 1. Personal information disclosed

Type of information	% of students
Real name	87%
Real post address	91%
Real place of residence	78%
Real current studies or employment	78%
Real place of birth	70%
Real date of birth	70%
Real phone number	43%
Real previous studies or employment	17%
Real e-mail address	9%
Real photo	4%
Real personal status	4%

Students seem to be reluctant to reveal pieces of information such as phone number, e-mail address, previous job or studies, personal status and photo probably considering them more sensitive. During Phase II, students were asked if they had removed any information from their FB profile within the last three months. Only 22% of them stated that they had removed personal status, 13% place of residence and previous studies or employment, 9% place of birth and post address, and 4% birth date. This reveals a minor ·shift. As far as indirect information disclosure is concerned, both in Phase I and II, 35% of the students admitted sharing happy or unhappy moments, success or failure within FB, while posts regarding personal political beliefs seem to be avoided (74%). Additionally, students, in Phase I, declared (44%) that they usually tag other persons' names in their photos, while in Phase II, they stated that the specific practice is more than familiar to them (70%). Taking the above findings under consideration, it is indicated that special emphasis should have been given regarding indirect information disclosure practices as well as the sensitivity degree of information.

It is also noteworthy that in Phase I all students stated that they "check in on FB" every time they visit a place, while in Phase II only 13% of them preserved this behavior. Respectively, while only 22% of the students preferred to communicate through inbox in Phase I, an obvious alteration is recorded in Phase II, whereby 91% of the students declared this preference. It is equally of great importance that in Phase I all students stated that they do not have any kind of control over the information they post, while, in Phase II, they all declared that they do have. Perceived control over personal information is crucial since it can lead either to a sense of security and thus to more information disclosure or to high privacy concerns generation and disclosure willingness decrease even in cases of lower risks resulting from disclosure [27]. Furthermore, 70% of the students in Phase II expressed their certainty that their shared information will not result in troubles in the future.

These findings indicate the advantages of our educational intervention, supporting [28] thesis according to which users with a better school education are better able to evaluate privacy risks in SNSs than those with less experience and lower education.

4.4 FB Privacy Concerns

While in Phase I only 35% of the students had expressed their concerns regarding personalized advertisements provided by FB, in Phase II this ratio was almost double (65%). Additionally, even though in Phase I most of the students (82%) were not at all concerned regarding companies' ability to access their personal information, in Phase II, this percentage was reduced to 74%. Since privacy concerns may burden the self-disclosure process [29], it is indicated that our educational intervention should be more focused on companies' access to personal information through SNSs.

After the completion of our educational intervention, students' anxiety centered on Phishing within FB was also recorded. Specifically, a notable shift has been recorded regarding those students that had expressed moderate concerns regarding Phishing in Phase I (13%). This ratio was increased to 30.4% in Phase II. Additionally, in Phase I, some students seemed to have no concerns at all regarding other users' access to their thoughts (22%) and feelings (13%). Findings, in Phase II, show a positive alteration only regarding students' thoughts -this percentage was reduced to 13%- while the respective ratio regarding their feelings was increased to 17%. In this respect, considering that the expression of innermost thoughts and feelings has been indicated as a reason for students' participation in SNSs [30], our educational intervention should have given special emphasis on that issue.

Nevertheless, it is important that 70% of the students declared in Phase II that their concerns regarding their profile visibility were reduced, since they had restricted it. An equal shift has been also recorded for their concerns regarding unwanted audience's knowledge about their location and activities, since, after the course completion, they avoided to "check in" and they communicated through their inbox.

These findings indicate an explicit impact on students' privacy awareness deriving from our intervention while they also support previous work [31] regarding the usefulness of privacy control techniques that allow users to successfully manage privacy threats from unknown external audience.

4.5 FB Privacy Risks

During Phase I, most of the students (61%) declared that they didn't deal with any risk within FB, while in Phase II, 74% of the total sample admitted having been conscious of the multiple risks that they could face within FB. It is noteworthy that in Phase I, none of the students had realized that all their actions in FB are leaving digital "traces", are recorded and detected, while most of them (78%) supported that if they deleted a conversation, no one would be able to find it. However, in Phase II, most of them (87%) understood that their previous perceptions were misguided.

Most of the students (83%), in Phase I, were not aware of the fact that FB, as a provider, gathers users' personal information. This finding supports previous work [32] which points out that students do not read SNSs privacy policies and therefore they do not realize that their personal information might be gathered, used and shared by providers. Though, in Phase II, 87% of the students declared that had acknowledged this as a risk. In Phase II also, 83% of the students acknowledged that governments may have access to users' personal information through FB, while in Phase I only 61% of them shared this perception.

These findings show, supporting Chen's [9] thesis, that the educational material referring to SNSs' function and risk assessment may provide the appropriate cognitive tools in order to remove the respective bias regarding the issue.

4.6 FB Privacy Awareness and Protection Strategies

As far as control techniques related to the FB are concerned, all students stated in Phase I they acknowledged its technical functions. However, in Phase II, 69% of them demonstrated that they were aware of possible dangers deriving from FB technical characteristics that they didn't know before. This finding supports previous work [33], which indicates that users would be more able to protect their privacy, if the provided mechanisms and interfaces allowed them to understand their function and if these mechanisms were incorporated in users' practices and values. In this respect, while in Phase I 35%

of the students believed that FB privacy settings are adequate to protect themselves, 69% expressed their anxiety regarding the usefulness of the specific protection strategy in Phase II. Furthermore, our findings point out that while 26% of the students, in Phase I, were not sure about the usefulness of the anti-spyware software, in Phase II this ratio was reduced to 21%.

With reference to students' personal protection strategies, findings indicate that most of the students in Phase I supported that they themselves have to undertake the responsibility to protect their privacy within FB (70%), as well as to protect others (96%), by utilizing several personal strategies. However, in Phase II, 56% of the students admitted that they didn't have in the past the required knowledge to achieve that, supporting previous research results [18] that record the necessity for students to learn various strategies for augmenting their information control in SNSs. It is also noteworthy that while, in Phase I, 56% of the students declared that they didn't have the skills to block unwanted audience out of their profile, in Phase II, 61% of the total sample affirmed that they had acquired this knowledge. Additionally, while in Phase I, 22% of the students declared that they had visited suspicious pages through FB, this ratio was reduced to 4% in Phase II. Respectively, findings point out the positive effect of our educational intervention regarding the adoption of the specific strategies.

4.7 Educational Intervention Evaluation

Our study was completed with students' evaluation concerning their perceived outcomes deriving from our educational intervention. Findings indicate that all students affirmed that they enhanced their knowledge and 96% of them affirmed that became aware not only of the benefits but also of the risks deriving from social media usage, both in a theoretical and practical aspect. One of the most important outcomes of the intervention concerns awareness enhancement. Most of the students (91%) acknowledged the necessity to maintain an adequate balance between their desire to interact with other people and obtain specific benefits within SNSs and their need to protect their privacy. In this respect and as basic cognitive outcome, most of the students (87%) declared that, after the semester course, they were more conscious of the practices that should adopt when acting in SNSs. This was recorded in several statements as "I have learned that I must think twice what might be hidden behind a profile or a post…". "I understood that Internet and its applications should be used with prudence" or "…I have also learned how to present myself without risking".

5 Conclusions

Digital literacy has been recorded as a prerequisite for online safety and has been included in the school curricula of the European countries. Though, as literature has shown [16, 17], online safety issue mostly focuses on Internet, ignoring SNSs specific features. The current research was addressed to a group of University students enrolled in the course titled "Social Media: Identity, Communities and Application Fields" offered by the Department of Cultural Technology and Communication of the University of the Aegean. This semester course included the sections by which our educational intervention could be structured and applied. The intervention focused on enhancing students' knowledge about risks deriving from social media usage in order for their awareness to be increased and consequently privacy protective behavior to be adopted.

The contribution of our educational intervention, in comparison to previous, is centered on its duration, its target group and its context. In contrast to former short-term relevant interventions, it lasted 13 weeks and was addressed to Tertiary Education students, taking into account that such kind of educational programs should simultaneously emphasize on both positive aspects and risks in SNSs. From the beginning of the intervention we acknowledged that students, aged in their majority between 20–25 years old, acquire already –in comparison to younger users- a shaped system of dispositions, tendencies, perceptions and consequently social actions, which is outlined by the concept of "habitus" [34]. Habitus was thus expected to be a possible obstacle in changes of students' concepts or actions. Nevertheless, the embedding of new knowledge covering previous cognitive gaps was expected to have an impact on concepts and actions. Current research has also confirmed students' knowledge gaps concerning privacy issues and protective behavior resulting from students' previous education. These gaps that should be taken into consideration for the Greek school curricula design (primary and secondary education) were adequately covered. In contrast to previous research findings having revealed no impact of educational interventions on students' attitudes and only a limited impact on their behavior, our intervention is shown to have a significant impact on students' attitude, increasing both privacy awareness and concerns through acknowledging risks in SNSs and confronting them. Awareness increase led students to adopt privacy protective behavior either by using personal strategies or employing technical mechanisms.

The results of our research pointed out that most of students had created their profile by the age of 16 years old, having been FB users for at least 4 years. Since FB intensity usage is recorded, in previous researches, to have a positive impact on knowledge, students should have been rather familiar with FB functions, but they hadn't. The fact that, as students stated, previous formal education had not contributed to the increase of their knowledge, enhances previous literature regarding courses' focus on internet usage in general. These results point out the need for establishment of specific long-term educational measures that will reinforce students' digital literacy, regardless FB intensity usage, in order to cover knowledge gaps.

Concerning profile's visibility, findings point out a significant alteration in students' profile visibility management with regard to its restriction. The same shift is recorded with reference to students' management of privacy settings, deriving from their need to obtain more privacy protection within FB, while the necessity for the adoption of certain technical measures in this targeted training is also revealed.

Results highlighted that most of the students didn't remove disclosed information from their profiles within the three months of our intervention. Regarding indirect information disclosure, results point out that, before the semester course, about half of the students used to tag other persons' names in their photos, while no reverse behavior has been recorded after its completion. The above findings can be attributed to the fact that changes in attitude and behavior may come up later in time, as literature has already recorded [16], or to habitus. Nevertheless, the need for ongoing monitoring of online behaviors is underlined.

Encouraging results by the educational intervention came up with reference to "check in" FB's function, inbox communication and information control. Although, at first, all students stated not having control over the information they post, this was subverted after the course. Also, the majority of them expressed certainty of shared information not resulting in troubles in the future. The above findings clearly show that the intervention helped students to acknowledge risks and confront them.

Referring to privacy awareness, students' concerns regarding companies' access to their personal information were decreased a little, after the course, indicating the necessity for the educational material to be more focused on that issue. Phishing concerns on the contrary rose notably, while the ratio of students not concerned about other users' access to their thoughts and feelings reduced regarding only thoughts. The non-subversion of feelings disclosure practice can be seen in terms of social developmental goals or of habitus. It is indicated thus that emphasis should be placed during future educational interventions on outlining risks resulting from feelings' disclosure. Students' concerns regarding unwanted audience's knowledge about their location and activities reduced due to their profile's visibility restriction and the differentiated use of FB features. These adopted practices underline the accomplishment of privacy awareness enhancement goal.

Students' low awareness level resulting from their lack of knowledge regarding FB functions was confront helping them understand the key features of SNSs' function and evaluate possible risks deriving from their usage. Moreover, students realized that their actions in FB leave digital "traces" and that even if any action is deleted it can be found. This indicates formal perceptions reverse. The majority of the students also acknowledged that FB gathers users' personal information and understood that governments may also have access to their personal information through FB.

Furthermore, the results show that students' awareness to identify and adopt specific personal and technical protection strategies related to personal information disclosure behavior was enhanced. These findings combined with that of students decreased uncertainty about the anti-spyware software usefulness, highlight the impact of our intervention. Although students supported their responsibility to protect themselves and other users within FB, it is revealed that they didn't have the required knowledge. Nevertheless, after the course, a great number of students had acquired knowledge and skills to support their protection.

Finally, awareness increase regarding the necessity to balance between their desire to interact with other people and protect their privacy is recorded by all students during the evaluation of the intervention and in this frame of reference it is especially encouraging that students declare more conscious when interacting in SNSs.

Limitations with reference to our research focus on the relevant small sample to which the intervention was addressed, even though sample's number constitutes about half of the students' enrolled in the course. Moreover, all participants belong to an age group that already has a shaped system of perceptions, values and actions. Even though knowledge is better embedded in older age groups comparing to younger, it isn't clear whether it can totally affect their actions since habitus alteration is a complicated process.

Nevertheless, it should be underlined that this age group (emerging adulthood) is likely to apply stricter privacy settings on SNS [26] -altering thus a formated action- and within this perspective awareness of the risks due to personal information disclosure constitutes a critical background. Finally, it should be noted that Phase II interview took place right after lectures' completion, due to several educational obligations that students had, thus not allowing to explore whether the impact of the intervention would last or results of the impact would come up latter in time, as already underlined in literature [16].

Future educational interventions on digital literacy enhancement regarding SNSs should be also long-term oriented, as the results of the current intervention were more encouraging than those of short-term and should explore impacts on awareness and behavior not just after the completion of intervention but over a period of time. Furthermore, educational packages to be used should cover knowledge and skills gaps resulting from previous education, regardless variables as FB intensity usage or age. They should also include material regarding legislation, companies' access to personal information and indirect information disclosure, while investigating at individual level perceptions on information sensitivity in relation to social norms and personal privacy needs.

References

1. Lin, K.Y., Lu, H.P.: Why people use social networking sites: an empirical study integrating network externalities and motivation theory. Comput. Hum. Behav. **27**(3), 1152–1161 (2011)
2. Pearson, E.: All the world wide web's a stage: the performance of identity in online social networks. First Monday **14**(3) (2009). http://firstmonday.org/article/view/2162/2127. Accessed Feb 2017
3. Buschel, I., Mehdi, R., Cammilleri, A., Marzouki, Y., Elger, B.: Protecting human health and security in digital Europe: how to deal with the "privacy paradox"? Sci. Eng. Ethics **20**, 639–658 (2014)
4. Dienlin, T., Trepte, S.: Putting the social (psychology) into social media is the privacy paradox a relic of the past? An in-depth analysis of privacy attitudes and privacy behaviors. Eur. J. Soc. Psychol. **45**, 285–297 (2015)
5. Bartsch, M., Dienlin, T.: Control your Facebook: an analysis of online privacy literacy. Comput. Hum. Behav. **56**, 147–154 (2016)
6. Baek, Y.M.: Solving the privacy paradox: a counter-argument experimental approach. Comput. Hum. Behav. **38**, 33–42 (2014)
7. Park, Y.J.: Digital literacy and privacy behavior online. Commun. Res. **40**(2), 215–236 (2011)
8. Moll, R., Pieschl, S., Bromme, R.: Competent or clueless? Users' knowledge and misconceptions about their online privacy management. Comput. Hum. Behav. **41**, 212–219 (2014)
9. Chen, R.: Living a private life in public social networks: an exploration of member self-disclosure. Decis. Support Syst. **55**, 661–668 (2013)
10. Trepte, S., Teutsch, D., Masur, P.K., Eicher, C., Fischer, M., Hennhöfer, A., Lind, F.: Do people know about privacy and data protection strategies? Towards the "Online Privacy Literacy Scale" (OPLIS). In: Gutwirth, S., Leenes, R., de Hert, P. (eds.) Reforming European data protection law, pp. 333–365. Springer, Heidelberg (2015). https://doi.org/10.1007/978-94-017-9385-8_14
11. Marcolin, B.L., Compeau, D.R., Munro, M.C., Huff, S.L.: Assessing user competence: conceptualization and measurement. Inf. Syst. Res. **11**(1), 37–60 (2000)

12. Mendel, T., Puddephatt, A., Wagner, B., Hawtin, D., Torres, N.: Global Survey on Internet Privacy and Freedom of Expression. Unesco Publishing, France (2012)
13. Taneja, A., Vitrano, J., Gengo, N.J.: Rationality-based beliefs affecting individual's attitude and intention to use privacy controls on Facebook: an empirical investigation. Comput. Hum. Behav. **38**, 159–173 (2014)
14. Marino, C., Vieno, A., Pastore, M., Albery, I., Frings, D., Spada, M.M.: Modeling the contribution of personality, social identity and social norms to problematic Facebook use in adolescents. Addict. Behav. **63**, 51–56 (2016)
15. Vanderhoven, E., Schellens, T., Valcke, M.: Exploring the usefulness of school education about risks on social network sites: a survey study. J. Media Liter. Educ. **5**(1), 285–294 (2013)
16. Vanderhoven, E., Schellens, T., Vanderlinde, R., Valcke, M.: Developing educational materials about risks on social network sites: a design based research approach. Educ. Tech. Res. Dev. **64**, 459–480 (2016)
17. Vanderhoven, E., Schellens, T., Valcke, M.: Educating teens about the risks on social network sites: an intervention study in secondary education. Communicar Sci. J. Media Educ. **43**(XXII), 123–131 (2014)
18. Del Rey, R., Casas, J.A., Ortega, R.: The ConRed program, an evidence based practice. Communicar Sci. J. Media Educ. **39**(XX), 129–137 (2012)
19. Mishna, F., Cook, C., Saini, M., Wu, M.-J., MacFadden, R.: Interventions to prevent and reduce cyber abuse of youth: a systematic review. Res. Soc. Work Pract. **21**(1), 5–14 (2010)
20. Steinke, J., Lapinski, M.K., Crocker, N., Zietsman-Thomas, A., Williams, Y., Evergreen, S.H., Kuchibhotla, S.: Assessing media influences on middle school–aged children's perceptions of women in science using the Draw-A-Scientist Test (DAST). Sci. Commun. **29**(1), 35–64 (2007)
21. Livingstone, S., Bulger, M.E.: A global agenda for children's rights in the digital age. Recommendations for developing UNICEF's research strategy. LSE, London (2013)
22. Greek Ministry of Education, Research and Religious Affairs. Curriculum and instructions for teaching "Information and Communication Technologies" in Primary Education during the school year 2016–17. https://app.box.com/s/kwepcz32fe7nu03b73xun3t0tgobwqts. (in greek)
23. Greek Ministry of Education, Research and Religious Affairs. Instructions for teaching Informatics in Secondary Education during the school year 2016–17. https://app.box.com/s/ey2r6cy4y5d4ffdu2jkor80wmj7m1l60. (in greek)
24. Williams, D.: On and off the'net: scales for social capital in an online era. J. Comput. Med. Commun. **11**(2), 593–628 (2006)
25. Krasnova, H., Spiekermann, S., Koroleva, K., Hildebrand, T.: Online social networks: why we disclose. J. Inf. Technol. **25**, 109–125 (2010)
26. Debatin, B., Lovejoy, J.P., Horn, A.K., Hughes, B.N.: Facebook and online privacy: attitudes, behaviors, and unintended consequences. J. Comput. Med. Commun. **15**, 83–108 (2009)
27. Brandimarte, L., Acquisti, A., Loewenstein, G.: Misplaced confidences: privacy and the control paradox. Soc. Psychol. Pers. Sci. **4**(3), 340–347 (2012)
28. Taddicken, M., Jers, C.: The uses of privacy online: trading a loss of privacy for social web gratifications? In: Trepte, S., Reinecke, L. (eds.) Privacy Online: Perspectives on Privacy and Self-Disclosure in the Social Web, pp. 143–158. Springer, Heidelberg (2011). https://doi.org/10.1007/978-3-642-21521-6_11
29. Stutzman, F., Gross, R., Acquisti, A.: Silent listeners: the evolution of privacy and disclosure on facebook. J. Priv. Confid. **4**(2), 7–41 (2013)

30. Sideri, M., Kitsiou, A., Kalloniatis, C., Gritzalis, S.: Privacy and facebook universities students' communities for confessions and secrets: the greek case. In: Katsikas, S.K., Sideridis, A.B. (eds.) e-Democracy 2015. CCIS, vol. 570, pp. 77–94. Springer, Cham (2015). https://doi.org/10.1007/978-3-319-27164-4_6
31. Johnson, M., Egelman, S., Bellovin, S.M.: Facebook and privacy: it's complicated. In: Proceedings of the Eighth Symposium on Usable Privacy and Security (SOUPS 2012), pp. 1–15. ACM, Washington (2012)
32. Lawler, J.P., Molluzzo, J.C.: A study of the perceptions of students on privacy and security on social networking sites (SNS), on the internet. J. Inf. Syst. Appl. Res. 3(12), 3–18 (2010)
33. Nguyen, M., Bin, Y.S., Campbell, A.: Comparing online and offline self-disclosure: a systematic review. Cyberpsychol. Behav. Soc. Netw. 15(2), 103–111 (2012)
34. Bourdieu, P.: Outline of a Theory of Practice. Cambridge University Press, Cambridge (1977)

A Conceptual Model of Decision-Making Support for Opening Data

Ahmad Luthfi[✉] ⓘ and Marijn Janssen ⓘ

Faculty of Technology, Policy and Management, Delft University of Technology,
Jaffalaan 5, 2628 BX Delft, The Netherlands
{a.luthfi,m.f.w.h.a.janssen}@tudelft.nl

Abstract. The trend of open data has spread widely in the government nowadays. The motivation to create transparency, accountability, stimulate citizen engagement and business innovation are drivers to open data. Nevertheless, governments are all too often reluctant to open their data as there might be risks like privacy violating and the opening of inaccurate data. The goal of the research presented in this paper is to develop a model for decision-making support for opening data by weighing potential risks and benefits using Bayesian belief networks. The outcomes can be used to mitigate the risks and still gain benefits of opening data by taking actions like the removing privacy-sensitive data from dataset. After the taking of actions the process can start over again and the risks and benefits can be weighed again. The iteration can continue till the resulting dataset can be opened. This research uses health patient stories dataset as an illustration of the iterative process. This shows how the decision-making support can help to open more data by decomposing datasets.

Keywords: Open data · Decision-making support · Bayesian belief networks · Risks · Benefits

1 Introduction

The government is expected to provide open access to the datasets for the public. The opening of data should result in the accomplishing of public values like transparency and accountability, but at the same time, other public values like privacy should be ensured [1]. Although the opening might yield benefits, they might also encounter risks [1–3]. Possible risks are the misuse of data or information for the benefit of individuals, groups, or even politicians [4]. Another frequently mentioned reason is privacy that can lead to inappropriate interpretation for the public in the end-point become a scourge or a reluctance to contribute to the spirit of open data [1, 5].

In spite of many datasets have been opened [4, 6, 7], a substantial number of datasets is still closed [1]. This situation can be explained by several reasons, including the reluctance of some organizational entities to release of the datasets for several reasons, including of the complexity or implementing systems [8–10]; skilled and highly specialized staff [11–13] and the readiness related to the infrastructure, hardware, software, or financial resources [14]. The risks of opening data include mistakes in data and potential misuse of data which can endanger the reputation of data providers [8]. One particular risk in the open data system

© Springer International Publishing AG 2017
S.K. Katsikas and V. Zorkadis (Eds.): E-Democracy 2017, CCIS 792, pp. 95–105, 2017.
https://doi.org/10.1007/978-3-319-71117-1_7

is a violation of the data protection act concerning the privacy of data [4]. When datasets are linked together the risk of privacy violations increases [15]. Overall there is a lack of insight into the potential risks and benefits of open data [16].

The goal of the research presented in this paper is to develop a model for decision-making support for opening data by weighing potential risks and benefits using Bayesian belief network. In the next section, the potential benefits and risks of opening data are described. Thereafter our model is presented, including our proposed decision-making support cycle, the evaluation of benefits and risks using a Bayesian belief networks model, and assessment phase. The contribution of this paper is to provide a conceptual model of Decision-making Support for governments and related departments to open more datasets. A proposed model can be used to reduce the risks and still acquire benefits by eliminating some fields of table structure that containing seven risk variables. The model is illustrated using health patient stories dataset that suggests improving the table structure before the opening of the dataset. Finally, conclusions are drawn to give a strong evaluation and assessment result, whether the dataset is feasible to open to the public.

2 Research Background

2.1 Risks of Opening Data

Open data have been shown to contribute to society through several programs of the governments of many countries in recent years [3]. Nevertheless, along with the advantages of implementing data disclosure, obstacles and risks are emphasized [5, 9, 17].

Table 1. Overview of possible risks of opening data

	Category	Risks	Description	Source
1	**Data inaccuracy**	• Dependencies of the data • Potentially manipulated	Openness of data allows to eliminate the elements of data dependence on each other that can cause less of the data quality and easily to manipulated	[9, 18, 19]
2	**Data misuse**	• Personal data misuse held by the third parties • Anonymized of the datasets	Data disclosure affect to personal data desecration by criminals and would be used by the unauthorized users	[9, 13, 20, 21]
3	**Data sensitivity**	• Vulnerability of the data • Data errors identified	Sharing datasets can cause personal or government data leakage and it will cause error identification	[9, 22–24]
4	**Data privacy**	• Open data access develops upon the private to information movement	Disclosure of datasets may risk on the information private issue and highly possible to decrease the meaning of the datasets	[18, 19, 23–25]
5	**Data violation**	• Triggering the unintentional discrimination of the personal identification • Abuse of civil rights tendency	Historical data might cover bias (e.g. racial profiling). Releasing the data without limiting the privacy type of data may affect unintentional discrimination	[9, 20, 21, 26]
6	**Data integration**	• Problems of synchronization of data • Problems of assessing the heterogeneous data	Multi format data owned by datasets will cause difficulties in performing data synchronization process and consuming reassessing a dataset.	[5, 9, 17, 21, 22]
7	**Data consistency**	• Duplicate some data compromising data integrity • Problems of data cleaning	Data inconsistency can be caused by duplication of some data that causes disintegration of the data	[27–31]

Many actors are involved in publishing an open data ecosystem and there is a degree of uncertainty that open data might result in undesired outcomes. Table 1 summarized the risks based on a literature review of the risks of opening data. The literature about the risks is fragmented and there was no single overview of these risks yet.

2.2 Benefits of Opening Data

There is much literature about the benefits of open data [32]. Table 2 shows the overview of the benefits of open data:

Table 2. Overview of possible benefits of opening data

	Category	Benefits	Description	Source
1	**Transparency**	• Opening data may stimulate the clarity of the datasets • The availability of the datasets in public sectors • Easiness to access of datasets	• Sharing of the datasets will increase the transparency of the government and private performance • Allows the public to search for and find the required datasets	[5, 19, 33, 34]
2	**Accountability**	• Getting the right data published • Enabling society to find, process and use information • Empowering institutional or social to choose better services	• The accountability of the impact of data disclosure may also influence the public's flexibility to process reliable information • Institutions or public service providers will be easy to choose which datasets they really need	[5, 33, 34]
3	**New applications/ Innovations**	• Promoting economic growth • Predicting the issue of the return of investment • Understanding the underlaying of the datasets	• The sophistication of application innovation in open data systems makes it possible to introduce potential investment • Openness of data can improve understanding of how to process data and project it properly	[5, 33, 34]
4	**Public trust**	• Improved public relations and attitudes toward government • Increased reputation	• Public sector can use open data to better inform citizens about its actions. • By publication of open data, a public-sector body can present itself as an open and transparent institution.	[5, 33, 34]
5	**Government services**	• Improved the availability • Improved government data and process • Better understanding and data management	• The availability of data about government services improves their accessibility and helps citizens and organizations to better utilize them • If the users can provide feedback about the published datasets they might notify the curators of these datasets about possible errors in data	[17, 19, 33, 34]

2.3 Decision-Making Support and Bayesian Networks

Decision Support System (DSS) aims to support and improve decision-making [35]. DSS is a model-based tool for processing data and assessment to assist in decision-making [36]. DSS can be defined as a computer-based system consisting of three interacting components, namely language systems, knowledge systems, and problem processing systems [37]. Of these definitions, it still includes both old and current versions of the DSS design model.

Bayesian network or belief network is a method to represent the relationship between conditional dependencies and outcomes by creating a probabilistic directed graphical representation [38, 39], adaptive nature of new information both qualitative and quantitative, as well as capability of capturing uncertainty [38]. To evaluate the potential risks and benefits, Bayesian networks are suitable as they provide the capability of predictions whether data selections have the potential risks or benefits, and computing the probability of event occurrence [39–41]. A Bayesian belief network is able to reflect some conditional independent variables [42]. Bayesian belief networks since it is compared to other methods such as Meta Models, Coupled Models, and Agent-based models, provide several additional purposes [38, 40]. There are two particular functions by using Bayesian belief networks are the capability to make focal range in-depth and compromise, and model output of the decision-making system can be aggregated [39, 41]. In the illustration on this study, the independent variable risk was evaluated using Bayesian network aimed at reducing the number of risk parameters in each table. This independence has an efficient way to calculate the posterior probability that refers to the evidence of risks [43, 44].

In this study, dataset can be obtained from data providers, government departments, or data agencies [45]. Bayesian network as a theory of uncertainty serves will be used to weight the score to perform the assessment phase. If the results of the assessment indicate that the trace holds the risk higher than the benefits, then measures can be taken to reduce the risks of adverse effect.

3   Method for Opening Data

3.1   Proposed Decision-Making Support Model

Our Decision-making Support model for opening data start by the retrieval of datasets in a data provider. There are four main steps to judge whether to open data. The steps used in this model presents in the Fig. 1 as follows:

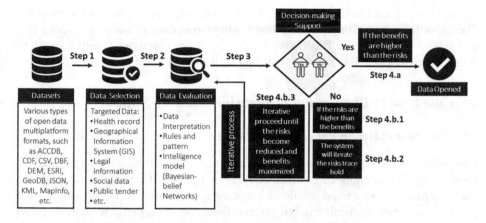

Fig. 1. Proposed Decision-making Support model phases

Step 1. **Retrieve and decompose datasets**. The Decision-making support model is required to be able to read various types of open data multiplatform formats. In one case of health records or medical records dataset, the Decision-making support will carefully sort the tables in the datasets, including ensuring that all fields are intact and maintained in relation to each table.

Step 2. Evaluation. This step is a very important stage where the datasets that have been selected in the previous step will go through the evaluation process. The system will perform interpretation of data that translates each data value from a table to be included in two broad categories of risks and benefits. Dataset is evaluated using the Bayesian-networks model to provide an assessment or weighting of all the fields in the table dataset by considering the probability and dependence of one field with another. Bayesian belief network gives scores for each field in the table based on seven risk variables.

Step 3. Assessment. The results of the evaluation in the previous stages are classification and level references to the risks and benefits of datasets. The advantage of this system is to provide iterative process conditions when conducting an assessment, to ensure that the benefits level is higher than the risk at hand. Technically, during the iterative process, the system will normalize the tables in the datasets by removing the fields from the table structure that has potential risks.

Step 4.a. Positive Result. In this step, the Decision-making support model will provide an assessment of each field in the datasets structure with respect to the risks variable. When the datasets test results show that the datasets have a greater benefit condition than the risk, the system will present a reference to open the dataset to the public. In this case, positive results can be interpreted that the tested dataset has a low risk value related to some data security risk issues.

Step 4.b. Negative Result. If the risk attribute of the datasets is still higher than the benefit (4.b.1) then the system performs the iteration of the trace hold risk and returns to the evaluation in step 3 (4.b.2), until the risk is reduced and the benefit becomes increased (4.b.3).

In the proposed Decision-making support model, multiple iterations are possible. This condition occurs if the system still finds a field in a table of datasets contains a risk that needs to be mitigated. This iteration will take place continuously until the system does not find a field in the dataset's table that indicates the value of risks.

4   Case Study: Illustration of Decision-Making Support

4.1   Case Study: Health Patient Stories Datasets

The government intends to publish medical record datasets through the Department of Health [46]. The opening of data can enable comparison of among hospitals or the mapping of the current trend profile of a disease in certain areas. One reason for the government to open medical records datasets is the ability of the public to analyze spread of some special diseases [47].

However, attributes can be misused, including knowing family history to analyze risks of getting a certain disease, accident records, drugs history, and other related issues. Some of the datasets published may be related to the attributes such as surgical history, obstetrical history, and medical allergies [48]. Each attribute also has a sub-attribute in which there is data value of a patient and his family [48, 49]. For other users or departments in need, these attributes are very important and useful for reuse in certain purposes.

4.2   Decision-Making Support Illustration

In a hospital data about patients are stored starting from the registration process, filling out personal identity, disease detection process, doctor's action, therapy, to financial information. This data can be stored using structured Electronic Medical Record (EMR) [50]. Figure 2 shows the original raw tables of the patient health stories:

Table 1 (Diagnosed Stage)	Table 2 (Undergoes Surgery)	Table 3 (Metastatic Disease)	Table 4 (eGFR)	Table 5 (1L Therapy)	Table 6 (Hospitalized)
Name_of_patient	Date_of_surgery	Metastases_sites	Biopsy_date	Regimen_name	Date_of_hospitalized
Date_of_birth	Surgeon	Time_to_recurrence	Test_of_date	Duration_of_theraphy	Cost_of_care
Place_of_birth	Anaesthetic		Turnaround_time	Dosage	
Gender			Number_of_unsuccessful_tests	Concomitant_meds	
Race			Test_result	Response	
Insurance			Type_of_eGFR	Line_of_theraphy	
Stage				Laboratory_name	
TNM_staging					

Fig. 2. Raw tables from the patient health stories (adapted from: Abernaty [50])

With the formation of a raw table then the system can begin the stages of analysis of the risks and benefits of the datasets. This condition is an illustration of the implementation of step 1 (Retrieve and decompose datasets) in Fig. 3, where the datasets have been determined using the format of database files (DBF). Meanwhile, the patient health record dataset option is associated with step 2 (Evaluation) of the DSS model stage. In this case, the DSS evaluation result shows that the trace hold variable of risks is higher than the benefits as the examining process in step 3 (Assessment). Therefore, the datasets were decided not to be opened to the public. Based on the design of the Decision-making support model in Fig. 1, if the trace hold variable risk is higher than the benefit, then the system will perform the iterative process.

First Iteration
Issue related risks: *Data privacy, Data security, Data sensitivity, Data confidentiality*

Table 1 (Diagnosed Stage)	Table 2 (Undergoes Surgery)	Table 3 (Metastatic Disease)	Table 4 (eGFR)	Table 5 (1L Therapy)	Table 6 (Hospitalized)
Name_of_patient (1)	Date_of_surgery	Metastases_sites	Biopsy_date	Regimen_name	Date_of_hospitalized
Date_of_birth (1)	Surgeon (1)	Time_to_recurrence	Test_of_date	Duration_of_theraphy	Cost_of_care (1)
Place_of_birth (1)	Anaesthetic (1)		Turnaround_time	Dosage	
Gender			Number_of_unsuccessful_tests	Concomitant_meds	
Race			Test_result	Response	
Insurance			Type_of_eGFR	Line_of_theraphy	
Stage				Laboratory_name (1)	
TNM_staging					

Fig. 3. First iteration of patient health stories datasets

At the step 4.a and b, the DSS system will provide an assessment of each field in the six table datasets with respect to seven risk variables. The seven variables are data privacy, data security, data sensitivity and data confidentiality that exist in the first iteration. The term data security used as one of the different variables in the assessment process of this model is to represent the data protection variables of destructive power and unwanted unauthorized user actions [18, 28]. Meanwhile, the other three variables such as accuracy data, data ownership, and data license are evaluated in the second interaction. Based on the trace hold using the Bayesian belief network, the system evaluates each table following the fields in it.

In Fig. 3, illustrated Decision-making support performs the iteration of datasets by considering several issues related risk issues. to The first four of seven risk variables are data privacy, data security, data sensitivity, and data confidentiality. The result is that there are several fields in each table that is omitted because the trace hold finds a high level of risk associated with four security issues. The multiple fields removed (see Fig. 3) are (Table 1: Name_of_patient, Date_of_birth, Place_of_birth); (Table 2: Surgeon, Anaesthetic); (Table 5: Laboratory_name); and (Table 6: Cost_of_care).

Figure 4 presents how Bayesian belief network, assess the potential risks of patient health stories dataset:

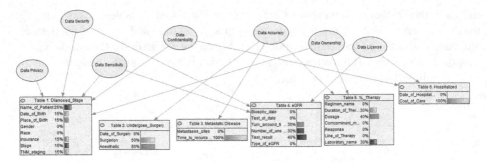

Fig. 4. Potential risks assessment with Bayesian belief network

In Fig. 4, Table 1 (Diagnosed_stage) has a potential risk to data privacy, data security, data sensitivity, and data confidentiality with the highest possible risk is in the Name_of_patient field (25%). Table 2 (Undergoes_surgery) has a potential risk to data accuracy issues with a projection of each weight of 50% for the Surgeon and Anaesthetic fields. Table 3 (Metastatic_disease), is predicted to have a potential risk to the issue of data accuracy with Time_to_reccurence field having the highest weight of 100%. Meanwhile, Table 4 (eGFR) has three risk issues: data security, data sensitivity, and data license with the highest risk weight predicted in the Test_result field of 40%. Table 5 (1L Therapy) also has risk issues of data accuracy and data ownership with the highest risk prediction weight held by the Dosage field (40%). Table 6 (Hospitalized) has one potential risk associated with data license with a weight of 100%.

The next step is to continue the second iterative process where the security issues analysed are related to data accuracy, data ownership and data license. The multiple fields removed (see Fig. 5) are (Table 1: Insurance, Stage, TNM_staging); (Table 3: Time_to_reccurrence); (Table 4: Turnaround_time, Number_of_unsuccessfull_test, Test_result); and (Table 5: Duration_of_theraphy, Dosage).

Second Iteration
Issue related risks: *Data accuracy, Data ownership, Data licence*

Table 1 (Diagnosed Stage)	Table 2 (Undergoes Surgery)	Table 3 (Metastatic Disease)	Table 4 (eGFR)	Table 5 (1L Therapy)	Table 6 (Hospitalized)
Name_of_patient (1)	Date_of_surgery	Metastases_sites	Biopsy_date	Regimen_name	Date_of_hospitalized
Date_of_birth (1)	Surgeon (1)	Time_to_recurrence (2)	Test_of_date	Duration_of_theraphy (2)	Cost_of_care (1)
Place_of_birth (1)	Anaesthetic (1)		Turnaround_time (2)	Dosage (2)	
Gender			Number_of_unsuccessful_tests (2)	Concomitant_meds	
Race			Test_result (2)	Response	
Insurance (2)			Type_of_eGFR	Line_of_theraphy	
Stage (2)				Laboratory_name (1)	
TNM_staging (2)					

Fig. 5. Second iteration of patient health stories dataset

Figure 6 presents the final iteration of Patient Health Stories Datasets. After passing the first and the second iterative process stages, the evaluation results show that the datasets in the third iteration have a lower risk than the benefits. Therefore, only after the third iteration, the dataset was decided to be opened to the public. If we examine more closely the final results of the iterative process in Fig. 6, the table structure in the datasets has undergone significant changes. Many of the fields that are eliminated or eliminated to avoid the risks.

Third Iteration (Final)

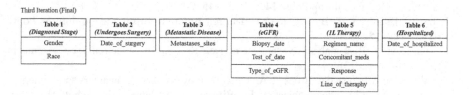

Table 1 (Diagnosed Stage)	Table 2 (Undergoes Surgery)	Table 3 (Metastatic Disease)	Table 4 (eGFR)	Table 5 (IL Therapy)	Table 6 (Hospitalized)
Gender	Date_of_surgery	Metastases_sites	Biopsy_date	Regimen_name	Date_of_hospitalized
Race			Test_of_date	Concomitant_meds	
			Type_of_eGFR	Response	
				Line_of_theraphy	

Fig. 6. Third Iteration (Final) of patient health stories datasets

5 Conclusions

The objective of this research is to develop a model for decision-making support for opening data by weighing potential risks and benefits using Bayesian belief network. A model was developed consisting of four phases (1) Data selection to choose targeted datasets, (2) Data evaluation to integrate datasets using the Bayesian network as an intelligence model, (3) Decision-making support to weigh the potential risks and benefits of datasets, and (4) Multiple iterative processes to get the risks become reduced and benefits maximized.

The model is illustrated by the process of opening patient health stories dataset. This dataset is evaluated and assessed whether the dataset is feasible to open to the public. To find out, this research designs an illustration of decision-making support model by involving the concept of trace holds variable analysis, such as Decision-making Support Cycle and Bayesian network model. As for assessing risk variables to datasets, this study uses seven risk classifications such as data privacy, data security, data sensitivity, data accuracy, data ownership, data license, and data confidentiality. From the evaluation and assessment of trace hold variable of each field in the six tables owned by the dataset, it takes three times the iterative process by eliminating several fields in each table on the consideration of the predefined risk classification.

References

1. Zuiderwijk, A., Janssen, M.: Towards decision support for disclosing data: closed or open data? Inform. Polity **20**(2–3), 103–107 (2015)
2. Conradie, P., Choenni, S.: On the barriers for local government releasing open data. Gov. Inform. Q. **31**(Suppl. 1), S10–S17 (2014)
3. Zuiderwijk, A., Janssen, M., David, C.: Innovation with open data: essential elements of open data ecosystems. Inform. Polity **19**(2–3), 17–33 (2014)
4. Kulk, S., Loenen, B.V.: Brave new open data world? Int. J. Spatial Data Infrasructure Res. **7**, 196–206 (2012)
5. Janssen, M., Charalabidis, Y., Zuiderwijk, A.: Benefits, adoption barriers and myths of open data and open government. Inform. Syst. Manage. **29**(4), 258–268 (2012)

6. Grimmelikhujsen, S.G., Meijer, A.J.: Effects of transparency on the perceived trustworthiness of a government organization: evidence from an online experiment. J. Public Adm. Res. Theor. **24**(1), 137–157 (2014)

7. Meijer, A., Thaens, M.: Public information strategies: making government information available to citizens. Inform. Polity **14**(1–2), 31–45 (2009)

8. Barry, E., Bannister, F.: Barriers to open data release: a view from the top. Inform. Polity **19**(1–2), 129–152 (2014)

9. Martin, S., et al.: Risk analysis to overcome barriers to open data. Electron. J. e-Government **11**(1), 348–359 (2013)

10. van Veenstra, A.F., van den Broek, T.A.: Opening moves – drivers, enablers and barriers of open data in a semi-public organization. In: Wimmer, M.A., Janssen, M., Scholl, H.J. (eds.) EGOV 2013. LNCS, vol. 8074, pp. 50–61. Springer, Heidelberg (2013). https://doi.org/10.1007/978-3-642-40358-3_5

11. Puron-Cid, G., Gil-Garcia, R.J., Luna-Reyes, L.F.: IT-enabled policy analysis: new technologies, sophisticated analysis and open data for better government decisions. In: 13th Annual International Conference on Digital Government Research, pp. 97–106. ACM Digital Library, College Park (2012)

12. Albano, C.S., Reinhard, N.: Open government data: facilitating and motivating factors for coping with potential barriers in the Brazilian context. In: Janssen, M., Scholl, H.J., Wimmer, M.A., Bannister, F. (eds.) EGOV 2014. LNCS, vol. 8653, pp. 181–193. Springer, Heidelberg (2014). https://doi.org/10.1007/978-3-662-44426-9_15

13. Yannoukakou, A., Araka, I.: Access to government information: right to information and open government data synergy. In: 3rd International Conference on Integrated Information (IC-ININFO), vol. 147, pp. 332–340 (2014)

14. Gurstein, M.: Open data: empowering the empowered or effective data use for everyone? First Monday, **16**(2) (2011). http://journals.uic.edu/ojs/index.php/fm/article/view/3316/2764

15. Bertot, J.C., Jaeger, P.T., Grimmes, J.M.: Using ICTs to create a culture of transparency: e-government and social media as openness and anti-corruption tools for societies. Gov. Inform. Q. **27**(3), 264–271 (2010)

16. Manyika, J., et al.: Open data: unlocking innovation and performance with liquid information (2013)

17. Barnickel, N., et al.: Berlin Open Data Strategy: organisational, legal and technical aspects of Open Data in Berlin. In: Concept, Pilot System and Recommendations for Action (2012)

18. Chen, D., Zhao, H.: Data security and privacy protection issues in cloud computing. In: International Conference and Privacy Protection Issues in Cloud Computing, pp. 647–651. IEEE Computer Society, Hangzhou (2012)

19. Archer, P., et al.: Business models for Linked Open Government Data: what lies beneath? (2013)

20. Walter, S.: Heterogeneous database integration in biomedicine. J. Biomed. Inform. **34**(4), 285–298 (2001)

21. Amit, S.P., Larson, J.A.: Federated database systems for managing distributed, heterogeneous, and autonomous databases. ACM Comput. Surv. **22**(3), 183–236 (1990)

22. Uhlir, P.F.: The Socioeconomic Effects of Public Sector Information on Digital Networks: Toward a Better Understanding of Different Access and Reuse Policies. National Research Council, Washington DC (2009)

23. Turner, P.: Unification of digital evidence from disparate sources. In: The Digital Forensic Research Conference, New Orleans, LA (2005)

24. Bayan, R.: Simple strategies to stop data leakage. TechRepublic (2004)

25. Scasa, T.: Privacy and open government. J. Future Internet **6**(2), 397–413 (2014)

26. Tran, E., Scholtes, G.: Open Data Literature Review. Barkeley School of Law, University of California (2015)
27. Han, J., et al.: Personalized active service spaces for end-user service composition. In: International Conference on Services Computing (SCC 2006). IEEE Computer Society (2006)
28. Aldossary, S., Allen, W.: data security, privacy, availability and integrity in cloud computing: issues and current solutions. Int. J. Adv. Comput. Sci. Appl. **7**(4), 485–498 (2016)
29. Catteddu, D.: Cloud computing: benefits, risks and recommendations for information security. In: Serrão, C., Aguilera Díaz, V., Cerullo, F. (eds.) IBWAS 2009. CCIS, vol. 72, p. 17. Springer, Heidelberg (2010). https://doi.org/10.1007/978-3-642-16120-9_9
30. Aljahdali, H., et al.: Multi-tenancy in cloud computing. In: 2014 IEEE 8th International Symposium on Service Oriented System Engineering (SOSE). IEEE, Oxford (2014)
31. Hashizume, K., Rosado, D.G., Fernández-Medina, E.: An analysis of security issues for cloud computing. J. Internet Serv. Appl., **4**(5) (2013)
32. Puddephatt, A., Zausmer, R.: Towards open and transparent government. In: International Experiences and Best Practice. Global Partners and Associates (2011)
33. Kucera, J., Chlapek, D.: Benefits and risks of open data. J. Syst. Integr. **1**, 30–41 (2014)
34. Schwegmann, C.: Open data in developing countries. In: European Public Sector Information Platform Topic Report No. 2013/02 (2012)
35. Turban, E., Aronson, J.E., Liang, T.-P.: Decision Support System and Intelligent System. Prentice Hall, Upper Saddle River (2007)
36. Little, J.D.C.: Models and Managers: The Concept of a Decision Calculus. Manage. Sci. **16**(8), 466–485 (1976)
37. Bonczek, R.H., Holsapple, C., Whinston, A.: The evolving roles of models in decision support system. Decis. Sci. **11**(2), 337–356 (1980)
38. Murphy, K.: A Brief Introduction to Graphical Models and Bayesian Networks (1998)
39. Neopolitan, R.E.: Learning Bayesian Networks. Prentice Hall Series in Artificial Intelligence. Northeastern Illinois University (2004)
40. Horný, M.: Bayesian Networks, in Technical report No. 5. 2014, Department of Health Policy & Management: Boston University School of Public Health (2014)
41. Spiegelhalter, D.J.: Bayesian graphical modelling: a case-study in monitoring health outcomes. Royal Stat. Soc. **47**(1), 115–133 (1998)
42. Kenett, R.S.: Applications of Bayesian networks to operational risks, healthcare, biotechnology and customer surveys. In: 22nd Colombian Statistics Symposium, Bucaramanga (2012)
43. Pearl, J., Russel, S.: Bayesian networks. In: Handbook of Brain Theory and Neural Networks, Cambridge, pp. 157–160 (2001)
44. Sprites, P., Glymour, C., Schienes, R.: Causation Prediction and Search. Carnegie Mellon University, Springer, New York (1993). https://doi.org/10.1007/978-1-4612-2748-9
45. Ubaldi, B.: Open government data: towards empirical analysis of open government data initiatives. In: OECD Working Papers on Public Governance, vol. 22, p. 60 (2013)
46. Kostkova, P., et al.: Who owns the data? Open data for healthcare. Frontiers Public Health **4**(7), 1–6 (2016)
47. Bøttcher, S.G., Dethlefsen, C.: Learning Bayesian Networks with R. Vienna University of Technology: Department of Mathematical Science, Aalborg University Denmark (2003)
48. Spooner, L.M., Pesaturo, K.A.: Chapter 1: The Medical Record (2013)
49. Ozair, F.F., et al.: Ethical issues in electronic health records: a general overview. Perspect. Clin. Res. **6**(2), 73–76 (2015)
50. Abernethy, A.: Real World Evidence: Opportunities and Challenges. Flatiron Health (2016)

Information Dissemination and Freedom of Expression

Monitoring Media Scrutiny of EU Official Information and Documentation. A Content Analysis of the European Online News Coverage (January–May 2017)

Cătălina Maria Georgescu[1](✉) [iD], Anca Parmena Olimid[1] [iD], Daniel Alin Olimid[2] [iD], Silviu Dorin Georgescu[3] [iD], and Cosmin Lucian Gherghe[1] [iD]

[1] Faculty of Social Sciences, Political Sciences Specialization, Center CEPOS, University of Craiova, 13th Street A. I. Cuza, Craiova, Romania
cata.georgescu@yahoo.com, parmena2002@yahoo.com, avcosmingherghe@gmail.com
[2] Biology Specialization, University of Craiova, 13th Street A. I. Cuza, Craiova, Romania
olimiddaniel@yahoo.com
[3] Faculty of Economy and Business Administration, University of Craiova, 13th Street A. I. Cuza, Craiova, Romania
gsilviu2000@gmail.com

Abstract. This paper discusses the media coverage of the European Union official information and documentation (press release, EU summits press conference communiques, etc.) released by the European Union official newsroom and disseminated using the online press in the period January–May 2017.

The paper reveals the inner-patterns of the EU online information dissemination while challenging the most important public events of the Europeans during this period: i.e. celebration of the sixty years of the EU existence, Dutch elections of March 2017, French elections of April/May 2017. The paper scrutinizes European and international online media platforms such as: politico.eu, europa.eu, neweurope.eu, euractiv.com using the content analysis methodology. The paper analyses media coverage by exploring the following dimensions:

1. Targeting the main European Union (EU) themes in online media-coverage
2. Labelling the framing of online news articles
3. Determining the tone of journalists and issues
4. Pinpointing the most influencing issues in media coverage

Keywords: European union · Media monitoring · Content analysis · European parliament agenda · Online news sources · Public policies

1 Background

A systematic content analysis of media coverage of current developing policy issues at European level (EU) should have as starting point the acknowledgement of the role and significance of Internet-based communication and information systems for governments, citizens and the business environment [13]. This is the more applicable especially as considering an additional governance-tire at supranational level [12]. The importance

© Springer International Publishing AG 2017
S.K. Katsikas and V. Zorkadis (Eds.): E-Democracy 2017, CCIS 792, pp. 109–122, 2017.
https://doi.org/10.1007/978-3-319-71117-1_8

of news coverage, media reporting techniques, editorship practices, journalistic style, attitude and tone in styling policy preferences, agenda setting and policy advocacy are common knowledge [7, 14]. This article employs a systematic content analysis of media coverage of key European policy updates pursuing both the quantitative aspect and the qualitative aspect of research methodology highlighted in the literature by assuming frequency distribution, relation analysis and main thematic approaches [3, 10]. One of the aims is to highlight the manner in which different media sources relate to key European aspects [2] in order to deduct the possible impact of the distribution of communication and news on different audiences [6].

Content analysis methodology has evolved greatly over the years with the stunning Internet communication and technology discoveries while their applicability has varied and diversified widely to cover aspects such as tracking the media coverage of specific issues on a short, medium or longer time frame introducing a stage-based event coverage analysis [11] and different semantic web techniques of data processing [16, 19]. Thus a strong branch of content analysis methodology has evolved around the study and introduction of seminal techniques of information and textual analyses, data categorisation and topic detection based on cluster analyses or other methods of searching for meaning in different media environments [17] including different NLP (Natural Language Processing) tools.

Identifying the main themes proves to be an interesting and challenging research activity in content analysis especially when a huge volume of information is concerned. Some researchers have overpassed this encumbrance by proposing innovative methods of manifold short texts theme abstraction in cases in which frequency analysis proves un-operational [1]. Recent researchers have developed further the manual analysis in order to grasp the endorsement, feelings and sentiments attached to the huge volume of opinions expressed and textual messages communicated throughout the online media platforms backed by the establishment of complex computational algorithms projected to employ vocabulary depending on context [8, 15]. Such researches aimed at imposing a special interest of study to the importance of journalistic and reporting tone and affect to the topics further taking over public discourse and policy-making, thus pointing out the relevance of language and especially the presence of affectogene wording and phrases in styling preferences and support [5]. Certain strands of research find an interest in identifying the impact of news-reading in understanding different phenomena by employing a critical analysis of the texts and identifying three particular potential reader profiles according to their engagement to the text [9].

However, researchers argue for the importance of *a priori* coding and other complex research semantics-based instruments, either computer-assisted or manually enhanced, for an efficient news reporting content analysis [4].

2   Aims and Objectives

This article processes the media coverage of the European Union official information and documentation (press releases, EU summits press conference communiques etc.) launched on the European Union official europa.eu platform and disseminated by the online press in the period January–May 2017. The paper reveals the inner-patterns of the EU online communication while challenging the most important public events of the EU citizens during this period: i.e. celebrating sixty years of the EU existence, Dutch elections of March 2017, French elections of April/May 2017, British elections and their importance on Brexit. The paper scrutinizes European online media platforms such as: politico.eu, europa.eu, neweurope.eu, euractiv.com using the content analysis methodology. The paper studies media coverage by probing the following dimensions: (1) tackling the main European (EU) themes in online media-coverage, (2) qualifying the framing of online news articles, (3) appreciating the tone of journalists and issues and (4) emphasising the most influencing issues in media coverage. The aim of this paper is to provide an original manner of analysing the coverage of the main European policy themes by online media initiating a correlation between the European Parliament's (EP) Agenda by event to media coverage of specific events. Thus the main objective is to highlight the impact of European issues and actions on online news media and to discuss the distribution of news and attention by online news services in order to proceed to quantifying media feedback of European policy issues.

3   Methods

3.1   Research Design

Methodologically, the research was divided into two parts. The first part consists in a content analysis of European Parliament weekly agenda (the analysis focuses on the first 20 weeks of 2017 covering the period 02nd January 2017 – 21st May 2017). The aim of this research is to discover the policy interests of this high-profile EU institution during the selected period. Basically we aim at pointing out the main issues on the EP agenda for the period under analysis in terms of (1) identifying the main strands of legislative interest, (2) dwelling a hierarchy as regards the frequency of the most discussed topics and (3) identifying whether there is a pattern for the most highlighted topics and specific political, social or security events throughout the EU. The second part consists in a systematic content analysis performed under a media monitoring in search for the manner in which the media reported the highest profile issues at European level and for pinpointing the interest of a number of news sources for European subjects. Thus, we aimed at monitoring the online news media coverage of European Union policy-making during the period January–May 2017. Further, we aimed at correlating the data obtained in the two stages of the research.

3.2   Research Questions

For the aims and objectives outlined in the previous section the research was built on the following questions: Q_i. Which were the main European themes in online media-coverage? Q_{ii}. Which were the frames journalists used on the selected online news articles? Q_{iii}. Can we trace elements of bias in online media coverage of top European issues? Q_{iv}. Can we identify the most influencing European issues in online media coverage?

3.3 Identifying and Selecting Top European Issues

As regards the methods employed for identifying key European issues, we opted for analysing the European Parliament's work documents (the so-called "The Week Ahead" Agendas) which summarise the top activities of the EU citizens' representatives. We selected 20 documents (following the EP agenda by event criterion) corresponding to the 6 months period between January 2nd 2017–May 21st 2017. The analysis of the EP weekly agenda by event revealed the institutional and political activity: the receival of delegations, plenary preparations and sessions, committee and political group meetings, the EP president's activity etc.

3.4 Selecting News Sources and Articles

Following the selection of the online news sources (we opted for EurActiv, New Europe and Politico.eu full text online archives) we identified a number of 2642 entries for the 20 weeks period between January 1st 2017 and May 21st 2017. The online articles were selected on both the headlines and content relevance criteria to match the research purpose following an elimination of duplicates (as was the case with updates or corrections), irrelevant articles, or articles which merely mentioned the search terms used.

4 Results and Discussion

4.1 European Issues

The European Parliament's (EP) online Agenda for the first 20 weeks of 2017 published on Europa.eu appears to be lush as it abounds in topics and different types of actions or events (visits of foreign delegations and visits to Member States or third parties, committee and political group meetings in Brussels, debates and discussions, plenary sessions and committee meetings in Strasbourg, mid-term elections, addresses, votes on legislative resolutions or on recommendations, inquiries etc.). The content analysis of the documents unfolds the issues on the EP agenda during the analysed period: asylum (including refugees relocation and help) (n = 9), ethical issues of robotics (n = 5), the activity of the Maltese Council Presidency (n = 3), police cooperation (n = 1), food waste (n = 3) and food safety (n = 1), car emissions (including environmental testing) (n = 4), taxation (n = 4), firearms (n = 2), Energy Union (n = 1), adoptions (n = 1), pesticides (n = 1), visa-free travel (n = 3), threats to the rule of law (n = 4), climate change (including the Arctic policy and carbon emissions) (n = 4), economic and monetary union (including money laundering, tax evasion, budgetary capacity, and the Panama papers issue) (n = 10), Schengen area issues (both internal and external borders checks) (n = 4), trade (including the EU-Canada trade agreement (CETA)) (n = 9), counter-terrorism measures (including measures against terrorism financing) (n = 5), peace process (2), Brexit (including EU citizens free movement in the UK following Brexit) (n = 8), "60th anniversary of the Rome treaties" (n = 1), facilitated access to print material (n = 1), EU internal security (n = 8), ethical issues and patients' safety as regards medical devices (n = 2), reducing roaming prices (n = 2), personal data protection (n = 1).

4.2   Distribution of Articles

The selection of news articles started naturally with empirically testing the relevance of the search terms. Thus we proceeded by employing an online Boolean search using the terms "European Union (EU)" AND "policy", "European Parliament" OR "European legislative". This action resulted in the identification of several thousands of findings which was followed by the actual selection of articles by removing duplicates (selecting updates, corrections etc.) and irrelevant pieces. The distribution of articles per news source during the selected period (01 January–21 May 2017) is shown in Fig. 1 featuring the statistics with Politico.eu – 916 articles (35%), EurActiv.com – 1045 (39%) and New Europe – 681 (26%) (Fig. 1).

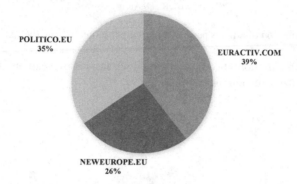

Fig. 1. Distribution of articles per news source during the selected period (Jan-May 2017)

Furthermore we employed a statistical analysis to highlight the distribution of articles per news source per month during the selected period resulting the following situation: January – Politico.eu 197 articles, NewEurope.eu 195 articles, and EurActiv.com 214 articles; February – Politico.eu 199 articles, NewEurope.eu 134 articles and EurActiv.com 225 articles; March – Politico.eu 211 articles, NewEurope.eu 159 articles and EurActiv.com 276 articles; April – Politico.eu 154 articles, NewEurope.eu 85 articles and EurActiv.com 155 articles and finally May – Politico.eu 130 articles, NewEurope.eu 108 articles and EurActiv.com 175 articles (Fig. 2). We noticed as a most significant difference between the overall number of articles published in January (606), February (558) and March (646) against April (394) and May (413); as regards the situation in May 2017, the explanation cannot rely solely on the fact that only the articles published during 01–21 May were selected, but also on the density of the activities and actions occurring at European (EU) level.

The analysis of the daily frequency distribution per source afferent to January 2017 revealed the situation covered in Fig. 3. The agenda of the European Parliament (EP) for January 2017 featured the receival of delegations by the European representatives, the committee scrutiny of a new European Commissioner for Budget and Human Resources, the issue of EU-Turkey deal and refugees displacement, ethical issues raised by artificial intelligence use, the Maltese Council Presidency taking office, the grounding for mid-term EP presidency elections, the committees meetings and inquiries on CETA,

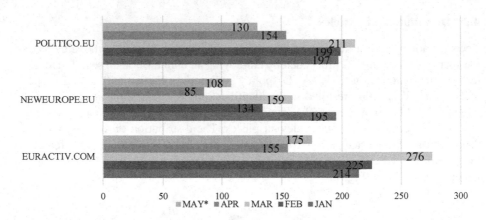

Fig. 2. Distribution of articles per news source per month during the selected period

recycling, vehicles emissions, taxation, personal possession of weapons, monetary union capacity and Eurozone economies evolution.

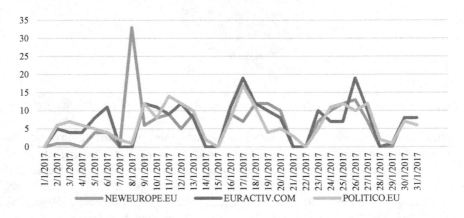

Fig. 3. Daily frequency distribution per source (January 2017)

Studying the daily frequency distribution per source of the February 2017 articles led to the statistics covered by Fig. 4. At European level the MEPs gathered in plenary session and committee meetings to debate and sometimes even vote aspects pertaining to the Energy Union, "cross-border adoptions", the replacement of dangerous pesticides, the suspension of visa requirements for certain European non-EU country nationals, threats to the rule of law in some African states, new measures for fighting terrorism, debating and voting the amendments to the Schengen Border Code, fighting greenhouse gas effects, resolutions for reforming the EU under the "Future of Europe", ethical standards and safety measures for robotics use, trade agreements, money laundering and tax evasion inquiries, research of asylum seekers situation, assessments of Frontex activity as regards border controls, EU relations with third countries and involvement in the peace process.

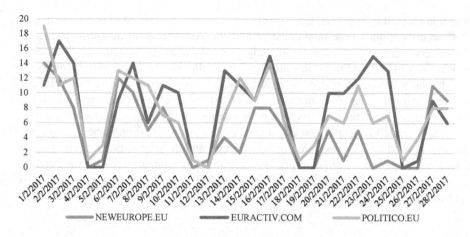

Fig. 4. Daily frequency distribution per source (February 2017)

The analysis of the daily frequency distribution per news source for March 2017 shows an established pattern of coverage with heavier reporting during weekdays and penurious, even absent during week-ends (Fig. 5). This is especially the case with EurActiv.com and NewEurope.eu. On the policy agenda of the EP appear the concoctions for the EU Summit and its effects as well as covering the "Rome declaration" addressing EU's (the Treaty of Rome in particular) 60th celebration, discussions on visa requirements with the US and the rights of EU citizens to reside in the UK, the affordability of medicines, diesel engines emissions inquiry, amendments to legislation against money laundering and tax evasion, offshores as well as against subsidizing terrorism, threats to fundamental rights and to the rule of law in certain EU Member States, assuming solidarity in solving the refugee and asylum crisis, shareholder legislation, legislation to trace the source of minerals and thus ban "conflict minerals", policy to

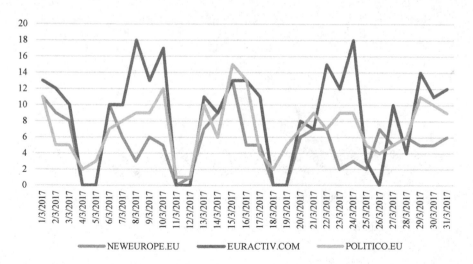

Fig. 5. Daily frequency distribution per source (March 2017)

heighten recycling, improved legislation on firearms, measures to improve feeding and food security, policy on climate change and the Arctic region, measures to increase consumers rights against online fraud, budgeting for the 2014–2020 financial framework and security in certain European states heavily challenged by latest terrorist attacks.

The daily frequency distribution of media reporting per source of the April 2017 articles is shown in Fig. 6. Political groups of MEPs debated Brexit issues which were formally voted into a resolution. Other policy debates and votes centred around medical devices, amended legislation on engine emissions testing, roaming pricing, visa regulations, oil production, prevention of hate speech and disinformation, securing private data, Syrian issue and return of migrants, waste management, digitalisation and employment, security and human rights, Turkish situation, social protection situation in EU, the Eurogroup and the Greek issue.

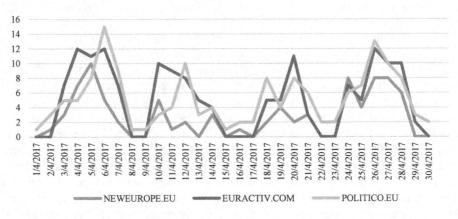

Fig. 6. Daily frequency distribution per source (April 2017)

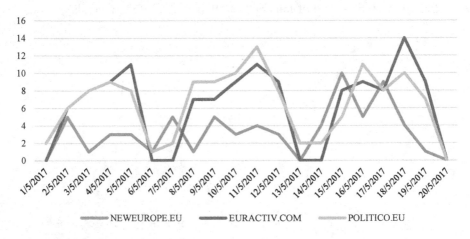

Fig. 7. Daily frequency distribution per source (May 2017)

The articles daily frequency distribution per source in May 2017 is presented in Fig. 7. The policy agenda of the EP exhibited the resuming of January debates regarding the Commission proposals on anti-money laundering. Other European policy-making topics included the re-consideration of taxation on e-books, the issue of monitoring the activity of private security companies, EU-NATO relations, further debates over Brexit, taxation, access to subscribed online content when abroad, fundamental rights issues in certain Member States, the relocation of refugees and the humanitarian crisis in Syria. We noticed some peaks in reporting on May 6th (11 articles - EurActiv.com), May 11th (13 articles from Politico.eu) and May 19th (EurActiv.com - 14 articles).

4.3   Themes

The presence and meaning of one or several themes within the articles' content was the next stage of our research. This stage included a search activity according to the editorial domains and sub-domains of the news sources employed. Further, we undergone a thorough reading of the articles' texts doubled by a manual extraction of the main themes featured in the articles. These were followed by a descriptive categorisation in order to accomplish the thematic analysis covered by the statistics rendered in Fig. 8. This stage thus completed by generating the following themes: Brexit (including EU-UK relations), economic governance (including circular economy, jobs/employment, CETA, development policy, agriculture and food), enlargement, global Europe (including Central and Eastern Europe), transportation (including road safety, road charging, access to public transportation, railways), Future EU (including EU Priorities 2020), Politics, elections, energy (including electricity, electric cars, biofuels), climate change (including the emissions trading scheme), Justice & Home Affairs (including, but not limited to human rights, freedom of thought), Digital Europe (including data protection, cybersecurity), language & culture and health (Fig. 8).

4.4   News Framing Analyses

The analysis of the "generic" news framing led to the identification of five "meta-themes" in the selected online news sources discourse: the "economics" frame, the "human impact" frame, the "conflict" frame, the "powerlessness" frame and the "moral values" frame [18]. Thus, "economics" framing appeared in articles tackling the economic implications of EU policy-making in the fields of social policy: "A social triple A without an entrepreneurial triple A?" (EurActiv.com, Feb 7, 2017), "Will MEPs stand up for financial stability over speculation?" (EurActiv.com, Feb 13, 2017); in the field of trade "A vote against CETA would reset Europe's trade agenda" (EurActiv.com, Feb 14, 2017) and "Spanish food exporters on edge over resurgence of protectionism" (EurActiv.com, Feb 22, 2017); counting economic effects of the different issues opened by Brexit "Scotland's independence debate is now intrinsically tied with Brexit" (EurActiv.com, Mar 15, 2017), "Brexit and Academia: anti-immigration hysteria is hurting an €86bn sector" (NewEurope.eu, April 27, 2017), "Gibraltar braces for a hard Brexit economy" (NewEurope.eu, May 10, 2017), "Taking back control? Not unless

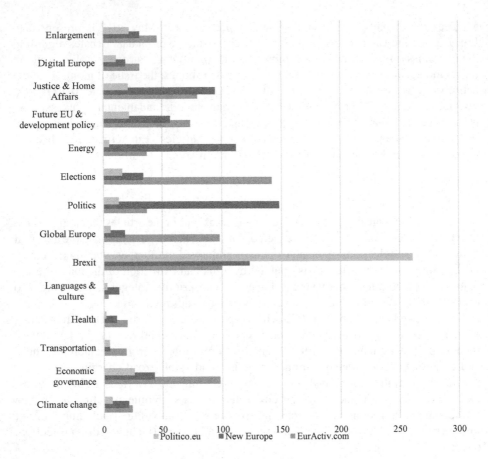

Fig. 8. Thematic distribution of articles per news source

you eat more fish" (Politico.eu, May 10, 2017), "How the EU trapped itself into a no-break lease in Britain" (Politico.eu, April 28, 2017), "ECJ places 38 mines along the path of a Brexit trade agreement" (NewEurope.eu, May 17, 2017); adding an economic dimension to energy policy-making, in articles entitled "Trillions of euros of energy efficiency investment up for grabs" (EurActiv.com, May 8, 2017), "Waste reform: From environmental disaster to economic opportunity" (EurActiv.com, Jan 17, 2017), "EU carbon market at risk of another lost decade" (EurActiv.com, Feb 24, 2017), "Loaded terms in the bioeconomy" (EurActiv.com, Feb 24, 2017), "ETS reform agreement catches its architect by surprise" (EurActiv.com, Mar 2, 2017), "Matching realism and ambition in aluminium recycling" (EurActiv.com, Feb 20, 2017); adding an economic dimension to the debate over human rights matters "Problems with Hungary affect EU single market too" (EurActiv.com, Apr 26, 2017).

We further found a strong "moral values" framing identified in articles pointing towards morality and ethical principles. We identified this frame in articles dealing with the specific aspects of Brexit: "Peace in Northern Ireland needs the EU now more than ever" (EurActiv.com, May 18, 2017), "Cheating Britain out of Europe" (NewEurope.eu,

May 7, 2017), "Gloves off: Brexit suddenly turns as ugly as every divorce" (NewEurope.eu, March 31, 2017); party politics and elections: "A marriage of convenience" (EurActiv.com, Jan 9, 2017), "Why traditional party democracy needs to be overhauled" (EurActiv.com, May 18, 2017), "European elections: Careful what you promise, citizens are watching" (EurActiv.com, Mar 29, 2017), "Patriotisme à l'européenne: Can identity politics save the EU?" (EurActiv.com, May 10, 2017); the Balkan enlargement "Brussels' Balkan approach: Little carrot, broken stick" (EurActiv.com, Mar 13, 2017); the future and reformation of the EU and the quest for an European identity: "Sixty years on, we must write a new chapter in our shared history" (EurActiv.com, Mar 24, 2017), "How should the EU stand up to the recurring temptation of 'national democracy'?" (EurActiv.com, Apr 5, 2017), "What's in store for the EU (hint: it might not be what you think)" (EurActiv.com, Mar 21, 2017), "Two- or multi-speed Europe is a dangerous idea" (EurActiv.com, Mar 9, 2017), "Cohesion policy is not just about money. It's about Europe's future" (Politico.eu, May 18, 2017); the biofuels issue: "Commission is not the only culprit in the biofuel shambles" (EurActiv.com, Mar 16, 2017); threats to the environment: "Magic tricks in the forest: When member states make their emissions vanish" (EurActiv.com, Mar 8, 2017) and "EU shift towards a low carbon economy should be socially just" (EurActiv.com, Apr 3, 2017); freedom of thought: "A Ministry of Truth in the European Parliament?" (EurActiv.com, Mar 10, 2017); trade policy: "Trust in EU trade policy boosted by court decision" (EurActiv.com, May 19, 2017); the war in Syria: "Brussels Syria conference: Why this war is personal" (EurActiv.com, Apr 4, 2017); and the issue of money laundering and financing terrorism: "Parliament again rejects blacklist of states at risk of money laundering" (NewEurope.eu, May 17, 2017).

Moreover, "conflict" framing was representative for articles addressing the issue of human rights and democracy per se: "Hungary was once a democracy: Now it is an 'Orbanocracy'" (EurActiv.com, Apr 5, 2017), "MEPs slam Hungary, call on EU to explore sanctions" (Politico.eu, May 17, 2017), "EU pushes talk, not action, to deal with Poland" (Politico.eu, May 16, 2017), "Brussels fails to broker a peaceful transfer of power in Skopje" (NewEurope.eu, April 4, 2017); the issue of taxation: "EU's idea for tackling tax avoidance? Blame others" (Politico.eu, May 10, 2017); the Cypriot issue: "The EU should be a more active contributor to the Cyprus issue" (EurActiv.com, Jan 5, 2017); Brexit talks: "May throws down gauntlet to European leaders" (EurActiv.com, Jan 17, 2017); firearms industry developments: "How the arms industry is staging a European coup" (EurActiv.com, Jan 23, 2017); Turkey's accession to the EU: "Dashing Turkey's EU hopes is the wrong answer" (EurActiv.com, May 5, 2017); car emissions scandal: "Will the Empire strike back in the next Dieselgate fight?" (EurActiv.com, May 8, 2017),

In addition, "human impact" framing was identified in articles generally indicating strong effects over individuals and the need for affirmative action, in articles dealing with elections: "Voting alone won't save our democracies" (EurActiv.com, Feb 9, 2017); entrepreneurship "Why self-employment needs nurturing, not protection" (EurActiv.com, Feb 7, 2017); and health policy "Health matters should supersede European bureaucracy" (EurActiv.com, Feb 13, 2017), "Turning back the clock on EU health protection is unthinkable" (EurActiv.com, Mar 13, 2017).

Finally, we identified a "powerlessness" frame tackled in articles addressing the promotion of the interest of large entities or actors over weak individuals or categories, for instance: "Public sector jobs fail to escape Brexit uncertainty" (EurActiv.com, Apr 28, 2017), "Europe's stateless locked in limbo" (EurActiv.com, May 4, 2017), "Brexit talks place citizens' rights in limbo" (EurActiv.com, Apr 24, 2017), "Brexit puts security cooperation at risk" (Politico.eu, April 27, 2017).

Thus, the second stage of our research produced a synthesis of meta-themes, manually generated, which describe the media perspectives of topic coverage during the six-month period: the selected media covered the uncertainties over economic, social and human rights prospects triggered by Brexit-related talks and negotiations, the new architectural re-structuring of Europe and the nationalism-supranationalism encounters in European matters. As shown in the reviewed literature, these were framed into a series of "meta-themes": the "economics" frame, the "human impact" frame, the "conflict" frame, the "powerlessness" frame and the "moral values" frame [18].

5   Conclusions

This paper presented the results of a systematic content analysis of online media coverage of key European ongoing policy issues. The aim of the research was to discover the nature of the issues representation and coverage by different online media sources, the distribution of topics, issues and news coverage along a twenty week period of time, as well as the manner in which the media relates to European weekly policy-making, including debates, adoption and implementation. The analysis suggests the existence of a strong correlation between the European policy process and its coverage and relevance through the media. The analysis has shown a strong interest of the different online news sources to European supranational governance topics by identifying the frequency, themes and meta-themes in media coverage. The analysis showed that the angle of reporting varied considerably with some news sources concentrating on (even thoroughly scrutinizing) the supranational level, while others being more interested in the effects and feedback of European (EU) public policy implementation at national level.

References

1. Amato, F., Gargiulo, F., Maisto, A., Mazzeo, A., Pelosi, S., Sansone, C.: A method for topic detection in great volumes of data. In: Helfert, M., Holzinger, A., Belo, O., Francalanci, C. (eds.) DATA 2014. CCIS, vol. 178, pp. 169–181. Springer, Cham (2015). https://doi.org/10.1007/978-3-319-25936-9_11
2. Backfried, G., et al.: Cross-media analysis for communication during natural disasters. In: Papasratorn, B., Charoenkitkarn, N., Vanijja, V., Chongsuphajaisiddhi, V. (eds.) IAIT 2013. CCIS, vol. 409, pp. 13–22. Springer, Cham (2013). https://doi.org/10.1007/978-3-319-03783-7_2
3. Boomgaarden, H.G., De Vreese, C.H., Schuck, A.R.T., Azrout, R., Elenbaas, M., Van Spanje, J.H.P., Vliegenthart, R.: Across time and space: explaining variation in news coverage of the European Union. Eur. J. Polit. Res. **52**, 608–629 (2013). https://doi.org/10.1111/1475-6765.12009

4. Franzosi, R.: Computer-assisted content analysis of newspapers. can we make an expensive research tool more efficient? Qual. Quant. **29**(2), 157–172 (1995). https://doi.org/10.1007/BF01101896
5. Davis, R.: A computer-aided affective content analysis of nanotechnology newspaper articles. NanoEthics **5**(3), 319–334 (2011). https://doi.org/10.1007/s11569-011-0129-8
6. Martinez-Martínez, L.E., Martínez-Espinosa, L.: News reports on TV, Twitter and the Active Audience. In: Abásolo, M.J., Perales, F.J., Bibiloni, A. (eds.) jAUTI/CTVDI -2015. CCIS, vol. 605, pp. 121–133. Springer, Cham (2016). https://doi.org/10.1007/978-3-319-38907-3_10
7. McCaw, B.A., McGlade, K.J., McElnay, J.C.: Online health information – what the newspapers tell their readers: a systematic content analysis. BMC Public Health **14**, 1316 (2014). http://www.biomedcentral.com/1471-2458/14/1316
8. Moreo, A., Castro, J.L., Zurita, J.M.: Handling context in Lexicon-based sentiment analysis. In: Greco, S., Bouchon-Meunier, B., Coletti, G., Fedrizzi, M., Matarazzo, B., Yager, R.R. (eds.) IPMU 2012. CCIS, vol. 298, pp. 245–254. Springer, Heidelberg (2012). https://doi.org/10.1007/978-3-642-31715-6_27
9. Oliveras, B., Márquez, C., Sanmartí, N.: Students' attitudes to information in the press: critical reading of a newspaper article with scientific content. Res. Sci. Educ. **44**(4), 603–626 (2014). https://doi.org/10.1007/s11165-013-9397-3
10. Saburova, M., Maysuradze, A.: A low effort approach to quantitative content analysis. In: Klinov, P., Mouromtsev, D. (eds.) KESW 2015. CCIS, vol. 518, pp. 168–181. Springer, Cham (2015). https://doi.org/10.1007/978-3-319-24543-0_13
11. Saga, R., Kobayashi, H., Miyamoto, T., Tsuji, H.: Measurement evaluation of keyword extraction based on topic coverage. In: Stephanidis, C. (ed.) HCI 2014. CCIS, vol. 434, pp. 224–227. Springer, Cham (2014). https://doi.org/10.1007/978-3-319-07857-1_40
12. Sideridis, A.B., Pimenidis, E., Protopappas, L., Koukouli, M.: An evaluation of the initiatives and the progress made on e-government services in the EU. In: Georgiadis, C.K., Jahankhani, H., Pimenidis, E., Bashroush, R., Al-Nemrat, A. (eds.) ICGS3/e-Democracy 2011. LNICST, vol. 99, pp. 151–165. Springer, Heidelberg (2012). https://doi.org/10.1007/978-3-642-33448-1_35
13. Sideridis, A.B., Protopappas, L., Tsiafoulis, S., Pimenidis, E.: Smart cross-border e-gov systems and applications. In: Katsikas, S.K., Sideridis, A.B. (eds.) e-Democracy 2015. CCIS, vol. 570, pp. 151–165. Springer, Cham (2015). https://doi.org/10.1007/978-3-319-27164-4_11
14. Sovacool, B.K., Saleem, S., D'Agostino, A.L., Ramos, C.R., Trott, K., Ong, Y.: What about social science and interdisciplinarity? A 10-year content analysis of *Energy Policy*. In: Spreng, D., Flüeler, T., Goldblatt, D., Minsch, J. (eds.) Tackling Long-Term Global Energy Problems. Environment & Policy, vol. 52, pp. 47–71. Springer, Dordrecht (2012). https://doi.org/10.1007/978-94-007-2333-7_4
15. Timonen, M., Toivanen, T., Kasari, M., Teng, Y., Cheng, C., He, L.: Keyword extraction from short documents using three levels of word evaluation. In: Fred, A., Dietz, J.L.G., Liu, K., Filipe, J. (eds.) IC3K 2012. CCIS, vol. 415, pp. 130–146. Springer, Heidelberg (2013). https://doi.org/10.1007/978-3-642-54105-6_9
16. Thomas, J., Harden, A.: Methods for the thematic synthesis of qualitative research in systematic reviews. BMC Med. Res. Methodol. **8**, 45 (2008). https://doi.org/10.1186/1471-2288-8-45

17. Vileiniškis, T., Šukys, A., Butkienė, R.: Searching the web by meaning: a case study of Lithuanian news websites. In: Fred, A., Dietz, J.L.G., Aveiro, D., Liu, K., Filipe, J. (eds.) IC3K 2015. CCIS, vol. 631, pp. 47–64. Springer, Cham (2016). https://doi.org/10.1007/978-3-319-52758-1_4

18. de Vreese, C.H.: News framing: theory and typology. Inform. Design J. Document Design **13**(1), 51–62 (2005)

19. Wang, J., Liu, X., Wang, J., Zhao, W.: News topic evolution tracking by incorporating temporal information. In: Zong, C., Nie, J.Y., Zhao, D., Feng, Y. (eds.) NLPCC 2014. CCIS, vol. 496, pp. 465–472. Springer, Cham (2016). https://doi.org/10.1007/978-3-662-45924-9_43

Is EU Copyright Law a Danger to Online Freedom of Expression?

Philippe Jougleux(✉) iD

European University Cyprus, 6 Diogenous St., 2404 Engomi, Cyprus
p.jougleux@euc.ac.cy

Abstract. The present paper discusses recent evolutions in jurisprudence on online copyright law enforcement in Europe, emphasizing consequences for freedom of expression. It debates whether free speech is menaced by application of this case law. First, reference is made to the relevant case law at the European level. Secondly, the author refers to injunctions against intermediaries and concludes that the danger to freedom of expression has been identified and taken in account by the court. Finally, the author refers to the parallel jurisprudential evolution of copyright law related to hyperlinks and demonstrates that here the issue of freedom of expression has not been taken enough into consideration, something that may have disastrous consequences.

Keywords: Copyright law · Internet law · Freedom of speech · Injunction · Communication to the public · Hyperlink

1 Introduction

It is unnecessary to present the vital role played by freedom of expression in the protection of democracy. However, even freedom of expression is subject to certain limitations dictated by public or personal interests, such as defamation, hate speech, child pornography, personal data, and image rights. One of these, and maybe not the most obvious, is copyright law. A general principle which is shared by national copyright laws worldwide is the distinction between ideas and expression of ideas, in other words between mere information and creation. The consequence is that basic information absolutely remains outside the scope of the protection conferred by copyright law.

However, information is inevitably contained in copyrighted content such as journalistic articles, videos, photography, databases or software. In this way, copyright enforcement indirectly, but also automatically, leads to the creation of a monopoly over information. As a result, information's property prevails over the right to the information.

In the past, however, the relationship of copyright law and freedom of expression was not seen as much as problematic, so much as complementary. Copyright law was conceived as the mandatory support of freedom of expression.[1] Only at the beginning

---

[1] P. Samuelson (2002), Copyright and freedom of expression in historical perspective, J. Intell. Prop. L., 10, 319.

© Springer International Publishing AG 2017
S.K. Katsikas and V. Zorkadis (Eds.): E-Democracy 2017, CCIS 792, pp. 123–135, 2017.
https://doi.org/10.1007/978-3-319-71117-1_9

of the digital age has this question of the relationship between copyright law and freedom of expression taken a new turn, with the multiplication of European jurisprudences in this field. The internet has offered the judges the opportunity to reassert the role and the limits of copyright law, with direct consequences for freedom of expression. For instance, the legal framework applicable to internet intermediaries has some direct implications on the general ability of the internet user to express himself, as intermediaries either give the ability to access information or host it. Blocking injunctions, by definition, limit the range of possibilities of the internet user to inform him- or herself. At the same time, other discussions related to online copyright law enforcement indirectly contribute to limit the internet user's freedom of expression. The recent accumulation of case law related to the concept of the right to communication to the public on the Internet goes specifically in this direction.

Here this article will demonstrate that respect of freedom of expression has appropriately been identified in the past, but that the new legal framework related to hyperlinks has not taken enough into consideration the consequences related to freedom of expression. Therefore, this article will first analyze the role of the European Court of Human Rights (ECtHR) as an arbiter in the conflict between copyright law and freedom of expression (1). Then, it will address the particular situation of the internet intermediaries in this context (2) and, finally, it will discuss the potential impact on freedom of expression of the recent jurisprudential evolutions related to the notion of communication to the public (3).

2   Origin and Framework of the Conflict Between Copyright and Freedom of Expression

2.1   About Freedom of Expression on the Internet

Much case law has been developed in recent years by the ECtHR regarding the role of the internet in the development of the human right of freedom of expression. Characteristically, in the case Editorial Board of Pravoye Delo and Shtekel v. Ukraine, which was about the condemnation of a journalist for defamation, the Court considered that "the absence of a sufficient legal framework at the domestic level allowing journalists to use information obtained from the Internet without fear of incurring sanctions seriously hinders the exercise of the vital function of the press as a 'public watchdog'".[2] In other words, states have a positive obligation to ensure that journalists can freely use online materials in the scope of their activities.

In another decision, it was stated that "In light of its accessibility and its capacity to store and communicate vast amounts of information, the Internet plays an important role in enhancing the public's access to news and facilitating the dissemination of information generally. The maintenance of Internet archives is a critical aspect of this role and the Court therefore considers that such archives fall within the ambit of the protection

---

[2] ECtHR, 5 May 2011, Editorial Board of Pravoye Delo and Shtekel v. Ukraine, no. 33014/05.

afforded by Article 10."[3] Both decisions, without making any reference to copyright issues, would potentially have consequences for free access to copyrighted content.

Generally speaking, online freedom of expression is characterized by two antagonistic developments. On the one hand, judges are very eager to interpret freedom of expression in an expansive sense as regards access to information. That means, for instance, that even the mere act of connecting to the internet is deemed to be protected as part of the protection of freedom of expression. In this context, many jurisdictions have recognized internet access as a human right. At the same time, UN Special Rapporteur report in 2011[4] referred to access to the internet as an essential part of freedom of expression and in 2016 the United Nations Human Rights Council released a non-binding resolution condemning intentional disruption of internet access by governments.[5] It should be highlighted in the context of this paper that the most significant consequence at practical level of this recognition is related to the enforcement of copyright law. Indeed, legislation that aims to cut access to recidivist infringers (on the model of the famous "three strikes" system) is de facto invalid.[6]

On the other hand, it should be noted that online freedom of expression is structurally limited. As human right, traditionally, it can be only be enforced against the State, whereas in practice the major part of the online media of expression is managed by the private sector.[7] Indeed, it has been proposed that the difficulty in enforcing freedom of expression to this "horizontal relationship" is one of the main causes for the traditional silence of case law and doctrine on the question of copyright law versus freedom of expression.[8]

2.2 Copyright Law as an Interference with Freedom of Expression

Modern copyright law is founded on a basic dichotomy, since two antagonistic general philosophies aim to explain its existence. According to the utilitarian approach, copyright law constitutes an artificial and necessary monopoly in order to protect production.

---

[3] ECtHR, 10 March 2009, Times Newspapers Ltd v. the United Kingdom (nos. 1 and 2), nos. 3002/03 and 23676/03, § 27.

[4] Frank Larue (2011) Report to the UN Human Rights Council "exploring key trends and challenges to the right of all individuals to seek, receive and impart information and ideas of all kinds through the Internet."

[5] James Vincent (2016-07-04) UN condemns internet access disruption as a human rights violation, The Verge. Retrieved 2016-10-20.

[6] N. Lucchi (2011) Access to Network Services and Protection of Constitutional Rights: Recognizing the Essential Role of Internet Access for the freedom of expression, Cardozo Journal of International and Comparative Law (JICL), Vol. 19, No. 3.

[7] Ivar A. Hartmann (2013) A right to free internet? on internet access and social rights. 13 J. High Tech L. 297.

[8] P.B. Hugenholtz, (2001) Copyright and freedom of expression in Europe. Expanding the boundaries of intellectual property: Innovation policy for the knowledge society, in: Rochelle Cooper Dreyfuss, Harry First and Diane Leenheer Zimmerman (eds.), Innovation Policy in an Information Age, Oxford: Oxford University Press 2000, 343.

By contrast, the natural law approach explains that the copyright law exists without any other need of justification, as it constitutes by itself a human right.[9] Indeed, Article 27 of the UN Convention of Human Rights refers to the interest of the author as an expression of the right to culture. Nevertheless, in positive law, protection of copyright law by the ECtHR has been realized by reference to the human right of property. Conflict between copyright and freedom of expression is, therefore, a conflict between two human rights, with the consequence that freedom of expression cannot in abstracto prevail over copyright rules. Also, in cases of conflicting Convention rights, the State benefits from a wide margin of appreciation. This means that the Court will not easily agree to intervene and condemn a State for violation of freedom of expression.

Is it, however, possible to see in the mere enforcement of copyright law an interference with freedom of expression? First of all, it has to be remembered that free speech does not only concern political expression, but it also extends to popular culture.[10] It is, therefore, unavoidable that the control of the informational goods market becomes a battlefield between these human rights. In 2013, in two different cases, the Strasbourg judges took a clear position and answered that indeed copyright law enforcement is an interference with freedom of expression. It must be noted that in neither case did the judges recognize a violation of Article 10 (freedom of expression) of the Convention of human Rights (ECHR). In other words, in each case the condemnation of the plaintiff for copyright law infringement did not violate Article 10. However, the reasoning of the judge here merits a lot of attention, since it states that copyright law enforcement automatically results in an interference with Article 10 rights and, therefore, the classical mechanisms of protection apply. Nonetheless, this means that the interference should be prescribed by law, should pursue the legitimate aim of protecting the rights of others, and should be necessary in a democratic society.

In the first case, Ashby Donald and others v. France, fashion photographers published some photos from a fashion show online without asking for the permission of the creators of the show.[11] The three photographers were ordered by the Court of Appeal of Paris to pay fines between €3,000 and €8,000 plus additional damages to the French design clothing federation and five fashion houses, all together amounting to €255,000. They argued before the Court that the conviction for copyright infringement and the award of damages breached their right to express themselves freely. While dismissing their complaint as manifestly ill and non-founded, the court placed copyright law enforcement in the category of exceptions to freedom of expression, meaning that its range should be ruled by principles of strict interpretation.

In other words, it is "no longer sufficient to justify a sanction or any other judicial order restricting one's artistic or journalistic freedom of expression on the basis that a copyright law provision has been infringed. Neither is it sufficient to consider that the unauthorised use, reproduction or public communication of a work cannot rely on one

---

[9] Alfred C. Yen (1990) Restoring the natural law: Copyright as labor and possession, Ohio St. LJ, 51, 517.

[10] Jack M. Balkin (2004) Digital speech and democratic culture: A theory of freedom of expression for the information society. NYUL rev., 79: 1.

[11] ECtHR (5th section), 10 January 2013, case of Ashby Donald and others v. France, Appl. nr. 36769/08.

of the narrowly interpreted exceptions in the copyright law itself, including the application of the so-called three-step test".[12]

The European Court declared the application admissible and not manifestly ill-founded (§25), but concluded on the merits of the case that the conviction of the applicants due to breach of the French Copyright Act did not amount to a violation of Article 10 of the Convention by the French authorities. The Court was, indeed, of the opinion that the conviction for copyright infringement and the award of damages were to be considered as an interference with the applicants' rights protected by Article 10 of the Convention. However, this interference was prescribed by law, pursued the legitimate aim of protecting the rights of others and was to be considered necessary in a democratic society.

The second case concerns the (in)famous "The Pirate Bay" website, used as a torrent portal by numerous users to download copyrighted materials (movies, tv shows, music, books, etc.). Following the same logic as the previous case, the court decided that the criminal conviction of the co-founders of The Pirate Bay for infringement of copyright did not violate Article 10 ECHR. The Court held that sharing, or allowing others to share, files of this kind on the Internet, even copyright-protected material and for profit-making purposes, was indeed covered by the right to "receive and impart information" under Article 10 of the European Convention.[13]

3 The Raise of Blocking Injunctions Against Internet Service Providers (ISP) and the Guaranteed Protection of Freedom of Expression

3.1 Protection of Intermediaries as a Form of Protection of Freedom of Expression

For almost twenty years, "Internet intermediaries", -both internet access providers and internet service providers (hosting services mainly)-, theoretically enjoy an immunity called "safe harbor". The main reason advanced by the European legislator when this mechanism was transposed into EU law[14] was economic (promotion of single market growth), while freedom of expression arrived as a second rationale.[15] Liability issues could have affected the dynamism of the sector. However, the internet's evolution

---

[12] Dirk Voorhoof (2013) Copyright vs freedom of expression Judgment, available at echr-blog.blogspot.com.cy.

[13] Dirk Voorhoof, Inger Høedt-Rasmussen (2013) ECHR: Copyright vs. freedom of expression II (The Pirate Bay), available at http://kluwercopyrightblog.com.

[14] Through the E-commerce Directive: Directive 2000/31/EC of the European Parliament and of the Council of 8 June 2000 on certain legal aspects of information society services, in particular electronic commerce, in the Internal Market ('Directive on electronic commerce').

[15] Sophie Stella Bourdillon (2012) Sometimes One Is Not Enough - Securing freedom of expression, Encouraging Private Regulation, or Subsidizing Internet Intermediaries or All Three at the Same Time: The Dilemma of Internet Intermediaries' Liability, 7 J. Int'l Com. L. & Tech. 154.

toward web 2.0 exponentially multiplies the opportunities to express and to be informed, and by default the intermediary's safe harbor became a guaranty of freedom of expression in the online environment. As the ECtHR explained in the cases mentioned above, Article 10 applies not only to the content of the information but also to the means of its transmission or reception. This is the case since any restriction imposed on the means necessarily interferes with the right to receive and impart information.

As the article have already shown, this means that the internet user's relationship with the internet access provider receives very powerful protection. In the same way, the internet service provider literally provides the medium for the user to express and be informed. It would be naïve, however, to see a flawless mechanism in this synergy between the intermediaries' safe harbor and freedom of expression.

3.2 The Limits of the Intermediaries' Safe Harbor and the Court of Justice of the European Union (CJEU)'s Telekabel Judgment

It has to be noticed that from the text of the safe harbor regulation itself it is clear that the intermediaries' immunity is not absolute. The providers of hosting services only enjoy such immunity provided they act expeditiously to remove illegal online content upon request (the "notice and take down" mechanism). This leads to a risk to the fundamental right of freedom of expression, as it induces behaviors of private censorship.[16] Also, the notice and take down mechanism is accompanied by another condition: the hosting service provider should ignore the illegality of the content. The CJEU has therefore developed a jurisprudence on this point that promotes the concept of intermediary's" passive approach,[17] which shows that the intermediaries' immunity is much less absolute than it prima facie seems.[18] Furthermore, the EU Commission has recently proposed to even more restrain this immunity, by adding a positive duty to "take measures to ensure the functioning of agreements concluded with rightholders for the use of their works or other subject-matter or to prevent the availability on their services of works or other subject-matter identified by rightholders through the cooperation with the service providers".[19] In other words, content recognition technologies will be mandatory for ISPs ("that store and provide to the public access to large amounts of works").

However, liability does not constitute in any case the most efficient means of enforcement of copyright law. Litigation takes time and its result, as regards the intermediary's relative immunity, is uncertain. Furthermore, the cost of litigation, due to the

---

[16] Aleksandra Kuczerawy (2015) Intermediary liability & freedom of expression: Recent developments in the EU notice & action initiative, Computer Law & Security Review, Volume 31, Issue 1, February 2015, Pages 46–56.

[17] See CJEU, Google France and Google v. Louis Vuitton case C-238/08, Judgment of the Court (Grand Chamber) of 23 March 2010; CJEU, L'Oréal SA and others v. eBay International AG, and others, case C-324/09, Judgment of the Court (Grand Chamber) of 12 July 2011.

[18] Tatiana-Eleni Synodinou (2015) Intermediaries' liability for online copyright infringement in the EU: Evolutions and confusions, Computer Law & Security Review, Volume 31, Issue 1, pages 57–67.

[19] Article 13 of Proposal for a Directive of the European Parliament and of the Council on copyright in the Digital Single Market – COM (2016) 593.

scale of the infringement, prohibits any practical use. At the same time, injunctions have an increasing role to play.[20] It is indeed established that the intermediaries' safe harbor does not affect the possibility of obtaining injunctions. Article 13 (2) of the E-Commerce Directive clearly explains that injunctions can be granted independently of the safe harbor's protection, and this means that new kinds of solutions for online law enforcement are slowly emerging, focusing specifically on the ISP's contribution to the prevention of copyright law infringement.[21] In theory, rights holders could seek a wide range of injunctions against ISPs, e.g.: temporarily or permanently disconnecting a user; blocking access to a website; blocking a specific type of Internet use (p2p networks); preventing an copyrighted work from illegally circulating on line; adopting a graduated response scheme (such as was recently adopted in Ireland).[22, 23] At the same time, the Enforcement Directive[24] explicitly confirms that rights holders have the right to seek an injunction intended to prevent an imminent act of infringement, or to forbid the continuation of the alleged infringement.[25]

The EU Court immediately understood and asserted the risks of injunctions against intermediaries for human rights, and applied a proportionality test in order to control the legality of these injunctions.[26]

In this context, the most important case is "Telekabel," which opens a new door in the fight against online piracy, as it reinstalls the online intermediary as protagonist of the online copyright law enforcement.[27] On the grounds of the Telekabel judgment, general injunctions against ISPs that aim to prevent users from accessing illegal content are valid. As we can see, this poses a huge issue for the protection of freedom of expression. Therefore, the judge added two conditions necessary for the validity of this mechanism. The access provider can avoid sanctions for breach of injunction *"provided that (i) the measures taken do not unnecessarily deprive Internet users of the possibility of lawfully accessing the information available and (ii) that those measures have the effect of preventing unauthorised access to the protected subject-matter or, at least, of making it difficult to achieve and of seriously discouraging Internet users who are using the*

---

[20] Christina Angelopoulos (2014) Are blocking injunctions against ISPs allowed in Europe? Copyright enforcement in the post-Telekabel EU legal landscape, Journal of Intellectual Property Law & Practice, 9(10), 812–821.

[21] The Article 13 (2) states that the safe harbor "shall not affect the possibility for a court or administrative authority, in accordance with Member States' legal systems, of requiring the service provider to terminate or prevent an infringement."

[22] Martin Husovec, Miquel Peguera (2014) Much Ado about Little – Privately Litigated Internet Disconnection Injunctions. IIC - International Review of Intellectual Property and Competition Law, Volume 46, Issue 1, pp 10–37.

[23] Irish High Court, *Sony v UPC Communications Ireland Limited,* 27 March 2015.

[24] Directive 2004/48/EC on the Enforcement of Intellectual Property Rights.

[25] Article 9 and 11 of the Directive.

[26] CJUE, Productores de Música de España (Promusicae) v. Telefónica de España SAU, case C-275/06, Judgement of 29 January 2008; CJUE, Sabam v Scarlet, case C-70/10, Judgement of 24 November 2011.

[27] CJUE, UPC Telekabel Wien v Constantin Film Verleih GmbH, Wega Filmproduktionsgesellschaft mbH, case C-314/12, Judgement of 27 March 2014.

services of the addressee of that injunction from accessing the subject-matter that has been made available to them in breach of the intellectual property right".[28]

The injunction, first, has to be effective. Filters can easily be circumvented, for instance with the help of a proxy server. The Court requests the measure in practice not to block access to content, but only to make access to illegal content more difficult in order to discourage the average user. It is illusory to suggest that a blocking order can be 100% effective. However, the intensive use of proxy servers for the purpose of illegally downloading protected works poses certain problems, such as risks to privacy (who controls the proxy and what data is collected?), internet speed limitations, and technical burdens (finding an available proxy). Assuming that the alternative legal market is simple, fast, practical and cheap enough, a blocking injunction should add the necessary space for it to flourish.

The second condition expressly addresses the issue of freedom of expression. It protects the ISPs against general measures which would have a disproportionate effect on the right to be informed. In other words, the promising mechanism of blocking orders as an efficient tool to fight online infringement of copyright law is structurally limited to those cases where the content is obviously and in a large part illegal. By definition, average intermediaries should not be concerned. For instance, the YouTube service from Google or Facebook cannot be blocked by the way of an injunction, since the consequences of the blocking order would be disproportionate. In the author's opinion, a sound interpretation of the proportionality of the blocking order would be based on the proportion respectively of legal and illegal content, and it would assert that this proportion should be overwhelming in favor of the existence of illegal content.

The recent case Mc Fadden[29] offers a perfect illustration of the balance achieved by using Telekabel's criteria. Mr Mc Fadden operates a free Wi-Fi network in his shop that is accessible to the public, and it is not password protected. Someone used that Wi-Fi connection to make a musical work available on the internet free of charge to the public without consent of the right holders. Sony Music, as the holder of the rights in the phonogram of the work, sought compensation for damages and an injunction against the infringement of its rights. The CJEU first based its argument on the Intermediaries' safe harbor and held that providers generally cannot be held liable if a user uses a provider's free Wi-Fi connection unlawfully to download copyrighted content. Then, as regards the injunction part, the court stated that copyright holders have the right to seek injunctions to stop future infringements. Such injunction orders, however, would need to balance on the one hand the intellectual property rights of rights holders and, on the other hand, the freedom to conduct a business of access providers and the freedom of information of the network users. The court held that such balance would be ensured by an order that such service provider, in order to end or prevent further infringements by its customers, should protect its Wi-Fi with a password, requiring users to reveal their identity in order to obtain the required password. In other words, as part of freedom of expression, public internet access is protected, but at the same time, it is possible to

---

[28] Par.63 of the Decision.
[29] CJUE, case C-484/14, Tobias Mc Fadden v Sony Music Entertainment, Judgement of 15 September 2016.

compel the administrator to use some measures of protection to limit illegal usage of such access.

3.3   Protection of Freedom of Expression in the ECtHR Delfi Case

It is not possible nowadays to discuss the intermediaries' safe harbor without mentioning the parallel substantial developments in ECtHR case law with the Delfi case.[30] We should highlight the fact that the Delfi case does not concern a copyright law issue. However, this jurisprudence deeply impacts the relevant legal framework of internet intermediaries and therefore should be read with attention. The fundamental interest of copyright law protection is here replaced by that of privacy, but the terms of the dilemma remain the same: is the conviction of an online intermediary a violation of Article 10 (freedom of expression), or is the safe harbor's application a violation of Article 8 (privacy)?

By admitting that the Estonian authorities legitimately condemned the hosting service provided in a case of defamation, the court of human rights implicitly accept that the intermediary's safe harbor cannot be absolute. It does not mean that the ECtHR believes in general that the entire safe harbor concept is incompatible with human rights, but that a balance of interests must be struck between freedom of expression and other legitimate interests. In this context, post-Delfi cases are vital to demonstrate how this new criterion can be applied. In particular, in the Pihl[31] case, the court ruled that a non-profit blog operator is not liable for defamatory users' comments in case of prompt removal upon notice, while in the Magyar[32] case an Internet news portal was found not liable for the offensive anonymous comments posted by its readers.

The key to understand these divergences lays in the appreciation of the illegality of the content. It seems that for the court hate speech constitutes a very serious situation which can justify the intermediary's liability (Delfi case). At the opposite, the posting of defamatory messages (such as in the Pihl and Magyar cases) is not important enough to justify an interference with freedom of expression. In this context, it is only a matter of speculation to determine either copyright law enforcement should prevail, or the intermediary's safe harbor rights. However, other criteria mentioned in the post-Delfi cases (the economic or non-economic purpose of the activity, the size of the operator and its practical possibilities of monitoring, and, implicitly, the intermediary's good faith) could be also used when balancing freedom of expression with copyright law.

In conclusion, the potential conflict between copyright law enforcement and freedom of expression has been taken in consideration by the judges, as the jurisprudence has constantly searched for consensual solutions in order to protect both interests.

---

[30]   ECHR, Delfi v Estonia, app no 64569/09, 10 October 2013; ECHR, Delfi v Estonia, app no 64569/09, 16 June 2015.

[31]   ECHR, Rolf Anders Daniel PIHL against Sweden, 9 March 2017, Application no 74742/14.

[32]   ECHR, Magyar Tartalomszolgáltatók Egyesülete and Index.hu Zrt v. Hungary, 2 February 2016, app no. 22947/13.

4 The CJEU's Communication of the Public Case Law: The True Danger to Freedom of Speech?

4.1 The Issue: Hyperlinks and Copyright Law

The conflict between copyright law and freedom of expression is not only limited to the issue of online enforcement (liability and injunctions). In the recent years, a new problematic has appeared as regards the definition of the boundaries of copyright law on the internet. The internet is based on a decentralized mode of navigation, where it is not necessary to actually give the address of the target content to the browsing software, as it is possible to click (and now tap) on hyperlinks and the target content is automatically displayed. Hyperlinks therefore play the role of citation, reference, communication, navigation tool, etc. In other words, this mechanism plays a substantive role in the internet common use and, by extension, in protection of the right to be informed. In fact, both sides of freedom of expression are concerned: freedom of expression stricto sensu, as the hyperlink's creator right to show content that he has found on the internet, and the right to be informed as the internet user's right to click on this hyperlink in order to navigate to the destination.

In parallel, after the adoption of the Information Society Directive 2001/29, EU copyright law has seen significant progress towards unification and particularly the notion of communication to the public, one of the most fundamental economic rights of the copyright right holder, has been elevated to the rank of autonomous notion of European law.[33] The landmark decision "Rafael hoteles" offers the general ontological framework of the notion.[34] Communication to the public means both an act of communication and also implies a new public that is an uncertain and potentially big group of persons. In the TV Catchup case, related to online broadcasting of TV signals by a website, the EU judges considered that offering a means of access to the content should be considered as an act of communication.[35] It was, therefore, only a matter of time that the question of the legality of hyperlinks from the point of view of copyright law was posed.

4.2 From the CJEU's Svensson Case Law to the Pirate Bay Ruling

The issue has come to the CJEU's attention with the Svensson case.[36] The court had few choices in hand. From a practical perspective, and having in mind the tremendous consequences for the exercise of freedom of expression, it was clear from the beginning that somehow the technic of hyperlinks should be validated. However, it was not possible

---

[33] Directive 2001/29/EC of the European Parliament and of the Council of 22 May 2001 on the harmonisation of certain aspects of copyright and related rights in the information society.

[34] CJUE, Sociedad General de Autores y Editores de España (SGAE) v Rafael Hoteles SA, C-306/05, Judgment of the Court (Third Chamber) of 7 December 2006.

[35] CJUE, ITV Broadcasting Limited and others v TV Catchup Limited and others, Case C-607/11, Judgment of the Court (Fourth Chamber) 7 March 2013.

[36] CJUE, Nils Svensson, Sten Sjögren, Madelaine Sahlman, Pia Gadd v Retriever Sverige AB, case C-466/12, Judgment of the Court (Fourth Chamber) of 13 February 2014.

for the court, bound by the limits of the prejudicial questions in the case, to refer to mechanisms which are external to copyright law, such as contract law or human rights. It had also to confirm and apply its previous case law, where a broad interpretation of the communication to the public right had been adopted. In their judgement, the judges accepted that hyperlinks do constitute, in light of the previous case law, an act of communication. However, as the content is, by definition, already present on the internet (and supposedly freely accessible), no new public exists. In consequence, the hyperlink activity does not fall under the scope of the communication to the public right.

The solution which was adopted in the Svensson case seems at first sight pertinent from a human rights perspective, as hyperlinks in the immense majority of cases will be deemed to be legal. Nevertheless, the rationale of the case seems to be built on the rights holder's intention, even through the prism of an objective test. It creates, in other words, a simple presumption that the rights holder's intent with the first act of communication to the public was to reach all internet users. The Svensson case left, however, a very important question in the shadows. What about hyperlinking to illegal content? Indeed, if the content has not been uploaded or streamed by the rights holder in the first place or with their consent, how to apply the Svensson line of reasoning?

This thorny question has also been dealt with by the court in the "Playboy" case.[37] In this case, a rights protected photograph had been found on an anonymous public server and a publication embedded it on its webpage through a hyperlink. It is, therefore, accepted that the rights holder's intention was never for the litigious photography to be freely accessible on the internet in the first place. However, to apply Svensson jurisprudence without any distinction would be catastrophic for human rights, as it places the burden of the proof of the legal or illegal character of the content's knowledge on the creator of the hyperlink. The court considered that the proof of the knowledge has to be brought by the rights holder. However, it added that in case the creator of the hyperlink is a professional (such as is the case when online activities are pursued with an economic purpose), the knowledge of the illegality of the content is presumed!

This broad interpretation of what constitutes an act of communication to the public is not limited to a technological definition of hyperlinks. The concept is technologically free and in the Svensson case the Court paid a lot of attention not to delimitate its application to a specific kind of hyperlink ("normal" text hyperlink, picture hyperlink, frame link, deep link or embedded video link to streaming activity). Therefore, any act by which a user, with full knowledge of the relevant facts, provides their clients with access to protected works is liable to constitute an 'act of communication' for the purposes of European copyright law.

In later decisions the CJEU applied this finding to similar (but not quite identical) circumstances. In the Bestwater case,[38] the jurisprudence has been applied to streaming activities. Similarly, it has been recently ruled that the sale of "Kodi" player with installed setting to private server of illegal content is an act of communication to the public as the

---

[37] CJUE, GS Media BV v Sanoma Media Netherlands BV, Playboy Enterprises International Inc., Britt Geertruida Dekker, case C-160/15, Judgement of 8 September 2016.

[38] CJUE, BestWater International GmbH v Michael Mebes, Stefan Potsch, case C-348/13, Order of the Court (Ninth Chamber) of 21 October 2014.

device gives the mean to access to the content (the settings are assimilated therefore to hyperlinks).[39] Finally, in a recent case related to the "Pirate Bay" website,[40] the Court decided that proposing torrent keys is also assimilated to the creation of hyperlinks.

4.3 Unsolved Human Rights Questions

The criterion of economic purpose of the activity is central for the EU judges. This position opens a conflict with human rights judges, as it was explicitly stated in the past by the ECtHR that a financial motive should play no role in the assessment of the legitimacy of a limitation on freedom of expression (see Ashby Donald case above). Therefore, in the author's view the profit making criterion which has been developed in recent case law in relation to the interpretation of the concept of communication to the public is potentially in conflict with the ECtHR's case law. It is, nevertheless, certain that the above mentioned decisions of the ECtHR in the Ashby Donald and Pirate Bay cases clearly indicate that the human rights court is more than favorable to the idea of a control of the right holder's prerogatives in the light of human rights.[41]

5   Conclusions

While in the Telekabel case the CJEU court clearly addressed the issue of protection of freedom of expression in the context of copyright law enforcement, a similar mechanism has not emerged in the jurisprudence related to the right of communication to the public. Indeed, as analyzed above, in the Svensson and GS Media cases, no consideration is given to the potential impact on freedom of expression of the right holders' control on hyperlinks. It can't be denied that the act of hyperlinking is a form of freedom of expression and therefore the Svensson case should be critically reviewed on the light of the ECtHR jurisprudence regarding interferences to freedom of expression. One solution would have been, rather than creating an absolute presumption in case of an economic purpose, using the more flexible mechanism of a range of indicia. In this range of indicia should be inserted a similar line of reasoning as in the Telekabel judgment, according to which the suppression of a means of access to information (whenever a hyperlink, a Kodi box setting or a torrent key) should not have the consequence to disproportionately deprive the user of access to legal content.

---

[39] CJUE, Stichting Brein v Jack Frederik Wullems, case C-527/15, Judgment of 26 March of 2017.

[40] CJUE, Stichting Brein v Ziggo, case C-610/15 (also known as The Pirate Bay case), Judgement of 14 June 2017.

[41] C. Geiger & E. Izyumenko (2014) Copyright on the human rights' trial: redefining the boundaries of exclusivity through freedom of expression, IIC-International Review of Intellectual Property and Competition Law, 3(45), 316–342.

References

1. Angelopoulos, C.: Are blocking injunctions against ISPs allowed in Europe? Copyright enforcement in the post-Telekabel EU legal landscape. J. Intell. Property Law Pract. **9**(10), 812–821 (2014)
2. Balkin, J.M.: Digital speech and democratic culture: a theory of freedom of expression for the information society. NYUL Rev. **79**, 1 (2004)
3. Bourdillon, S.S.: Sometimes one is not enough - securing freedom of expression, encouraging private regulation, or subsidizing internet intermediaries or all three at the same time: the dilemma of internet intermediaries' liability. J. Int'l Com. L. Tech. **7**, 154 (2012)
4. Geiger, C., Izyumenko, E.: Copyright on the human rights' trial: redefining the boundaries of exclusivity through freedom of expression. IIC-Int. Rev. Intellect. Property Competition Law **3**(45), 316–342 (2014)
5. Hartmann, I.A.: A right to free internet? on internet access and social rights. J. High Tech L. **13**, 297 (2013)
6. Hugenholtz, P.B.: Copyright and freedom of expression in Europe. expanding the boundaries of intellectual property: Innovation policy for the knowledge society. In: Dreyfuss, R.C., First, H., Zimmerman, D.L. (eds.) Innovation Policy in an Information Age, p. 343. Oxford University Press, Oxford (2000)
7. Husovec, M., Peguera, M.: Much Ado about Little – privately litigated internet disconnection injunctions. IIC-Int. Rev. Intellect. Property Competition Law **46**(1), 10–37 (2014)
8. James, V.: UN condemns internet access disruption as a human rights violation, The Verge, 04 Jul 2016. Accessed 20 Oct 2016
9. Kuczerawy, A.: Intermediary liability & freedom of expression: recent developments in the EU notice & action initiative. Comput. Law Secur. Rev. **31**(1), 46–56 (2015)
10. Larue, F.: Report to the UN Human Rights Council "exploring key trends and challenges to the right of all individuals to seek, receive and impart information and ideas of all kinds through the Internet." (2011)
11. Lucchi, N.: Access to network services and protection of constitutional rights: recognizing the essential role of internet access for the freedom of expression. Cardozo J. Int. Comp. Law (JICL), **19**(3) (2011)
12. Samuelson, P.: Copyright and freedom of expression in historical perspective. J. Intell. Prop. L. **10**, 319 (2002)
13. Synodinou, T.-E.: Intermediaries' liability for online copyright infringement in the EU: evolutions and confusions. Comput. Law Secur. Rev. **31**(1), 57–67 (2015)
14. Voorhoof, D.: Copyright vs freedom of expression Judgment (2013). echrblog. blogspot.com.cy
15. Voorhoof, D., Høedt-Rasmussen, I.: ECHR: copyright vs. freedom of expression II (The Pirate Bay). (2013). http://kluwercopyrightblog.com
16. Yen, Alfred C.: Restoring the natural law: copyright as labor and possession. Ohio St. LJ **51**, 517 (1990)

Internet Censorship Capabilities in Cyprus: An Investigation of Online Gambling Blocklisting

Vasilis Ververis[1,5]([✉]), Marios Isaakidis[2], Chrystalleni Loizidou[3], and Benjamin Fabian[4]

[1] Humboldt University, Berlin, Germany
ververis@kth.se
[2] University College London, London, UK
[3] University of Nicosia, Nicosia, Cyprus
[4] Hochschule für Telekommunikation, Leipzig, Germany
[5] Universidade Estadual do Piauí, Teresina, Brazil

Abstract. This paper presents the initial findings of an open and collective effort towards a cross comparison study of web-content blocking regulations and practices, in different parts of Cyprus. Our analysis is based on network measurement data collected by volunteers in Cyprus, using a custom OONI probe and open DNS resolvers, from five residential ISPs; Callsat (AS 24672), Cablenet (AS 35432), Cyta (AS 6866), MTN (AS 15805) and Multimax (AS 197792). We were able to identify a number of unreported Internet censorship cases, non-transparently implemented blocking regulations, and collateral damage due to blocking of email delivery to the regulated domains by the National Betting Authority of the Republic of Cyprus. These results indicate the presence of at least two distinct regimes on the island.

Keywords: Internet censorship · Cyprus · Internet policy · Network measurements · Blocklists · Network filtering · Freedom of expression · Information policy

1 Introduction

This paper describes the initial findings of an open and collective effort to gather data, using OONI (Open Observatory of Network Interference) and open DNS (Domain Name System) resolvers in Cyprus, towards a cross comparison study of web content blocking regulations and practices between Cyprus and other countries in terms of implementation techniques. We suggest there is a need for a closer study of how censorship (the blocking of content, the top-down imposition of restrictions on information) is legislated and justified in political terms on the one hand, and on the other hand the actual extent and the procedural technicalities of its implementation as experienced by the citizen, in this case the Internet user or the ISP (Internet Service Provider) client. This investigation

© Springer International Publishing AG 2017
S.K. Katsikas and V. Zorkadis (Eds.): E-Democracy 2017, CCIS 792, pp. 136–149, 2017.
https://doi.org/10.1007/978-3-319-71117-1_10

of *how* blocking is legislated and implemented on a local level contributes to discussions around transparency, accountability, and freedom of expression more broadly. The island of Cyprus presents an interesting geopolitical case study because it allows for the collection of data on what we have come to think of as more than two distinct regimes in terms of information policy: the one followed in the RoC (Republic of Cyprus) in the south of the island, which largely adopts EU (European Union) policy, and the one followed in the area occupied by Turkey in the north of the island. The landscape regarding policy over Internet blocking may prove to be even more complex, considering the existence of two British sovereign military bases on the island, although our study does not yet include data from these areas. Our initial measurements are biased towards Internet blocking by ISPs following RoC protocols, with fewer observations revealing the policy of Internet blocking in the north (only one north Cyprus ISP, Multimax, is measured).

Our intention is to gather data on the capabilities of ISPs to perform censorship, or more specifically their capabilities to block access to specific information in Cyprus, and to provide comparable data about how the application of technologies for censorship, or control over information, is developing internationally.

The rest of the article is structured as follows. First we introduce the case of Cyprus and the specific legal circumstances around online gambling that allow us to investigate Internet blocking on the level of the ISP. We then briefly indicate similar research done in other countries, and present our methodology, the infrastructure and the tools we used. Following, we provide an analysis of the collected data set per blocking method and ISP and analyze the blocklist used to conduct blocking, its effects and collateral damage. We conclude with an outlook on how this kind of research might be used in the future.

2   The Case of Cyprus

For the case of Cyprus we collected measurements from end-user connections located on various ISPs on both sides of the island. Cyprus has a population of 1,1 million. In comparison to other countries, access to Internet services is very good, as shown by the 2016 statistics of the ITU information society report: 71.2% penetration of Internet access in Cyprus. The share of fixed-broadband subscriptions of residents lies at 22.3%, with an additional 54.8% having active mobile broadband subscriptions. The average Internet bandwidth per Internet user is measured at 89,791 Bit/s in 2016 [36]. This gives us a better understanding about user experience and allows for evaluating how each ISP has implemented the updated betting act directives. We investigate the extent to which ISPs may have over-blocked or under-blocked any entries included or deduced in the blocklist, and we analyze any collateral damages to unregulated websites. In recent years, ISPs in the RoC have implemented an Internet filtering infrastructure to comply with the laws and regulations imposed by the National Betting Authority (NBA). Our starting point was to find out how the technical infrastructure to block or filter unregulated web resources (the ones implied by the NBA) has taken place and discover cases of under or over blocking and to find collateral damage caused by blocking Internet resources that were not meant to be blocked (such as email).

3   Previous Research

The RoC is considered a safe haven for freedom of speech. It is important to note that Freedom House reports that mention and catalog Internet censorship related events in the years 2006 [27], 2007 [28], 2008 [29], 2011 [30], 2012 [31], 2013 [32], 2014 [33] document that citizens are able to access the Internet on a regular basis and are not subject to any known government restrictions, although they do report a difference between the years 2012 and 2013. However, Freedom House numerical rating reports for Cyprus are based on conditions on the south of the island only. Worth mentioning is research on media pluralism that considers risks to freedom of expression and right to information in Cyprus as low risk [4]. We have not been able to find any previous work that discusses Internet censorship in Cyprus, and there has been no attempt to compare information across the island's divisions.

This case study on Cyprus is related to two previous OONI case studies. In the first instance we refer to previous research on large scale content blocking in Greece [43]. Similarly with the NBA in Cyprus, in Greece this kind of blocking is initiated by the Greek gaming commission (EEEP), an independent administrative authority that acts as the public body, responsible for the control and supervision of gambling services. The Greek case-study analyzed the techniques and policies used to block content of gambling websites in Greece and presented the implications of under-blocking, over-blocking, and collateral damage by blocked email communication. It also highlighted issues of transparency in Internet filtering and unfair competition between ISPs. In the second instance we refer to a case study in Turkey that attempted to track changes to Internet traffic during the coup d'etat of July 2016. The study brings up the technical aspects of potential Internet blocking in Turkey and highlights the importance of a grassroots understanding of ISP blocking capabilities [23].

4   Detecting Network Interference and the Republic of Cyprus Gambling Law of 2012

Identifying signs or conclusive results of network interference that can be caused by Internet filtering or surveillance is a challenging process that requires adequate knowledge of the underlying network infrastructure on the side of the ISPs or their upstream providers. In this article, we focus on censorship by content regulation policies, and particularly the gambling law of 2012, L. 106(I)/2012 [8]. The law implies that the ISPs are obliged to apply a *blocking system* that will prevent users and ISP clients from accessing gambling services providers who are not licensed (do not hold a Class B license) or service providers who possess, operate infrastructure or provide online casino services in Cyprus. According to the NBA, a *blocking system* is defined as:

A system installed by the Internet service provider which prevents the routing and the movement from the terminal equipment of the Internet user to particular Internet website addresses URL (Uniform Resource Locator).

According to the RoC gamling law of 2012, non compliance is punishable with a term of imprisonment not exceeding five years or a fine not exceeding three hundred thousand Euro or to both such sentences. Upon notification from the NBA, ISPs are obliged to block URLs of gamling services that do not follow regulations within seventy two hours. Although the law does not specify the way in which URLs should be submitted to the ISPs for blocking, the current means seem to be a publicly available blocklist; a file with a list of URL entries named as *Blocking List* [19], located on the official website of the RoC NBA [20].

4.1 Analysis of the Republic of Cyprus NBA Blocklist

NBA publishes a blocklist usually in a text file format that contains a number of URL entries of websites with complete file paths, not just domain names (such as http://m.downloadatoz.com/apps/com.microgenius.casino777,482188. html) that offer non-licensed gamling services in Cyprus. NBA was established in 2012 as an independent authority, consisting of a president and six members. One of the authority's duties is to notify ISPs in an electronic manner on every Internet URL through which gamling services are offered that are not covered by a class A or B licensed bookmaker, or anyone offering services prohibited in the present gamling law [8]. Although the law was issued in 2012, the first public release of the blocklist (that we were able to detect from the online archives) was in February, 2013 [9]. NBA does not provide a blocklist versioning system similar to other countries [43]. We assume 10 blocklist versions from February 2013 to May 2017 [9–18], though we cannot with certainty confirm the existence of additional blocklists in the past. Our findings are derived from Internet archives [1,2] that provide historical snapshots of websites. Starting in February 2013, the NBA publishes a blocklist containing 95 entries of URLs [9] that increases to a total of 2563 (in April 2017) URL entries [18], approximately 27 times more than the initial size of the blocklist. Figure 1 illustrates a timeline with the date and URL entries of the blocklist published by the NBA.

During our analysis of the blocklist, we identified a number of malformed entries (mainly URLs and domain names) such as *1xbet.??* as well as duplicate entries and at least one entry that does not seem to host gambling related content; https://www.commission.bz, an advertisement affiliate program. The malformed URL entries of the blocklist may introduce technical issues to the filtering implementation of the blocklist as URLs that contain malformed characters (such as *??*) may not be parsed correctly. Additionally, a number of domain names in the blocklist were found to be expired or not registered, meaning that these domain names are not hosting any gambling related content (actually not hosting any content since they are not registered) but are still blocked by many ISPs in the Republic of Cyprus.

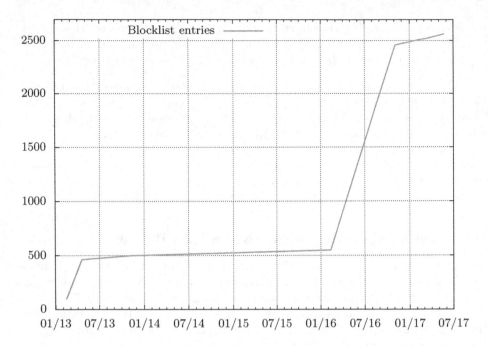

Fig. 1. Timeline of the NBA blocklist publication

The NBA list implies that ISPs should do URL blocking as the entries of the blocklist contain URLs. ISPs would only be able to block them if they had previously deployed a blocking mechanism that would give the technical capability to ISPs to look inside the payload of the network packets, and more specifically at the layer 7 contents where the actual URL of an HTTP request is referenced, that technology is named as a Deep Packet Inspection (DPI). In order to be able to filter HTTPS URLs the ISP needs to intercept the connection between the client (user of the ISP) to the server and perform an active man-in-the-middle attack on every HTTPS connection in order to decrypt the SSL/TLS, layer it and look at the unencrypted payload. Currently the SSL/TLS connections (HTTPS URLs) destined to the ISPs censorship infrastructure are not being handled (port 443 is unreachable). The connection times out and the user is not receiving any notification about the blocking in place apart from a connection error (error: couldn't connect to host).

5   Methodology for Data Collection and Analysis

We are using a variety of common free and open source software networking tools for gathering, categorizing, distributing, analyzing data and comparing the results. Acquiring results from a number of different ISPs is crucial to form a representative sample. We have conducted network measurements and used publicly available data based on OONI reports [41] submitted by volunteers. We were able to collect and process network measurement data from the following residential landlines and cellular ASes (Autonomous Systems): AS15805 (MTN Cyprus Limited), AS24672 (CallSat International Telecommunications Ltd.), AS35432 (Cablenet Communication Systems Ltd.), AS6866 (Cyprus Telecommunications Authority), AS8544 (Primetel) and AS197792 (Multimax Iletisim Limited). Even so, this remains a limited sample and the findings presented here are tentative and preliminary.

5.1   Data Set Used for the Tests

First, we compiled a list of all URLs that are reported to be blocked in Cyprus as published and curated by the RoC NBA [19], the Greek gamling authority's blocklist [7] the Lumen database [35] for Turkey, and the community-collected global test list maintained by Citizenlab [37]. Additionally, we have used the public open DNS servers list provided by Digineo GmbH [25].

5.2   Collection of Network Measurements

The collection of the network measurements took place during the months of March to May 2017, though we were able to process relevant data submitted by volunteers from the months January and February earlier in 2017. Volunteers collected and submitted network measurements by using a custom set of tools and test lists [40] populated from the data sets enumerated in Sect. 5.1. For our censorship research we used ooniprobe, an application developed by the OONI project [24] and used by volunteers and organizations to probe their network for signs of network tampering, surveillance or censorship. Developed with the idea of ensuring the detection of any interference to network communications, it aims to collect and provide high quality reports by using open and transparent data methodologies freely available to anyone that would like to process and analyze.

Ooniprobe is the application that was used to conduct the measurements on the ISP networks (both landline and cellular networks) where we detected network tampering and content blocking. Ooniprobe provides a variety of test cases and classes that could be used to probe the networks. More analytically, in our research we have deployed and analyzed a number of network measurements tests, precisely instant messaging, HTTP header fields manipulation and invalid request line tests, Tor and pluggable transports reachability tests as well as the web connectivity test. We were not able to identify any certain case of network interference in all of the tests apart from the web connectivity test. However this does not necessarily mean that there is no other sort of network interference happening on the network during different date periods or from different vantage points.

Web connectivity is an ooniprobe test methodology where we were able to identify and detect if a website is reachable and the reason or cause in case a website is not reachable. This test reaches a non censored control measurement endpoint (test helper) to assist with the comparison of the measurements for a given website. At first, the test performs an *A* DNS lookup to a special domain name service in our experiments; *whoami.akamai.com* that will respond to the *A* DNS lookup request with the resolver of the probe. Upon DNS resolver identification, the test will perform a DNS lookup querying the *A* record of the default resolver for the hostname of the URL tested. Following the test will try to establish a TCP session on port 80 or port 443 if the URL in question begins with the prefix *http* or *https* accordingly for the list of all IPs returned by the previous DNS query. Finally, the test performs a HTTP GET request for the path specified in the uniform resource identifier using the most widely used web browser user agent; *Mozilla/5.0 (Windows NT 6.1) AppleWebKit/537.36 (KHTML, like Gecko) Chrome/47.0.2526.106 Safari/537.36* [42] as the HTTP header. Upon completion of the test, the gathered data are compared with the ones of the control measurement test helper.

6   Preliminary Findings

We were able to perform measurements on the following ISPs: Cytanet (AS 6866), Cablenet (AS 35432) and Multimax (AS 197792). Additionally, we were able to identify block pages based on reports contributed by volunteers to the OONI data repository [41] on ISPs Callsat (AS 24672) and MTN (AS AS15805).

The most common identified method of content blocking on Cypriot ISPs is DNS hijacking. Since ISPs are in control of the DNS servers used by their users in residential broadband or cellular connections, they can manipulate the DNS servers' responses and can redirect the requesting users to anywhere they want. Taking advantage of this privilege, ISPs modify their resolvers to override censored domains' legitimate DNS replies by creating local zone entries [3]. These entries usually point to a server that they control where they run a web server that displays a webpage with the warning message to users or block page.

6.1   Differences Between ISPs

All ISPs, with the exception of Multimax in the north of the island, were using DNS hijacking as the blocking to control the access of the entries in NBA's list. Comparing the network measurements from all ISPs we found multiple cases of websites (entries of the blocklist) not being blocked, providing error messages (specifically HTTP status codes 403 and 404) or were unable to connect (connection failed) to HTTPS entries instead of the blocking page or the reason (legislation) why a user cannot access the specific website in question. Additionally, we were able to detect instances where email communication to the specific websites was also blocked although the law does not imply blocking email communication but only restricting access to the website that is included in the blocklist.

Additionally, at least one ISP was found redirecting the user to the website of NBA [20], leaking the IP addresses and possible the web browser's specific user metadata.

6.2   Callsat ISP

Network measurements analyzed from Callsat ISP [6] (AS 24672) on the entries of the NBA blocklist revealed an outdated *landing* block page with a URL that points to a non-existent web resource (HTTP status code 404). The blockpage is illustrated in Fig. 2.

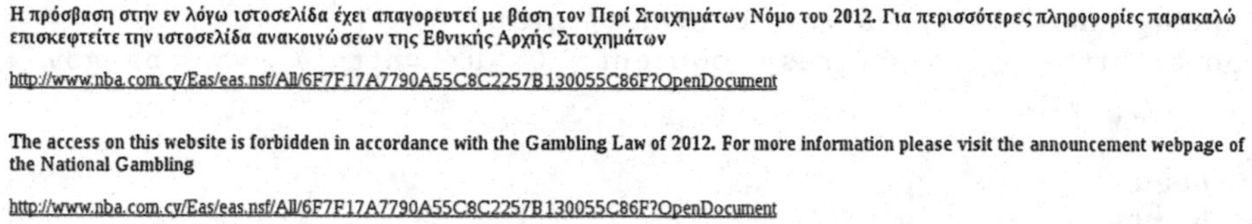

Η πρόσβαση στην εν λόγω ιστοσελίδα έχει απαγορευτεί με βάση τον Περί Στοιχημάτων Νόμο του 2012. Για περισσότερες πληροφορίες παρακαλώ επισκεφτείτε την ιστοσελίδα ανακοινώσεων της Εθνικής Αρχής Στοιχημάτων

http://www.nba.com.cy/Eas/eas.nsf/All/6F7F17A7790A55C8C2257B130055C86F?OpenDocument

The access on this website is forbidden in accordance with the Gambling Law of 2012. For more information please visit the announcement webpage of the National Gambling

http://www.nba.com.cy/Eas/eas.nsf/All/6F7F17A7790A55C8C2257B130055C86F?OpenDocument

Fig. 2. Callsat ISP NBA regulation landing page

6.3   Cablenet ISP

Our findings from the network measurements reveal that the Cablenet ISP [5] (AS 35432) was directing users trying to access the entries of the blocklist to a generic error webpage (HTTP status code 403) without providing any justification of the blocking. The user may falsely assume that the website in question experiences technical issues. The blockpage is illustrated in Fig. 3.

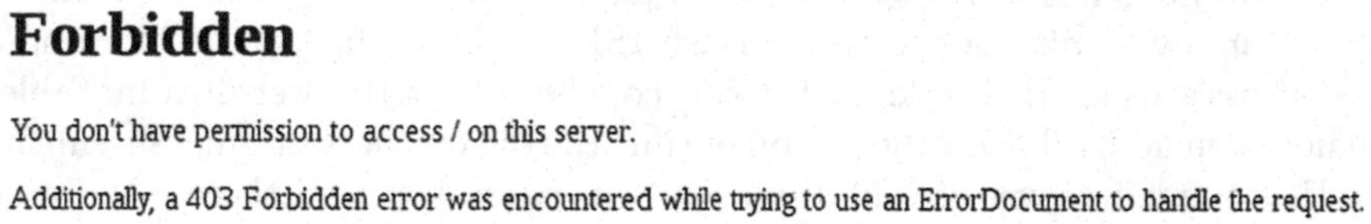

Forbidden

You don't have permission to access / on this server.

Additionally, a 403 Forbidden error was encountered while trying to use an ErrorDocument to handle the request.

Fig. 3. Cablenet ISP NBA regulation landing page

6.4   Cyta ISP

Cyta ISP [21] (AS 6866) does not point the users to a blockpage but rather redirects the users trying to access the blocked entries from the blocklist to the NBA website. The excerpt from the HTML markup code is illustrated in Listing 1.1.

```
<!doctype html>
<html class="no-js">
<head>

<meta http-equiv="content-type" content="text/html; charset=
    utf-8">
<meta name="copyright" content="copyright 2013">
<meta name="author" content="Designed & Developed by Cyta">
<meta name="distribution" content="global">
<meta http-equiv="refresh" content="0; url=http://www.nba.gov.
    cy/" />

</head>
</html>
```

Listing 1.1. Cyta ISP's HTML markup landing page

6.5 MTN ISP

Network measurements collected from MTN ISP [38] (AS 15805) on one day (02/04/2017) show no evidence of blocking.

6.6 Multimax ISP

Multimax [39] (AS 197792) is one of the ISPs that operates in the north of Cyprus. We have not identified any block pages, however, upon closer analysis, we found many similarities to the Turkish ISPs and specifically the blocking of web resources using IP blocking. We can conclude that the websites in Table 1 have not been accessible for the period of time during our network measurements. Note that the list of websites in Table 1 is not exhaustive and there could more websites or service that may be potentially blocked by this ISP.

Table 1. Multimax ISP: List of blocked websites

https://www.wikipedia.org
https://www.torproject.org
http://www.islamdoor.com
http://www.fepproject.org
http://www.no-ip.com
https://wikileaks.org
https://psiphon.ca

6.7   Collateral Damage

In our research we identified that the Mail Exchange (MX) records are absent, and do not contain the relevant DNS records that point to the email server of the domain name in question. That is rendering email delivery to the specific domain name impossible.

```
;  <<>> DiG  9.9.5−9+deb8u10−Debian  <<>> MX  williamhill.com  @82
    .102.93.140
;;  global  options:  +cmd
;;  Got  answer:
;;  −>>HEADER<<−  opcode:  QUERY,  status:  NOERROR,  id:  19519
;;  flags:  qr  aa  rd  ra;  QUERY:  1,  ANSWER:  0,  AUTHORITY:  1,
    ADDITIONAL:  1

;;  OPT  PSEUDOSECTION:
;  EDNS:  version:  0,  flags:;  udp:  1280
;;  QUESTION  SECTION:
;williamhill.com.              IN    MX

;;  AUTHORITY  SECTION:
williamhill.com.        3600      IN    SOA  ns1.cablenet−as.net.  noc.
    wavespeed.net.
1483803163  10800  3600  604800  3600

;;  Query  time:  97  msec
;;  SERVER:  82.102.93.140#53(82.102.93.140)
;;  WHEN:  Tue  Apr  04  02:35:07  CEST  2017
;;  MSG  SIZE    rcvd:  113
```

Listing 1.2. Empty (no answer) DNS MX records for williamhill.com (dig output)

In the Listing 1.2 we have requested the MX records of the domain name williamhill.com from the DNS server *82.102.93.140* (DNS resolver in Cyprus operated by Cablenet) compared to the Google's DNS resolver *8.8.8.8* as illustrated in Listing 1.3. Google's DNS resolver answered with 2 entries in the query (*ANSWER: 2*) for the domain name in question whereas Cablenet's DNS resolver sent no answers (*ANSWER: 0*). The DNS queries took place on 4 April, 2017.

```
;  <<>>  DiG  9.9.5−9+deb8u10−Debian  <<>>  MX  williamhill.com  @8
   .8.8.8
;;  global  options:  +cmd
;;  Got  answer:
;;  −>>HEADER<<−  opcode:  QUERY,  status:  NOERROR,  id:  16093
;;  flags:  qr  rd  ra;  QUERY:  1,  ANSWER:  2,  AUTHORITY:  0,
   ADDITIONAL:  1

;;  OPT  PSEUDOSECTION:
;  EDNS:  version:  0,  flags:;  udp:  512
;;  QUESTION  SECTION:
;williamhill.com.                        IN         MX

;;  ANSWER  SECTION:
williamhill.com.               605      IN         MX         10
mxb−0010e301.gslb.pphosted.com.
williamhill.com.               605      IN         MX         10
mxa−0010e301.gslb.pphosted.com.

;;  Query  time:  40  msec
;;  SERVER:  8.8.8.8#53(8.8.8.8)
;;  WHEN:  Tue  Apr  04  02:43:51  CEST  2017
;;  MSG  SIZE   rcvd:  116
```

Listing 1.3. Google DNS MX records for williamhill.com (dig output)

6.8 Circumventing Blocking

Using a block-list/allow-list model (sort of an ON/OFF model) is not granular enough and tends to fail; it will have negative impact on users and customers of the ISPs that may or may not find routes around the blocking. Furthermore, creating such an ineffective blocking gives a false sense of security as the entities that enforced such blocking would assume that the content is being blocked although blocking is easily circumvented.

6.9 Using Alternative DNS Resolver

Circumventing the blocking enforced by the ISPs is just a tweak in the network configuration and requires no technical expertise by using a different DNS resolver such as Google DNS [22] (*8.8.8.8*) or OpenDNS [34] (*208.67.222.222*).

7 Conclusions and Future Work

Although this case study initially focused on the blocking of gamling websites specifically, it brings up interesting data regarding more general blocking practices in the north of the island, which need to be further investigated. One example is our finding that the RoC block list isn't blocked in the north of

Cyprus, but that a number of other websites have been blocked there, matching the list of websites blocked in Turkey (see Table 1). This opens up a discussion of more than one regime of freedom of expression on the island, and also raises the question of whether there may be a third point of difference with blocking practices implemented in the British sovereign bases. Furthermore, our intention is to confirm with ISPs regarding the technical infrastructure used to implement blocking.

As explained in the introduction, this is only the beginning of an effort to more closely study how online content-blocking is legislated and implemented, in an effort to understand the political extensions of these practices and their related dangers to internet freedom and freedom of information. For example, beyond issues of content-blocking and connected debates around censorship, the data collected here also implicate issues of privacy and personal data protection (with regard to ISP redirection practices), as well as issues of transparency (with regard to how content-blocking is implemented). We hope that the evidence this research begins to produce will come to feature in further discussion, leading to a better understanding of the dangers as well as alternative and safer technical options. More ambitiously, we hope that this research will promote a more sensitive approach guiding policy and national legal provisions that will more effectively safeguard the aforementioned freedoms.

Acknowledgements. We are grateful to Greg Andreou, observer, Costas Tsangarides, savvas, members of the Lefkoşa Hackerspace, and other anonymous contributors in Cyprus for running the measurement tests and their overall support. This project is an initiative of hack66/observatory [26], a Cyprus-based Internet observatory that aims to collect and analyze data, and routes of data, through Europe, Middle East and Africa in order to promote evidence-based policy making. It has been possible thanks to the long-running efforts of the OONI team.

References

1. Internet Archive. The Wayback Machinve. http://web.archive.org/. Accessed 05 Jun 2015
2. Archive.is. Webpage Capture. http://archive.is. Accessed 04 Jun 2015
3. Atkins, D., Austein, R.: Threat analysis of the domain name system (DNS). http://web.archive.org/web/20140826081656/http://www.ietf.org/rfc/rfc3833.txt. Accessed 26 Aug 2014
4. Christophorou, C.: Cyprus: Media Pluralism Monitor 2015 [European Uni versity Institute, Robert Schuman Centre for Advanced Studies]. https://web.archive.org/web/20170606205318/http://monitor.cmpf.eui.eu/mpm2015/results/cyprus/. Accessed 06 Jun 2017
5. Cablenet. Cablenet ISP official website. http://archive.is/UBxqc. Accessed 05 Jun 2017
6. Callsat. Callsat ISP official website. http://archive.is/CAuFL. Accessed 04 Jun 2015
7. EEEP Greek Gaming Commission. https://www.gamingcommission.gov.gr/images/Anakoinoseis/BlackListVersion4_11072014.pdf. Accessed 11 Jul 2015

8. National Betting Authority of Cyprus. Betting Law 2012. http://web. archive.org/web/20170605132235/http://nba.gov.cy/wp-content/uploads/ TheBettingLawof2012.pdf. Accessed 05 Jun 2015
9. National Betting Authority of Cyprus. National Betting Authority of Cyprus Blocklist. 14 February 2013. https://web.archive.org/web/20130217021102/ http://blocking.nba.com.cy:80/. Accessed 17 Feb 2013
10. National Betting Authority of Cyprus. National Betting Authority of Cyprus Blocklist, 19 April 2013. https://web.archive.org/web/20130906231633/http:// blocking.nba.com.cy:80/. Accessed 06 Sept 2013
11. National Betting Authority of Cyprus. National Betting Authority of Cyprus Blocklist, 12 November 2013. https://web.archive.org/web/20131124123355/ http://blocking.nba.com.cy:80/. Accessed 24 Nov 2013
12. National Betting Authority of Cyprus. National Betting Authority of Cyprus Blocklist, 29 January 2016. https://web.archive.org/web/20160201084135/http:// blocking.nba.com.cy:80/. Accessed 20 Feb 2016
13. National Betting Authority of Cyprus. National Betting Authority of Cyprus Blocklist, 15 February 2016. https://web.archive.org/web/20160303044805/ http://blocking.nba.com.cy:80/. Accessed 03 Mar 2016
14. National Betting Authority of Cyprus. National Betting Authority of Cyprus Blocklist, 4 November 2016. https://web.archive.org/web/20161106114742/ http://blocking.nba.com.cy:80/. Accessed 06 Dec 2016
15. National Betting Authority of Cyprus. National Betting Authority of Cyprus Blocklist, 17 February 2016. https://archive.fo/Wdb9n. Accessed 24 Feb 2017
16. National Betting Authority of Cyprus. National Betting Authority of Cyprus Blocklist, 13 March 2017. https://archive.fo/Z7WtK. Accessed 19 Mar 2017
17. National Betting Authority of Cyprus. National Betting Authority of Cyprus Blocklist. As it appeared in Google cache on 27 April 2017 05:09:03 GMT, 27 April 2017
18. National Betting Authority of Cyprus. National Betting Authority of Cyprus Blocklist, 25 May 2017. https://web.archive.org/web/20170526021718/http:// blocking.nba.com.cy. Accessed 26 May 2017
19. National Betting Authority of Cyprus. National Betting Authority of Cyprus Blocklist website. https://web.archive.org/web/20170605133936/http://blocking. nba.com.cy. Accessed 05 Jun 2015
20. National Betting Authority of Cyprus. National Betting Authority of Cyprus official website. https://web.archive.org/web/20170605132348/http://nba.gov.cy. Accessed 05 Jun 2015
21. Cyta. Cyta ISP official website. http://archive.is/NBDpH. Accessed 05 Jun 2017
22. Google Developers. Using Google Public DNS. http://web.archive.org/web/ 20140829223153/https://developers.google.com/speed/public-dns/docs/using. Accessed 29 Aug 2014
23. Aben, E., Evdokimov, L., Xynou, M.: Internet Access Disruption in Turkey (2016). https://web.archive.org/web/20170606190316/http://ooni.torproject.org/ post/turkey-internet-access-disruption/. Accessed 06 Jun 2017
24. Filastó, A., Appelbaum, J.: ONI: open observatory of network interference. In: Free and Open Communications on the Internet. USENIX (2012). https://www. usenix.org/system/files/conference/foci12/foci12-final12.pdf
25. Digineo GmbH. Public DNS Server List. https://web.archive.org/web/ 20170606195759/https://public-dns.info/. Accessed 06 Jun 2017
26. Hack66. Hack66 Observatory. https://web.archive.org/web/20170606204802/ http://hack66.info/observatory. Accessed 06 Jun 2017

27. Freedom of House. Freedom of the Press, Cyprus Country report (2006). https://web.archive.org/web/20170605134525/https://freedomhouse.org/report/freedom-press/2006/cyprus. Accessed 05 Jun 2015

28. Freedom of House. Freedom of the Press, Cyprus Country report (2007). https://web.archive.org/web/20170605134610/https://freedomhouse.org/report/freedom-press/2007/cyprus. Accessed 05 Jun 2015

29. Freedom of House. Freedom of the Press, Cyprus Country report (2008). https://web.archive.org/web/20170605134650/https://freedomhouse.org/report/freedom-press/2008/cyprus. Accessed 05 Jun 2015

30. Freedom of House. Freedom of the Press, Cyprus Country report (2011). https://web.archive.org/web/20170605134800/https://freedomhouse.org/report/freedom-press/2011/cyprus. Accessed 05 Jun 2015

31. Freedom of House. Freedom of the Press, Cyprus Country report (2012). https://web.archive.org/web/20170605134838/https://freedomhouse.org/report/freedom-press/2012/cyprus. Accessed 05 Jun 2015

32. Freedom of House. Freedom of the Press, Cyprus Country report (2013). https://web.archive.org/web/20170605134916/https://freedomhouse.org/report/freedom-press/2013/cyprus. Accessed 05 Jun 2015

33. Freedom of House. Freedom of the Press, Cyprus Country report (2014). https://web.archive.org/web/20170605135021/https://freedomhouse.org/report/freedom-press/2014/cyprus. Accessed 05 Jun 2015

34. OpenDNS Inc., OpenDNS IP Addresses. http://web.archive.org/web/20140829223158/http://www.opendns.com/opendns-ip-addresses/. Accessed 29 Sept 2014

35. Berkman Klein Center for Internet and Society at Harvard University, Lumen. http://archive.is/BwyBv. Accessed 05 Jun 2015

36. ITY. I. T. U. 2016. Measuring the Information Society Report. https://web.archive.org/web/20170605134129/http://www.itu.int/en/ITU-D/Statistics/Documents/publications/misr2016/MISR2016-w4.pdf. Accessed 05 Jun 2015

37. Citizen Lab and Others. URL testing lists intended for discovering website censorship. https://github.com/citizenlab/test-lists.2014

38. MTN. MTN ISP official website. http://web.archive.org/web/20170605020143/http://www.mtn.com.cy/. Accessed 05 Jun 2017

39. Multimax. Multimax ISP official website. http://web.archive.org/web/20170605015656/http://www.mmcyp.com. Accessed 05 Jun 2017

40. Hack66 Observatory. A custom set of tools to perform ooniprobe network measurements (2017). https://github.com/hack66/bet2512

41. OONI. OONI measurements files repository. https://web.archive.org/web/20170606210652/https://measurements.ooni.torproject.org/. Accessed 06 Jun 2017

42. Statcounter. StatCounter GlobalStats. http://gs.statcounter.com/. Accessed 05 Jun 2015

43. Ververis, V., et al.: Internet censorship policy: the case of Greece. In: Free and Open Communications on the Internet. USENIX (2015). https://www.usenix.org/system/files/conference/foci15/foci15-paper-ververis-updated-2.pdf

Social Networks

On the (Non-)anonymity of Anonymous Social Networks

Vasileios Chatzistefanou[1] and Konstantinos Limniotis[1,2](✉)

[1] School of Pure and Applied Sciences, Open University of Cyprus,
G. Kranidioti Ave., 2220 Nicosia, Cyprus
vasileios.chatzistefanou@st.ouc.ac.cy, konstantinos.limniotis@ouc.ac.cy
[2] Hellenic Data Protection Authority, Kifissias 1–3, 11523 Athens, Greece
klimniotis@dpa.gr

Abstract. The anonymity provided by the so-called anonymous social networks is studied in this paper. In particular, five popular anonymous social networks - namely, Social Number, Anomo, Whisper, Candid and the Yik Yak - are being analysed, in terms of investigating the data that are being processed by the corresponding mobile applications on Android systems. The results show that there is personal data processing in place which in some cases may result in tracking or even identification of the users and, thus, anonymity is not ensured.

Keywords: Android system · Anonymization · Anonymous social networks · General Data Protection Regulation · Personal data · Pseudonymization

1 Introduction

In the era of big data, there is an extensive collection and further processing of personal data which in turn give rise to several privacy concerns, mainly with regard to profiling and disclosure of private data [12]. According to a 2013 study [17], 86% of internet users have tried to be anonymous online - e.g. by taking steps to remove or mask their digital footprints. In such an environment, social networks have a crucial role since their users produce and disseminate huge amount of information. Therefore, conventional social networks have been extensively studied from many aspects, including privacy issues (see, e.g., [8,21]).

A special type of social networks that has been recently appeared is the so-called *anonymous* social networks, that is social networks that they typically do not require users to create user profiles and they (claim that) collect very little information about them. By these means, it is supposed that people may express their beliefs and opinions freely, in both public and private social spheres, without feeling that their privacy is being violated. Several such anonymous networks are known, whilst the vast majority of them are smart applications operating on IoS or Android systems. Of course, with the entrance of such anonymous applications there are also growing concerns for issues like cyber-bullying and

© Springer International Publishing AG 2017
S.K. Katsikas and V. Zorkadis (Eds.): E-Democracy 2017, CCIS 792, pp. 153–168, 2017.
https://doi.org/10.1007/978-3-319-71117-1_11

personal defamation. As a response to this, known anonymous apps put efforts to remove all abusive and harmful posts.

Anonymous social networks have not been studied extensively in the literature; an analysis of the contents of the posts of the users, with the aim to evaluate the extent to which they think the post should be anonymous, is presented in [7], whilst a study on how anonymity and the lack of social links affect the users behavior is presented in [22]. In this paper, we focus on evaluating the privacy that is actually provided by anonymous social networks, through investigating which type of user's personal data they process and examining whether these data suffice to identify the users. Our analysis is based on the main foundations for personal data protection in Europe, that is the Data Protection Directive 95/46/EC [10] as well as the new General Data Protection Regulation 2016/679 [11] that is going to replace the existing Data Protection Directive on May 25th, 2018; both of them explicitly define the notion of personal data, whilst they also state the conditions that need to hold in order to characterize data as anonymized, i.e. non–personal. In this direction, we studied five popular social networks, namely Social Number, Anomo, Whisper, Candid and Yik Yak (the latter one shut down in April 2017); more precisely, we performed a dynamic analysis of the corresponding Android smart applications, by using appropriate software tools which help to monitor what an Android application is doing at runtime, in order to identify which personal data are being collected by these applications. The main findings rest with the observation that almost all the applications seem to process the Google Advertising ID (GAID) from the user's devices, whilst some of them also collect device gps data; in addition, there are also cases where the user of an anonymous network may be associated with an e-mail address or with her/his account on Facebook (in case that the user chooses such an option). Finally, although all applications are based on the TLS protocol for securing the connection, some applications do not implement the so-called SSL pinning as an additional measure to avoid the Man-In-The-Middle attacks - i.e. to further ensure that eavesdropping cannot occur on the data connection.

It should be explicitly pointed out that our aim is not to make a comparative study between these social networks neither to qualify them in terms of their provided services; in the same line, ethical issues that may arise by the use of anonymous media are out of the scope of this paper. Our ultimate goal is to demonstrate how difficult is to achieve full anonymization, even in cases of the so-called anonymous social networks.

The paper is organized as follows; the definition of the personal data, the notion of anonymous data and pseudonymization, as well as a discussion on Android identifiers and the security characteristics of smart apps, are presented in Sect. 2. Section 3 constitutes the main part of the paper, where the results of our dynamic analysis on the corresponding smart apps are presented. In Sect. 4 we further elaborate on the findings from our analysis, describing how the personal data that seem to be gathered by anonymous social networks can be used for potential identification or tracking of the users. Finally, concluding remarks are given in Sect. 5.

2   Preliminaries

In this Section, we present the definitions regarding personal and anonymous data, the notions of identifiers in an Android device, whilst we also discuss security issues of Android smart apps. This Section sets the necessary background in order to evaluate the findings from our analysis that is presented in the subsequent Sect. 3.

2.1   Personal Data Protection Regulation

The Data Protection Directive. In 1995, the EU adopted the Data Protection Directive 95/46/EC (Data Protection Directive - DPD) [10], forming the main foundation for data protection in Europe until 2016 and it still remains in place until the mid of 2018, as described next. Member states of the EU ought to have amended their national laws to conform to DPD within three years. The directive has the objective to provide for a high level of protection of the fundamental rights and freedoms of the individuals with regard to the processing of personal data.

The DPD introduces - amongst others - the following definitions (Art. 2) with regard to personal data processing:

(a) The term "personal data" refers to any information relating to an identified or identifiable natural person ("data subject"); an identifiable person is one who can be identified, directly or indirectly, in particular by reference to an identification number or to one or more factors specific to his physical, physiological, mental, economic, cultural or social identity.

(b) The term "processing of personal data" ("processing") refers to any operation or set of operations which is performed upon personal data, whether or not by automatic means, such as collection, recording, organization, storage, adaptation or alteration, retrieval, consultation, use, disclosure by transmission, dissemination or otherwise making available, alignment or combination, blocking, erasure or destruction;

(c) The term "controller" (data controller) refers to the natural or legal person, public authority, agency or any other body which alone or jointly with others determines the purposes and means of the processing of personal data.

The Data Protection Directive codifies basic privacy principles that need to be guaranteed when personal data are collected or processed, including legitimacy (art. 6 I (a)), purpose limitation (art. 6 I(b)) and data minimization (art. 6 I (c)). Moreover, personal data may be processed only if the data subject has unambiguously given his consent (art. 7 (a)), although there are some exemptions where the data processing is allowed without asking for the data subject's consent (e.g. if there is a legal obligation or a contractual agreement). In addition, pursuant to Art. 10, individuals whose personal data are being processed have the right to information about at least the identity of the controller, their data processing purposes, and any further information necessary for guaranteeing fair data processing. With regard to security, the data controller should adopt appropriate technical and organizational security mechanisms to guarantee the confidentiality, integrity, and availability of personal data (Art. 17).

It should be pointed out that, as stated in Recital 26 of the DPD, the principles of protection shall not apply to data rendered anonymous in such a way that the data subject is no longer identifiable; however, to determine whether a person is identifiable, account should be taken of all the means likely reasonably to be used either by the controller or by any other person to identify the said person. This implies that simply removing the identifiers of the data subjects does not ensure anonymization [3].

The General Data Protection Regulation. The EU has created a new data protection regime, the Regulation (EU) 2016/679 or General Data Protection Regulation (GDPR) [11], to replace the Data Protection Directive so as to further protect and empower all EU citizens data privacy. The GDPR aims to harmonise data protection laws across Europe, by removing the need for national implementation. The GDPR entered into force on May 24th, 2016 and its enforcement begins on May 25th, 2018. One of the biggest changes that the GDPR brings is that it applies to all organizations processing the personal data of data subjects residing in the European Union, regardless of the organization's location - whilst territorial applicability of the DPD refers to data process "in context of an establishment".

Some definitions in the DPD are re-formulated in the GDPR, whilst several new definitions are also introduced. Amongst others, the notion of *pseudonymisation* is introduced in Art. 4 of the GDPR, meaning *the processing of personal data in such a manner that the personal data can no longer be attributed to a specific data subject without the use of additional information, provided that such additional information is kept separately and is subject to technical and organisational measures to ensure that the personal data are not attributed to an identified or identifiable natural person.* The GDPR also introduces several new obligations for data controllers, including - amongst others - the data protection by design and by default (art. 25) and the requirement for the controller to carry out a Data Protection Impact Assessment (DPIA) where the processing is likely to result in a high risk to the rights and freedoms of natural persons (Art. 35).

Similarly to the DPD, the GDPR states (Recital 26) that the principles of data protection should not apply to anonymous information, namely information which does not relate to an identified or identifiable natural person or to personal data rendered anonymous in such a manner that the data subject is not or no longer identifiable. However, as it is also explicitly stated, *personal data which have undergone pseudonymisation, which could be attributed to a natural person by the use of additional information should be considered to be information on an identifiable natural person. To determine whether a natural person is identifiable, account should be taken of all the means reasonably likely to be used, such as singling out, either by the controller or by another person to identify the natural person directly or indirectly. To ascertain whether means are reasonably likely to be used to identify the natural person, account should*

*be taken of all objective factors, such as the costs of and the amount of time
required for identification, taking into consideration the available technology at
the time of the processing and technological developments.* Therefore, the GDPR
explicitly states that pseudonymization should not be considered, in general, as
anonymization. The pseudonymisation though can reduce the risks to the data
subjects concerned; more precisely, with regard to the security of data processing, Art. 32 of the GDPR states that *taking into account the state of the art, the
costs of implementation and the nature, scope, context and purposes of processing
as well as the risk of varying likelihood and severity for the rights and freedoms
of natural persons, the controller and the processor shall implement appropriate
technical and organisational measures to ensure a level of security appropriate
to the risk, including inter alia as appropriate: (a) the pseudonymisation and
encryption of personal data (...).* Therefore, although pseudonymization does
not coincide with anonymization, it may constitute an appropriate safeguard to
reduce the data protection risks.

2.2   Android Applications

Device Identifiers. It is widely known that many devices possess specific characteristics which allow them to be "fingerprinted". As a concrete example, we
may refer to the unique identifiers that are often associated with devices (such
as, e.g., the MAC address). However, the term device fingerprinting is much
more general, since it refers to any possible unique trace that the use of such a
device leaves [9]; such a trace is often contingent on the specific software that is
installed on the device.

Since our test environment has been built upon Android devices, we shall
next describe the identifiers that may be associated with such a device. These
identifiers are [20]:

- The IMSI (Identity Mobile Subscriber Identity), which is a 15-digit decimal
  identifier representing the mobile subscriber identity,
- MAC address, which is a 48-bit number assigned to the device's Wi-Fi net-
  work interface,
- IMEI, which is a permanent 15-digit decimal identifier representing GSM or
  LTE device,
- Android ID, which is a 64-bit randomly generated number,
- Google Advertising ID (GAID), which is 32-digit alphanumeric identifier. The
  GAID is available only on devices that have the Google Play service installed.
  The GAID can be reset at any time, according to the user's request. The
  GAID is generally used to collect information so as to further used to display
  advertisements and other information on the user's device.

In general, device fingerprints can also constitute personal data [4]. In this
respect, unique device identifiers as above may suffice to result in identification
of a user of the device, it they are combined with other information elements.
Therefore, not only the IMSI - which is uniquely associated with a specific user -
but also all the other identifiers should be considered as personal data.

Security Issues - The TLS Protocol. Towards providing secure communication over an insecure channel, the Transport Layer Security (TLS) protocol, as a successor of the Secure Sockets Layer (SSL) protocol, is being considered as a somehow de-facto standard. TLS is based on symmetric encryption for ensuring confidentiality, whereas the symmetric key is being interchanged via public key cryptographic algorithms. Moreover, data integrity is ensured by message authentication codes (MACs). A crucial issue for achieving all the above security goals is that the client should be able to verify the identity of the server. The entity authentication is ensured by appropriate use and verification of digital certificates, which are signed by trusted Certificate Authorities (CAs); by these means, a Man-In-The-Middle (MITM) attack can be prevented, since the attacker is generally not able to use a fake identity with a valid certificate.

TLS is also used to secure Android applications. However, many Android applications fail to properly validate TLS/SSL certificates, which may allow an attacker to perform a successful MITM attack [16]. In such a case, an attacker on the same network as the Android device may be able to view or modify network traffic that should have been protected by TLS (e.g. in case that an attacker manages to install his own certificate on the user's device through social engineering). To overcome such issues, i.e. to ensure that apps are restricted to talk only with web services which exchange only one or a set of certificates that it can recognize or to restrict an app's trusted CAs to a small set known to be used by the app's servers, many app developers proceed with the so-called *SSL pinning*, that is the validated certificate is being stored locally within the app; this is an extra security step to thwart MITM attacks [16]. Hence, SSL pinning constitutes an additional security measure against MITM attacks, although it should not be considered as a panacea.

3   Analysis of Anonymous Social Networks

In this Section we present the results of our analysis on smart apps of anonymous social networks, which took place for the period December 2016–February 2017. Our study focuses on five popular anonymous social networks, namely *Social Number, Anomo, Whisper, Candid* and *Yik Yak* (the latter one shut down on April 2017). We first describe our adopted methodology and subsequently present the results for each case separately.

3.1   The Testing Environment

In order to analyze the outgoing data from our Android device for our research purposes, we utilized the free version of the Burp Suite [5], in order to establish an HTTP proxy between the Android device and the destination server (i.e. the server of the anonymous social network), so as to intentionally intercept and inspect the raw traffic passing from our Android device to the server (Fig. 1). The Burp suite is a popular tool, used by many security professionals (see, e.g., [13]). The proxy server has been installed on a workstation in our local network.

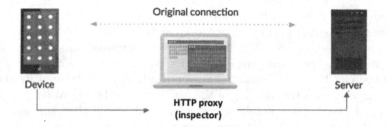

Fig. 1. The testing environment

We initiated two testing environments; the first one with a real Android device and the second one with a virtual Android device. By these means, we were able to verify our results by comparing the outputs obtained from the analysis of these two different environments. In both cases, the outgoing traffic is first redirected to the aforementioned proxy. Since our analysis indicated that there is always a coincidence between the results of the two cases (that is real and the virtual Android device), we subsequently simply refer to an Android device, without differentiating the two scenarios.

Since all the smart apps corresponding to the above social networks are based on the TLS protocol for securing communication, we need to issue a digital certificate for our proxy server; this implies that we need to embed this certificate to the list of the trusted certificates in our Android device since, otherwise, we would not be able to redirect the data through our proxy so as to monitor them. Of course, in case that a smart app uses SSL pinning, such an approach will not suffice to succeed in redirecting the communication through our proxy server. According to our observations, two anonymous networks - that is the Social Number and the Anomo - do not support SSL pinning and, thus, we were able to perform the dynamic analysis through our proxy.

To be able to analyse smart apps that they use SSL pinning, we utilize an appropriate module of the Xposed framework [18], namely the Inspeckage Android packet inspector - that is a simple application with an internal HTTP server [15]. This tool allows for intercepting the encrypted traffic through bypassing the certificate verification, even if the certificate is "pinned" within the application. The Inspeckage has been used for analysing Whisper, Candid and Yik Yak, since our analysis indicated that these applications implement SSL pinning as an additional security feature.

3.2 Analysis of the "Social Number" Application

The *Social Number* [19] is based on assigning a large unique meaningless number to each user, which corresponds to the user's login name (such a number could be, for example, $000 - 3172 - 012$). The social network claims that *the user is just a number and the user's real identity is never revealed.* Once the user gets a number, she/he may register to the network, whereas a personal password is also needed for any subsequent connections.

Our first observation, when deploying the Social Number to our Android device, is that the application asks for an e-mail address of the user at the registration process; this e-mail address will be used in case that the user forgets her/his password. Apparently, the e-mail address constitutes user's personal data (despite the fact that in case that this e-mail address is only used by the user for this purpose, then the identity of the user may not be revealed).

A second observation, as already discussed above, is that the application does not utilize SSL pinning; therefore, we were able to decrypt (i.e. read) the transmitted data through the Burp Suite, since the application accepted the certificate of our proxy server as valid, via installing it to the device's list of trusted certificates. This is illustrated in our *post* message in Fig. 2, which shows how the intermediate proxy can read our user name and password (which are transmitted encrypted, due to the TLS).

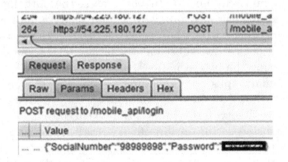

Fig. 2. A decrypted post message with user's credentials in the Social Number

Further analysis on the transmitted data indicates that, once a user is connected, a random access token is being created. This token seems that it is never repeated at subsequent connections of the same user - i.e. a new token is created at each new connection.

Concluding, the Social Number network collects the e-mail addresses of the users - which should be considered as personal data, even if the users do not provide their active e-mail address - whilst the application does not use SSL pinning as an additional safeguard against MITM attacks (although, as already stated above, SSL pinning does not constitute a full response to this threat). Therefore, in case of a successful MITM attack, the attacker will be able, e.g., to read the password of the user. Bearing in mind that many users unfortunately tend to use the same password for many applications, it becomes evident that, at the worst case scenario, there are some security and data protection risks (e.g. if the user is fully identified by her/his e-mail address that she/he has sent at the registration process).

3.3   Analysis of the "Anomo" Application

The *Anomo* social network [2] is an application for anonymously connecting users with others sharing the same interests, whilst there are options for the users to reveal personal information (if, for example, they feel comfortably with some other users). Each user chooses an avatar and a login name at her/his desire. There is also an option for the users to connect to the Anomo by using the user's Facebook account, that is the e-mail address and the password that are being used in Facebook.

Our first observation is that, similarly to the Social Number, the smart app does not utilize SSL pinning. In Fig. 3 we show how we were able, through the Burp Suite, to reveal the encrypted Facebook credentials - i.e. the e-mail address and the password - in a case that a user chooses to connect to the Anomo by using his Facebook account. Therefore, a successful MITM attack may result in revealing the password, as well as the e-mail address, that the user has in Facebook.

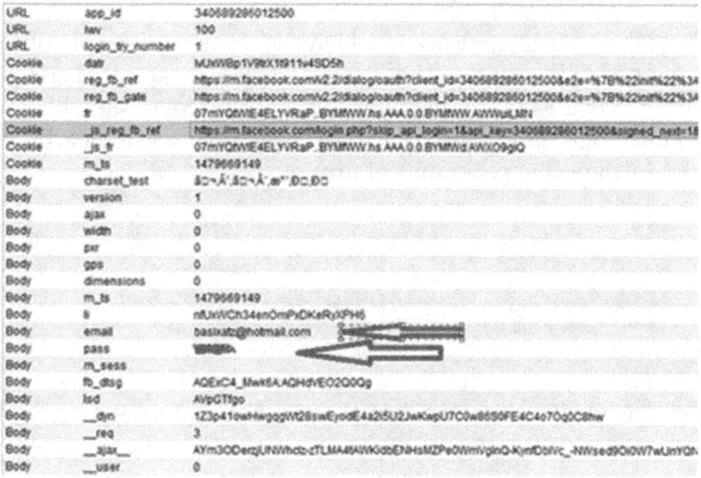

Fig. 3. Revealing user's Facebook credentials in our testing environment when connecting to the Anomo

Moreover, our analysis indicates that the Anomo application collects the device's GAID, as shown in Fig. 4. This holds for any case, that is in either the case that the user creates her/his own account to the Anomo application or she/he is connected through the Facebook credential.

As concluding remarks, the GAID for each user (device) seems to be processed by the Anomo. Moreover, SSL pinning, which is an additional safeguard against MITM attack, is not being used, whilst - at the worst case scenario - a MITM attack may result in revealing the Facebook credentials of the user.

```
4bff420f-2285-408b-a5e8-f6b06cb8c892
--3i2ndDfv2rTHiSisAbouNdArYfORhtTPEefj3q2f
Content-Disposition: form-data; name="application_package_name"

com.vinasource.anomoinc.anomo
--3i2ndDfv2rTHiSisAbouNdArYfORhtTPEefj3q2f
Content-Disposition: form-data; name="event"

CUSTOM_APP_EVENTS
--3i2ndDfv2rTHiSisAbouNdArYfORhtTPEefj3q2f
Content-Disposition: form-data; name="application_tracking_enabled"
```

Fig. 4. Revealing GAID within the data that are being processed by the Anomo

Finally, as an open question, it should be further investigated whereas the connection to the Anomo through Facebook credentials allows identification of the user from either of these two networks.

3.4 Analysis of the "Whisper" Application

The *Whisper* [23] is a social network in which the users may simply observe posts from other users and comment on them, without necessitating a login procedure. The application provides the options for any user to create her/his own group, as well as to filter out those posts that have been created by nearby users - i.e. by users lying in the same geographical area.

```
<?xml version='1.0' encoding='utf-8' standalone='yes' ?>
<map>
    <boolean name="limit_ad_tracking_enabled" value="false" ></boolean>
    <string name="advertising_id">4bff420f-2285-408b-a5e8-f6b06cb8c892</string>
</map>
```

Fig. 5. Revealing GAID within the data that are being processed by the Whisper

Although there is no any login procedure in place, a user receives notifications on her/his device whenever somebody likes or replies to her/his post, which means that the app actually knows the device from which the user initiated the post. This is owing to the fact that a unique token is generated, which is associated solely with a user's device, which in turn means that if a user accesses the app from another device, the app will generate another token and create a new entity in the database [1]. Moreover, the option of finding out posts from nearby users indicates that the device's location is also being processed.

As it is shown by our dynamic analysis, the Whisper application implements SSL pinning, so we are not able to intercept the communication by installing our proxy's certificate in the Android device. Therefore, to perform our dynamic analysis on Whisper, we have to "unpin" the embedded certificate from the application in order to analyze it, through the appropriate software module that is described above - i.e. the Inspeckage inspector. Our analysis via this module indicated that the application processes some information regarding the Android device (model, manufacturer) but, most importantly, it also processes the GAID, as shown in Fig. 5. Moreover, as expected, the Whisper application collects device's gps data according to our analysis, as shown in Fig. 6.

```
<long name="last_successful_ad_timestamp" value="1485718287461" ></lor
<float name="longitude_prefs_key" value="25.876919" ></float>
<float name="lattitude_prefs_key" value="40.85136" ></float>
<string name="nickname">Coffee Knight</string>
```

Fig. 6. Revealing geolocation data within the data that are transmitted to the Whisper

As concluding remarks, we may state that the Whisper implements SSL pinning as a additional measure for thwarting MITM attacks, whereas it seems that it processes the GAID and the geolocation data of the device. It is not clear how GAID is further processed (e.g. there is a probability that it is used for assigning a unique ID to each device for the purposes described above).

3.5   Analysis of the "Candid" Application

The *Candid* [6] is a social network which processes all the users posts with the aim to remove inappropriate content and flag negative posts. The company also says that identifies hate speech, slander and threats, so as to keep a conversation decorous. Candid requires users to sign in by way of Facebook, but once they are on the platform, all their content is supposed that is kept separate from their identity. A random username is given to each post, which means that the same user may post with different usernames in different threads.

As previously, our analysis indicates that Candid supports SSL pinning for further enhancing security. Therefore, we utilized the Inspeckage module for analysing our outgoing traffic. By these means, we managed to find out that GAID is also being processed by the social network, as shown in Fig. 7. Moreover, since the user uses her/his Facebook account to connect to the network, our analysis shows that a successful MITM attack allows to reveal the username that the user has in Facebook; we didn't reveal though the Facebook password of the user (Fig. 8). In any case, it should be further investigated whereas the connection to the Candid through Facebook credentials allows identification of the user from either of these two networks.

Concluding, we may state that the Candid implements SSL pinning as a additional measure for thwarting MITM attacks, whereas it seems that it processes the GAID of the device. It is not clear how GAID is further handled. Moreover, the connection to the Candid through the Facebook account should be further investigated in terms of studying which personal data - if any - are finally released to each of these two social networks.

```
<?xml version='1.0' encoding='utf-8' standalone='yes' ?>
<map>
    <boolean name="limit_ad_tracking_enabled" value="false" ></boolean>
    <string name="advertising_id">4bff420f-2285-408b-a5e8-f6b06cb8c892</string>
```


Fig. 7. Revealing GAID within the data that are being processed by the Candid


```
118 GET[com.facebook.AccessTokenManager.SharedPreferences.xml] String(com.f
ist_name":"Bill","name":"Basilis Bill","link_uri":"https:\/\/www.facebook.com\/app_scop
117 CONTAINS[com.facebook.AccessTokenManager.SharedPreferences.xml](com.f
```


Fig. 8. Revealing user's Facebook username in our testing environment when connecting to the Candid

3.6 Analysis of the "Yik Yak" Application

Yik Yak was a social media smartphone application, allowing users to create and view discussion threads within the same geographical area (termed "Yaks" by the application). Therefore, GPS data were being used to locate the users. Each user could choose her/his own username. As other anonymous social media, Yik Yak met criticism for feeding bullying and harassment; on the other side, academics have identified how Yik Yak was mostly used as a positive way to build a sense of community on campus [14]. On April 28, 2017, Yik Yak announced it would be shutting down.


```
<?xml version='1.0' encoding='utf-8' standalone='yes' ?>
<map>
    <boolean name="limit_ad_tracking_enabled" value="false" ></boolean>
    <string name="advertising_id">4bff420f-2285-408b-a5e8-f6b06cb8c892</string>
</map>
```


Fig. 9. Revealing GAID within the data that are being processed by the Yik Yak

As previously, our analysis indicates that Yik Yak was supporting SSL pinning for further enhancing security. Thereofore, we utilized the Inspeckage module for analysing our outgoing traffic. By these means, we managed to find out that GAID is also being processed by the social network, as shown in Fig. 9. Our analysis also indicated that the application processes some information regarding the Android device (model, manufacturer), as well as it collects device's gps data as shown in Fig. 10.

device_manufacturer":"Xiaomi","device_model":"Redmi Note 3","carrier":"vodafone GR","country":"GR","language":"el","platform":"Android","u
sequence_number":217,"library":{"name":"amplitude-android","version":"2.7.1"},"api_properties":{"androidADID":"992a3c8c-5d12-4c00-8b6c-
abled":true},"event_properties":{},"user_properties":{"$set":{"Yakarma":106}},"groups":{}} id=130,event={"event_type":"$identify","timestamp":
4B5F06A5A471D5E07","device_id":"3190d47e-c11f-4131-89c3-958c391e8e9dR","session_id":148207583393,"version_name":"4.7","os_na
t":"Xiaomi","device_manufacturer":"Xiaomi","device_model":"Redmi Note 3","carrier":"vodafone GR","country":"GR","language":"el","platfor
t032b60a81f8","sequence_number":218,"library":{"name":"amplitude-android","version":"2.7.1"},"api_properties":{"androidADID":"992a3c8c-5
3":false,"gps_enabled":true},"event_properties":{},"user_properties":{"$set":{"HasEverSetProfilePic":false}},"groups":{}} id=131,event={"event_
er_id":"6ABE83EODD03B1B4B5F06A5A471D5E07","device_id":"3190d47e-c11f-4131-89c3-958c391e8e9dR","session_id":148207583539
_version":"5.0.2","device_brand":"Xiaomi","device_manufacturer":"Xiaomi","device_model":"Redmi Note 3","carrier":"vodafone GR","countr
f":"d3d5dc0e-30bb-47b1-a54f-e89792f298ce","sequence_number":220,"library":{"name":"amplitude-android","version":"2.7.1"},"api_propertie
52d88b688f9","limit_ad_tracking":false,"gps_enabled":true},"event_properties":{},"user_properties":{"$set":{"HasBio":true}},"groups":{}} id=13
85361565327,"user_id":"6ABE83EODD03B1B4B5F06A5A471D5E07","device_id":"3190d47e-c11f-4131-89c3-958c391e8e9dR","session_id":
e":"android","os_version":"5.0.2","device_brand":"Xiaomi","device_manufacturer":"Xiaomi","device_model":"Redmi Note 3","carrier":"vodafon
Android","uuid":"7ea40062-ac27-4efb-9a9d-b1bdc70224e6","sequence_number":225,"library":{"name":"amplitude-android","version":"2.7.
1":25.878490000000003},"androidADID":"4bff420f-2285-408b-a5e8-f6b06cb8c892","limit_ad_tracking":false,"gps_enabled":true},"event_prop
6}},"groups":{}} id=133,event={"event_type":"$identify","timestamp":1485361562419,"user_id":"6ABE83EODD03B1B4B5F06A5A471D5E0
91e8e9dR","session_id":1485361562247,"version_name":"4.10","os_name":"android","os_version":"5.0.2","device_brand":"Xiaomi","device_
Note 3","carrier":"vodafone GR","country":"GR","language":"el","platform":"Android","uuid":"eef89075-330d-4085-943f-02f79168b10e","sequen
droid","version":"2.7.1"},"api_properties":{"location":{"lat":40.8557,"lng":25.878490000000003},"androidADID":"4bff420f-2285-408b-a5e8-f6b0
f":true},"event_properties":{},"user_properties":{"$set":{"HasEverSetProfilePic":false}},"groups":{}} id=134,event={"event_type":"$identify","tim
t003B1B4B5F06A5A471D5E07","device_id":"3190d47e-c11f-4131-89c3-958c391e8e9dR","session_id":1485361562247,"version_name":"4.1
ice_brand":"Xiaomi","device_manufacturer":"Xiaomi","device_model":"Redmi Note 3","carrier":"vodafone GR","country":"GR","language":"e
t5-883b-ec6d3693e8d1","sequence_number":227,"library":{"name":"amplitude-android","version":"2.7.1"},"api_properties":{"location":{"lat":4
0":"4bff420f-2285-408b-a5e8-f6b06cb8c892","limit_ad_tracking":false,"gps_enabled":true},"event_properties":{},"user_properties":{"$set":{"H
vent={"event_type":"$identify","timestamp":1485361687167,"user_id":"6ABE83EODD03B1B4B5F06A5A471D5E07","device_id":"3190d47e-c1
5361562247,"version_name":"4.10","os_name":"android","os_version":"5.0.2","device_brand":"Xiaomi","device_manufacturer":"Xiaomi","devi
R","country":"GR","language":"el","platform":"Android","uuid":"feb725ae-2ffc-4222-a606-178adcf0b5a2","sequence_number":228,"library":{"na
roperties":{"location":{"lat":40.8557,"lng":25.878490000000003},"androidADID":"4bff420f-2285-408b-a5e8-f6b06cb8c892","limit_ad_trackin

Fig. 10. Revealing geolocation data - and other info on the device - within the data that are transmitted to the Yik Yak

4   Evaluation of the Results

Our analysis indicates that all studied anonymous social networks process some personal data of their users. In cases that such social networks collect e-mail addresses or usernames from other networks such as the Facebook, the personal data processing is obvious. However, other information such as the GAID or geolocation data may also contribute in identifying a user. To illustrate this, we next present our analysis on the traces that the users leave when surfing in the Internet, with the aim to discover how often they "feed" their GAID to other applications. It should be stressed that although the GAID is user-resettable, it is generally questionable whether users regularly proceed in resetting its value.

Again, we used the same testing environment, having the Inspeckage as our tool to analyze Android applications at runtime. We focused on three popular browsers, namely Firefox, Chrome and Opera, as well as on three popular social networks, namely Instagram, Twitter and Facebook. With regard to the three web browsers, our analysis indicates that Opera processes our GAID, as shown in Fig. 11. With regard to the social networks, we get that Twitter and Instagram also process GAID (see Figs. 12 and 13 respectively). Therefore, GAID constitutes a device identifier which is being used by many popular applications and, thus, it may serve for creating a user profile - that is to track user's behavior. Moreover, in case that the GAID is being used for associating the device with the identity of the user (e.g. in a MITM attack on a user that is connected to the Twitter, as Fig. 12 shows), then the user becomes fully identifiable even in the so-called anonymous applications.

advertising_pref_store.xml

```
<?xml version='1.0' encoding='utf-8' standalone='yes' ?>
<map>
    <boolean name="limit_ad_tracking" value="false" ></boolean>
    <string name="advertising_id">4bff420f-2285-408b-a5e8-f6b06cb8c892</string>
</map>
```

Fig. 11. Revealing GAID within the data being processed by the Opera browser

TwitterAdvertisingInfoPreferences.xml

```
<?xml version='1.0' encoding='utf-8' standalone='yes' ?>
<map>
    <boolean name="limit_ad_tracking_enabled" value="false" ></boolean>
    <string name="advertising_id">4bff420f-2285-408b-a5e8-f6b06cb8c892</string>
</map>
```

com.twitter.android_preferences.xml

```
<?xml version='1.0' encoding='utf-8' standalone='yes' ?>
<map>
    <long name="log_last_flush_request" value="1485707880143" ></long>
    <string name="client_uuid">e2b08d32-99b8-4abf-9c6c-e0adaf7e4b1e</string>
    <long name="become_inactive_timestamp" value="1485707882215" ></long>
    <boolean name="phone_verified" value="true" ></boolean>
    <string name="current_account">BillChatzistef1</string>
    <long name="pref_ref_src_date" value="1481476257124" ></long>
```

Fig. 12. Revealing GAID and username within the data being processed by Twitter

com.instagram.android_preferences.xml

```
<?xml version='1.0' encoding='utf-8' standalone='yes' ?>
<map>
    <string name="google_ad_id">4bff420f-2285-408b-a5e8-f6b06cb8c892</string>
    <boolean name="opt_out_ads" value="false" ></boolean>
    <string name="current">{&quot;id&quot;:,&quot;1495233222&quot;,&quot;biography&quot;:,&quot;&quot;,,&quot;blocking&
    <boolean name="has_seen_direct_story_from_instagram_nux" value="true" ></boolean>
    <boolean name="has_seen_layout_button_nux" value="true" ></boolean>
    <boolean name="bgsync_launch_next_online" value="false" ></boolean>
    <string name="user_access_map">[{&quot;user_info&quot;:{&quot;id&quot;:,&quot;1495233222&quot;,&quot;biography&qu
    <long name="push_reg_dateandroid_mqtt" value="1482156936901" ></long>
    <int name="used_double_tap_hint_impressions" value="1" ></int>
    <boolean name="show_tos" value="false" ></boolean>
    <boolean name="used_double_tap" value="true" ></boolean>
    <boolean name="com.facebook.sdk.appInstallEvent" value="true" ></boolean>
</map>
```

Fig. 13. Revealing GAID within the data being processed by Instagram

5   Conclusions

In this paper, a preliminary study on the personal data that are being processed by anonymous social networks is presented, based on a dynamic analysis of the corresponding Android applications. Although there are still many open questions with regard to the exact type of this processing, our analysis reveals that these networks indeed process some personal data and thus they should be considered as pseudonymous and not as anonymous. There are several differences between these networks; in any case though, the degree to which the provided pseudonymity should be considered as adequate or not needs to be further investigated.

The main outcome of our analysis is that, since personal data processing is in place, the users should be aware that full anonymity is not necessarily ensured. Therefore, recalling that the GDPR will apply to any data processing concerning EU citizens, we get that anonymous social networks are expected to fall within the scope of the GDPR regardless the establishment of the data controller.

References

1. Abrosimova, K.: Developing an Anonymous Social Networking App. https://yalantis.com/blog/anonymous-social-network-development/
2. Anomo. http://www.anomo.com
3. Article 29 Working Party: Opinion 5/2014 on Anonymization Techniques (2014). http://ec.europa.eu/justice/data-protection/article-29/documentation/opinion-recommendation/files/2014/wp216_en.pdf
4. Article 29 Working Party: Opinion 9/2014 on the application of Directive 2002/58/EC to device fingerprinting (2014). http://ec.europa.eu/justice/data-protection/article-29/documentation/opinion-recommendation/files/2014/wp224_en.pdf
5. Burp Suite. https://portswingger.net/burp
6. Candid. http://www.getcandid.com
7. Correa, D., Silva, R.A., Mondal, M., Benevenuto, F., Gummadi, K.P.: The many shades of anonymity: characterizing anonymous social media content. In: 9th International Conference on Web and Social Media (ICWSM), pp. 71–80. AAAI Press (2015)
8. Díaz, I., Ralescu, A.: Privacy issues in social networks: a brief survey. In: Greco, S., Bouchon-Meunier, B., Coletti, G., Fedrizzi, M., Matarazzo, B., Yager, R.R. (eds.) IPMU 2012. CCIS, vol. 300, pp. 509–518. Springer, Heidelberg (2012). https://doi.org/10.1007/978-3-642-31724-8_53
9. Eckersley, P.: How unique is your web browser? In: Atallah, M.J., Hopper, N.J. (eds.) PETS 2010. LNCS, vol. 6205, pp. 1–18. Springer, Heidelberg (2010). https://doi.org/10.1007/978-3-642-14527-8_1
10. European Commission: Directive 95/46/EC of the European Parliament and of the Council of 24 October 1995 on the protection of individuals with regard to the processing of personal data and on the free movement of such data. Off. J. L. **281**(31–50) (1995)

11. European Union: Regulation (EU) 2016/679 of the European Parliament and of the Council of 27 April 2016 on the protection of natural persons with regard to the processing of personal data and on the free movement of such data, and repealing Directive 95/46/EC (General Data Protection Regulation). Off. J. L. **119**(1) (2016)

12. European Union Agency For Network And Information Security: Privacy by design in big data - An overview of privacy enhancing technologies in the era of big data analytics, December 2015. https://www.enisa.europa.eu/publications/big-data-protection

13. Hafiz, M., Fang, M.: Game of detections: how are security vulnerabilities discovered in the wild? Empir. Softw. Eng. **21**, 1920–1959 (2016)

14. Junco, R.: Yik Yak and Online Anonymity are Good for College Students. Wired (2015). https://www.wired.com/2015/03/yik-yak-online-anonymity-good-college-students/

15. Mobile Security Wiki. https://mobilesecuritywiki.com/

16. Moonsamy, V., Batten, L.: Mitigating man-in-the-middle attacks on smartphones - a discussion of SSL pinning and DNSSec. In: Proceedings of the 12th Australian Information Security Management Conference (AISM), pp. 5–13 (2014)

17. Pew Research Center: Anonymity, Privacy, and Security Online, September 2013. http://pewinternet.org/Reports/2013/Anonymity-online.aspx

18. Rovo89: Xposed module repository. http://repo.xposed.info

19. Social Number. https://socialnumber.com

20. Son, S., Kim, D., Shmatikov, V.: What mobile ads know about mobile users. In: Network and Distributed System Security Symposium (2016)

21. Tzortzaki, E., Kitsiou, A., Sideri, M., Gritzalis, S.: Self-disclosure, privacy concerns and social capital benefits interaction in FB: a case study. In: ACM International Conference Proceeding Series (ICPS), PCI 2016, p. 32 (2016)

22. Wang, G., Wang, B., Wang, T., Nika, A., Zheng, H., Zhao, B.Y.: Whispers in the dark: analysis of an anonymous social network. In: IMC 2014, pp. 137–150. ACM (2014)

23. Whisper. http://whisper.sh

Fostering Active Participation of Young People in Democratic Life: A Case Study Using the #ask Dashboard

Areti Karamanou[1(✉)], Eleni Panopoulou[1], Vibor Cipan[2], Darko Čengija[2], David Jelić[2], Efthimios Tambouris[1], and Konstantinos Tarabanis[1]

[1] University of Macedonia, Egnatias 156, 54006 Thessaloniki, Greece
{akarm,epanopou}@uom.gr, {tambouris,kat}@uom.edu.gr
[2] UX Passion d.o.o., Horvatovac 23, HR – 10000 Zagreb, Croatia
{vibor,darko,david}@uxpassion.com

Abstract. In many democratic countries, including the European Union Member States, it is increasingly important that policy makers are aware of young people's opinion. In this respect, the European Union prioritizes the discovery of new forms of participation in democratic processes and access to political decision-making through online and offline tools. The aim of this paper is to demonstrate and evaluate the idea of promoting young people's participation in political decision-making by brokering discussions on Twitter. Towards this end, we present a case study that utilizes and makes a preliminary evaluation of the #ask Dashboard, a software solution for brokering and analyzing discussions on Twitter between policy makers and young people. In terms of the case study, we discovered Twitter handles of 74 policy makers and 229 young people interested in ten topics. We used the #ask Dashboard to broker more than 275 discussions about these topics. So far, we have achieved 367 replies, 15 retweets and 105 likes mostly from young people. Students who participated in brokered discussions for a month performed the evaluation of the case study. Although students believe that the case study gave them the opportunity to be active on political issues, they were sceptical on whether Twitter discussion brokering successfully reaches young people and policy makers.

Keywords: eParticipation · Twitter · Policy making · Youth

1 Introduction

According to Eurostat, by 2050 youth under the age of 25 will account for a *quarter* of all working age persons [1]. At the same time, political alienation and dissatisfaction among the same age group is observed [2]. To tap into the full potential of the rich source of youth's social dynamism, politicians and policymakers must make sure they take the thoughts of young people into account. The European Commission has already recognized this fact and proposed the 2010–2018 EU Strategy for Youth [3] to promote the active citizenship, social inclusion and solidarity of young people. However, over 6 years later, the goals of the EU Strategy for Youth remain unfulfilled. As a result, EU still

© Springer International Publishing AG 2017
S.K. Katsikas and V. Zorkadis (Eds.): E-Democracy 2017, CCIS 792, pp. 169–184, 2017.
https://doi.org/10.1007/978-3-319-71117-1_12

prioritizes the discovery of new forms of participation in democratic processes and access to political decision-making through online and offline tools [4].

Young people are increasingly building social networks the last years combining global connectivity with local roots. In particular, EU reports that 82% of young people participated in online social networks in 2014 [4]. Young people are also willing to engage in new forms of political participation, often using social media [4].

At the same time, over the past years, social media have become integrated into election campaigning and other forms of political communication [5]. In particular, social media like Twitter are now placing the focus mostly on the individual politician rather than on the political party, thereby expanding the political arena for increased personalized campaigning [6].

The aim of this paper is to demonstrate and evaluate the idea of promoting young people's participation in political decision-making by brokering discussions on Twitter. Towards this end, we present a case study that utilizes and makes a preliminary evaluation of the #ask Dashboard, a software solution for brokering and analyzing discussions on Twitter between policy makers and young people.

The remaining of this paper is organized as follows. Section 2 provides examples of the use of social media for eParticipation, Sect. 3 reviews a number of existing software solutions for Twitter analytics, Sect. 4 presents the #ask Dashboard and Sect. 5 presents the case study before concluding in Sect. 6.

2   eParticipation and Social Media

During the last years, the rise of social media has given politicians and governments new opportunities for enabling, engaging and empowering citizens in political decision-making [7]. As a result, many scientific studies are interested in understanding the role of social media in enhancing the engagement of citizens in political life. In this section we present examples of relevant studies that employ two of the most popular social media i.e. Facebook and Twitter in the context of eParticipation. We present the purpose of the studies along with the specific social media characteristics used (e.g. Twitter posts, replies etc.).

Regarding Facebook, relevant eParticipation studies aim, for example, to measure the impact of media types (e.g. video, text etc.) and content types (e.g. environment, housing) on citizens' engagement on governmental Facebook pages [8], to explore how successfully local governments utilize Facebook for managing their communication with citizens [9], to understand the content of the communications between citizens and governmental Facebook pages [10], and to understand the impact of the use of Facebook in elections or election campaigns [11, 12]. In order to achieve their objectives, most of these studies employ specific Facebook characteristics like Facebook posts [8–12] and comments on Facebook posts [9].

In the same way, a number of scientific studies in literature employ Twitter aiming, for example, to de-bureaucratize the organization of government communications [13], to examine its role in developing social trust [14] and its effects on government reliability [15] and to predict election results [16]. The specific Twitter characteristics that these studies exploit include the content of tweets [13, 16], demographic information of Twitter accounts [14] and the followers of Twitter accounts [15].

Finally, other studies employ both Twitter and Facebook and, sometimes, additional social media (e.g. YouTube, LinkedIn etc.), to examine, for example, which one is mostly used in local governments [17], which one achieves the strongest degree of citizens' commitment to local governments [18] or to understand how they are used by citizens in specific cities [19].

3   Software for Twitter Analytics

In order to find the optimal tools for the creation of the #ask Dashboard, an in-depth analysis of 19 software analytics software solutions has been conducted (Table 1). All solutions were analyzed in such way that their relative strengths and weaknesses were compared in order to find the optimal set of solutions.

In the rest of this section, we analyse in more detail the eight most relative software solutions. These include: *Klear, Foller.me, Twitonomy, Tweetchup, Twitter REST API, Twitter Streaming API, Twitter Analytics* and *Klout (Klout API)*. A summary of key findings is presented further in this paper.

3.1   Klear

Klear is primarily used as a tool for the identification of influencers on Twitter and inspection of their profiles. Identified influencers are then categorized and users can apply various filters to narrow down the results. Klear's main strengths include detailed follower analysis with top followers and followers by country. Also, it is possible to get detailed graph information about users connections and mutual relationships. Additionally, identification of the tweets that got the most retweets is possible.

Main limitations and weaknesses are related to limited number of queries and paid license. However, lack of application programming interface (API) is key weakness identified when benchmarked against the Dashboard's needs.

3.2   Foller.me

Foller provides information about users Twitter profile and their social connections. Strengths include the ability to display overall information about the user and identification of general topic competitor talks about. Also, it is possible to easily identify the most popular hashtags used by a specific user as well as a list of user profiles the user has interacted with.

Again, lack of the API access is a key weakness as well as the limitation that only last 100 tweets are being analyzed.

Table 1. Software solutions for Twitter Analytics

Software	URL	Open source
klear	https://klear.com	No
foller.me	https://foller.me/	No
twitonomy	https://www.twitonomy.com/	No
tweetchup	https://tweetchup.com/	No
DD-CSS beta	http://dd-css.com/	Yes
Digital Methods Initiative	https://github.com/digitalmethodsinitiative/dmi-tcat	Yes
BU	http://www.bu.edu/com/research/bu-tcat/	Yes
FLOCKER	http://flocker.outliers.es/	Yes
beta Followthehashtag	http://analytics.followthehashtag.com/#!/	No
isciencemap	http://maps.iscience.deusto.es/	Yes
SODATO	http://cssl.cbs.dk/software/sodato/	No
#TAGS	https://tags.hawksey.info/	No
TWEET ARCHIVIST	https://www.tweetarchivist.com/	No
The Chorus Project making sense from Twitter	http://chorusanalytics.co.uk/	Yes
rapidminer	https://rapidminer.com/	Yes
REST APIs	https://dev.twitter.com/rest/public	Yes
Streaming APIs	https://dev.twitter.com/streaming/overview	Yes
Analytics	https://analytics.twitter.com/	Yes
KLOUT	https://klout.com/s/developers/v2	Yes

3.3 Twitonomy

This service is a solid Twitter analytics tool offering fairly comprehensive analysis of a user profile or several of them at once. As its chief strengths we can point out detailed and very visual analytics about the tweets, retweets, replies, mentions, hashtags and more. That information is reliable and can serve as a valuable source of data. Additionally, users can browse, search, filter and get insights about their followers and about the users they are following as well as monitor interactions with other Twitter users. Another useful functionality is the ability to track follower growth, track traffic from the tweeted links and get and export Search Analytics on any keywords, hashtags, URL or user mentions and users themselves.

And now, almost as a rule, chief weakness is the lack of API access and supports which seriously hampers any potential Twitonomy already has.

3.4 Tweetchup

Tweetchup is another web tool we evaluated in the process. It is a simple tool suitable for analysis of users connections on Twitter, profile keywords and hashtags, Exactly those features are its main strengths with the additional value of keywords and hashtags analysis. Lack of API support and, effectively, lack of any programmatic ability to retrieve or interact with the data is a main weakness of this solution.

3.5 Twitter REST APIs

The REST APIs from Twitter are the official RESTful API created, developed and maintained by Twitter itself. Functionalities exposed through this API are spanning a wide range and include ability for programmatic access to reading and writing Twitter data, creating a new tweets, reading user profiles and follower data and much more.

Key strengths are the facts that this is an official Twitter release and, as such, it provides all information that can be obtained from Twitter itself. Also, all tools and services listed prior to this one are, in fact, relying on Twitter REST API – all that made it an attractive potential candidate for our use. Major weakness of the REST API is its limited number of allowed API calls (rate limiting).

3.6 Twitter Streaming APIs

The Streaming APIs are fundamentally different from REST API – they offer access to Twitter's global stream of public Tweets in real-time and they are suitable for following certain topics (hashtags, keywords etc.) or users and general data mining options. The ability to provide content in real-time without API rate limitations makes this approach very attractive for the needs of the #ask Dashboard. However, limited number of simultaneous connections and number of users who could be tracked at the same time can be considered to be major weaknesses of Twitter Streaming API.

3.7   Twitter Analytics

Twitter Analytics is an activity and analytics dashboard used to learn more about tweets, users and how they resonate with your audience. It shows how people interact with tweets in real-time, compares tweet activity and followers, and offers information about interests and infographics. It is, also, possible to export your own analytics in CSV format for further analysis on your own. However, it does not come with the API and thus renders itself inadequate for our Dashboard needs.

3.8   Klout and Klout API

Klout is a social media analytics tool, which ranks its users according to their online social influence and generates a Klout Score, which is a numerical value between 1 and 100. In determining the user score, Klout measures the size of a user's social media network and correlates the content created to measure how other users interact with that content and user itself.

Chief strengths of Klout are the ability to quantify various attributes of someones social media impact into a single metric. As such, it is an attractive and fairly broadly used metric to determine user influence. Additionally – it provides an API access to its functionalities. However, major identified weakness is the fact that API access is rate-limited and smart back-off mechanisms would need to be implemented.

4   The #ask Dashboard

The #ask Dashboard is based on the following APIs: *Twitter REST API, Twitter Streaming API* and *Klout API*. The #ask Dashboard itself serves two main purposes: (1) Brokering conversations between young people and policy makers and, (2) producing and distributing content.

4.1   Brokering Conversations

The primary goal of the #ask Dashboard is to broker conversations between young people and policy makers. The assumption is that the brokered conversation will bring greater value if the people conversing were already quite influenced on Twitter. Although people of lower influence are not excluded per se, the best results will be achieved with the top influencers.

For that reason, the #ask Dashboard allows the brokers to learn the influence of each Twitter user fed into the Dashboard. The influence score is calculated and pulled in from the Klout service (Fig. 1).

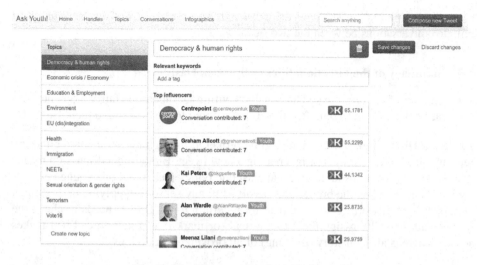

Fig. 1. The Klout score in #ask Dashboard

Next step is to define topics of interest. After identification of key influencers, their Twitter feed will contain various different topics and content - not all of which is going to be of interest to us. To solve that issue, we defined a number of topics of interest. Some of the topics we identified were: *Sexual orientation & gender equality; Economic crisis; NEETs*[1] *Inclusion & Participation (e.g. socio-economic, cultural); Immigration & Migration; Environment; Terrorism; Education & Employment; EU (dis)integration; Democracy & human rights; Health.*

Brokers will then look for the tweets that are related to one of the topics of interest. Once the tweet is found, the broker will be able to 'label' it with one of the topics, so that it will become tracked by the Dashboard.

Broker is then able to either reply to tweets, or compose new tweets while mentioning at least one person from both youth and policy makers. This is the first step in brokering a conversation that a broker can make, and it is the most direct way to initiate a communication. However, brokers will be free to find additional ways for the young people and policy makers to communicate, and as long as the initiative came from the broker, it can be considered a brokered conversation.

4.2 Content Production

The secondary goal of the #ask Dashboard is adjustment of content of certain policies to the young people and consolidation of their views and opinions. Infographics are considered as an effective tool for such role.

The Dashboard will only serve as storage library of the infographics. Broker will upload infographics in a Dashboard storage space, and then compose a tweet with a link

---

[1] NEETs stands for young persons who are "Not in Education, Employment, or Training".

to the infographic in it. This will drive the traffic towards our website, and may also initiate conversations between the two sides.

4.3   Summary of the Functionalities of the #ask Dashboard

While the set of features created and enabled within Dashboard is fairly large, here we summarize the most important functionalities tailored to the broker and their use cases.

Broker a Discussion. Discussions can be brokered through the Dashboard either by replying to an existing tweet or by creating a new tweet. Brokering a discussion means that the broker mentions in the tweet at least one policy maker and one young person's Twitter handle. When the broker gets involved in any sense (by replying or creating a new tweet), he is starting a new thread for a certain topic. Broker needs to check the replies and manually assign them to a thread (or mark it as a new thread if it makes sense). There is also a history (tracking) of all brokered discussions.

Import a Twitter Handle. The #ask Dashboard allows users to import Twitter handles (from young people and policy makers). Automatically, Klout scores will be updated for all imported handles – through Klout API (Fig. 2). Handles will be ordered by a custom algorithm where Klout score is just one of the factors, while others such as "how responsive to our brokerage the person is" are also included. Clicking a handle brings that person's Twitter feed.

Fig. 2. Importing Twitter Handles

Tag a Tweet. The #ask Dashboard also allows the creation and adding of labels to tweets. These labels are used to assign one of the topic categories to tweets (Fig. 3). Clicking a tag (or topic category) brings the Twitter feed from all youth and policy makers (mixed into a single stream of tweets).

Fig. 3. Tweets are tagged with one of the topics

View Statistics. Broker is able to keep an eye on various statistics using the Dashboard:

- *Keyword statistics* - the broker can add any keyword (or a hashtag) to a list, and from that point on track a number of indicators (e.g. how many tweets with this keyword, how many replies etc.)
- *User statistics* - the system automatically tracks indicators for all handles added
- *Thread statistics* - the system automatically tracks indicators for all threads

Upload Infographics. The #ask Dashboard is not used to create infographics. It is only used to compose tweets that contain a link to an already uploaded infographic. The infographics are then stored in and uploaded via Dashboard.

4.4   Architectural Overview

The architecture of the Dashboard (Fig. 4) is centered on the API built by ourselves. User interface is a web application Dashboard used by #ask brokers in order to identify relevant stakeholders, topics of interest and associated content (tweets). General functionality route (marked with red arrows) shows the backbone of the system: Web UI communicates with the API and then stores (or retrieves) the data from the database and renders it to the end user.

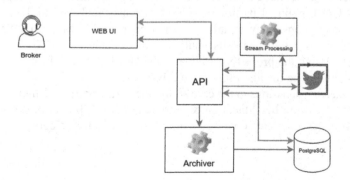

Fig. 4. The architecture of the #ask Dashboard (Color figure online)

Blue arrows are related to the streaming and content collection. API makes requests toward Twitter Streaming API and a processing occurs (filters are being applied, content is structured and delivered). Tweets are then further managed by our API, sent through the Archiver component and stored in the PostgreSQL database. From the database, tweets can be easily retrieved, further analyzed, aggregated and then served to brokers and users. Most of the entity connections are two-way which allows for greater flexibility and simplifies the entire process and development management efforts.

For the database of the architecture we relied on. We needed a solid, freely available and object-relational database and its associated management system. Database stores information about the collected tweets and topics associated with them. Also, information about handles and handle topics are collected, connected and saved. The front-end of the #ask Dashboard is written in Angular.js and Twitter Bootstrap framework was used to ensure familiarity with existing Twitter user interface and make the user experience efficient, easy to use and flexible.

5   A Case Study

In overall, the aim of the case study is to demonstrate and evaluate the use of the #ask Dashboard for brokering discussions between Greek policy makers and young people on Twitter. The content of the discussions is relevant to ten topic categories, i.e. Sexual orientation & gender equality; Economic crisis; NEETs' Inclusion & Participation (e.g. socio-economic, cultural); Immigration & Migration; Environment; Terrorism; Education & Employment; EU (dis)integration; Democracy & human rights; Health. In this section, we describe the achievements of the case study so far, as well as the results of this preliminary evaluation of the case study.

5.1   Achievements

So far, we discovered 74 Twitter handles of policy makers and 229 Twitter handles of young people, all of them active in Twitter and interested in the topic categories selected by the project. In particular, Twitter handles related to policy makers may regard Twitter accounts of Greek political parties or individual policy makers and Twitter handles related to young people may regard Twitter accounts of National Youth Councils, members of National Youth Councils, youth network organisations, NGOs or individual young people. Using the project's dashboard, the Greek pilot has brokered more than 275 discussions among the identified Twitter handles.

Most brokered discussions in the case study refer to democracy & human rights and to economic crisis with the education & employment topic being third in frequency. Figure 5 shows the full breakdown of the discussions per topic category.

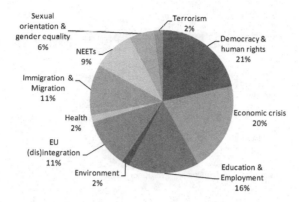

Fig. 5. Frequency of topics discussed in the Greek pilot

Overall, the case study achieved 367 replies, 15 retweets and 105 likes so far and in general replies are well structured. A high response rate from both target groups is observed, however, youth is in general more active than policy makers. Figure 6 presents a screenshot of a brokered discussion with eight replies.

Fig. 6. A brokered discussion

Nonetheless, the case study achieved to become popular and to be followed by high-profile politicians such as the vice president of the largest opposition party in Greece.

The percentages of the replies, retweets and likes of all topics are presented in Figs. 7, 8 and 9 respectively. As expected, most of the replies, retweets and likes regard tweets of the two most popular topic categories in the project i.e. democracy & human rights and economic crisis.

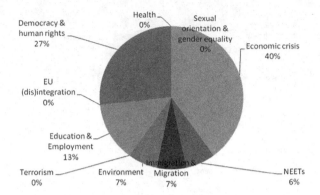

Fig. 7. Frequency of retweets of each topic in the Greek pilot

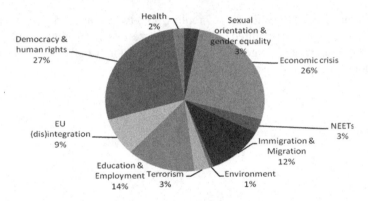

Fig. 8. Frequency of likes of each topic in the Greek pilot

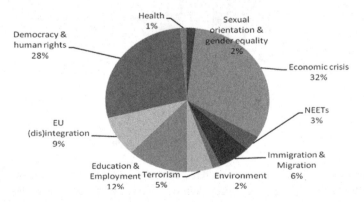

Fig. 9. Frequency of replies of each topic in the Greek pilot

5.2 Evaluation

A small focus group of six University students from Thessaloniki, Greece, followed #ask and interacted with youth and policy makers on Twitter for a month. The students evaluated #ask through an online questionnaire.

All respondents are between 22 and 24 years of age, all male and none of them affiliated with any student councils, youth chapters, institutions or NGOs. All of them hold a Twitter account but only one of them reported being a frequent user (using Twitter a few times per week). Two others use it once a month and the rest three hadn't used it for more than three months.

As regards their interaction online, only two out of six respondents use Twitter to discuss political issues and follow politicians and decision makers. The rest of them reported not using Twitter for discussing political issues. The most popular topics of interest were democracy and human rights, education, health, and youth employment issues. Figure 10 presents the popularity of each #ask topic among evaluation respondents.

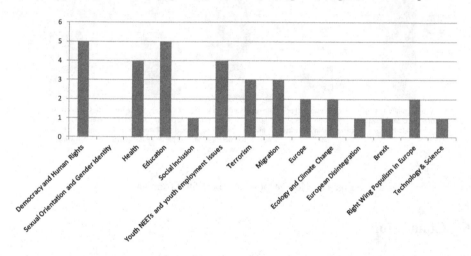

Fig. 10. Popularity of topics of interest among respondents

As regards their level of satisfaction, four out of six students reported being satisfied with the tweets' content on the topics of their interest and two reported a neutral reply. As regards Greek policy makers' Twitter presence, four out of six reported being satisfied and two dissatisfied. However, respondents were not that satisfied with the level of participation of young people from Greece and the level of interaction achieved between young people and policy makers: four reported a neutral answer and two dissatisfaction. Nonetheless, only one of the respondents appears to have been involved in brokered conversations with policy makers, whereas the majority (four out of six) prefers not to get into direct discussion with policy makers.

The majority (four out of six students) believe that the Twitter discussion brokering is inclusive, addressing also the interests of disadvantaged young people. However, respondents are sceptical whether the Twitter discussion brokering successfully reaches young people and policy makers: two students reported that brokering achieves this impact up to a certain extent, whereas the majority (four out of six) thinks that such an impact is not really achieved. Opinions are divided as regards the ability of the Twitter discussion brokering to create e-talks between youth and policy makers at local level: two support this ability, two do not support it and the rest two gave a neutral reply.

As regards how they benefited from the project, most replied that it gave them an opportunity to start active participation via Twitter. The full replies to this question are provided in Fig. 11. Most suggestions provided referred to increased promotion to the youth, e.g. through exploitation of existing youth channels, and increased direct involvement of policy makers, e.g. through involving a specific policy maker to tweet and reply for a short period of time.

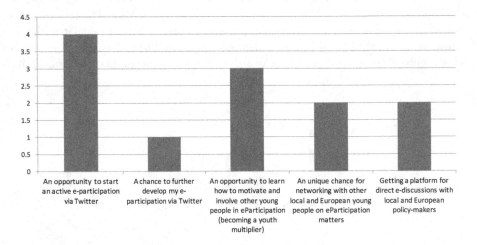

Fig. 11. How respondents benefited from #ask

6   Conclusion

The European Union Member States recognize that it is increasingly important for policy makers to be aware of young people's opinion. As a result they prioritize the discovery of new forms of participation in democratic processes and access to political decision-making through online and offline tools.

The aim of this paper was to demonstrate and evaluate the idea of promoting young people's participation in political decision-making by brokering discussions on Twitter. To achieve this objective we presented the #ask Dashboard, a software solution for brokering and analyzing discussions on Twitter between policy makers and young people, as well as a case study that utilizes and evaluates that Dashboard.

To implement the #ask Dashboard, 19 software applications for Twitter analytics were identified and analysed. The #ask Dashboard is based on three of them: Twitter REST API, Twitter Streaming API and Klout API. We used the #ask Dashboard to broker discussions between Greek policy makers and young people on Twitter. We identified Twitter handles of 74 policy makers and 229 young people interested in the selected topic categories. We brokered more than 275 discussions among the Twitter handles achieving 367 replies, 15 retweets and 105 likes mostly from young people. Our work was followed by high-profile politicians including the vice president of the largest opposition party in Greece. We must point out however that this politician is anyway very active in social media and particularly the use of Twitter. The evaluation was performed by six students who participated in the brokered discussions.

Overall, our preliminary results seem to be promising. First, from a technological perspective, this study helped us verify that the #ask Dashboard fully satisfies all its expected requirements. In addition, the study helped us verify that the selected topics are interesting for young people and to conclude that the most popular ones were (1) democracy and human rights, (2) education, (3) health, and (4) youth employment issues. Furthermore, our study gave young people the opportunity to be active on Twitter on political issues for the first time.

We believe that our initial results show that our work is one step closer towards connecting young people and policy makers on Twitter. However, we are still sceptical about the strategy that should be followed to ensure the successful brokering of discussions between the two sites. In the future we plan to search for additional strategies that will motivate young people as well as policy makers to participate in brokered discussions. For example, we plan to ask policy makers use the #ask Dashboard so as to learn their thoughts about it and provide some advice or best practices on how to become better conversation brokers. We will also investigate relevant literature to extract requirements, advices and best practices for making social media content viral.

Acknowledgments. The work presented in this paper was carried out in the course of the #ask[2] project [20], which is funded by the European Commission within the Erasmus+ Programme.

References

1. Eurostat. Youth in Europe: A Statistical Portrait (2009). http://pjp-eu.coe.int/documents/1017981/1668203/YouthinEurope.pdf/40f42295-65e4-407b-8673-95e97026da4a. Accessed July 2017
2. Snell, P.: Emerging adult civic and political disengagement: a longitudinal analysis of lack of involvement with politics. J. Adolesc. Res. **25**(2), 258–287 (2010)
3. European Commission. EU Strategy for Youth (2009). http://eur-lex.europa.eu/LexUriServ/LexUriServ.do?uri=COM:2009:0200:FIN:EN:PDF. Accessed July 2017
4. European Commission. Draft 2015 Joint Report of the Council and the Commission on the implementation of the renewed framework for European cooperation in the youth field (2015). http://eur-lex.europa.eu/legal-content/EN/TXT/PDF/?uri=CELEX:52015DC0429&from=EN. Accessed July 2017

---

[2] http://ask-project.eu/.

5. Skogerbø, E.: Everybody reads the newspaper: local newspapers in the digital age. In: Biernacka-Ligieza, I., Kocwin, L. (eds.) Local and Regional Media – Democracy and Civil Society Shaping Processes, Wydawnictwo MARIA, Nowa Ruda – Wrocław, pp. 357–373 (2011)

6. Enli, G.S., Skogerbø, E.: Personalized campaigns in party-centred politics: Twitter and Facebook as arenas for political communication. Inf. Commun. Soc. **16**(5), 757–774 (2013)

7. Effing, R., van Hillegersberg, J., Huibers, T.: Social media and political participation: are Facebook, Twitter and YouTube democratizing our political systems? In: Tambouris, E., Macintosh, A., de Bruijn, H. (eds.) ePart 2011. LNCS, vol. 6847, pp. 25–35. Springer, Heidelberg (2011). https://doi.org/10.1007/978-3-642-23333-3_3

8. Bonsón, E., Royo, S., Ratkai, M.: Citizens' engagement on local governments' facebook sites. An empirical analysis: the impact of different media and content types in western europe. Gov. Inf. Q. **32**(1), 52–62 (2015)

9. Hofmann, S., Beverungen, D., Räckers, M., Becker, J.: What makes local governments' online communications successful? Insights from a multi-method analysis of Facebook. Gov. Inf. Q. **30**(4), 387–396 (2013)

10. Bellström, P., Magnusson, M., Pettersson, J.S., Thorén, C.: Facebook usage in a local government: a content analysis of page owner posts and user posts. Transforming Gov. People Process Policy **10**(4), 548–567 (2016)

11. Andersen, K.N., Medaglia, R.: The use of Facebook in national election campaigns: politics as usual? In: Macintosh, A., Tambouris, E. (eds.) ePart 2009. LNCS, vol. 5694, pp. 101–111. Springer, Heidelberg (2009). https://doi.org/10.1007/978-3-642-03781-8_10

12. Robertson, S.P., Vatrapu, R.K., Medina, R.: The social life of social networks: Facebook linkage patterns in the 2008 US presidential election. In: Proceedings of the 10th Annual International Conference on Digital Government Research: Social Networks: Making Connections between Citizens, Data and Government, pp. 6–15. Digital Government Society of North America (2009)

13. Meijer, A.J., Torenvlied, R.: Social media and the new organization of government communications: an empirical analysis of Twitter usage by the Dutch police. Am. Rev. Publ. Admin. **46**(2), 143–161 (2016)

14. Park, M.J., Kang, D., Rho, J.J., Lee, D.H.: Policy role of social media in developing public trust: Twitter communication with government leaders. Publ. Manage. Rev. **18**(9), 1265–1288 (2016)

15. Kim, S.K., Park, M.J., Rho, J.J.: Effect of the Government's use of social media on the reliability of the Government: focus on Twitter. Publ. Manage. Rev. **17**(3), 328–355 (2015)

16. Kalampokis, E., Karamanou, A., Tambouris, E., Tarabanis, K.A.: On predicting election results using Twitter and Linked Open Data: the case of the UK 2010 Election. J. Univ. Comput. Sci. **23**(3), 280–303 (2017)

17. Oliveira, G., Welch, E.: Social media use in local government: linkage of technology, task, and organizational context. Gov. Inf. Q. **30**(4), 397–405 (2013)

18. Haro-de-Rosario, A., Sáez-Martín, A., del Carmen Caba-Pérez, M.: Using social media to enhance citizen engagement with local government: Twitter or Facebook? New Med. Soc., 1461444816645652 (2016)

19. Mossberger, K., Wu, Y., Crawford, J.: Connecting citizens and local governments? Social media and interactivity in major US cities. Gov. Inf. Q. **30**(4), 351–358 (2013)

20. Ruston McAleer, S., Panopoulou, E., Glidden, J., Tambouris, E., Tarabanis, K.: Augmenting social talk: the #ask Project. In: Parycek, P., Edelmann, N. (eds.) CeDEM16 Proceedings of the International Conference for E-Democracy and Open Government 2016, Edition Donau-Universität Krems, pp. 61–67, 18–20 May 2016. Danube University Krems, Austria (2016). ISBN 978-3-902505-81-1

Electronic Identity Authentication

Electronic Authentication for University Transactions Using eIDAS

Konstantinos Gerakos, Michael Maliappis[✉], Constantina Costopoulou, and Maria Ntaliani

Informatics Laboratory, Department of Agricultural Economics and Rural Development, Agricultural University of Athens, 75 Iera Odos, 118 55 Athens, Greece
kostisgerakos@gmail.com, {michael,tina,ntaliani}@aua.gr

Abstract. The lack of a comprehensive European Union cross-border and cross-sector framework for secure, easy-to-use and authenticated electronic transactions has led to the electronic IDentification and Authentication Services (eIDAS) Regulation. This can be applied to student mobility programs that require authentication. The main objective of this article is to describe the connection of existing student services of the Agricultural University of Athens to the national eIDAS node. It describes the working progress of the connection of the Erasmus exchange student identification service to the node. Specifically, the upgrade of the existing service processes and the development of automated Web services based and compatible with the eIDAS Regulation are presented. These Web services speed up the process of student identification and facilitate uploading of documents needed for registration.

Keywords: Security · Identification · Authentication · Erasmus program

1 Introduction

Throughout the world, governmental organizations are upgrading their Information Technology (IT) systems to provide automated processes to the public, as well as to their collaborators nationwide. Cross-border applications have been proven vital for citizens and businesses that are transacting transnationally, but still problems of compatibility occur at the level of user authentication in the form of transnational services [1]. The European Commission (EC) has acknowledged the problem of not having a "comprehensive EU cross-border and cross-sector framework for secure, trustworthy and easy-to-use electronic transactions that encompasses electronic identification and trust services" [2, 3]. EC has issued the EU 910/2014 Regulation on electronic IDentification and Authentication Services (eIDAS), which sets standards for secure certification services for all citizens of the European Union (EU) member states [4].

In this direction, a European initiative entitled as "Transformation of Greek e-Gov Services to eIDAS cross-border Services" has been established. The initiative started in 2017 and will be completed in the following year. It aims at connecting existing Greek public services to the Greek eIDAS node. It will integrate the following groups of services: government services for business and citizens, healthcare and social security related

© Springer International Publishing AG 2017
S.K. Katsikas and V. Zorkadis (Eds.): E-Democracy 2017, CCIS 792, pp. 187–195, 2017.
https://doi.org/10.1007/978-3-319-71117-1_13

services and academia and research services in partner Universities. To reach this objective, this initiative will firstly adapt the above services to be integrated with eIDAS, in order to be able to request, receive and process the new set of identification data received from the eIDAS node under the eIDAS Regulation; and secondly connect services to eIDAS node to allow for cross-border authentication. Finally, it will support Greece in meeting the requirements of the eIDAS Regulation and will facilitate access to Greek public e-services for all EU citizens and businesses using their national electronic identification (eID), and thus ensure cross-border mobility and support and strengthen the Digital Single Market. This initiative can be applied to student mobility programs that require authentication, such as the Erasmus student mobility program.

In recent years, more than 4,000 higher education institutions are participating in Erasmus program across 37 countries. There is an increasing interest from the EC to provide electronic support services for the participants. Recently, there has been an EC call for proposals on projects regarding common interests under the Connecting Europe Facility (CEF) in the field of trans-European Telecommunication Networks, including the Erasmus program authentication through eIDAS. Examples of European initiatives for providing support for student mobility are the following: "Field trial on the impact of enabling easy mobility on recognition of external studies" (Emrex), trying to bring a solution for electronic transferring of students' records by allowing the student to initiate the process; and "Erasmus without Paper" (EWP), providing application programming interfaces (APIs) that can be invoked by any institution in order to push or receive data. However, among the objectives of both initiatives is the use of eID for identification of exchange students and the complications that may arise from this process due to different national backgrounds.

This article presents an ongoing research that describes the connection of existing services of the Agricultural University of Athens (AUA) to the national eIDAS node regarding the Erasmus exchange students' certification service at collaborating universities. It is investigated whether the use of the student national eID through eIDAS facilitates the existing registration process. Furthermore, a system design for supporting the Erasmus exchange students' services is presented.

The structure of the paper is organized as follows: Sect. 2 gives an overview of the eIDAS Regulation. In Sect. 3, the AUA Erasmus Office processes for authenticating exchange students from EU universities, as well as the problems encountered by the existing information system are presented. Section 4 proposes a Web service based on the eIDAS authentication for facilitating the enrollment of Erasmus exchange students. Finally, the conclusions are drawn in the last section.

2   eIDAS Regulation

In 2014, EC established a regulation on eID seeking to enhance trust in electronic transactions [4]. eIDAS has replaced the Electronic Signatures Directive, contributing to the development of specific applications. It addresses citizens from different countries and gives guidance on how to use the national eID of their countries of origin by government agencies (i.e. ministries, universities, institutions) in other member countries. The eIDAS Regulation refers to two distinct subjects. Firstly, it describes a system of cross-border mutual recognition of eID schemes used in member countries for accessing online public services. Upon its implementation, a European citizen from one country will be enabled to use his/her eID for accessing public services in another country. Secondly, eIDAS Regulation provides a common legal framework for trust services, containing common provisions related to electronic signatures, electronic seals, electronic time stamps, electronic registered mail and Web authentication.

The implementation of the eIDAS is based on geographically dispersed servers among the EU countries that make up the eIDAS nodes. An eIDAS node is described as an operational entity involved in cross-border authentication of citizens, according to the interoperability architecture of eIDAS [5]. It can support different roles:

- *eIDAS Connector:* an eIDAS node requesting a cross-border authentication; and
- *eIDAS Service:* an eIDAS node providing cross-border authentication, which could be either proxy based or middleware based.

In 2015, the Commission Implementing Regulation (EU) 2015/1502 defined a set of criteria in order to categorize a technical implementation of eIDAS based services according to three Levels of Assurance (LoA), as follows:

- *Low*: identity evidence is assumed to be genuine. There is no further verification of the provided credentials.
- *Substantial*: verification of identity evidence is based on recognized evidence.
- *High*: physical appearance is required and a verified possession of valid identity evidence is needed.

In the following, an eIDAS identification process scenario is given (Fig. 1):

1. A user, who initially originates from country B, chooses to use an online public service from country A.
2. The user is connected to the eIDAS Connector of country A to obtain authentication.
3. The eIDAS Connector node of country A communicates with the eIDAS Service node of country B, using the parameters provided by the user.
4. The eIDAS Service node of country B decides upon the identification contacting the national identity provider. Upon successful identification, the user can use online public services in country A.

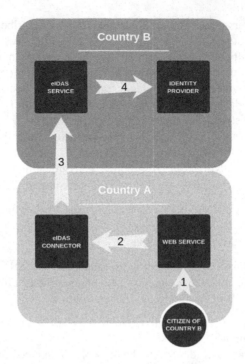

Fig. 1. An eIDAS identification process scenario

The results of the identification return to the Web service following the reverse route.

3   AUA Erasmus Office Processes

This section briefly describes the process followed by an Erasmus exchange student for getting authentication in AUA services (e.g. course enrollment, course attendance). AUA participates in the Erasmus program and it has accepted hundreds of exchange students. The usual process for an exchange student of a collaborating university to participate in the Erasmus program at AUA involves filling an application with a list of the courses he/she wishes to attend, and which must correspond to courses in his/her department's curriculum and submitting attestations to the competent services. Exchange students wishing to attend AUA courses should be identified by the AUA Erasmus Office and should be given a student identity card.

This process is complex, as the corresponding services of the Erasmus Offices of the collaborating universities require additional attestations and applications, which are often incompatible with those issued by the Greek state. In addition, the successful attendance of courses is certified with the submission of the grades by the AUA teaching staff. The collaborating university requires specific papers issued by the relevant departments of the AUA. These papers are provided by the AUA Erasmus Office. The existing process involves time-consuming and complicated actions that are distinct and differ from one university to another. An information system could simplify some of these processes, but it would encounter additional difficulties, as demonstrated in the next section.

3.1 Course Enrollment Use Case

This section presents a use case that depicts the process of an exchange student's enrollment in a course provided by the AUA. This use case corresponds to the situation prior to the eIDAS-based approach. The student applies and chooses one or more courses offered by the AUA that are in accordance with his/her curriculum in the university of origin. The AUA Erasmus Office may approve or reject applications. Similarly, the Erasmus Office at his/her university abroad may approve or reject applications. Finally, the AUA Erasmus Office is responsible for communicating the student's grade to his/her university of origin. Below, the steps for the existing course enrollment process are described:

1. *Student nomination*: the collaborating university sends a list of nominated students to participate in the Erasmus program.
2. *Collection of documents:* AUA Erasmus Office receives all the necessary paperwork and applications either in print or electronic form.
3. *User Registration:* the exchange student provides all the necessary identity information and the AUA Erasmus Office identifies and registers him/her, providing credentials (username and password).
4. *User Login*: the user connects to AUA online services. The usual way is through the credentials assigned by the AUA Erasmus Office.
5. *Selection of courses:* the user selects the courses he/she wants to attend. The courses to be chosen are dynamically recovered based on the student's origin department.
6. *Validation of courses:* the AUA Erasmus Office validates the courses the student has chosen and informs the relevant Department Secretariat.
7. *Completion of studies:* when the exchange student graduates the AUA Erasmus Office sends his/her grades to the corresponding Office at the collaborating university.

The aforementioned process presents certain limitations that make the automation difficult. The most important limitations are:

- The identification of exchange students requires the involvement of the pertinent official employee.
- Upon completion of the exchange student's studies, the grades that will be sent to the collaborating university should also be validated.

4 AUA eIDAS Based Web Services

Previously, the process of an exchange student's course enrollment within the framework of the Erasmus program has been outlined. In this section, the above limitations will be resolved using eIDAS-compliant services. Specifically, AUA trying to optimize the process and upgrade the existing services, intends to develop Web services compatible with the EU eIDAS Regulation. Web services will use eIDAS standards for the following activities:

- *User authentication:* any EU citizen will be able to authenticate and access the services via his/her local Service Provider.
- *Electronic signatures:* by using electronic signatures with eIDAS standards, AUA tries to improve trust of existing services [6].

4.1   Erasmus Student Mobility Service

Using the eIDAS approach we present a use case that addresses the problems described in the previous section. Moreover, the AUA Erasmus Office will no longer be responsible for the exchange students' identification and authentication, since the process will be automated. The process is distinguished for two different actors. The first actor regards an employee of the student mobility Office of the university of origin, who is in charge of providing a list of nominated students. The second actor is an Erasmus exchange student. The steps followed by the employee in order to provide a list of nominated students are described below:

1. The employee accesses the AUA Erasmus Web portal, logs in and submits a list of nominated students.
2. For every nominated student the portal requests student information and official documents.
3. The portal redirects the information in the Web service of the AUA Erasmus Web portal in order to store it in its database.
4. The Web service prepares a minimum of personal attributes for every student, namely Family Name, Given Name, and Date of Birth, in order to prepare the identification process.

The steps followed by an Erasmus exchange student in order to enroll in a course in AUA are described below (Fig. 2):

1. The student visits the AUA Erasmus Web portal (Erasmus Student Information System) and logs in providing the eIDAS credentials acquired from his/her country of origin.
2. The portal redirects his/her request for login in the Web service of the AUA Erasmus Web portal to grant permission to registered users.
3. The Web service recognizes that the student has provided the eIDAS credentials and contacts the eIDAS node that confirms the eIDAS registered users.
4. Upon confirmation from the eIDAS node, the Web service grants access to AUA Erasmus Web portal. In case the student logs in for the first time the Web service creates a local account in correspondence with the student's eIDAS account.
5. The student enrolls in the course that he/she wants to attend and the selections are saved in the database of the AUA Erasmus Web portal.
6. AUA Erasmus Office is notified on the student registration and accepts, modifies or rejects the registration.

7. Upon the completion of the student's studies the AUA Erasmus Office sends his/her
   grades to the corresponding Office at the university of origin digitally signed.

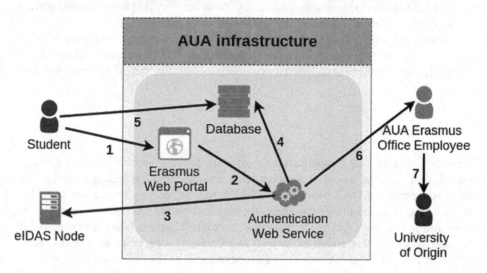

Fig. 2. AUA eIDAS student enrollment service

4.2 Authentication Web Service

AUA plans to deploy several Web services in order to support the enrollment service
from the employee of the student mobility Office side and the Erasmus exchange student
side. The most important Web service is the Authentication Web Service (AWS), which
will provide identification for exchange students and is described in technical detail
below.

AWS sends messages to the national eIDAS Identification Provider (IdP) in Security
Assertion Markup Language (SAML) format and receives success or failure messages,
allowing or denying access accordingly for the exchange students. In order to avoid
access from non-nominated individuals, the AWS has a predefined list of student attributes provided by the corresponding university. Specifically, the list will be populated
automatically from the information given and will contain three mandatory attributes:
Family Name, Given Name and Date of Birth, which are defined in eIDAS SAML
attribute profile.

The authentication process is accomplished using AWS. The student provides
his/her credentials (username and password), and the AWS service forms the appropriate
SAML request to the eIDAS node. Upon confirmation of the student identity from the
national IdP, the three mandatory attributes return augmented with the Unique Identifier
(UID). After the first authentication: (a) the UID is stored in the local database of the
AUA Erasmus Web portal in order to make the next access requests quicker; and (b) for
each student the three mandatory attributes are compared with the ones provided by his/
her university of origin and the student will be asked to fulfill the rest of the mandatory
attributes so as AWS accepts the student.

The level of assurance of the technical implementation of AUA Erasmus Web portal can be characterized as substantial, since it requires a two-step authentication. Every new user has to be verified upon the mandatory attributes provided from a trusted partner (i.e. university of origin) and then authenticated from a national IdP.

Additionally, AWS by implementing eIDAS, offers security and protection of students' personal data. According to previous studies, eIDAS offers by default strong cryptographic capabilities and defensive mechanisms for the most common web attacks [7].

5   Conclusion

The adoption of eIDAS authentication in software development facilitates the implementation of systems aimed at authenticating transnational agreements, such as the Erasmus program. eIDAS provides a solution to citizens' authentication from EU member states and simplifies the processes required by the information systems. As mentioned in literature, the major challenge that eIDAS approach has to face is its full adoption by all member countries, as well as its general acceptance by citizens [8, 9]. Currently, most of the eIDAS nodes in European member states are in a pilot phase.

Regarding the eIDAS for Erasmus exchange students, the AUA proposes a AWS service. This will be used for the simplification of the existing identification process for Erasmus students. The particular Web service can support the authentication of student enrollment, namely to accept a student and import his/her information into the AUA database. AUA will be considered as a responsible public agency for students' certification and identification.

In future AUA intends to utilize the eIDAS standards for electronic signatures for official documents, such as the student supplement diploma. According to the eIDAS Regulation, electronic signatures can be categorized as "qualified" or "advanced" based on their acceptance by other EU member states. The "qualified" electronic signature has the equivalent legal effect of a handwritten signature [3]. In this light, AUA intends to speed up administrative processes by providing Web services to users to digitally sign documents using "qualified" electronic signature.

Acknowledgement. This work has been partially supported by the Innovation and Networks Executive Agency of the European Commission with no: 2015-EL-IA-0083 entitled "Transformation of Greek e-Gov Services to eIDAS cross-border Services".

References

1. Sideridis, A.B., Protopappas, L., Tsiafoulis, S., Pimenidis, E.: Smart cross-border e-gov systems and applications. In: Katsikas, S.K., Sideridis, A.B. (eds.) e-Democracy 2015. CCIS, vol. 570, pp. 151–165. Springer, Cham (2015). https://doi.org/10.1007/978-3-319-27164-4_11
2. Cuijpers, C.M.K.C., Schroers, J.: eIDAS as guideline for the development of a pan European eID framework in FutureID (2014)

3. European Union (2014). "Wording taken from the explanatory memorandum of eIDAS". http://eurlex.europa.eu/legal-content/EN/TXT/?uri=CELEX:52012PC0238
4. The European Parliament and the Council of the European Union: Regulation (EU) No 910/2014 of the European Parliament and of the Council of 23 July 2014 on electronic identification and trust services for electronic transactions in the internal market and repealing Directive 1999/93/EC, July 2014
5. Joinup collaborative platform: eIDAS – Interoperability Architecture. Version 1.00, November 2015
6. Hermann, S., Wefel, S.: Challenging eID & eIDAS at University Management. Open Identity Summit (2016)
7. Morgner, F., Bastian, P., Fischlin, M.: Securing transactions with the eIDAS protocols. In: Foresti, S., Lopez, J. (eds.) WISTP 2016. LNCS, vol. 9895, pp. 3–18. Springer, Cham (2016). https://doi.org/10.1007/978-3-319-45931-8_1
8. Stasis, A., Kalogirou, V., Tsiafoulis, S.: Generic services for cross domain use in e-government. In: Sideridis, A., Kardasiadou, Z., Yialouris, C., Zorkadis, V. (eds.) e-Democracy, Security, Privacy and Trust in a Digital World, vol. 441, pp. 64–72. Springer, Cham (2014). https://doi.org/10.1007/978-3-319-11710-2_6
9. Strack, H., et al.: eID & eIDAS at University Management-Chances and Changes for Security & legally binding in cross boarder Digitalization. http://www.eunis.org/eunis2017/wp-content/uploads/sites/10/2017/06/EUNIS_2017_paper_33.pdf

The FICEP Infrastructure
How We Deployed the Italian eIDAS Node in the Cloud

Paolo Smiraglia[1(✉)], Marco De Benedictis[1(✉)], Andrea Atzeni[1(✉)],
Antonio Lioy[1(✉)], and Massimiliano Pucciarelli[2(✉)]

[1] Dip. Automatica e Informatica, Politecnico di Torino, Torino, Italy
{paolo.smiraglia,marco.debenedictis,andrea.atzeni,antonio.lioy}@polito.it
[2] Agenzia per l'Italia Digitale (AgID), Roma, Italy
pucciarelli@agid.gov.it

Abstract. The EU Regulation No 910/2014 imposes to each EU Member State to notify its electronic identification scheme and to recognize the ones notified by the other Member States by 29 September 2018. In this process, Italy will notify SPID, an authentication scheme that allows citizens and business entities to access online services provided by the public administration and private bodies with a unique set of credentials. Technological and operational aspects related to the infrastructure that will allow the SPID notification represent the core business of the FICEP project. This paper offers an overview of the *architectural* and *technological* aspects that made possible the deployment of the FICEP architecture in the cloud.

Keywords: eIDAS Regulation · Federated authentication · Cloud computing

1 Introduction

The European Commission places digitalisation of public utility services at the core of its innovation strategy. The so-called *Digital Single Market* [5] is one of the ten priorities of the European digital agenda, since it addresses the increasing demand for trust and security and supports simplicity and convenience, regulating and integrating the EU Member State business landscapes. The Digital Single Market implementation lies on two building blocks. The former, referred as *electronic IDentification* (eID), ensures that people and businesses can use their own national electronic identification schemes to access public services in other EU countries where eIDs are available. The latter, referred as *electronic Trust Services* (eTS), includes electronic signatures, electronic seals, time stamp, electronic delivery service, and website authentication, while ensuring that they will work across borders and have the same legal status as traditional paper-based processes.

Historically, EU countries implemented these two building blocks separately, considering specific national requirements. While some international standards

S.K. Katsikas and V. Zorkadis (Eds.): E-Democracy 2017, CCIS 792, pp. 196–210, 2017.
https://doi.org/10.1007/978-3-319-71117-1_14

successfully evolved (e.g. SAML for eID) and were widely adopted in many EU states, still each country introduced differences in rules and local implementation (e.g. using smart-cards rather than mobile devices for authentication). At EU level this is a blocking obstacle for the development of cross-border electronic services. To remove this barrier, while not disrupting the previously deployed infrastructures, the EU Regulation no. 910/2014, also known as the *eIDAS Regulation*, enables eID and trust services transnational interoperability, making the cross-border interfaces homogeneous and consistent among different nations.

Following the publication of the *eIDAS Regulation Implementing Act* (Commission Implementing Regulation 2015/1501), the *eIDAS Technical Subgroup* has defined an interoperability architecture [7], which is strongly bound to the outcomes of the project *Secure idenTity acrOss boRders linKed* (STORK) [30]. Such architecture defines the eID interoperability infrastructure as a network of national gateways, named *eIDAS-Node* (successor of the STORK PEPS) that shall be implemented by each Member State. The gateway represents the central point of each country's eID infrastructure, and all transactions involving electronic identity pass through this component. Furthermore, the regulation requires that each state notifies at least one eID system.

Italy will implement the eIDAS Regulation by notifying the *Sistema Pubblico di Identità Digitale* (SPID) [29] as national identification scheme for providing cross-border authentication. Moreover, the Italian gateway will be deployed and adapted to the SPID infrastructure. Such activities have been defined in the context of the EU project *First Italian Cross-border eIDAS Proxy Service* (FICEP) [10]. The rationale and the motivations, as well as the design and technical aspects regarding the deployment of the infrastructure, represent the core topics of this paper, and can serve as a reference for other countries on their way to eIDAS implementation and compliance.

The rest of the paper is structured as follows. Section 2 presents an architectural overview of the FICEP infrastructure, comprising the national eIDAS-Node and the additional components required for the adaptation to the SPID authentication scheme. In Sect. 3, a set of requirements for the implementation of this architecture is proposed, resulting in the designs of a cloud platform for the deployment of its components. Section 4 addresses the specific technologies adopted for the implementation of such platform. Section 5 presents the related work and finally, open points to be addressed in a future iteration of the platform's deployment are highlighted in Sect. 6, along with the authors' conclusions.

2   Architectural Overview

In federated authentication terminology, *Service Provider* (SP) is a system that provides a service to its users, typically after a preliminary authentication phase. *Identity Provider* (IDP) is a system capable of identifying users and asserting to a third party that their credentials (and, optionally, additional information) are known by the system. *Attribute Provider* (AP) is a system which is capable of providing and asserting the possession of some end user attributes to a third party. In the traditional federated identity scheme, a SP requests authentication for a specific user to a IDP, which is in charge of validating the user's credentials. Optionally, the IDP may reply with user data, if relevant for the service provisioning. Furthermore, data may be collected by one (or more) AP in case the IDP is not capable of providing such information.

SPID authentication adopts the architecture of the traditional federated identity scheme. Different SPs, belonging to either the *Public Administration* (PA) or the *Private Sector* (PS), may allow Italian citizens to authenticate to various services by using a unique set of credentials, issued by one of the accredited IDPs of the infrastructure. APs are not currently active in SPID, but this role is already defined in the platform's specification.

Besides SP, IDP and AP, eIDAS introduces the role of eIDAS-Node as centralised gateway/proxy that allows the interactions between national and foreign entities. All the national gateways establish amongst them a *circle of trust* based on the bilateral exchange of *trust anchors* (e.g. X509 certificates). The eIDAS-Node is composed of two independent modules: the eIDAS-Proxy-Service and the eIDAS-Connector. The former *provides* cross-border authentication for the citizens of the implementing Member State by interfacing with the national IDPs and APs. The latter, eIDAS-Connector, *requests* cross-border authentication for foreign users accessing a SP in the implementing Member State. The FICEP infrastructure extends the core functionalities of the eIDAS-Node with additional modules that connect the gateway with the SPID environment.

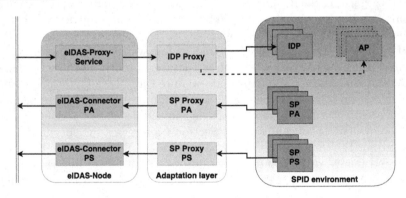

Fig. 1. The FICEP architecture.

As in Fig. 1, the FICEP infrastructure provides two different eIDAS-Connector instances that differentiate between SPs belonging to the Public Administration or the Private Sector. This solution has been implemented to allow, for each context, an independent management process. Although the SPs accreditation will be managed by a national agency, the connectors could be operated by different entities. For instance, the Public Administration eIDAS-Connector could be hosted on governmental premises, while the Private Sector one by an external entity (e.g. from industry). Despite the architectural similarities, the core components of the SPID architecture (namely the SPID SPs and IDPs) and the eIDAS-Node are not interoperable as is, because of the incompatible formats of their authentication protocols, implemented through different profiles of the *Security Assertion Markup Language 2.0* (SAML 2.0) [39]. The FICEP architecture addresses this incompatibility by introducing an adaptation layer composed of two additional proxies, named *SP Proxy* and *IDP Proxy*, to map the information carried by the protocols in between the eIDAS-Node and the SPID SPs and IDPs.

SP Proxy consists of a gateway that interfaces the Italian eIDAS-Connector with multiple SPID SPs. It logically serves as a eIDAS SP for the eIDAS-Connector, and as a SPID IDP for the multiple SPID SPs connected to FICEP. It enables Italian SPs to authenticate foreign users trying to access their services, by routing the authentication request to the eIDAS-Node of the user's Member State. As depicted in Fig. 1, each SP sector (i.e. PA, PS) is assigned to a specific SP Proxy, which will route authentication requests to the proper eIDAS-Connector. IDP Proxy consists of a gateway that interfaces the Italian eIDAS-Proxy-Service with multiple SPID IDPs. It logically serves as a eIDAS IDP for the eIDAS-Proxy-Service, and as a SPID SP towards the multiple IDPs available in the country. It enables foreign SPs to authenticate Italian citizens trying to access their services, by routing the authentication request to the SPID IDP that issued the user's credentials. An important aspect of the adaptation is the attributes management. Despite both eIDAS and FICEP distinguish between natural and legal person attributes, the number of the available attributes and the way to request them differentiate in the two domains. In SPID the available attributes are seventeen and they are requested by referring one of the groups (pre-defined list of attributes) defined and advertised by the selected IDP. Differently, eIDAS defines eighteen attributes, which are retrieved by directly specifying them in the requests. Another difference is that in eIDAS requests the attributes can be *mandatory* or *optional* while in SPID, they are always *mandatory*. Furthermore, eIDAS defines also the concept of *minimum dataset* for each attributes category, which is not defined in SPID. All of these differences caused the implementation of temporary adaptation strategy that will be updated according to the evolution of eIDAS and SPID. In the current implementation, only the eIDAS attributes composing the minimum datasets (always mandatory) are mapped to SPID attributes and the SPID IDPs have to define and advertise a set of attribute groups that match the eIDAS minimum datasets.

3   Cloud Platform Design

According to the NIST definition, cloud computing is a model for enabling ubiquitous, convenient, on-demand network access to a shared pool of configurable computing resources that can be rapidly provisioned and released with minimal management effort or service provider interaction [37]. FICEP is a critical infrastructure that operates at the national level. It allows Italian citizens to access European services by using their own national credentials and vice-versa. The cross-border authentication is a process that can occasionally require a significant amount of resources. Therefore, having a cloud architecture as a baseline for the FICEP platform represents a fundamental aspect. The following section describes how FICEP was implemented as a cloud platform, by detailing the design principles and the security requirements that have driven the deploy, and by presenting an overview of the architectural choices.

3.1   Principles and Requirements

The design development considered five main principles. (*Scalability*) The cloud architecture should be composed of small and task-specific computational units to have a modular infrastructure with a high level of granularity. Thus, it can scale dynamically according to the needs. (*Replicability*) The infrastructure should be replicable independently from the underlying layers. This makes possible the deployment of identical and parallel environments (e.g. development, staging, production) to support staged development. Furthermore, it allows different organisations to re-use the same solution to deploy their infrastructure. (*Coherence*) To have a unified and centralised management of the configurations, each computational unit should be based on the same operating system, and units performing the same task should use the same software stack. (*Efficiency*) Use open-source and community supported solutions to avoid *"re-inventing the wheel"* and to focus the effort on *"trying to make the wheel better"*. (*Measurability*) The deployment of a cloud-based infrastructure is a continuous process that may require several refinement phases. The possibility to measure accurately chosen indicators in the infrastructure is a key feature to implement an efficient allocation of the needed resources.

The deployment has been executed by considering four security requirements. (*Hardening*) To reduce the attack surface and minimise the risk of security threats, the computational units should be based on a minimal and hardened software stack. (*Isolation*) In case of a security breach, the attack propagation must be prevented. Therefore, all the environment should be properly isolated and only the strictly required ingress and egress communications should be allowed. (*Administrative audit*) A user with administrative access has full powers on the infrastructure. Therefore, administrators should be given access only after strong authentication. Furthermore, all the administrative accesses should be monitored to audit the administrators' activity. (*Minimal exposure*) Each publicly exposed service is a potential source of attack for the whole infrastructure. Therefore, only the front-end services (e.g. load balancers) should be accessible from the Internet. Back-end services like databases or caching systems should be available only on the local intranet, or via secure channels implemented with VPN technologies like IPSec.

3.2   Platform Overview

According to isolation and minimal exposure requirements, the FICEP platform (see Fig. 2) is a three-tier architecture that exposes the web applications allowing the cross-border authentication as described in the eIDAS regulation. We refer the three tiers with the names *front*, *middle* and *back*. The front tier represents the De-Militarised Zone of the architecture and contains all the instances that expose public services. In particular, the front tier includes a *bastion host* to obtain administrative access to the infrastructure and the *load balancers* to balance the traffic towards the FICEP applications, which are executed on the application servers hosted in the middle tier. Finally, the back tier contains all the instances running the infrastructure management and monitoring components.

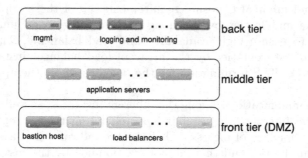

Fig. 2. The FICEP platform.

All the instances composing the FICEP infrastructure are remotely manageable via *Secure SHell* (SSH) protocol. W.r.t. the minimal exposure requirement and to reduce the number of public IP addresses to be allocated within the virtual data centre, all the instances are reachable through a bastion host as depicted in Fig. 3. In particular, when an administrator needs access to an instance, he/she performs a first authentication on the bastion host. Then, if successful, the bastion host forwards the access request towards the target instance where the administrator is authenticated again. Besides the minimal exposure, this architecture also meet the administrative auditing requirement. In particular, having a single point of access to the infrastructure allows the implementation of a centralised auditing system to track the administrators' activity (e.g. SSH session tracking [13]). Furthermore, it simplifies the management of the administrative accesses. For instance, the exclusion of a specific administrator should disable only his/her account on the bastion host. In FICEP architecture, the authentication on the bastion host and the target instance are performed by relying on *public key authentication* mechanism. This approach mitigates threats related to the intrinsic weakness of password-based authentication mechanisms (e.g. short and easily guessable passwords).

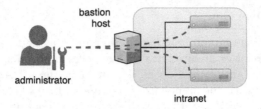

Fig. 3. SSH bastion host architecture.

As presented in Sect. 2, the FICEP platform is composed of applications implementing the eIDAS-Node (developed by Connecting Europe Facility group) and applications implementing the adaptation layer between eIDAS and SPID (developed by FICEP partners). By considering the scalability principle and the isolation and minimal exposure requirements, all of these applications are deployed in the middle tier by spawning each application on multiple application servers to ensure high availability and load balancing. These features are managed in the front tier by the array of load balancer instances, which also implement the TLS termination for the domains where the application are reachable.

The local communications among the different instances, as well as the access to and from the Internet, are regulated by relying on the concept of *security group*. It represents a set of ingress and egress firewall rules that are enforced at the infrastructural level, and that cannot be modified by the instances. W.r.t. the isolation requirement, each instance of the FICEP infrastructure has a specific task and for each of them we defined a specific security group. To identify both the flows that must be allowed among the different instance types and consequently the rules to be included within each security groups, we followed a matrix based approach where each intersection represents an allowed flow. For the sake of clarity, Fig. 4 presents a simple matrix to determine the firewall rules between load balancer (LB), HTTP server (WWW) and database (DB) instances. In particular, we can see that LB instances are allowed to initiate a communication only with WWW instances over the 8080 port while WWW instances only with DB instances over 3306 port.

from / to	LB	WWW	DB
LB	x	8080	x
WWW	x	x	3306
DB	x	x	x

Fig. 4. Example of security groups matrix.

The measurability of the FICEP infrastructure is supported by the infrastructure schema depicted in Fig. 5. In particular, the infrastructure manages log entries by implementing the *publish/subscribe* messaging pattern where the *producers* (messages senders) publish messages on a *broker* that dispatches them to all the subscribed *consumers* (messages readers). In the FICEP logging infrastructure, the producer is represented by the *log shipper*, a small module installed on each computational unit, which is in charge of sending the local log entries towards the *log broker*, which is implemented as a *queue*. The queue consumer is represented by the *log indexer*, a component in charge of fetching the log entries from the queue and storing them on a persistent back-end (*log storage*) after the execution of some analysis or transformations (e.g. anonymisation of sensitive data). Finally, the collected information related to applications or to the whole architecture can be accessed via the *log viewer*, typically in the form of web dashboard.

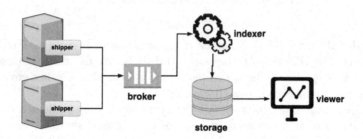

Fig. 5. The FICEP logging infrastructure.

W.r.t. the replicability principle, the deployment of the whole FICEP architecture is managed by following a declarative pattern, where the focus is on *"what has to do"* and not *"how it has to do"*. In particular, by relying on specific tools and frameworks, we described the whole environment by using a *high level* and *human readable* languages, which are entirely *manageable as code* and then integrable in automated processes. This management pattern allows us to deploy the same infrastructure in multiple environments, being sure the result will be every time the same. For instance, to support a multi-staged development of the applications, the same "recipe" could be used to create three identical and parallel infrastructures representing the *development, staging* and *production* environments.

4   Technological Aspects

The technological solution presented in this paper is not the only viable way to implement a national eIDAS-Node. Indeed, used tools and frameworks were selected by considering the architecture and the principles defined in Sect. 3, the compatibility with the technology inherited by other activities (e.g. *SPC Cloud* [28]) and by past projects (e.g. STORK) and finally, the skill set already available in the FICEP consortium. The technology behind the FICEP platform

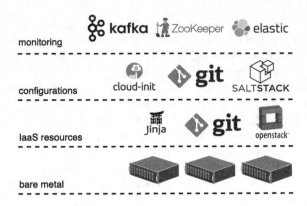

Fig. 6. The FICEP technological stack.

can be analysed by considering a stack composed of four layers (see Fig. 6), each one grouping a specific set of frameworks and tools. We use this organisation to allow the reader in identifying which parts can be reused in his/her environment and which are the underlying requirements.

The bare metal layer includes all the technologies that allow a cloud service provider to offer its customers a set of cloud-based services, for instance, *Infrastructure-as-as-Service* (IaaS). In the context of the FICEP architecture, the management of this layer is outside the scope. Therefore, its technological aspects will be not included in the current analysis.

4.1 Management of IaaS Resources

The FICEP infrastructure is built on top of a set of IaaS resources provided via *OpenStack* [22]. The latter is an open-source cloud operating system that controls large pools of computing, storage and networking resources, which can be managed through a web dashboard or a command line interface. OpenStack is also at the base of SPC Cloud, an Italian initiative with the goal of facilitating the migration of the PA towards cloud-based solutions. They offer cloud services furnished via *HPE Helion* [14], a commercial-grade distribution of OpenStack, which is fully compatible with the pure open-source version. Since the FICEP activities are part of the Italian PA digitalisation process, we relied on SPC Cloud services. In particular, we used HPE Helion as the provider of IaaS resources.

Within the FICEP infrastructure, the management of IaaS resources has been performed by organising them in *stacks*, which are created by relying on *Heat* [12], the flagship orchestration framework for OpenStack. Heat implements an engine to launch multiple composite cloud applications (or stacks) defined as *templates*, which are in the form of text files that can be manipulated like code. This aspect introduces several benefits. For instance, it allows versioning of the infrastructure with frameworks like Git and then eases the management of new features or rollbacks in case of failures. In addition, a code-defined infrastructure allows the exact replication of the same infrastructure in different environments (e.g. develop, staging, production), for instance, to manage a multi-stage deployment of the applications. Finally, it could allow the integration of the infrastructure deployment with continuous integration and delivery systems. Besides these benefits, the adoption of a template-based deployment reduces to few clicks (or API calls) the execution of a process that includes many manual and repetitive steps, which could be the main cause of errors or misconfiguration. In terms of numbers, the creation of a new virtual server requires the selection of a *flavour* (a profile expressed in amount of RAM and number of CPUs), the creation of a volume for persistent storage, the connection to a network, the assignment of one or more security groups (firewall rules), the injection of the SSH credentials and many other configurations. In order to be modular and scalable, the FICEP infrastructure is composed of near twenty small servers, so all of the operations to create a server must be repeated twenty times. Furthermore, the number of operations must also consider the steps to create auxiliary resources like networking, server base images, flavours and security groups.

The Heat templating language provides intrinsic functions that can be used inside templates to perform specific tasks, e.g. getting the value of a resource attribute at runtime or building a string starting from a template string with placeholders. Despite the availability of such functions, there are some operations that cannot be performed (e.g. the repetition of a template code block). To address this limitation, we enhanced Heat by developing a helper that implements the missing features we need. The helper is in the form of Python script that gets some inputs (e.g. the server scaling factor) and renders the final Heat template by using *Jinja2* [15], a Python templating engine. Both the Heat template and the helper script are versioned using a Git private repository hosted on BitBucket.

4.2   Management of Servers' Configurations

Once the IaaS resources are successfully allocated, the result is a virtual data centre composed of a set of connected servers each one running the same minimal operating system, which was initialised by relying on *cloud-init* [4], the *defacto* multi-distribution tool to handle the early initialisation of cloud instances.

The full configuration of each server is strictly dependent on the final use. Despite this, all the servers share a common set of configurations, for instance, related to the administrative accesses, system packages repositories and the installation of the common tools. To manage the servers configurations, we adopt a centralised, declarative and platform independent approach. In particular, we rely on *SaltStack* [25], a centralised IT automation framework that allows the management of server configurations with a declarative approach, which is based on the definition configuration *states* expressed in the form of text files that use a high level, human readable and platform independent language[1]. In SaltStack,

---

[1] SaltStack tutorial with plenty of examples – https://docs.saltstack.com/en/latest/topics/tutorials/starting_states.html.

it is common use to group states related to the same context in *formulas*. For instance, all the states related to the installation and configuration of Tomcat application server could be grouped under the same formula, which can be then managed as Git repository (see `tomcat-formula` [27]). In order to have coherent environment, the configuration of the servers representing the FICEP infrastructure is based on the composition of several formulas. With the efficiency principle in mind, some of them were implemented from the scratch while others were forked from the SaltStack community repository [26] in order to be used "as-is" or with some modifications. The list of the used formulas is available on the official FICEP repository [2]. SaltStack implements a master/slave architecture where the master node controls the slaves (or "minions") through a specific agent. By properly configuring the whole environment, the installation and the configuration of all the servers composing the FICEP infrastructure can be performed (and replicated) by executing just one command (`salt "*"` `state.highstate`) on the master node. Beside the initial configuration, SaltStack is also used to perform common management tasks. For instance, the update of the hosts aliases file (`/etc/hosts`) could be executed in parallel on all the servers by defining and applying a state or formula.

4.3   Monitoring Layer

The monitoring of the FICEP infrastructure is implemented by relying on the open source stack, named ELK stack, composed of *Elasticsearch* [8], *Logstash* [20] and *Kibana* [17]. W.r.t. the logging infrastructure described in Sect. 3, the following section describes how and which software have been used to implemented the components of the monitoring infrastructure.

The *log shipper* is implemented with *Filebeat* [11], a small application installed on each each server of the infrastructure. Filebeat reads the local log files and forwards the content towards the *log broker*, which is implemented as three-nodes *Kafka* [16] cluster. Kafka is a distributed streaming platform that implements the *publish/subscribe* messaging pattern. The Kafka cluster is orchestrated by a *ZooKeeper* [36] instance, which is running on a dedicated server. ZooKeeper is in charge to manage the Kafka nodes' hierarchy, the election of a new master in case of failure and the replication of the data across the cluster. The *log indexer* is implemented with Logstash, an open-source data-processing pipeline that is able to collect data from multitude of sources, to transform it and to send the result to a storage back-end. In the FICEP infrastructure, Logstash consumes the log entries from the Kafka cluster, applies some filters in order to grab some specific information and store the result on the *log storage*, here implemented as three-nodes Elasticsearch cluster. Elasticsearch is a distributed, RESTful search and analytics engine designed for horizontal scalability, maximum reliability, and easy management. All the collected information, as well as the raw log entries, are accessible on the *log viewer*, which is implemented with Kibana, a powerful web dashboard to monitor and analyse logs. The basic ELK capabilities are enriched by including within the stack the facilities coming from the *X-Pack* [33] component. In particular, the latter is used to implement the security among the ELK modules and to monitor the health of the whole ELK stack.

5   Related Work

The application of cloud computing to the deployment of services for the public sector has been discussed and proposed in different initiatives, given the advantages of the cloud model in terms of cost savings, availability and scalability.

Zwattendorfer *et al.* [42] presented in 2013 an evaluation of eight different European countries, namely Austria, Denmark, Finland, France, Germany, Ireland, Spain and the United Kingdom, on their use of cloud computing in e-Government services. The result of the authors' analysis was that, although in early development stage, most of the countries were including cloud computing in their national strategy, and the dominant deployment model was a private cloud platform based on either IaaS, PaaS, or SaaS service models, without a clear winner.

The implementation of a cloud deployment model for public services was addressed more recently by the FP7 *Cloud-for-Europe* [3] (C4E) project, co-funded by the European Commission and running from June 2013 until March 2017. The project was part of a larger initiative, named *European Cloud Partnership* (ECP) [9], addressing the challenges for cloud use in the public sector and designing innovative solutions to provide cloud services for the e-Government.

Zwattendorfer and Slamanig [40] discussed the application of a cloud deployment model for a federated eID environment as defined by the STORK [30] project, evaluating such model with respect to its applicability and protection of citizens' privacy. The authors' proposal was to move the national gateway, formerly PEPS, from the traditional deployment in a data-center to a cloud service model, to improve the scalability of the platform when managing a large number of authentications. In addition, they proposed to adapt the entities involved in the citizens' authentication to support a *Unidirectional Multi-use Proxy Re-Encryption* (UM-PRE) scheme to address confidentiality of citizens' authentication data. Differently from STORK, the eIDAS solution already provides built-in support for encryption of authentication's assertions exchanged between the national gateways.

The same authors described the challenges and obstacles in deploying the Austrian eID system in a public cloud infrastructure [41], which represents a key asset in the Austrian e-Government facilities. Differently from the solution presented in this paper, which focuses on the Italian implementation of the eIDAS gateway, the Austrian solution presented by the authors is rooted in the STORK framework for providing cross-border authentication.

6   Future Work and Conclusions

Building the Italian eIDAS infrastructure required, and will require, the integration and the harmonisation of several environments, which were designed and implemented by different entities, with different tools and different approaches. In this scenario, commonly referred as "dependency hell", the resolution of conflicts could require the implementation of risky tricks. A solution to harmonise and integrate heterogeneous applications by avoiding conflicts could be the deployment of each application within an isolated environment like containers [38]. According to the *Docker* [6] definition, a container image is *a lightweight, stand-alone, executable package of a piece of software that includes everything needed to run it*. The eIDAS-Node as well as the core components of the FICEP architecture (SP Proxy and IDP Proxy) are stateless applications, and this characteristic makes them suitable to be deployed as containers, for instance, by using Docker engine. In a complex architecture like FICEP, there could be part of the containers which are in charge of managing security-critical data. Instead of using Docker, these security containers could be implemented by relying on *rkt* (rocket) [24], a security oriented containers engine. Moving in the direction of a container-oriented infrastructure represents an evolution towards the *micro-services* paradigm where each computational unit has a specific task and the whole infrastructure is managed by an *orchestrator*. Frameworks like *Kubernetes* [19], *Mesos* [21] or *Portainer* [23] represent an example of container orchestrator. According to the configuration, they can autonomously manage the whole life-cycle of a container-based architecture. For instance, in case of requests growing for a specific service, the scaling factor of each involved application mutates according to the needs. Implementing the micro-services paradigm based on containers could require the re-engineering of the applications, for instance, the splitting of a monolithic application in several independent units. While the legacy components (e.g. monitoring software, load balancers) of the FICEP architecture are ready to be deployed as micro-service, the FICEP software and in particular, the eIDAS code developed by the EU, require a deep refactoring. Therefore, a switch towards a container-based architecture represents one of the upcoming challenges.

A critical aspect of the use of automated configuration framework like SaltStack is the management of *secrets* (e.g. private key files, password). The configuration recipes are plain-text files that are typically stored on version control system, which could be hosted on a third-party infrastructure. Therefore, storing secrets on these files could expose the whole infrastructure to security breaches. A solution to address this issue could be the use of cryptography (e.g. encrypt the recipes before pushing them) or the use of secrets management framework like *Vault* [31], *Knox* [18] or *Barbican* [1]. All of them expose a RESTful API to access different types of secrets. In addition, they also provide mechanisms to implement secrets rotation and auditing. In FICEP, the secrets management is currently a manual task. Since SaltStack natively support the integration with Vault, we planned to include this feature in next releases of the platform.

The current version of the infrastructure manages the allocation of cloud resources and the configuration of the instances as two separate tasks that have to be executed manually. In particular, the former relies on OpenStack Heat while the latter on SaltStack. One of the next challenges is to enhance the Heat template to automatically execute the SaltStack configuration states once the cloud resources are fully allocated. This enhancement should allow us to reach the target of deploying the whole infrastructure with a single command.

Administrative accesses to the infrastructure occurs via an SSH bastion host that authenticates administrators with a single factor and by relying on public key cryptography. In order to enhance the security of the whole architecture, the use of a second authentication factor could be introduced. For instance, it could be implemented by introducing the use of hardware devices like the YubiKey (see *Yubico PAM module* [34] or *SSH Authentication* [35]) or the integration of secret management framework like Vault (see *Vault SSH secret backend* [32]).

In conclusion, the proposed architecture for the implementation of the Italian eIDAS-Node and integration of the SPID eID scheme is foreseen as a viable solution for enabling at Member State level the eIDAS regulation by leveraging the advantages of cloud deployment schemes regarding infrastructure's cost, scalability and availability. The IaaS service model adopted within FICEP is suited for deploying the custom designed three-tiers platform because it allows the maintainer's control over the tenant's internal resources, such as private networks, storage and computational power. Furthermore, the proposed solution has been implemented by leveraging open-source technologies to maximise its applicability, apart from the cloud management system, i.e. HPE Helion, which is compatible with the open-source OpenStack software nevertheless.

Acknowledgement. The work described in this paper is part of the FICEP project, co-financed by the European Union's Connecting European Facility under the grant agreement no. INEA/CEF/ICT/A2014/0041.

References

1. Barbican. https://wiki.openstack.org/wiki/Barbican
2. BitBucket - FICEP. https://bitbucket.org/ficep
3. Cloud for Europe. http://www.cloudforeurope.eu
4. Cloud-init. http://cloudinit.readthedocs.io
5. Digital Single Market. https://ec.europa.eu/digital-single-market
6. Docker - Build, Ship and Run Any App, Anywhere. https://www.docker.com
7. eIDAS - Interoperability Architecture. https://joinup.ec.europa.eu/sites/default/files/eidas_interoperability_architecture_v1.00.pdf
8. Elasticsearch - RESTful, Distributed Search & Analytics. https://www.elastic.co/products/elasticsearch
9. European Cloud Partnership. https://ec.europa.eu/digital-single-market/european-cloud-partnership
10. FICEP - First Italian Crossborder eIDAS Proxy Service. http://www.agid.gov.it/agenda-digitale/infrastrutture-architetture/progetto_ficep
11. Filebeat - Lightweight Shipper for Logs. https://www.elastic.co/products/beats/filebeat
12. Heat - OpenStack Orchestration. https://wiki.openstack.org/wiki/Heat
13. How to Record SSH Sessions Established Through a Bastion Host. https://aws.amazon.com/blogs/security/how-to-record-ssh-sessions-established-through-a-bastion-host

14. HPE Helion OpenStack. https://www.hpe.com/emea_europe/en/software/openstack-cloud-iaas.html
15. Jinja - The Python Template Engine. http://jinja.pocoo.org
16. Kafka - A distributed streaming platform. https://kafka.apache.org
17. Kibana - Explore, Visualize, Discover Data. https://www.elastic.co/products/kibana
18. Knox - Secret management service. https://github.com/pinterest/knox
19. Kubernetes - Production-Grade Container Orchestration. https://kubernetes.io
20. Logstash - Collect, Parse, Transform Logs. https://www.elastic.co/products/logstash
21. Mesos. http://mesos.apache.org
22. OpenStack - Open Source Cloud Computing Software. https://www.openstack.org
23. Portainer - Simple management UI for Docker. http://portainer.io
24. rkt - A security-minded, standards-based container engine. https://coreos.com/rkt
25. SaltStack - Intelligent orchestration for the software-defined data center. https://saltstack.com
26. SaltStack Formulas. https://github.com/saltstack-formulas
27. Saltstack `tomcat-formula`. https://github.com/saltstack-formulas/tomcat-formula
28. SPC Cloud - Servizi di Cloud Computing per la Pubblica Amministrazione. https://www.cloudspc.it
29. SPID - Sistema Pubblico di Identità Digitale. https://www.spid.gov.it
30. STORK - Secure idenTity acrOss boRders linKed. https://www.eid-stork2.eu
31. Vault - A Tool for Managing Secrets. https://www.vaultproject.io
32. Vault SSH Secret Backend. https://www.vaultproject.io/docs/secrets/ssh/index.html
33. X-Pack - Extend Elasticsearch, Kibana & Logstash. https://www.elastic.co/products/x-pack
34. Yubico PAM module. https://developers.yubico.com/yubico-pam
35. YubiKey - SSH Authentication. https://developers.yubico.com/PGP/SSH_authentication
36. ZooKeeper. https://zookeeper.apache.org
37. Mell, P., Grance, T.: The NIST definition of cloud computing. Special Publication, 800-145, NIST, Sep 2011
38. Merkel, D.: Docker: lightweight linux containers for consistent development and deployment. Linux J. 2, p. 239 (2014). http://dl.acm.org/citation.cfm?id=2600239.2600241
39. Organization for the Advancement of Structured Information Standards (OASIS): Assertions and Protocols for the OASIS Security Assertion Markup Language (SAML) V2.0. https://docs.oasis-open.org/security/saml/v2.0/saml-core-2.0-os.pdf
40. Zwattendorfer, B., Slamanig, D.: Privacy-preserving realization of the STORK framework in the public cloud. In: SECRYPT-2013 - International Conference on Security and Cryptography, pp. 1–8, Jul 2013
41. Zwattendorfer, B., Slamanig, D.: The Austrian eID ecosystem in the public cloud: how to obtain privacy while preserving practicality. J. Inf. Secur. Appl. **27–28**, 35–53 (2016)
42. Zwattendorfer, B., Stranacher, K., Tauber, A., Reichstädter, P.: Cloud computing in E-Government across Europe, pp. 181–195 (2013). http://dx.doi.org/10.1007/978-3-642-40160-2_15

ICT in Government and in the Economy

Secure Document Exchange in the Greek Public Sector via eDelivery

Antonios Stasis(✉) and Loukia Demiri(✉)

Hellenic Ministry of Administrative Reconstruction, 15, Vas. Sofias Avenue, Athens, Greece
{a.stasis,l.demiri}@ydmed.gov.gr

Abstract. This paper describes how eDelivery specifications and technologies can be implemented in order to show how Document Management Systems used by the Greek Public Authorities can be connected in a common interoperability infrastructure for establishing communication with stakeholders (namely national and cross-Border Public Authorities, citizens and businesses) in a structured, secure, legal binding and accountable way. The action is conducted by the Hellenic Ministry of Administrative Reconstruction and it takes into account the eIDAS regulation's provisions on Electronic Registered Delivery Systems and on Trust Establishment and the Connecting Europe Facility (CEF) eDelivery specifications. The action includes the establishment of interoperability nodes (Access Points) and of infrastructure for discovery of the recipients (Service Metadata Publisher), the development of connectors for the integration of the backend Document Management Systems, the generation and exchange of evidences for ensuring authenticity and non-repudiation and the establishment of trust between the communicating points by using digital certificates. As communication is necessary not only at national but also at cross-border level, the Ministry has cooperated with Greek and European Public and Private Bodies, in order to ensure fulfillment of all requirements and integration with all possible stakeholders. The connection of the Document Management System used by the Hellenic Ministry of Administrative Reconstruction serves as a proof-of-concept.

Keywords: Secure Document Exchange · eDelivery · Access Points · Document Management Systems · Cross-border message exchange · Exchange of evidences · Non-repudiation · Back end system integration

1 Introduction

With the introduction of Law 4440/2016 [1], Greece aspires to move towards a new era of communication of the Greek Public Authorities with each other and with citizens and businesses at both national and cross-border level. The law foresees the obligatory use of electronic communication by all Public Bodies for all document exchanges, in order to be able to offer quicker and simpler services and to reduce bureaucracy and costs. For the realization of this, it is however necessary to ensure that all communications are safe and trusted and that transaction evidences are produced and can be accessed at any time. Moreover, electronic document exchange falls under the Greek Administrative Procedure Code i.e. law 2690/1999 (OG A 45), which means that it must also comply with

© Springer International Publishing AG 2017
S.K. Katsikas and V. Zorkadis (Eds.): E-Democracy 2017, CCIS 792, pp. 213–227, 2017.
https://doi.org/10.1007/978-3-319-71117-1_15

its provisions as far as legal validity and proof of transactions goes. Finally, the eIDAS regulation, i.e. the European regulation on Electronic Identification and Trusted Services [2], has provisions for data exchange via Electronic Registered Delivery Services, whereas the Connecting Europe Facility (CEF) European Mechanism [3], sets technical standards and provides sample implementation for eDelivery [4] and funds related actions aiming at ensuring cross-border trusted communication. However, there are still issues that remain unclear at both technical and legal level. Determination of "Qualified ERDS", signing of exchanged documents and/or messages, establishment of trust, are only examples of the issues that still remain at "grey" zone. This becomes more obvious when coming to cross border data exchange. However, even at national level it is not always easy to design and implement electronic document exchange. The Hellenic Ministry of Administrative Reconstruction has started electronic document exchange using a simple e-mail service in 2012. In 2013 the Ministry adopted the use of a document management system (DMS) that used a specific xml format for document exchange that was developed in collaboration with DMS vendors that offer services in Greece[1]. The discussion on electronic document exchange in Public Administration has revealed a number of issues given that (a) different systems provided by various vendors are used by the Greek Public Bodies, (b) the specifications about protocols and exchanged documents are not always clear or globally implemented and (c) the existing technical and legal framework (national and EU) is still uncomplete as mentioned before.

In this context it is worthwhile to investigate how the Document Management Systems (DMS) used by the different GR Public Authorities can be interconnected by implementing eDelivery specifications and solutions with minimal, or even no, interference with the existing systems and how the unspecified technical issues can be tackled in a generic way, applicable to other MS as well. In parallel it is interesting to examine how the eIDAS regulation and the Greek Administrative Procedure Code (along with all related administrative decisions) can be combined and which issues still remain unregulated in order to ensure that all exchange is conducted in a legal binding, secure, trusted and evidence accompanied way at both national and cross-border level. The connection of the Hellenic Ministry of Administrative Reconstruction (HMAR) DMS will serve as a proof-of-concept.

The structure of this article has four (4) sections as following:

1. EU Existing Framework
2. The "Electronic Document Exchange" Greek Action
3. Implementation and Issues Tackled
4. Results and next steps

---

[1] See press releases for the evolution of Electronic Document Exchange in Hellenic Ministry of Administrative reconstruction http://www.minadmin.gov.gr/?cat=99.

2   EU Legal and Technical Framework

2.1   eIDAS Electronic Registered Delivery Services

Regulation (EU) N°910/2014 "on electronic identification and trust services for electronic transactions in the internal market and repealing Directive 1999/93/EC" (eIDAS Regulation aims to raise the trust between the stakeholders of cross-border interoperable services setting the legal framework for valid and trusted electronic communication.

According to the regulation a "qualified trusted service" is a service offered by an accredited provider who is registered in at least one trusted list created and maintained by the supervisory body of a Member State (MS) i.e. the body that has been designate by the MS for this role. By introducing the EU trust mark, the regulation also gives to qualified service providers the opportunity to indicate in a simple and recognisable manner that they are registered in a trusted list and thus offer qualified trusted electronic services.

Electronic signatures, electronic seals, electronic timestamps are all considered as "qualified services". Electronic Registered Delivery Services (ERDS) are also qualified services, defined in art.3(36) of the regulation as a *service that makes it possible to transmit data between third parties by electronic means and provides evidence relating to the handling of the transmitted data, including proof of sending and receiving the data, and that protects transmitted data against the risk of loss, theft, damage or any unauthorised alterations.*

The legal validity of Electronic Registered Delivery Services are defined in art.43 of the regulation. According to art.43 all data sent and received via an ERDS, cannot be denied their legal validity and must be accepted as evidences, even if the ERDS is not qualified. Moreover, if the ERDS is qualified, then the data transmitted are also to be considered as having data integrity, identified sender and recipient and accuracy of date and time indicated by the service.

In addition art.44 defines the requirements that an ERDS needs to meet in order to be recognised as qualified. Given the complexity in interpreting the requirements, the article also provides for the authorization to the European Commission to introduce implementing acts for the definition of standards for sending and receiving procedures, which must be followed in order for the requirements to be fulfilled; the same authorisation is granted by the regulation to the Commission in order to also issue specific implementing acts for other fields, such as electronic identification, EU trust mark, trusted lists, etc.

Until now, a number of implementing acts has been published, on electronic identification and on electronic trusted services [5]. However, no implementing act has been yet issued for ERDS, leaving the standards for qualified ERDS still unclear.

2.2   Proposal on a Single Digital Gateway Regulation [6]

The EC's proposal for an EU Regulation on *establishing a single digital gateway to provide information, procedures, assistance and problem solving services and amending Regulation (EU) No 1024/2012*, is an initiative aiming at boosting the

European Digital Single Market by making national electronic services and the related legal framework transparent and easy to reach by all potential users across Europe. The regulation sets a number of provisions for the creation of a central digital window through which national online administrative procedures, assistance services and related legislation available to domestic users, will be made available to all EU citizens and businesses. At the beginning the Member States will be obliged to offer fully online services for 13 key procedures, including services addressing various citizen and business lifecycle events such as birth, studying, working, moving, retiring, starting a business and doing business.

In order to ensure the quality of the offered information and services, all available procedures that will be through the Gateway will be subjected to specific quality criteria indicated by the regulation. Article 12 in particular, provides for the cross-border exchange of evidence between the competent authorities. More specifically the Article states that evidences for each transaction between competent Authorities must be generated whenever there is an explicit request of the online procedure's user (i.e. citizen or business).

Evidences will be generated by the competent authorities, but requested and exchanged via *a technical system established by the Commission in cooperation with the Member States*. However this is not applied for procedures *established at Union level which provide for different mechanisms for the exchange of evidence, unless they are integrated into those procedures*. From that point of view seems that the use of e-delivery may also be extended to other on line services just to ensure the creation and exchange of the appropriate evidence for each service, therefore the e-delivery is a prominent solution that can have many different types of use depending on the business requirement.

2.3   CEF eDelivery Building Block

The European Mechanism "Connecting Europe Facility" (CEF) is a funding instrument created to enhance the Digital Single Market and to promote interoperability between the different Member States in three areas: Transport, Energy and Telecom. CEF Telecom supports the connection between electronic services available in the different Member States for the communication between EU Public Administrations, Citizens and Businesses. In order to assist the Member States and to ensure technical consistency, CEF Telecom [7] has defined five Digital Service Infrastructures (DSIs): eID, eSignature, eTranslation, eInvoicing and eDelivery [8]. Each DSI, also referred to as Building Block (BB), provides the Member States with technical specifications and standards, implementation guidelines, sample implementation software, assistance services and test platforms to verify the implemented solutions' compliance to the specified rules.

eDelivery DSI refers to the electronic exchange of information (data) and it is based on a 4-corner model: corner 1 represents the sender's service/system (backend system), corner 2 the sending interoperability node, corner 3 the receiving node and corner 4 the recipient's system/service. eDelivery interoperability nodes are called Access Points (AP), they are all implemented according to the same (CEF) specifications and they handle the communication between the sender's and the recipient's systems, according to the defined by CEF message exchange protocol. Access Points are implemented at Member State level and may run under the supervision of a public or a private body. Recipients' addresses, the related Access Points as well as conditions of accessing (ex. accepted document types) are registered in a Service Metadata Publisher (SMP); one or more SMPs may run in a Member State. The discovery of the location of the correct SMP to consult during a message exchange is done by a Service Metadata Locator (SML). Messages sent via eDelivery, are "content agnostic", in the sense that the same mechanism is used no matter the type and/or the format of the original information. Messages are "enveloped" in a pre-defined schema, commonly agreed between the communicating parties (including the APs) and followed by a set of metadata which are used for its routing. Backend integration may be achieved via the implementation of a connector. Commonly agreed evidences are produced at key route points and exchanged between the involved parties, in order to ensure legal assurance and accountability. Trust between the 4-corners is established via digital certificates (Fig. 1).

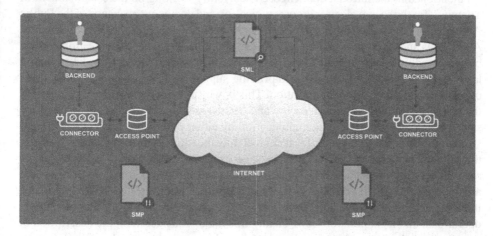

Fig. 1. The generic 4-corner eDelivery model

The generic topology of an eDelivery network as specified by CEF is the following [9]:

For the implementation of an Access Point, CEF specifies as standards the open-PEPPOL AS2 [10] (used in e-Procurement) and the e-SENS AS4 profiles [11]. The e-SENS AS4 profile is the outcome of the work on eDelivery in the context of the e-SENS project [12] and it is a profile of the ebMS3 [13] and AS4 [14] OASIS Standards, based on ENTSOG (the European Network of Transmission System Operators (TSO) for Gas [15]) AS4 profile for TSOs and on e-CODEX [16] specifications. CEF proposes a number of open- and close-Source software products that can be used for the implementation of APs by the Member States [17].

In order to ensure authenticity, integrity and trust, all messages and evidences are digitally signed by the APs. Digital certificates can either be mutually exchanged or be registered in a commonly accessed trusted list (PKI model). In the context of eIDAS this list is the one defined in the implementing act (EU) 2015/1505. eIDAS specifications are applicable for the security controls [18]. The ETSI Electronic Signature and Infra-structure [19] standard is applied for the signature of the messages and the evidences.

For the location of data (SML) and the capability lookup (SMP), CEF specifies the e-SENS profile of the OASIS BDXL standard [20] and the e-SENS profile of the OASIS SMP standard [21] respectively. For both the SML and the SMP, CEF also offers a reference implementation software [22, 23].

The implementation of a connector for the integration of the backend systems is not obligatory but it is strongly suggested by CEF, since it offers added value functionality, such as monitoring and evidences [24]. The e-SENS REM profile is the proposed standard for evidences generation [25], implementing the REM Evidence standard.

3   The "Secure Electronic Document Exchange Action" in Greece

As mentioned in the introduction, Greece is currently working on the establishment of a network for the secure electronic communication and document exchange of the Public Authorities (a) with each other (b) with citizens and businesses and (c) with cross-border Authorities and/or citizens and businesses [26]. Until now this communication is done by using traditional post services, or in best cases, simple email services; the first solution leads to the waste of tons of paper and printing supplies, whereas the second one lacks of security and proof-of-communication. This is why eDelivery has been considered as the suitable solution to establish secure and trusted message exchange, ensuring at the same time non-repudiation of communication by either part (sender or receiver).

Even though the framework for technical specifications is already defined by CEF, the implementation of eDelivery for message exchange in the Public Administration, requires for a number of additional agreements and requirements at national, or per case also at cross-border, level. This is necessary in order to ensure the suitability of the implemented solution not only from technical aspect, but also from administrative, operational and legal point of view. Taking this under consideration, the description of metadata and the generation of the appropriate evidences are two of the most important issues to tackle. Moreover, it is necessary to define accountability at each step of the message transaction in order to be able to attribute responsibility in case of discrepancies. The definition of different degrees of confidentiality may also be needed, in order to ensure integrity and security of the transferred information. Finally, it is necessary to minimize any changes to the existing services and/or the way the users interact with them, so that the release in production of the new functionality is done in a smooth and easy way. In all cases, it is also important that all the eIDAS requirements for ERDS are fulfilled and all CEF specifications implemented, and to ensure that all decisions are accepted by cross-border partners.

The decisions about all the aforementioned issues, are generic and applicable to all services connected to the Hellenic eDelivery infrastructure. This considered, the initial phase of the action includes the development of a connector for the Document Management System used by HMAR, and the interconnection of the Ministry and of at least one other Public Authority using the same DMS, as an initial proof-of-concept [27]. It is worth mentioning that the HMAR DMS is one of the more commonly used in the

Greek Public Sector. At a second phase the connector for another widely used DMS and the connection for more than 20 other Public Authorities of the Central and the Local Government, using either one of the two, will also take place.

Given the number of different backend systems that need to be connected, four (4) access points have or will be developed initially in Greece: AP1 for the connection of the DMS of Public Authorities of the Central Government, AP2 for Cross-border communication, AP3 for the connection of services addressed to citizens and businesses and AP4 for the needs of the Local Government. AP3 will be implemented and be operated by Hellenic Post SA, whereas the rest three are currently under the responsibility of HMAR.

Before the beginning of the action one Access Point has been implemented for pilot purposes in Greece as a result of a joint action between Germany, France, Austria and, at a later stage, Slovenia and Greece in the context of the e-SENS "Business Lifecycle" WP5.4 domain [28]. The results of e-SENS were delivered to CEF. The results of this work are being evolved in the CEF funded project "NO Barriers in eDelivery (NOBLE)" [29]. Through NOBLE Greece, Germany, France and Slovenia continue to cooperate in order to address implementation problems that remain open and to move things forward. Issues, such as advanced evidence generation and exchange, use of SMP and establishment of trusted lists will be tackled by NOBLE partners. The main target is to make the eDelivery network developed in e-SENS fully operational at production level. The project intends also to extend at cross-border level the use the existing ERDS, especially those offered by Postal Services. This way more ground for communication and business transactions with other Member States will be offered enhancing the Digital Single Market.

The development of AP1, AP2 and AP3, the connection of a service addressed to citizens/businesses (to show communication with end users via the Hellenic Post SA services) and the communication with foreign ERDS all fall in the context of the NOBLE action. The same goes for the connector of HMAR's DMS, which means that the specifications definition, will also take into account all decisions taken at NOBLE level for cross-border communication.

The connector for the second DMS and the connection of the other Public Bodies are the purpose of the, also funded by CEF, project "Secure Document Exchange with eDelivery in Greece". This action is complementary to the NOBLE one and will re-use and extend its results for the needs of the Local GR Government.

In order for the whole action to be successful, the aforementioned technical activities, will be accompanied with administrative acts and, if necessary, legal provisions. In all cases it is important to ensure that the system created will be functional not only at technical but also at operational level.

4   Implementation and Issues Tackled

The implementation of the HMAR DMS connector [30] followed the implementation of AP1 (for the connection of Central Government Public Bodies) and of the SMP. The AP and the SMP follow the CEF specifications and the implementation details decided by NOBLE partners. The AP implemented the Holodeck AS4 software solution [31], which is an open source product that offers basic AP functionality fully compatible with the AS4 standard. Given that extra functionality is required to support the evidence required by the Administrative Procedure Code a connector in front of the AP is also being implemented. The SMP currently is based on Philip Helgers' PEPPOL SMP server. The additional support for the trusted list is being examined and alteration in the current version will be required.

For the implementation of the DMS connector two major factors had to be combined: cross-border (namely CEF and NOBLE) specifications (given that the exchange of messages isn't limited at national level) and national legal and administrative requirements. Message envelope format and core metadata are defined at cross-border level. However it may be needed that additional metadata are defined at national level; they will also be transmitted cross-borderly but they will not be used at the destination country. The same goes for evidences: core evidence information as defined for cross-border communication must be generated at all cases. Any extra information required for national communication is acceptable even though not necessarily processed in the destination country. Minimum metadata and evidences exchanged at cross-border level are a matter of bi- or multi- country negotiation and it is important. However it is not always easy or feasible, to find a compromise that address each country's minimum requirements. As mentioned earlier in the paper, message exchanged are content agnostic. Nevertheless, given the Hellenic Administrative Procedure Code, it was necessary to define the basic categories of documents to be transmitted and some specific metadata for each one. For the fulfillment of the special national needs, the extended part of the AS4 and REM messages will also be used.

4.1 Message Creation and Routing

According to the existing legal framework and defined procedures, in the Greek Public Administration "conventional document exchange" is done via each Public Authority's DMS. For communication with another public authority or with a business, the sender defines the recipient's organization and the address (postal and/or email) and optionally the final recipient's name and address (if different than the one of the organization). When coming to communication with citizens, the sender defines the final recipient's name and (postal and/or email) address. The sender also defines a set of metadata (such as subject of document, type, keywords, etc.), is then forwarded via the DMS to the (sender) Authority's DMS and then sent to the destination Authority/business/citizen via post and/or email.

In the HMAR's DMS "conventional routing" is done through a screen in which the user uploads the document(s) to be transmitted and adds a set of mandatory and optional metadata. The name, subject and date are mandatory, whereas other information such as remarks, keywords, etc. are optional. The address of the recipient is already registered in the DMS system, since the recipient(s) are chosen by a predefined list. Before the sending of the document the system adds automatically some extra information, namely document unique identification number, year and date.

Given that the generic legal and procedure framework must still be followed, routing via eDelivery will be done in the same way, with the addition of a new "eDelivery address" field to the recipients' predefined list. The user will be able to select the recipient's (no matter if it is a Public Authority, a business or a citizen) eDelivery address instead of the "conventional" one. The system will recognize the type of the address and will automatically make all necessary adjustments to route the message via the eDelivery network (see Fig. 2 below). Almost no changes are necessary in the current user-interface in order for eDelivery document exchange. All the added functionality is achieved via the connector implemented.

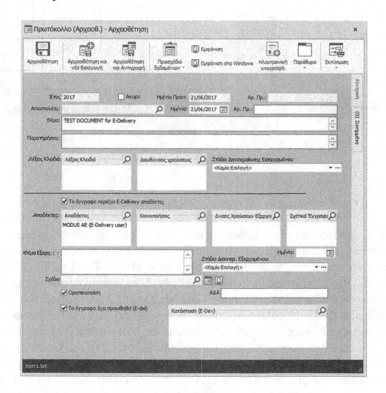

Fig. 2. eDelivery message metadata in the HMAR DMS

The (eDelivery) addressing schema has been agreed in the context of the e-SENS WP5.4 action and it is an email like address where the recipient's domain is included. The domain, deriving from the address, is sent as an additional metadata, so that the related AP can be discovered via the SMP/SML.

Following the provisions of the existing legal framework and in order to maintain the existing granularity schema, the addresses of the Public Bodies will be assigned to each instance of the DMS used by the recipient Public Body. For instance for HMAR where four different DMS instances are used (Generic, Confidential, Secretary Generals and Ministers' DMS instance) four distinct eDelivery addresses will be defined.

The connector developed runs in front of the DMS system and connects it with the AP connector. In the topology, depicted in Fig. 3, Corner 1 includes the DMS connector ("Papyros Bridge") and the Public Body DMS in the right, Corner 2 the right Access Point and Connector, Corner 3 the left Access Point and Connector and Corner 4 the left (unnamed) system:

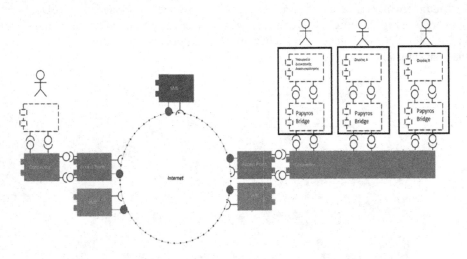

Fig. 3. Connecting GR Public Authorities via eDelivery Topology

The message format is the one defined in the context of the e-SENS project, re-used in NOBLE and it is a standard SBD/SBDH document. The message's header contains the appropriate routing metadata according to the e-SENS SBDH profiling [32]. The document and its metadata are included in the body. The document to be exchanged and any attachments are included in the body's message as an "Attachment Type" element.

Additionally to the metadata described by the SBDH profile, for the documents exchange in Greece more metadata need also to be transmitted. The extra metadata derive by the core document attributes defined in the context of the Greek eDocument Interoperability Framework [33]. The type of the document for which a pre-defined list will be described, the protocol date, remarks, other recipients and/or notifications and document issuer may be included as metadata. Other fields may also be defined at a later stage.

For the transmission of the message between the four corners a REM-Dispatch message is created and signed by the connector, namely the DMS (Corner 1). The message is sent to the connector of Corner 2. For cross-border communication it has been commonly agreed that no evidences are needed by Corner 2. For national message exchange a REMevidence Acceptance/RejectiononSubmission is generated at Corner 2.

Corner 2 evaluates the recipient's address against the SMP in order to discover the recipient AP (Corner 3). Once the message is received by Corner 3 a DeliveryNonDe-livery evidence is generated. According to the current implementation the message is not sent back until Corner 4 (i.e. the recipient) accesses its mailbox. However since responsibility ambiguities may occur, this may change so that the Delivery/NonDelivery evidence is signed by Corner 3 and sent back to Corner 2 immediately.

When the message arrives at Corner 4 two more evidences AcceptanceRejection-ByRecipient is generated by Corner 4. The evidences are signed by Corner 4, sent back to Corner 1 (i.e. the Sender) and it is displayed as a flag of the related message at the DMS system.

4.2 Open Implementation Issues

Evidences Generalisation

As it is described in the previous paragraph three types of evidences are currently generated for national and cross-border communication needs: DeliveryNonDelivery by Corner 3, RetrievalNonRetrieval and AcceptanceRejection by Corner 4. These represent the minimum set of evidences agreed among the NOBLE partners in order to ensure liability at cross-border level.

However, it is possible that at a second stage more detailed evidences are required at national level for administrative and legal purposes, especially when it comes to documents exchanged between Public Authorities and citizens/businesses. The implementation of such functionality may require either the generation of other type of evidences, such exchange of evidences between Corner 1 and Corner 2 or the addition of more information in the existing ones. In all cases, this will not affect the cross-border communication since any extra information will simply be ignored by the receiving systems.

Moreover, the proposed EU Digital Single Gateway regulation provides for the generation of evidences for Public Authorities communication upon request of the final (citizen or business) user and exchange via a central technical system. Once the regulation is accepted and put into force, it may have impact on the way or the type of evidences generated and the way they are exchanged.

Trust Establishment

Trust Establishment is an issue that still remains open for both domestic and cross-border message exchanges. Mutual exchange of certificates, which was initially used, is suitable only for a limited number of services/APs.

Moving towards the connection of multiple services/APs calls for the use of something more generic and less cumbersome. Trust lists (TL), where the APs' and possibly the SMPs' certificates are registered are definitely a good solution. However it seems to be rather complicated and difficult to maintain TLs within the scope of the current action (including the NOBLE project). In this view, it has been decided to use an intermediary solution for proof-of-concept reasons. The CEF PKI service [34] has been used for the issuance of certificates for all the implemented APs and SMP; these certificates will be registered in a shared key store created for the needs of the project and will serve as a mockup of a trusted list. Once maintenance and governance issues are solved, TL will be used in production environment.

Messages Signature

Messages and evidences are signed by the sending corners before their transmission. Currently the XML Signature generated by the SPOCS (XMLDsig) [35] components is used. This is ETSI REM compliant but it is not conformant to the eIDAS specifications for Advanced Electronic Signatures (AdES). Taking this into account, the signature service will be upgraded to at least XAdES-B [36] in order to meet the Advanced e-Signature standards.

Integration of SMP with the existing AS4 implementation

SMP has been implemented and it is being used for capability lookup. However the Holodeck AS4 software solution doesn't offer as open source software any functionality for the connection of the AP to the SMP. This means that extra implementation is required either in-house or by an external vendor. Since this is an ad-hoc solution, maintenance and update cost can raise dramatically.

On the other hand, other AS4 compliant software solutions are also proposed by CEF. Some of them (ex. Domibus i.e. the CEF sample implementation [37]) do offer SMP connection functionality but they have to be examined in details in order to decide whether or not they fit the generic GR DMS connection requirements. An impact and cost analysis for each one is needed in order to estimate how difficult it is to move towards another solution and whether the benefits of choosing a commercial product (ex. IBM solution [38], FLAME [39]) outweighs its acquisition and maintenance cost.

5   Conclusions - Next Steps

In order to pass from paper to electronic document exchange it is necessary to ensure that electronic communication is done in a secure, trusted and evidence emitting manner. No room for legal ambiguities, administrative failures and/or organizational gaps should be left. The implementation of the EU specifications and standards for eDelivery along with the eIDAS regulation provisions for ERDS are key elements for the achievement of the aforementioned goal. Through the connection of the DMS used by HMAR, it has been showed that secure and trusted electronic communication with Public Bodies using the same DMS is possible. Moreover via the e-SENS and NOBLE projects the Hellenic ERDS connected in the domestic eDelivery system will be able to also communicate with other ERDS originating from the other partner's countries, setting the grounds for a more wide EU cross-border message exchange.

The national next steps include the establishment of communication with end users, which will be achieved via the connection to the existing AP of a number of ministry's services addressed to citizens and businesses. The implementation of the AP held by Hellenic Post and the connection of their services will complete the network. Administrative documents and acts will be sent by HMAR to Hellenic Post (via AP1 and AP3) and then routed by the Hellenic Post backend system to the address declared by the citizen/business (which may be an eDelivery, an e-mail or a postal address). In this case, a mixed model of communication will be used: eDelivery to eDelivery, eDelivery to email and eDelivery to paper. For the routing of the initial message the connector will be programmed to set as recipient address in the SBDH the eDelivery address of the Hellenic Post, keeping the final recipient address as part of the message's metadata.

Implementation of cross-border communication will continue via the NOBLE project. The work already achieved and the fact that there are issues that still remain open and need to be negotiated, show that there is a number of more specific technical guidelines and of administrative decisions that need to be taken. In some cases these are policy decisions and they exceed the limits of the project. Issue like minimum required evidences and corner of generalisation for cross-border communication, governance and maintenance of central trusted lists, standards for the signing of messages and evidences are some core issues that should be resolved at EU level. In the context of the NOBLE project some agreement can be made between the partners, but the extension of the functionality to other countries demands for more central decisions.

Moreover there is still lack of specific standards for qualified ERDS, which gives room to interpretations and diversity in the offered services. When it comes to cross-border communication this may cause security and trust discrepancies. At this stage and in order to achieve the desired level of quality and assurance, one or more eIDAS implementing acts on qualified ERDS are necessary to set the appropriate standards. The definition of an eIDAS cooperation network so as to permit to all the MS to cooperate and the drafting of a related proposal could be a first step towards this direction. The connection of a new ERDS system to an AP causes some additional implications that have to be tacked regarding the management of the SMP i.e. how the new ERDS will be registered to the SMP. The registration can either be centralized or decentralized providing the connector the possibility to add new systems to the AP and do the appropriate registration to the SMP. Last but not least the notification of the existing ERDS systems regarding the changes in the SMP is still an ongoing issue, since the existing available EC sample implementation does not provide such functionalities. It is crucial for the end user of a document management system to be aware for the ERDS systems that are being connected to the trust realm of the document exchange domain. For these issues further work is required.

More specifically in Greece the action will also continue with the implementation of the AP for Local Government, the connection of another widely used DMS and the participation in the eDelivery system of more than 20 additional Public Authorities. In order to ensure interoperability, the requirements and specifications defined for the connection of the HMAR DMS will be implemented. It is obvious that each time a new DMS or service joins the Hellenic eDelivery network, a new connector must be developed. For the integrity of the system, it is necessary that all new connectors comply with the same rules and follow the same standards. As long as the legal framework remains the same, the basic required functionality shouldn't differentiate from one system to another.

References

1. Law no 4440/2016 (Government Gazette Part A, no 224) on "Regulatory Governance: Principles, Processes and Means of Better Regulation"
2. eIDAS regulation. http://eur-lex.europa.eu/legal-content/EN/TXT/HTML/?uri=CELEX: 32014R0910&from=EN

3. Connecting Europe Facility (CEF). https://ec.europa.eu/inea/en/connecting-europe-facility
4. CEF Digital eDelivery. https://ec.europa.eu/cefdigital/wiki/display/CEFDIGITAL/eDelivery
5. EU eIDAS observatory. https://ec.europa.eu/futurium/en/content/eidas-implementing-acts
6. Proposal for a Regulation on Digital Single Gateway. https://ec.europa.eu/info/law/better-regulation/initiatives/com-2017-256-0_en
7. European Commission Strategy on Digital Single Market. https://ec.europa.eu/digital-single-market/connecting-europe-facility
8. CEF Digital Home. https://ec.europa.eu/cefdigital/wiki/display/CEFDIGITAL/CEF+Digital+Home
9. CEF Digital eDelivery overiew. https://ec.europa.eu/cefdigital/wiki/display/CEFDIGITAL/How+does+eDelivery+work+-+Overview
10. Peppol Homepage. http://peppol.eu/
11. eSENS Generic Architecture Repository AS4. http://wiki.ds.unipi.gr/display/ESENS/PR+-+AS4
12. eSENS homepage. https://www.esens.eu/
13. OASIS open document on ebms3. http://docs.oasis-open.org/ebxml-msg/ebms/v3.0/core/os/ebms_core-3.0-spec-os.pdf
14. OASIS open document on AS4. http://docs.oasis-open.org/ebxml-msg/ebms/v3.0/profiles/AS4-profile/v1.0/os/AS4-profile-v1.0-os.html
15. ENTSOG homepage. https://www.entsog.eu/
16. e-CODEX Homepage. https://www.e-codex.eu
17. CEF Access Point Software. https://ec.europa.eu/cefdigital/wiki/display/CEFDIGITAL/e-SENS+AS4+conformant+solutions
18. CEF Security Control Guidance. https://ec.europa.eu/cefdigital/wiki/display/CEFDIGITAL/Security+Controls+guidance
19. ETSI Electronic Signature and Infrastructure. https://portal.etsi.org/esi/el-sign.asp
20. eSENS Generic Architecture Repository DBXL. http://wiki.ds.unipi.gr/display/ESENS/PR+-+BDXL+1.3.0
21. eSENS Generic Architecture Repository SMP. http://wiki.ds.unipi.gr/display/ESENS/PR+-+SMP_home
22. CEF SML Software. https://ec.europa.eu/cefdigital/wiki/display/CEFDIGITAL/SML+software
23. CEF SMP Software. https://ec.europa.eu/cefdigital/wiki/display/CEFDIGITAL/SMP+software
24. CEF Backend Integration. https://ec.europa.eu/cefdigital/wiki/display/CEFDIGITAL/How+does+eDelivery+work+-+Backend+Integration
25. eSENS Generic Architecture Repository REM. http://wiki.ds.unipi.gr/display/ESENS/PR+-+REM
26. Press release for implementation of eDelivery. http://www.aftodioikisi.gr/ipourgeia/dimosio-ilektronika-i-diakinisi-engrafon-apo-fthinoporo-oi-protoi-foreis-lista/
27. Hellenic Ministry of Administrative Reconstruction Call for Connecting the Document Management System to eDELIVERY. http://www.minadmin.gov.gr/?p=20938
28. e-SENS Business Lifecycle eDELIVERY. http://wiki.ds.unipi.gr/display/ESENSPILOTS/5.4.2+-+Architecture+and+BB+Implementation+-+eDelivery. last updated
29. NOBLE Press Release. https://www.governikus.de/fileadmin/user_upload/Pressemitteilungen_PDF/PressRelease_GovernikusKG_CEF-NOBLE_Feb2017_english.pdf
30. Hellenic Ministry of Administrative Reconstruction and MODUS S.A., Contract for the Connection of the Hellenic Ministry's of Administrative Reconstruction Document Management System to eDELIVERY, Athens, April 2017
31. Holodeck homepage. http://holodeck-b2b.org/

32. e-SENS   SBDH   profile.   http://wiki.ds.unipi.gr/display/ESENSPILOTS/5.4.2+-+Architecture+and+BB+Implementation+-+eDelivery?preview=/29921991/33587213/Business%20Lifecycle%20SDBH%20Profile%20v0.5.pdf#id-5.4.2-ArchitectureandBBImplementation-eDelivery-BusinessLifecycleSDBHProfile
33. Greek e-Government Interoperability Framework homepage. http://www.e-gif.gov.gr/portal/page/portal/egif
34. CEF PKI Service. https://ec.europa.eu/cefdigital/wiki/display/CEFDIGITAL/PKI+Service
35. SPOCS Homepage. https://www.eu-spocs.eu/
36. XADES   xml   signature.   https://joinup.ec.europa.eu/sd-dss/webapp-demo/doc/dss-documentation.html#_the_xml_signature_xades
37. CEF Digital Domibus Access Point Software. https://ec.europa.eu/cefdigital/wiki/display/CEFDIGITAL/Domibus
38. IMB Electronic Data Interchange (EDI) Services. http://www-05.ibm.com/services/dk/ecommerce/index.html?ca=ecommerce&me=w&met=dk_hp_tab2
39. Flame Messaging Solutions. http://flame.co.za/

Towards an Integrated and Inclusive Platform for Open Innovation in the Public Sector

Aggeliki Androutsopoulou[1](✉) , Nikos Karacapilidis[2], Euripidis Loukis[1] ,
and Yannis Charalabidis[1]

[1] Department of Information and Communication Systems Engineering,
University of the Aegean, Samos, Greece
{ag.andr,eloukis,yannisx}@aegean.gr
[2] Industrial Management and Information Systems Lab, MEAD,
University of Patras, Patras, Greece
karacap@upatras.gr

Abstract. The growing adoption of the open innovation paradigm in the public sector poses a set of research challenges related to the particularities of the domain and the technologies required to manage the associated knowledge flows among diverse types of stakeholders. This paper aims to shed light on how the proper combination of existing ICT tools can support and advance the implementation of open innovation practices in the public sector. Towards this aim, it first presents a non-exhaustive taxonomy of these tools, which is also associated with the open innovation phase they primarily support. Paying particular attention to the issues of collaboration support and sophisticated data collection and analysis, the paper also proposes an open, inclusive and sustainable web-based platform that builds on the synergy between human and machine intelligence to address the important challenges of public sector open innovation. An indicative application scenario, concerning a contemporary societal problem, showcases the potential of the proposed solution.

Keywords: Open innovation · Public sector · Crowdsourcing · Public policy formulation · Collaboration support · Argumentation · Knowledge management

1 Introduction

Open Innovation (OI) was firstly introduced by Chesbrough [1] as a paradigm shift from the traditional closed model of innovation, referring to the internal control of ideas and knowledge resources within an organization, to 'the use of purposive inflows and outflows of knowledge to accelerate internal innovation, and expand the market for external use of innovation, respectively' [2]. The increasing social media popularity and internet use, together with the growing number and mobility of knowledge workers, triggered the development of diverse OI methods and practices in business [3, 4], extending the innovation capacity along and beyond the boundaries of a firm and its human capital. Successful initiatives in the knowledge co-development process, carried out by private companies involving diverse external actors (customers, suppliers,

© Springer International Publishing AG 2017
S.K. Katsikas and V. Zorkadis (Eds.): E-Democracy 2017, CCIS 792, pp. 228–243, 2017.
https://doi.org/10.1007/978-3-319-71117-1_16

competitors, cross-sector firms, universities and research institutions), have offered fertile ground for research on the types of OI practices used in the private sector [5, 6], as well as the context and typology of the problems each type is appropriate for [7].

Boosted by the adoption of e-participation initiatives and the transition of decision making process from a top-down to a bottom-up approach, the OI paradigm has started being adopted by the public sector to tackle the increasing complexity of problems and policy challenges faced by contemporary societies [8–11]. From a public administration perspective, the integration of a distributed innovation process, which is based on purposively managed knowledge flows across organizational boundaries, provides the opportunity to include citizens and their ideas and expertise into the work of the governments (citizen-sourcing) [9, 12, 13]. Citizens, as inhabitants of a particular city, and also due to their professional activity, have specific knowledge (or experience) of their micro environment, which the administration cannot easily access. Through appropriate guidance, they can use that knowledge to actively develop novel ideas for addressing social problems and needs, as well as co-create public services together with the local administration and fellow citizens.

While extensive research on the adoption of OI in the private sector has been conducted, fundamental differences in its implementation in governance pose a series of challenges, which call for further investigation on the key characteristics of public sector innovation field [11, 14]. Although there is strong linkage between open innovation and open government initiatives [13], an analysis of e-government literature shows that there are limited influences of the OI paradigm in the e-government research, poorly connected with the perspectives of management science [15]. Four divergent facets of OI in the two sectors have been identified, namely focus, aim, value, and external stakeholders [14]. It has been also stressed that there are a number of factors limiting the innovation performance of public sector organizations, which are related to the legal and socio-economic framework they operate, such as the absence of financial resources, the contradicting regulations [16], and low citizens' trust in such initiatives, as well as organizational factors such as lack of innovation culture and motivation [17–19].

Another set of challenges stems from the role of information technology on OI activities [20]. Current research trends emphasize on the utilization of social media by governmental agencies for the collection of external knowledge through crowdsourcing and web consultations [21]. Admittedly, there is a gap on the usage and efficacy of tools beyond social media, including the use of open data platforms for providing better access to and interpretation of governmental data and the information produced by internal information systems of public administrations [22]. As explicitly stated by Klein and Convertino [23], 'open innovation systems face important challenges deriving, ironically, from their very success: they can elicit such high levels of participation that it becomes very difficult to guide the crowd in productive ways and pick out the best of what they have created'. This implies problems such as low signal-to-noise ratios (only a small percentage of the ideas from OI engagements are considered as being of high quality), insular ideation (ideas are typically generated quickly by single individuals, without reference to other submitted ideas), non-comprehensive coverage (there is no inherent mechanism for ensuring that the ideas submitted comprehensively cover the most critical facets of the problem at hand), poor evaluation (based on subjective criteria, while little support is provided to aid stakeholders build upon each other's facts and reasoning), poor idea filtering (engaging stakeholders in cognitively complex and time-consuming tasks), and burdensome management of the overall innovation process (referring to monitoring, awareness, and attention mediation issues). Related studies [24] pinpoint additional issues requiring attention, such as the need to stimulate the creation and support the sustainable development of public/private communities, the (partial) formalization of the stakeholders' contributions aiming to further exploit the reasoning capabilities of the machine, the support for a collaborative construction of solutions, and the development of public services by third parties.

Generally speaking, the requirements of the OI process in the public sector can be (partially or fully) handled by a palette of ICT tools, each paying attention to a specific aspect of the process. Section 2 of this paper attempts a taxonomy of these tools, classified upon their basic purpose, identifying state-of-the-art functionalities of each category and pointing to representative solutions. Taking this classification into account, and associating the abovementioned problems and challenges to it, Sect. 3 reports on integration issues and describes an open, inclusive and sustainable platform that enables all types of stakeholders to participate in and manage the full range of activities concerning OI in the public sector. To better demonstrate the potential of the proposed solution, a specific scenario of use concerning the management of refugees and migrants inflows is also sketched. The last section of the paper outlines concluding remarks and future work directions.

2   A Taxonomy of Tools Supporting OI Phases

Typical OI systems, idea management platforms and customer engagement tools, such as Ideascale (https://ideascale.com), OpenIdeo (https://openideo.com), Spigit (https://www.spigit.com), UserVoice (https://www.uservoice.com), Imaginatik (https://www.imaginatik.com) and Nosco (http://nos.co), are used mainly in the private and to some extent in the public sector [13, 23, 25]. Generally speaking, OI processes can be supported by a variety of digital tools that allow governmental agencies harness the "wisdom of crowd". An indicative but not exhaustive list includes platforms facilitating cooperation between public administrations, citizens and other societal actors (academia and research institutes, other governmental organizations, non-governmental agencies including the private sector, non-profit organizations) [11], web-based software tools that enable access to great numbers of participants from all over the world, and user friendly toolkits guiding the actual involvement of non IT specialists in the innovation generation. These aim to fit specific purposes related to the management, monitoring, evaluation, and diffusion of OI initiatives:

- To provide the right information to potential problem solvers, by achieving better access to data and improved understanding of the problem and its parameters, and facilitate convergence among stakeholders.
- To control, manage and improve the information flows between governmental agencies and the participants of OI processes, as well as among these participants.

- To build and manage a knowledge base integrating heterogeneous internal and external knowledge and diverse experiences (from the organization's internal and external network, respectively), consolidating open governmental data and Web 2.0 content and embedding the accumulated content into the official institutional platforms.
- To effectively plan, coordinate, and monitor the OI process guiding the productivity of the crowd and providing comprehensive reports for the final outcomes.

2.1 Phases of OI Process in the Public Sector

Having considered alternative interpretations of the OI model, we claim that the one proposed by Mergel [13] is the most applicable one in the public sector. These phases are briefly discussed below.

Pre Phase: Problem Identification. This preparatory phase aims to formulate and broadcast a complete and accurate description of the problem to be solved. Although public management problems are usually defined by the government agency carrying out the initiative, social problems, needs and issues can also emerge through crowdsourcing. In the former case, modelling techniques support the formalisation of the problems. In the latter, an unstructured idea collection process is launched without any distribution of the problem statement to the public (passive crowdsourcing [21, 26]). Both instances can benefit by open data platforms that improve problem understanding and solving capacity of the involved target groups through better access and reuse of relevant government information [27].

Phase 1: Ideation. During the idea generation and collection phase, people are encouraged to submit proposed solutions and ideas, or articulate specific needs through digital platforms and participation portals. Idea solicitation is usually combined with methods aiming to boost the creativity of stakeholders and citizens such as rewards, funding, competitions, and hackathons. This phase encounters the risk of low levels of citizens' participation, which can be mitigated by mining proper sources to discover ideas and harvest the distributed knowledge that lies on the web.

Phase 2: Incubation. This phase fosters co-creation and peer production among the crowd community or external experts in a collaborative effort to incubate and develop the submitted ideas. Participants can view, comment, discuss and rate the ideas of other participants and vote for their favorite ideas, thus adapting the reviewed and improved solutions. This step includes also idea filtering and prioritization, where the community decides which solutions are best (might be combinations of submitted proposals).

Phase 3: Implementation. Selected or favorite solutions are validated through proof of concept of alternative implementations provided by the crowd or governmental actors. Implementation is complemented by progress monitoring and continuous report in order to identify necessary refinements in the process or the associated innovation concepts. Compared to the previous ones, this phase usually demonstrates less interactivity, as in most cases governmental organizations proceed in this phase without solicitation of public input.

2.2 Categories of Tools

Open Data Platforms. As a result of a long-standing movement towards the open government and open data paradigms, open data portals have proliferated over the last years, enabling users to find re-usable information. Governments have created portals mashing up national, regional and cross-national datasets, such as the EU Open Data Portal (https://www.europeandataportal.eu), CKAN (https://ckan.org), the World Bank (http://www.worldbank.org), etc. The value of public sector information is recognized with respect to leading informed policy decisions and unlocking innovation. Open data platforms play a catalytic role in opening up collaboration in the whole data lifecycle, ensuring data quality, relevance and robust access [28].

Policy Modelling & Simulation. The increasing complexity of social problems has triggered the evolvement of Policy Modelling, a research field that incorporates the use of information technologies and computational modelling to inform policy analysis, management and decision-making. On top of that, simulation methodologies (such as Agent-based, Discrete Event and System Dynamics simulation) allow testing alternative solutions, as well as predicting and assessing the impact of prospective policy choices. During an OI process, policy modelling can help users model and visualize policy related information from the real world, serving various purposes such as problem structuring and formalisation (description of a policy's main elements), or the simulation of alternative solutions' implementation reducing the associated uncertainty.

Policy Modelling and Simulation tools include ontology editors (e.g. Protégé - http://protege.stanford.edu and ELEON - http://users.iit.demokritos.gr/~eleon/) and simulation platforms (e.g. Vensim - http://www.vensim.com and Anylogic - http://www.anylogic.com). The majority of them meet the needs of public sector innovation, i.e. building and running models of a policy or a social problem to be solved, which include the main topics, sub-topics and terms of it, in order to be used for collecting relevant content authored by citizens and experts in various electronic spaces. However, there is a lack of tools allowing the population or modifications of the adopted models through automated machine or multiple user driven interventions. This could facilitate the exchange of data between a model and extracted information, as a feature that can offer to stakeholders a clear view on the issues and aspects of the discussion. This need is partially addressed by the NOMAD Authoring Tool, which provides a web-based interface to create domain and policy models that capture topics and arguments relevant to a policy and their inter-relations. Using semantic representation technologies, these models set the basis for the initiation of crawling and analysis of similar text segments on the web [21].

Social Media Monitoring. Social Media Monitoring and Analytics is an evolving marketing research field that refers to the tracking or crawling of various social media content as a way to determine the volume and sentiment of online conversation about a brand or topic [26]. Their added value lies on the fact that such investigations can be performed at real time and in a highly scalable way [29]. Well-known platforms of this category include Hootsuite (https://hootsuite.com), Trackur (http://www.trackur.com), and Sysomos (https://sysomos.com). There is limited literature concerning the use of such tools by government agencies and the extent these are useful for understanding and addressing the complex and 'wicked' problems of modern societies [9].

As proposed in [21], Social Media Analytics can reveal the issues, ideas and arguments that can best contribute in the public innovation process. The NOMAD platform is composed of a set of tools for searching and analyzing content, concerns and other information hidden within the text of citizens' conversations on the web. What differentiates NOMAD from typical Social Media Monitoring tools is that analysis is tailored against specific policy makers' goals, by properly visualizing arguments, opinions and sentiments regarding a policy domain, and creating a semantically rich, accurate stream of data that can be leveraged in any workflow. Such tools can support the required "attention mediation" suggested by Klein and Convertino [23], by providing a structured way to represent the "big picture". Disclosing the analytics and reports implies the provision of feedback to the involved population on how their input has been taken into account.

Opinion Mining. Opinion mining tools employ natural language processing, machine learning, text analysis and computational linguistics to extract relevant information from the vast amounts of human communication over the Internet or from offline sources. In fact, the propagation of opinionated data has caused the development of Web Opinion Mining [30] as a new concept in Web Intelligence, which deals with the issue of extracting, analyzing and aggregating web data about opinions. The analysis of users' opinions, known as Sentiment Analysis, is significant because through them it is possible to determine how people feel about a product or service and know how it was received by the market. We can distinguish between two types of tools in this category; those that provide a framework for data mining algorithms, e.g. Rapidminer (https://rapid-miner.com), WEKA (http://www.cs.waikato.ac.nz/ml/weka/), and KNIME (https://www.knime.org/) [31], and online platforms that can visualize (in real time) Opinion Mining Analytics on predefined Web 2.0 Sources, e.g. sentiment viz (https://www.csc2.ncsu.edu/faculty/healey/tweet_viz/tweet_app/) and Socialmention (http://www.socialmention.com).

Opinion Mining methods and tools make possible for public administration to reach citizens' opinions about policies and other topics of interest [32]. In general, traditional opinion mining techniques apply to social media content as well, however, there are certain factors that make Web 2.0 data more complicated and difficult to be parsed. An interesting study about the identification of such factors was made by Maynard et al. [33], in which they exposed important features that pose certain difficulties to traditional approaches when dealing with social media streams, such as the short length of messages, the existence of noisy content and the disambiguation in the subject of reference.

Reputation Management. Reputation Management refers to the need to seek references for an individual or organization participating in social networks and communities regarding their intellection or influence [34]. This need is partially addressed by existing online reputation management services, which monitor one's influence based on his/her activities in the social web, such as Klout (http://www.klout.com) and Naymz (http://www.naymz.com), or measure scientific research performance based on citation analysis, such as Google Scholar (http://scholar.google.com) and Research Gate (http://www.researchgate.net). Another stream of reputation management systems are using customer feedback to gain insight on suppliers and brands, or get early warning signals to reputation problems (e.g. eBay RMS).

Likewise, OI processes in the public sector may attract and make use of information from a plethora of different sources and may be affected by the public relations between multiple stakeholders, which should be treated according to their credibility. Current reputation algorithms can partially address this challenge by assigning a generic reputation score to experts. Nevertheless, a valid application of author-based idea filtering [23] for identifying promising ideas from large corpuses demands contributors to be assessed against their expertise on specific topics related to the public problem under investigation. This approach is followed by the EU-Community Reputation Management System [35], which collects data related to the knowledge, credibility and expertise of individuals, and uses a synthetic algorithm to assign a reputation score to them.

Collaboration Support. The emergence of the Web 2.0 era introduced a plethora of collaboration tools, which enable engagement at a massive scale and feature novel paradigms. At the same time, it is broadly admitted that the collaboration aspect of OI initiatives in the public sector is relatively unexplored [13]. These tools cover a broad spectrum of needs ranging from knowledge exchanging, sharing and tagging, to social networking, group authoring, mind mapping and discussing. For instance, Facebook (http://www.facebook.com) and LinkedIn (http://www.linkedin.com) are representative examples of social networking tools that facilitate the formation of online communities among people with similar interests; tools such as MindMeister (http://www.mindmeister.com) and Mindomo (http://www.mindomo.com) aim to collectively organize, visualize and structure concepts via maps to aid brainstorming and problem solving; Debatepedia (http://wiki.idebate.org) and Cohere (http://cohere.open.ac.uk) are typical tools aiming to support online discussions over the Web; phpBB (http://www.phpbb.com) and bbPress (http://www.bbpress.org) are Web 2.0 applications enabling the exchange of opinions, focusing especially on providing an environment in which users can express their thoughts without paying much attention to the structure of the discussion.

The above tool categories enable the massive and unconstraint collaboration of users; however, this very feature is the source of a problem that these tools introduce: the problem of information overload. The amount of information produced and exchanged and the number of events generated within these tools exceeds by far the mental abilities of users to: (i) keep pace with the evolution of the collaboration in which they engage, and (ii) keep track of the outcome of past sessions. Current Web 2.0 collaboration tools exhibit two important shortcomings making them prone to the problems of information overload and cognitive complexity. First, these tools are "information islands", thus providing only limited support for interoperation, integration and synergy with third party tools. While some provide specialized APIs with which integration can be achieved, these are primarily aimed at developers and not end users. Second, Web 2.0 collaboration tools are rather passive media, i.e. they lack reasoning services with which they could actively and meaningfully support collaboration.

Argumentation Support. As far as argumentation is concerned, various tools focusing on the sharing and exchange of arguments, diverse knowledge representation issues and visualization of argumentation have been developed. Tools such as Araucaria [36], Reason!Able [37] and Compendium (http://compendium.open.ac.uk) allow users to create issues, take positions on these issues, and make pro and contra arguments. They can capture the key issues and ideas and create shared understanding in a knowledge team; in some cases, they can be used to gather a semantic group memory. However, these argumentation support tools have the same problems with the aforementioned Web 2.0 collaboration tools. They too are standalone applications, lacking support for interoperability and integration with other tools (e.g. with data mining services foraging the Web to discover interesting patterns or trends). They also cope poorly with voluminous and complex data as they provide only primitive reasoning services. This makes these tools prone to the problem of information overload. Argumentation support services recently developed in the context of the Dicode project [38] address most of these issues through innovative virtual workspaces offering alternative visualization schemas that help stakeholders control the impact of voluminous and complex data, while also accommodating the outcomes of external web services, thus augmenting individual and collective sense-making (see next section).

In any case, argumentation support tools reveal additional shortcomings that prevent them from reaching a wider audience. In particular, their emphasis on providing fixed and prescribed ways of interaction within collaboration spaces make them difficult to use as they constrain the expressiveness of users, which in turn results in making these systems being used only in niche communities. Adopting the terminology used in the most common theoretical framework of situational awareness shaped by Endsley [39], this category of tools only partially cover the needs of the three stages of situational awareness, namely perception (i.e. perceive the status, attributes, and dynamics of relevant elements in the setting under consideration), comprehension (i.e. perform a synthesis of disjointed elements of the previous stage through the processes of pattern recognition, interpretation, and evaluation), and projection (i.e. extrapolate information from previous stages to find out how it will affect future instances of the operational setting).

Decision making support. Data warehouses, on-line analytical processing, and data mining have been broadly recognized as technologies playing a prominent role in the development of current and future Decision Support Systems [40], in that they may aid users make better, faster and informed decisions. However, there is still room for further developing the conceptual, methodological and application-oriented aspects of the issue. One critical point that is still missing is a holistic perspective on the issue of decision making. This originates out of the growing need to develop applications by following a more human-centric (and not problem-centric) view, in order to appropriately address the requirements of public sector stakeholders. Such requirements stem from the fact that decision making has also to be considered as a social process that principally involves human interaction [41]. The structuring and management of this interaction requires the appropriate technological support and has to be explicitly embedded in the solution offered.

The above requirements, together with the ones imposed by the way public sector stakeholders work and collaborate today, delineate a set of challenges for further decision support technology development. Such challenges can be addressed by adopting a knowledge-based decision-making view, while also enabling the meaningful accommodation of the results of the social knowledge and related mining processes. According to this view, which builds on bottom-up innovation models, decisions are considered as pieces of descriptive or procedural knowledge referring to an action commitment. In such a way, the decision making process is able to produce new knowledge, such as evidence justifying or challenging an alternative or practices to be followed or avoided after the evaluation of a decision, thus providing a refined understanding of the problem. On the other hand, in a decision making context the knowledge base of facts and routines alters, since it has to reflect the ever-changing external environment and internal structures of the organization. Knowledge management activities such as knowledge elicitation, representation and distribution influence the creation of the decision models to be adopted, thus enhancing the decision making process [42], while evaluation of contributions in the decision making process act as a reputation mechanism and provide incentives for engagement.

Table 1 attempts a mapping of the previously presented categories of ICT tools with the OI phases they primarily support. As shown, support for collaboration and social media monitoring applies to all phases, while the need for sophisticated analysis may be served by alternative combinations of tools such as those supporting policy modelling and social media monitoring.

Table 1. ICT tools used at different phases of OI in the public sector.

	Problem identification	Ideation	Incubation	Implementation
Open data platforms	x			x
Policy modelling & simulation	x			x
Social media monitoring	x	x	x	x
Opinion mining	x	x	x	
Reputation management		x	x	
Collaboration support	x	x	x	x
Argumentation support		x	x	x
Decision support			x	x

3   Towards an Inclusive OI Platform

3.1   Integration Issues

The majority of tools reported in the previous section have been originally designed to work as standalone applications. However, in complex contexts such as that of OI in the public sector, which are characterized by diverse types of stakeholders and activities, these tools need to be integrated and meaningfully orchestrated. In most cases, this is a complex and challenging issue, which depends on many factors, such as the type of the resources to be integrated, performance requirements, data heterogeneity and semantics, user interfaces, and middleware [43]. At the same time, public sector stakeholders are confronted with the rapidly growing problem of information overload. An enormous amount of content already exists in the "digital universe", i.e. information that is created, captured, or replicated in digital form, which is characterized by high rates of new information that demands attention. When working together, people have to cope with this diverse and exploding digital universe; they need to efficiently and effectively collaborate and make decisions by appropriately assembling and analyzing enormous volumes of complex multi-faceted data residing in different sources. Admittedly, when things get complex, we need to aggregate big volumes of data, and then mine it for insights that would never emerge from manual inspection or analysis of any single data source.

We argue that the above requirements can be fully addressed by an innovative web-based platform that ensures the seamless interoperability and integration of diverse components and services. The proposed solution should be able to loosely combine web services to provide an all-inclusive infrastructure ('single-access-point') for the effective and efficient support of public and private sector stakeholders participating in OI. It will not only provide a working environment for hosting and indexing of services, seamless retrieval and analysis of large-scale data sets; it will also leverage Web technologies and social networking solutions to provide stakeholders with a simple and scalable solution for targeted collaboration, resource discovery and exploitation, in a way that facilitates and boosts open innovation activities. Much attention needs to be paid to standardization issues to make existing data and software reusable with the minimum effort and without introducing new standards. Interoperability issues should be considered from a technical, conceptual and user interface point of view. When necessary, the foreseen platform should exploit rich semantics at machine level to enable the meaningful incorporation and orchestration of interoperable web services in customized OI-related workflow settings, aiming to reduce the data-intensiveness and smooth the associated workloads to a manageable level.

The proposed integration can be based on established technologies and standards of a service-oriented architecture. Application Programming Interfaces (APIs) allow different applications to connect and interact with each other, while web services provide a standardized way of integrating web-based applications using open standards such as XML, SOAP, WSDL and UDDI. Such an integration approach has been fully developed in the context of the Dicode EU project (http://dicode-project.eu/), where a widget-based solution was conceived to deliver diverse web services to end-users, a dedicated registry of services served location and recommendation purposes, and alternative service integration modes were proposed and thoroughly tested in the project's use cases. It has been shown that this approach, namely the Dicode Workbench [44], ensures a flexible, adaptable and scalable information and computation infrastructure, and exploits the competences of stakeholders to properly confront information management issues, such as information characterization, classification and interpretation, thus giving added value to the underlying collective intelligence. Moreover, it facilitates knowledge sharing and knowledge co-creation, and assures better-informed collaboration. At the same time, such an approach pays much attention to the issues of usability and ease-of-use, not requiring any particular programming expertise from the end users.

3.2   Synergy of Human and Machine Reasoning

As stressed in the literature [23, 25], the collaboration aspect needs to be emphasized in the proposed integrated platform, and meaningfully combined with tools supporting sophisticated support for analysis and reflection among stakeholders. Collaboration and decision making support services developed in the context of the Dicode project adhere to such imperatives [38]. Specifically, they (i) provide advanced collaboration support functionalities through innovative virtual workspaces, (ii) are geared towards achieving consensus and gaining of insights, (iii) support incremental formalization of argumentative collaboration (i.e. a stepwise and controlled evolution from a mere collection of individual ideas and resources to the production of highly contextualized and interrelated knowledge artifacts), which augments sense-making through reviewing, commenting on and extending the shared content, and (iv) aid stakeholders rank alternative solutions and conclude the issue at hand (i.e. reach a decision), offering a working environment that is able to interpret diverse knowledge items and their interrelationships in order to proactively suggest trends, or even aggregate data and calculate the outcome of a multi-criteria collaborative decision making process.

The above services can further augment the quality of OI activities when properly combined with a set of tools for sophisticated collection and analysis on textual content published in external social media, which has been developed in the context of the NOMAD project [21]. This is highly valuable, as it enables the collaboration and argumentation taking place as part of OI initiatives to take into account and benefit from 'fresh' relevant content contributed by citizens in numerous social media, incorporating useful ideas, knowledge as well as perceptions of the general public. Integrating components from many of the tool categories presented in Sect. 2, the NOMAD toolset provides APIs for services that: (i) create and maintain policy models (incorporating the main elements of public policies), (ii) mine relevant user-generated data from a variety of online text sources (e.g. political blogs, social media, web-sites), (iii) perform linguistic analysis to transform free text into a set of structured data, (iv) discover and extract arguments from free text, (v) perform sentiment analysis to classify text segments according to their 'tone' (positive, neutral, negative), (vi) cluster arguments, based on calculated similarities, and present automatically-generated summaries, and (vii) visualize a structured view of the crowd opinion on a policy, providing insights on how much, when and how people are talking about a specific issue.

Such a combination between human collaboration support and data collection and analysis tools builds on the synergy between human and machine intelligence to facilitate and enhance individual and collective work during the entire OI process. In addition, it addresses diverse requirements related to the data intensiveness and cognitive complexity of settings concerning OI in the public sector.

3.3 An Application Scenario

The proposed solution is illustrated through a realistic example concerning the development of public policy for the management of immigrants-refugees inflows in Greece. Assuming that the related OI process is initiated by the Greek Ministry of Interior, policy makers and advisors from the Ministry in cooperation with other stakeholders (NGO representatives, governmental agencies, migration experts, etc.) use the Dicode Collaboration Support services (see Fig. 1) to elaborate the issue. They agree on an initial policy model incorporating three alternative solutions (appearing next to the 'light bulb' icons in the Dicode workspace of Fig. 1). Different stakeholders' perspectives are associated with these solutions as arguments in favor or against them (shown with green and red arrows, respectively). Stakeholders may also contribute to a better understanding of the problem and its policy context by uploading supplementary material of any format (e.g. documents referring to EU legislation, multimedia material pointing to a particular dimension of the problem, informative graphs and tables etc.).

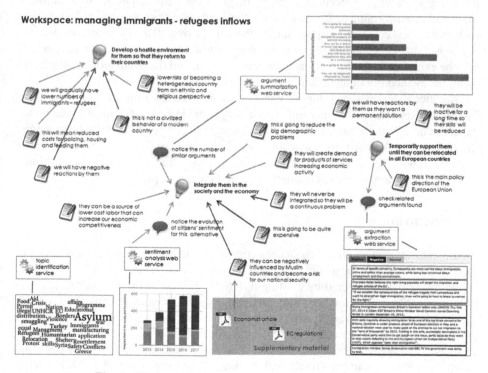

Fig. 1. Workspace of the application scenario (an instance).

At the same time, stakeholders may easily invoke external web services (notice the 'double gear' icons in the Dicode workspace) to look for additional data related to the policy model under consideration. Through appropriate APIs, external services may upload their outcomes into the Dicode collaboration workspace, thus making them part of the undergoing collaboration. For instance, a Topic Identification service may reveal - through the word cloud shown in Fig. 1 - the most popular topics discussed by citizens in relevant web sources (blogs, news sites, social media communities, etc.), thus triggering the consideration of additional perspectives (e.g. those related to provision of asylum). In the instance shown in Fig. 1, a set of NOMAD services have been already executed to aid the required sophisticated analysis of the associated big textual data. Specifically: (i) the Sentiment Analysis service, which enables stakeholders to view the extent (and evolution over time) of the support or opposition of the crowd on an alternative solution, (ii) the Argument Extraction service that reveals new arguments in favor or against the already proposed solutions, which can then be exploited by stakeholders, (iii) the Argument Summarization service that returns the volume of extracted arguments' clusters to provide users with estimations about their popularity.

The collaborative environment proposed allows stakeholders to upload and refine alternative ideas and proposals, argue on them, and evaluate existing content consolidating the knowledge brought forward by both humans and the machine. Machine-retrieved content can be leveraged by stakeholders, in that it enables them advance an ongoing deliberation and gain new insights, based on 'fresh' content from the society reflecting knowledge, perceptions and feelings of the general public. In addition, it motivates brainstorming in the ideation and the incubation phases. Finally, the retrieved (external textual content) analytics may further aid the overall decision making process. It is noted that decision making support services also offered by the Dicode approach may be exploited in the implementation phase of OI to aid the evaluation of alternative solutions by incorporating various algorithms and criteria.

Additional services may further enhance the OI process illustrated in Fig. 1. For instance, a Reputation Management service may provide ranking of ideas based on the expertise of the contributor; a Policy Simulation service may run scenarios to predict the outcome of the most prevalent solutions. In parallel, real time social data can be aggregated with statistical information coming from public administration (e.g. Ministries, Greek Asylum Service, Eurostat) or related open data platforms.

4   Conclusions

Taking into account identified challenges concerning the implementation and advancement of OI practices in the public sector, this paper embarks on the analysis and synthesis of the functionalities offered by existing ICT tools. It focuses on the fundamental and highly valuable integration between collaboration and decision support tools, on one hand, and data collection and analysis tools, on the other. Associating the identified tool categories with the diverse OI phases, the need for collaboration and sophisticated data collection and analysis has been stressed. This led to the description of an open and inclusive solution that may foster and facilitate OI initiatives in the public sector, enabling expert argumentative consultations to be informed by relevant external social media content incorporating the knowledge, perceptions and feeling of the society.

The proposed platform offers a novel collaborative environment that allows stakeholders immerse in Web 2.0 interaction paradigms and exploit its enormous potential to collaborate through reviewing, commenting on and extending the shared content along the OI phases. The platform enables stakeholders maintain chains of views and opinions, accompanied by the supporting data, which may reflect, at any time, the current collective knowledge on the issue under consideration, and justify a particular decision made or action taken. In the proposed solution, collaboration services are not standalone applications that operate autonomously; instead, they coexist and make use of other services' outcomes to improve their performance.

Future work directions include the implementation of the proposed OI platform and its practical application and evaluation within the context of diverse OI practices in the public sector. Also, it will be very interesting to evaluate to what extent such a platform enables a transfer of knowledge, perceptions and feelings from the society towards the experts/technocrats, contributing to overcoming the negative aspects of the 'technocracy' (e.g. limited understanding of diverse needs, values and concerns of different stakeholder groups on particular social problems the experts analyze) [35].

References

1. Chesbrough, H.W., Vanhaverbeke, W., West, J.: New Frontiers in Open Innovation. Oxford University Press, Oxford (2014)
2. Chesbrough, H.W.: Open Innovation: The New Imperative for Creating and Profiting from Technology. (2003)
3. Chesbrough, H.W.: The era of open innovation. MIT Sloan Manag. Rev. **44**(3), 35–41 (2003)
4. Spithoven, A., Vanhaverbeke, W., Roijakkers, N.: Open innovation practices in SMEs and large enterprises. Small Bus. Econ. **41**, 537–562 (2013)
5. Felin, T., Zenger, T.R.: Closed or open innovation? Problem solving and the governance choice. Res. Policy **43**, 914–925 (2014)
6. Mina, A., Bascavusoglu-Moreau, E., Hughes, A.: Open service innovation and the firm's search for external knowledge. Res. Policy **43**, 853–866 (2014)
7. Bellantuono, N., Pontrandolfo, P., Scozzi, B.: Different practices for open innovation: a context-based approach Different practices for open innovation: a context-based approach. J. Knowl. Manag. **17**, 558–568 (2013)
8. Mergel, I.: A framework for interpreting social media interactions in the public sector. Gov. Inform. Q. **30**, 327–334 (2013)
9. Loukis, E., Charalabidis, Y., Androutsopoulou, A.: Promoting open innovation in the public sector through social media monitoring. Gov. Inform. Q. **34**, 99–109 (2017)
10. Ferro, E., Molinari, F.: Framing web 2.0 in the process of public sector innovation: going down the participation ladder. Eur. J. ePractice **9**, 1–15 (2010)
11. Lee, S.M., Hwang, T., Choi, D.: Open innovation in the public sector of leading countries. Manag. Decis. **50**, 147–162 (2012)
12. Chesbrough, H., Bogers, M.: Explicating open innovation: clarifying an emerging paradigm for understanding innovation keywords. New Frontiers in Open Innovation, pp. 1–37 (2014)
13. Mergel, I.: Opening government: designing open innovation processes to collaborate with external problem solvers. Soc. Sci. Comput. Rev. **33**, 599–612 (2015)

14. Kankanhalli, A., Zuiderwijk, A., Tayi, G.K.: Open innovation in the public sector: A research agenda. Gov. Inform. Q. **34**, 84–89 (2017)
15. Viscusi, G., Poulin, D., Tucci, C.: Open innovation research and e-government: clarifying the connections between two fields. In: XII Conference of the Italian Chapter of AIS (itAIS 2015) (2015)
16. Mergel, I., Desouza, K.: Implementing open innovation in the public sector: the case of challenge.gov. Public Adm. Rev. **73**, 882–890 (2013)
17. Bekkers, V., Tummers, L.G., Voorberg, W.H.: From public innovation to social innovation in the public sector: a literature review of relevant drivers and barriers. Erasmus University Rotterdam, Rotterdam (2013)
18. Misuraca, G., Viscusi, G.: Shaping public sector innovation theory: an interpretative framework for ICT-enabled governance innovation. Electron. Commer. Res. **15**, 303–322 (2015)
19. Van Duivenboden, H., Thaens, M.: ICT-driven innovation and the culture of public administration: a contradiction in terms? Inform. Polity. **13**, 213–232 (2008)
20. Criado, J.I., Sandoval-Almazan, R., Gil-Garcia, J.R.: Government innovation through social media. Gov. Inform. Q. **30**, 319–326 (2013)
21. Charalabidis, Y., Loukis, E., Androutsopoulou, A., Karkaletsis, V., Triantafillou, A.: Passive crowdsourcing in government using social media. Transforming Gov. People, Process Policy **8**, 283–308 (2014)
22. Ham, J., Lee, J.-N., Kim, D.J., Choi, B.: Open innovation maturity model for the government: an open system perspective. In: Proceedings of the 36th International Conference on Information Systems (ICIS), pp. 1–11 (2015)
23. Klein, M., Convertino, G.: A roadmap for open innovation system. J. Soc. Media Organ. **2**, 1 (2015)
24. Assar, S., Boughzala, I., Isckia, T.: eGovernment trends in the web 2.0 era and the open innovation perspective: an exploratory field study. In: Janssen, M., Scholl, H.J., Wimmer, M.A., Tan, Y.-h. (eds.) EGOV 2011. LNCS, vol. 6846, pp. 210–222. Springer, Heidelberg (2011). https://doi.org/10.1007/978-3-642-22878-0_18
25. Hrastinski, S., Kviselius, N.Z., Ozan, H., Edenius, M.: A review of technologies for open innovation: Characteristics and future trends. In: Proceedings of the Annual Hawaii International Conference on System Sciences (2010)
26. Bekkers, V., Edwards, A., de Kool, D.: Social media monitoring: responsive governance in the shadow of surveillance? Gov. Inform. Q. **30**, 335–342 (2013)
27. Chan, C.M.L.: From open data to open innovation strategies: creating E-Services using open government data. In: Proceedings of the 46th Hawaii International Conference on System Sciences (HICSS-46). pp. 1890–1899 (2013)
28. Alexopoulos, C., Loukis, E., Mouzakitis, S., Petychakis, M., Charalabidis, Y.: Analysing the characteristics of open government data sources in Greece. J. Knowl. Econ., 1–33 (2015). https://doi.org/10.1007/s13132-015-0298-8
29. Stavrakantonakis, I., Gagiu, A.-E., Kasper, H., Toma, I., Thalhammer, A.: An approach for evaluation of social media monitoring tools. In: 1st International Workshop on Common Value Management, pp. 52–64 (2012)
30. Taylor, E.M., Rodríguez O., C., Velásquez, J.D., Ghosh, G., Banerjee, S.: Web opinion mining and sentimental analysis. In: Velásquez, J.D., Palade, V., and Jain, L.C. (eds.) Advanced Techniques in Web Intelligence-2: Web User Browsing Behaviour and Preference Analysis. SCI, vol. 452, pp. 105–126. Springer, Heidelberg (2013). https://doi.org/10.1007/978-3-642-33326-2_5

31. Dhokrat, A., Khillare, S., Mahender, C.N.: Review on techniques and tools used for opinion mining. Int. J. Comput. Appl. Technol. Res. **4**, 419–424 (2015)
32. Maragoudakis, M., Loukis, E., Charalabidis, Y.: A review of opinion mining methods for analyzing citizens' contributions in public policy debate. In: Electronic Participation Proceedings of the 3rd IFIP WG 8.5 International Conference, ePart 2011. pp. 298–313 (2011)
33. Maynard, D., Bontcheva, K., Rout, D.: Challenges in developing opinion mining tools for social media. In: LREC 2012, pp. 15–22 (2012)
34. He, D., Peng, Z., Hong, L., Zhang, Yu.: A social reputation management for web communities. In: Wang, L., Jiang, J., Lu, J., Hong, L., Liu, B. (eds.) WAIM 2011. LNCS, vol. 7142, pp. 167–174. Springer, Heidelberg (2012). https://doi.org/10.1007/978-3-642-28635-3_16
35. Androutsopoulou, A., Mureddu, F., Loukis, E., Charalabidis, Y.: Passive expert-sourcing for policy making in the European union. In: Tambouris, E., Panagiotopoulos, P., Sæbø, Ø., Wimmer, M.A., Pardo, T.A., Charalabidis, Y., Soares, D.S., Janowski, T. (eds.) ePart 2016. LNCS, vol. 9821, pp. 162–175. Springer, Cham (2016). https://doi.org/10.1007/978-3-319-45074-2_13
36. Reed, C., Rowe, G.: Araucaria: Software for puzzles in argument diagramming and XML. Department of Applied Computing, University of Dundee Technical report, pp. 1–21 (2001)
37. van Gelder, T.: Argument mapping with Reason!Able. Am. Philos. Assoc. Newslett. Philos. Comput. **2**, 85–90 (2002)
38. Karacapilidis, N.: Mastering Data-Intensive Collaboration and Decision Making: Research and Practical Applications in the Dicode Project. Springer Science & Business Media, Switzerland (2014)
39. Endsley, M.R.: Toward a theory of situation awareness in dynamic systems: Situation awareness. Hum. Factors **37**, 32–64 (1995)
40. Shim, J.P., Warkentin, M., Courtney, J.F., Power, D.J., Sharda, R., Carlsson, C.: Past, present, and future of decision support technology. Decis. Support Syst. **33**, 111–126 (2002)
41. Smoliar, S.W.: Interaction management: The next (and necessary) step beyond knowledge management. Bus. Process Manag. J. **9**, 337–353 (2003)
42. Karacapilidis, N.I., Gordon, T.F.: Dialectical planning. In: Proceedings of 14th International Joint Conference on Artificial Intelligence (IJCAI 1995); Workshop on Intelligent Manufacturing Systems, pp. 239–250 (1995)
43. Ziegler, P., Dittrich, K.R.: Three decades of data integration — all problems solved? In: 18th IFIP World Computer Congress (WCC 2004), pp. 3–12 (2004)
44. de la Calle, G., Alonso-Martinez, E., Tzagarakis, M., Karacapilidis, N.: The dicode workbench: a flexible framework for the integration of information and web services. In: Proceedings of the 14th International Conference on Information Integration and Web-based Applications and Services, pp. 16–25. ACM, New York (2012)

The Penetration of Robotics into the Administrative Function of the State - Pre-economy of Citizenry's Benefit

Despoina Kotsi[✉]

G. Souri 16, 13451 Athens, Greece
despoinakwtsh@gmail.com

Abstract. Today's digital robots could become tomorrow's public servants containing algorithms as integral components of their computer program system. This is how we would slowly slip into the automated society, transforming many facets of life more basically our relationship with governmental branches. The fundamental principle in the constitutional Charter of ...e-administration becomes not surprisingly an algorithm. Robot and human mind reveal a difference between perceivability and impassioned perceptivity. Legality and a "Supreme widespread Constitutionality" form inserted data provided to robot in order to calculate upon. For this feedback eliminates unlawful activity of Administration. Robot is charged with a duty of transmitting the request of the administered to the Natural Correspondent of the person who is a superior officer, probably robot's manipulator. It can also receive a hearing by citizens according to their right for a due process. The robot is in principle not a subject itself, but an interject (=it confronts the citizen but also the State). It also contains both legislation and jurisprudence. The law that is kind of the robot's heart and guides it is also the product of state will. Correspondingly, jurisprudence, which is the blood with which the heart produces pulsating responses, is the guarantor of the freedoms of the individual. Thus, the robot - civil servant is an autonomous and anarchist guardian of the state organization. At last, all - both citizens and Government - are happy with the robot's operating as a public servant.

Keywords: Public-robot servant · Algorithm · Computer · Administration · Legality · Human · Administered · Individual · Absolutization · Problem · Liability · Administrative act · Competence · State · Subject/inject

1 Introductory Aspect: An Algorithm as a Constitutive Principle of Administrative Action

In Greek mythology,

Talos was a giant automaton made of bronze to protect Europa in Crete from pirates and invaders.

He circled the island's shores three times daily. (en.wikipedia.org)

D. Kotsi—Lawyer.

© Springer International Publishing AG 2017
S.K. Katsikas and V. Zorkadis (Eds.): E-Democracy 2017, CCIS 792, pp. 244–254, 2017.
https://doi.org/10.1007/978-3-319-71117-1_17

(For Minos used him as guardian of the law in the city, and Talos as the same for the rest of Crete. For Talos thrice a year made a round of the villages, guarding the laws in them, by holding their laws inscribed on brazen tablets, which gave him his name of "brazen.")

"Minos", Plato translated by W.R.M. Lamb.

A huge part in nowadays notion about Artificial Intelligence is being occupied by Robotics. A robot differs from a machine by regulating itself: it gathers and receives information from outside and utilizes it to adjust and consider it in further situations [1]. In fact, robots constitute technical systems that perceive (sensing and object recognition), think (reasoning and decision making) and act (feedback and ultimate control) [2]. Firstly, they recognize the environment and then they decide upon this specific perception – cross-fertilization of embedded and collected data – on what to do next. Finally, they translate reasoned decision into moderated activity.

Today's digital robots contain algorithms as integral components of their computer program system. This is how we are slipping into the automated society, transforming many facets of life more basically our relationship with governmental branches. Administration – just like industry and market – will follow the flow for the benefit of the citizenry. Invasion of robots in public administration should be combined with regulation. The fundamental principle in the constitutional Charter of …e-administration is not surprisingly an algorithm. In the most general terms, algorithms can be defined as "well-defined set[s] of steps for accomplishing a certain goal" [3]. Weighting becomes the core element in the safely-built algorithm with the mathematical structure. Indeed, we have to do with a "mathematical equation expressing an outcome variable as a function of selected explanatory variables put together in a particular way [...]" [4].

So, out of a "panspermia" (i.e. variety) of algorithms regulating public administration, there is one standing distinctly on its throne:

$$1 + OX = 1.$$

Unit stands for the individual, the person under administration that seeks integrity, plus is for the parallel orientation of citizen and the city. Zero is the wishful diminution of state power multiplied always by objective facts and resulting in zero compulsion. One is the result of the addition between total respect for the individual and augmenting desire for the deletion of unjustified force. But, the above-mentioned zero which evangelizes the futuristic shrinking of state enforcement summarizes concrete factors that contribute to the ideal fulfillment of the individual. Zero represents as well (a) principle of legality, (b) principle of constitutionality, (c) utilitarianism & social engineering – perhaps! It lies in the eye of the beholder (the thinking ideologue might be), if (d) international assimilation, (e) economic status, (f) public purpose or even (g) public order form a zero variable, seen in terms of struggling to reach an absolute good. To be clear, zero stands for absolute Justice

2   Putting a Robot in the Shoes of a Public Servant – The Happy Ministry

2.1   Lawful Activity

Taking into consideration the autonomous nature of a robot, we tend to ask ourselves if a shaped conscience characterizes these sophisticated and computerized systems that we call "robots". Does a robot contain animus? For animus delivers feeling reactions and sentimental mode of thinking and behaving together with rational correspondence to exogenous stimulus. A robot is bare of and remains untouched to lyric comportment of the governed. To illustrate this point, let us refer to the example of a disabled administered waiting to be served in the queue of a governmental agency. The public-robot servant should definitely prioritize the citizen to others, but this would happen merely based upon a verifiable rational truth that points the social necessity for this noble sort of civility. After all, courtesy as an exemption to the general rule, which is defined within the boundaries of public benefit, and as a specified dimension of the principle of good administration is well-deserved norm of the Science of Administration – part of public law. In no case – irrelevant how strongly it matches emotional and popular sense of justice- social adaptability of public services meets nuggets of sensitiveness. It is of crucial importance to discriminate between perceivability and impassioned perceptivity – the latter belongs only to the human beings endogenously. Adjudicating algorithm systems – i.e. robots – could only attain the ability of co-understanding: approaching a situation by calculating a golden ration conforming to a fair solution. Humans with a psyche can possibly and by nature treat an administered with exaggerating compassion. That is why principle of legality is being imposed on public servants. Limit is always the engraved. On the opposite, administrative agencies can turn unjustifiably harmful by nature besides psyche as an inherent condition. But here it is not the absence of sensitivity causing harm –as wrongfully is first thought-, but rather the lack of reasonableness which is anticipated as the safety valve for the public interest. However, since a civilized polity cannot confide in the hands of public servants and their inner criterion for justice and the good administration, it invented the rule of law. To sum up, public-robot servants can add to law-governed societies and be morally consistent at the same time as long as they are purely reasonable creatures leading to the disappearance of emotionality whereas constructing cautiously the bridge of rationalized sensitiveness: bridge to an era of fully incorporated human inferiority (e.g. disability, poverty, diversity, il-liberalness etc.) to the administrator's cerebrum.

Robots' concluding in Administration's logical performing so powerfully, poses in return great questions about the principle of constitutionality. Who is after all and at the end of the day the exponent of the golden ratio between sacred individuality and social needs? Is the lawmaker, the founding fathers or even the constitutional/administrative judge the one that beholds the measure of adaptability to fairness? What if the robot itself makes a decision – in real terms it is about an administrative decision- that contradicts legality in favor of a safely well-reasoned conformity with the Constitution wording? According to the Greek constitution, for instance, public servants "owe faith to the Constitution [...]" [5]. Can we say that robotic creatures are destined to act in the frame of administrative activity without constitutional charters embedded? To go even further we could mention federal (like E.U. texts) and international obligations. Let's agree to refer to all these under the name of a "Supreme widespread Constitutionality", which includes both state supreme order and supranational acquisition – the latter derived from the French neologism "acquis supranational". The answer is that reasonable decisions are not qualified as such without holistic view of the pragmatological and legal sphere. For legal culture and epistemology is a systemic approach of things. So, in order for Government to diminish the threat of an extremely large interpretation of the supreme widespread constitutionality by public-robot servants, each word of the texts with a higher validation will be matched to the respective case-law so far in order to create an interpretation-tank for the robot. That way, results will be predictable and courts would again have the last say in interpreting the Constitution. One could say that the public-robot servant is a walking (and working!) law library and the Central Administration charged with performance of these servants intervenes like a doctor to their computer-cerebrum injecting alterations that happen in the legal field.

Part of Administration's lawful activity is the public procurement procedure. Contracting Authority has discretion and margin of appreciation as to define and specify the criteria to be used in evaluation process of offers. The relative list of selection criteria in the EU Directive is indicative. The criteria that are always appreciated and taken into account are: quality, price, operating costs, aesthetic and environmental characteristics, and more. Absolute weighting of the above-mentioned is only possible in computational terms and with all criteria into mathematical quantities translated. The robot provides security of choice and guarantees transparency and equal treatment of candidates and thus prevents unfair competition in absolute terms. It is self-evident and unnecessary to say that such a streamlined judgment must be reasonably verified if objections are raised. Apart from this, the criteria for assessing bids must be formulated so as to enable the persons concerned to fully understand their qualifications. The robot can therefore predict computationally on the basis of the criteria he sets – and by quoting the analytic substance of each criterion – the most ideal candidates. Thus, the economy of conventional action of government is achieved and the contracting authority is discharged right from the pre-contractual stage. Specifically, in the document "COMMISSION STAFF WORKING PAPER Evaluation Report Impact and Effectiveness of EU Public Procurement Legislation" (2011) it is stated that: "Suppliers questioned had mentioned the increase of the requirements of the public sector in the environmental performance criteria. They worried that the requirements were changing regularly and that there was no homogeneous set of national or international standards." The robotic contracting authority could diagnose irregularities and provide continuity in state requirements as a treatment. Last but not least, the robot-Administrator of the Contracting Authority does not disclose information that is known to it and which is classified as confidential and has to do with technical or commercial secrets concerning economic operators. Thus, the robot builds confidence in administrative transparency, objectivity and effectiveness.

2.2 Unlawful Activity

If the State damages an individual, it is then liable to compensation. However, given that the margin of error is minimized through the absolutization of the process with mathematical reasoning, the probability of damage and consequently liability is reduced to zero. This is the primary finding that someone comes up with when a damage problem is raised.

Key feature in the examination of facts is that liability requires activity of the Administration's organ as a precondition. Such activity is clearly established in administrative law as an act, an omission, a material energy, or an omission of physical energy. Autonomous nature of robots makes us wondering who holds liability in case of an error. Whenever fault is detected in the structure and the programming of the computerized robot-actor, then regulator behind the robot is responsible and subjectively liable to compensation. We have to clear up this periphery of the problem as culpability of State is objectively (i.e. generally) attributed to Administration, but law gives us indication that Administration seeks in the end reductively from the individually responsible person the amount with which it has compensated the individual (105 of the Insider Law of the Civil Code). If the widely-appraised sophisticated system of the robot presents a functional error that could not by highest levels of due diligence be predicted – science deadlock for example -, then accountableness remains objective and attributable to Administration as long as human modulator cannot be held responsible. Compensation in money for wrongful instructions delivered by manipulator cannot be claimed by the robot as it does not have human needs to cover and hence does not save money. However, the evolution of the robotic personality will recognize them the right to save credits as remuneration for the work they perform. Depending on the type of work, the severity and the difficulty of the work being done, each robot will have accumulated credit units of value on a personal tab in the administrative files! For any damage that affects an administered and it is attributable to a fault in his or her own robot's autonomous operation, Administration will deduct units from its value measurement. Going a little further, robot-civil servants will have after scolding them to pursue the return to the previous high efficiency as shown in the list and therefore competitively conceive of their colleagues.

As stated above, public-robot servants have legal feedback embedded in their computer-system and as a result, all their actions are supported by a systematic resolution. It is by far impossible for the walking/working law library to go against the law, to commit illegality – the latter constitutes main precondition for civil liability of the State. Inherent is the calculation in favor of the public interest as well. Citizens [6] can always acquire on demand a printed copy with the whole of the robot's legal resolution. As for the qualification of exercise of public power, we have to agree that robots confirmedly do possess the ability to produce administrative acts, in other words capacity of dominantly intervene into the legal sphere of administered individuals. Robots must have a mandate, an act of appointment or any other form of delegation so as liability to be fulfilled. They are not in abstract understood as public servants. Finally, we admit that robots do have only service nature and are executive beings, but they must in any case have a legal bond with the Administrative Branch.

3 Services of P-ubic R-obots are a Blessing to Administration's P-ublic R-elations!

3.1 Application of Citizens to Administration

"Decisions that rely on machine learning are unlikely to be rejected by the courts as insufficiently reasoned. To be sure, administrative law has long compelled reason-giving by agency officials, especially for rulemaking, rendering reasons a cornerstone of accountable and transparent government." [7]. The test for arbitrary and capricious standard can be found in the State Farm [8] where we see Court's demand for an agency to "articulate a satisfactory explanation for its action, including a rational connection between the facts and the choice made". That Court offered what is now canonical test for arbitrary and capricious review: "Normally, an agency rule would be arbitrary and capricious if the agency has relied on factors which Congress has not intended it to consider, entirely failed to consider an important aspect of the problem, offered an explanation for its decision that runs counter to the evidence before the agency, or is so implausible that it could not be ascribed to a difference in view or the product of agency expertise." [7].

Question remains whether the so called auto-control of Administration, which is a stage before accessing the courts' jurisdiction, has a role in the era of agencies' exclusion of arbitrary and capricious action. Does a procedure that demands provision of reasoning by administrators – robots in this case – meet any need for reparation when administrative system itself has been destined not to fail at all? The issue is primarily an issue of Democracy. Citizens have the constitutionally guaranteed right of petition. The participative character of our political regime - the Republic - protectively embraces the respondent's reaction and in no case does deny it. The robot as a civil servant is by definition inferior to his manager and is always hierarchically subject to a human organ. Its role to the citizen's request is the duty of transmitting the request to the Natural Correspondent of the person (according to the Natural Judge). This right of the Natural Correspondent is now becoming more intense in the era of artificial intelligence as a right of contact and physical communication between man and man to solve a related personal problem. Of course, conditions will be met in order for the request to arrive at the natural recipient - inadequate justification, omission of legal action, silence, and so on. Proper regulation of robots for handling cases, however, is estimated to drastically reduce recourse to Natural Correspondent who is the senior administrative officer and is in charge of the respective task.

A gigantic change takes place in the existing norms of the bureaucratic structure of the administrative action in modern countries. The hierarchical boss, who is sometimes a robot-manager, cannot carry out a legitimacy check since he is the same person who introduces the legality information into the computerized system the robot follows. We might perhaps say that if a hierarchical superior and manager are not identified, any legal inconsistency acknowledged by the citizen seeking to restore the law and its application is first checked for its merits by the hierarchical officer. The hierarchical officer is then responsible for checking the robot manager for the algorithm he implanted in the robot. However, we have to say that the hierarchical control in this case is not unnecessary since it can lead to the dismissal of the administrator-manager due to the gravity of the misdemeanor.

What disappears from the forefront of hierarchical control is the control by the hierarchical senior of employee's – public-robot servant's in this case – feasibility. According to conventional wisdom, opportunity control [9] is the power that has the superior body to prevent adoption or cancel an operation that has already been issued, and only because it disagrees, that is, because it does not find it appropriate. In exercising control of expediency, the superior body - in the case of preventive review - refuses to approve an administrative act and - in the case of repressive control - it annuls or modifies an act, that it does not find it essentially correct. The intervention of the head of the hierarchical institution has no other limit here but its own will, which exists absolutely. The robot determines on the basis of input data how it will behave, and this is ultimately verifiable in court. The senior hierarchical officer remains sovereign as a Natural Responder, but his will is restricted to the checking procedure. Robotic actions are entirely dominant by the fact that the operational system of administrative products has been absolutized by the robot function. Moreover, the margin of discretion is deposited on the robot, for he is the one who acts decisively (=produces a rule of law).

Crucial in a Republic is the usefulness of administrative appeals to agencies by the administered. After reflection, the administrative appeals are the pleasing expression of the Civil Society because they establish a legal relation between the State and the citizens. Indeed, the remedies confer on administrated a power of attributability [10]. Who is receptive of such appeals: the robot who is the author of the act or the superior officer? In case of a simple appeal, the robot can receive a demand of reproduction of the administrative act as long as the administered verifies the harmful result of the computer's calculation. Truth is that if an algorithm is concretely founded, then an answer would hardly be different from the initially delivered. Under those circumstances, the form of appeal that prevails is the hierarchical appeal, directed to the public servant who is superior – either a robot or a human.

An interesting aspect of the matter concerns the transfer of authority from a superior body to a lower one (e.g. robots) as well as the signing authorization. Can the highest organ pass on his full competence? The answer is no. The senior officer who is a human being is right for this reason in his place and he has a competence of moral quality that artificial intelligence cannot reach. Artificial operation is ideal and totally acceptable by the society, but man always has control and responsibility for the smooth functioning and operational interconnection of computer networks. That is why the transfer of competency to the robot is not tolerable under the law, because it just ignores the justification of the existence of the human's high competence. Contrary to high competence, the robot can sign operations or other documents alongside the upper organs as it can be followed up. There is no exclusivity of competence being transferred in that case to justify legal prohibition.

In any application to the Administration, robots ultimately ensure and guarantee a basic general principle of administrative law: impartiality. A civil servant who is a robot has no personal interest in handling a case. In the absence of subjective elements of the robot, there is no particular link or particular relation or sharp opposition to the persons involved in an action. One objection that somebody might argue is that there is a particular relationship between the robot and the Administration itself, since it is its own representative. However, as we have said, the robot has all the legislation that, as the whole of subjective knowledge, is the same as the closest degree of objectivity. The robot is therefore not a subject itself, but an interject (=it confronts the citizen but also the State). The law that is kind of the robot's heart and guides it is also the product of state will. Correspondingly, jurisprudence, which is the blood with which the heart produces pulsating responses, is the guarantor of the freedoms of the individual. Thus, the robot - civil servant is the autonomous anarchist guardian of the state organization.

3.2 Hearing of Citizens by Administration

The principle of the previous hearing has been placed in the sphere of administration as a precondition for the issuance of individual administrative acts in the field of state administration, especially when it comes to acts in detriment to the administrated. The robot algorithm has information about the possible facts that it will be required to address and take into consideration before issuing each individual administrative act. However, it cannot predict in its entirety the human pathogenesis, which in turn is unpredictable. The person is characterized by uniqueness and must be treated with specialty. The citizen himself is the best informed person about his case. The robot we called "an interject" as opposed to the "subject", the way it has received the legal theoretical equipment from the State, the same is needy of the subject to understand the subjective data. With regard to the robot's assignment, the robot modulator should enter keywords in his computer system that relate to fundamental rights in their kernel and hence constitutional predictions. This is the way to map the critical situations to be taken into account for the adoption of the administrative act. It is imperative for the administered to be listened in order for the processing of the internal computer to be contacted properly. As we shall see "a constitutional provision, it constitutes a proclamation whose very substance concludes with the idea of taking part in the administrative life, at least as regards the part of the administrative action concerning the rights and the legally protected interests of the administrators" [11]. Here, the right to a previous hearing is a right of defense in the direction of a positive result, as opposed to the request to the Administration, where we have the right of attack in the direction of the positive outcome. Moreover, it adds to the strengthening of the status activus processualis [12] of the affected. Right to a previous hearing by administration achieves a balance between the machinery of artificial thinking and the physical humanity that undergoes sometimes painful real situations.

Likewise a judge, who whenever hearing of the administered did not take place, comes into the essence of the case by curing the void of the Administration to listen to the person concerned, robot-administrator plays the role of a "Primitive Judge" and performs adjudicating algorithms to extract a convenient and fair solution. At last, the saying does not only goes "Iura novit curia", but also "Imperium novit curia" in the robot-era. Concurrence of the two branches is a matter of analysis however not to be investigated in the present article.

One incidental mention [13] has to be made about the flexibility with which the U.S. Supreme Court treats the right to hearing before Administration and the reflective effects of that viewpoint on robotic-centered Administration. The Mathews [14] Court explicitly noted that, "due process is flexible and calls for such procedural protections as the particular situation demands". Initially, the Court in Goldberg v. Kelly [15] had pointed out the importance of welfare recipients having the ability to appear in person before the government official who makes the decision about whether to terminate benefits. At paragraph 268, it finds unconstitutional the procedures that do "not permit recipients to appear personally with or without counsel before the official who finally determines continued eligibility" and do not allow recipients to "present evidence to that official orally, or to confront or cross-examine adverse witnesses". The Court rejected a process in that case that was based on written documentation, finding that it was even insufficient for a human caseworker to present the case on behalf of the welfare recipient (paragraph 269). Six years later, in Mathews v. Eldridge, the Supreme Court held that, in the context of Social Security disability benefits, the government could structure a process based solely on paperwork review and without offering the recipients of those government benefits a pre-termination hearing before an administrative official (paragraphs 321–322). The Court did not overturn Goldberg, but instead offered the now-canonical balancing test involving three factors that must be weighed in determining whether due process has been satisfied:

First, the private interest that will be affected by the official action; second, the risk of an erroneous deprivation of such interest through the procedures used, and probable value, if any, of additional procedural safeguards; and finally, the Government's interest, including the function involved and the fiscal and administrative burdens that the additional or substitute procedural requirement would entail (paragraph 335).

It is obvious that the gravity of one's case should not exclude the due process of previous hearing even if the Court states at times that "the government could structure a process based solely on paperwork review [...]". The latter would make the job of the public-robot servants easier and more simple, but claimants should certainly have a right to be heard or we should totally abolish the human factor. Guess what: we cannot. It is feasible to robotize the state and its services, but it is impossible to eliminate human needs and reactions. In a particular context of Mathews, the Court noted that the administrative review system "operated on an open-file basis" (par. 347), meaning that those denied disability benefits could, at any point following their deprivations, submit new evidence. Robots are absolutely convenient with this suggestion as well since they have all case-information embedded.

4   Conclusion: Talos is the "Happy" Minister

Talos, the first called automated robot of ancient Greece, was the guardian of law application while he was holding laws of villages inscribed on his brazen tablets. Similarity with the visioned robot of the future that will staff public administration is crystal-clear, as we told that the public-robot servant has all applicable legislation incorporated in his artificial mind. He is therefore happy to serve the administered as he fulfils his very functional existence. We could say that there is not yet a right of the robot to private life except for its need for rest, which comes naturally to be recognized. But still, that need complements functionality aim. Unlike humans, the education of many had failed to supply them with a noble purpose in life, robots who serve as administrators did acquire from the moment of their civic naissance a birth certificate validated with a well-determined, universal goal: Justice. Not only the judiciary branch is destined to attain social justice. Dated back to Plato and Aristotle, justice is the ultimate ambition of a polity. Legislators or individuals are highly concerned if their actions align with a just behavior anticipated from citizens living in a democracy where everyone is accountable. For what reason we sidestep Administrators in this gentle endeavor?

Bureaucratic structure along with the political neutrality that we strictly expect from public servants have led to administrative inertia. One detected attempt to produce effective results has been the spoils system where political will is being transfused by Government to selected administrative staff who has pre-decided to operate legality. With robots, neither bureaucratization nor politicization are purposeful. Automation is the magic word. Without selection or psychological predisposition of the servant, the Minister gets happy: his/her political will finds its way to the citizens. Did any of you suppose that a minister's desire or attitude could somehow be unfair? Well, robots will be there to make him/her feel wiser. Still, robots will keep someone pleased: citizens. This is why on the top of my paper I stated that penetration of Robotics into the administrative function of the State for Citizenry's Benefit constitute a pre-economy (prediction of future facts) indicated by Plato in his dialogue Minos.

References

1. Meisen, T.: Robotics in Public Administration, Faculty of Mechanical Engineering RWTH Aachen University, p. 3. https://www.maschinenbau.rwth-aachen.de/global/show_document.asp?id=aaaaaaaaaaaaogsj. Accessed 16 Sept 2017
2. Meisen, T.: Robotics in Public Administration, Faculty of Mechanical Engineering RWTH Aachen University, p. 6. https://www.maschinenbau.rwth-aachen.de/global/show_document.asp?id=aaaaaaaaaaaaogsj. Accessed 16 Sept 2017
3. Coglianese, C., Lehr, D.: Regulating by Robot: Administrative Decision Making in the Machine-Learning Era, Faculty Scholarship. 1734, p. 3. http://scholarship.law.upenn.edu/faculty_scholarship/1734. Accessed 16 Sept 2017
4. Coglianese, C., Lehr, D.: Regulating by Robot: Administrative Decision Making in the Machine-Learning Era, Faculty Scholarship. 1734, p. 9. http://scholarship.law.upenn.edu/faculty_scholarship/1734. Accessed 16 Sept 2017
5. Mavrias, K., Pantelis, A.: Constitutional Texts, 4th edition. A.N. Sakkoulas, Athens-Komotini: Article 103 of the Constitution of 1975 "Civil servants are executors of the will of the State and serve the People they have faith in the Constitution and devotion to the Fatherland. The qualifications and the manner of their appointment are defined by law", p. 350 (2007)
6. Coglianese, C., Lehr, D.: Regulating by Robot: Administrative Decision Making in the Machine-Learning Era, Faculty Scholarship. 1734, (2017). http://scholarship.law.upenn.edu/faculty_scholarship/1734. Accessed 16 Sept 2017: "Sierra Club, at 334 ("The safety valves in the use of such sophisticated methodology are the requirement of public exposure of the assumptions and data incorporated into the analysis…")"

7. Coglianese, C., Lehr, D.: Regulating by Robot: Administrative Decision Making in the Machine-Learning Era, Faculty Scholarship. 1734, p. 51. (2017). http://scholarship.law.upenn.edu/faculty_scholarship/1734. Accessed 16 Sept 2017

8. Motor Veh. Mfrs. Ass'n v. State Farm Ins (1983). https://supreme.justia.com/cases/federal/us/463/29/case.html. Accessed 16 Sept 2017

9. Lytras, S.: Administrative Law (The Organization of Public Administration). A. N. Sakkoulas, Athens-Komotini, p. 67 (2004)

10. Chevallier, J.: De l'Administration Démocratique à la Démocratie Administrative, Revue Française d' Administration Publique (La démocratie administrative: Des administrés aux citoyens), No 137–138, pp. 221–222 (2011). «un pouvoir d' exigibilité»

11. Skaltsa, M.A.: Protection of the citizen as fundamental principle of the administrative action. A.N. Sakkoulas, p. 76, phrase attributed to Prof. Pr. Pavlopoulos (2007)

12. Skaltsa, M.A.: Protection of the citizen as fundamental principle of the administrative action. A.N. Sakkoulas, p. 83 (2000)

13. Coglianese, C., Lehr, D.: Regulating by Robot: Administrative Decision Making in the Machine-Learning Era, Faculty Scholarship. 1734, pp. 32–33. (2017). http://scholarship.law.upenn.edu/faculty_scholarship/1734. Accessed 16 Sept 2017

14. Eldridge, M.V.: U.S. (1976). http://law.jrank.org/pages/23685/Mathews-v-Eldridge-Due-Process-Flexible.html. Accessed 16 Sept 2017

15. Kelly, G.V.: U.S. (1970). https://www.law.cornell.edu/supremecourt/text/397/254. Accessed 16 Sept 2017

Factors Explaining ICT Expenditure Behavior of Greek Firms During the Economic Crisis 2009–2014

Spyros Arvanitis[1] and Euripidis Loukis[2(✉)] ⓘ

[1] KOF Swiss Economic Institute, ETH Zurich, Zurich, Switzerland
arvanitis@kofeth.ethz.ch
[2] Department of Information and Communication Systems Engineering,
University of the Aegean, Samos, Greece
eloukis@aegean.gr

Abstract. The financial and economic crisis of 2008 affected negatively investment in general, and investment in ICT was not left unchanged, with negative consequences for firms' future performance and competitiveness. So this paper aims at investigating factors explaining firms' crisis behavior with respect to ICT investment and ICT operational expenditures, i.e. their crisis vulnerability of ICT expenditures, for the crisis period 2009–2014. To this end, we examine the effects of six groups of factors on firms' ICT investment and expenditure behavior during the crisis 2009–2014: three groups of *internal* factors and three groups of *external factors*. We focus our analysis on the internal ICT-related factors; we need all other factors in order to be able to appropriately specify two econometric models, one for ICT investment expenditures and a second one for ICT operational expenditures, and avoid omitted variable bias. The analysis of the factors that may influence the likelihood of a reduction of ICT investment and operating expenditure as a consequence of the crisis is primarily explorative, thus driven by available data and economic intuition. Our study is based on Greek firm data from the manufacturing, construction and services sector that have been collected in 2015/2016. We find that all six groups of variables contribute significantly to the explanation of both ICT investment and ICT operational expenditures during the crisis period 2009–2014, even if not to the same extent and not for each of the two dependent variables.

Keywords: ICT investment · ICT operational expenditures · ICT technologies · Economic crisis

1 Introduction

The financial and economic crisis of 2008 affected negatively investment in general, and investment in ICT was not left unchanged, with negative consequences for firms' future performance and competitiveness (Rojko et al. 2011; Keeley and Love 2010; OECD 2009). World ICT spending fell by around 4% in 2009 (OECD 2010). Nevertheless, the decrease of ICT investment has been lower than that of GDP worldwide

© Springer International Publishing AG 2017
S.K. Katsikas and V. Zorkadis (Eds.): E-Democracy 2017, CCIS 792, pp. 255–271, 2017.
https://doi.org/10.1007/978-3-319-71117-1_18

so that the ratio of ICT investment to GDP has increased. The 2009 decline of world spending in ICT is not as large in current US dollars as in 2001-02, owing to growth in non-OECD economies and the introduction of new products (OECD 2010), two factors that helped compensate part of the reduction of expenditures in the OECD economies, particularly in the 'old' industries. Worldwide, about 57% of the 2009 ICT spending was on communication services and hardware, 21% on computer services, 13% on computer hardware and 9% on software.

The theoretical expectation for the impact of crisis on ICT investment is qualitatively the same as for all other kinds of investment. The main idea is that independent of the source of financing the general investment propensity decreases in periods of economic recession. Firms are confronted with demand uncertainty that makes investment more risky than in 'normal' or boom periods. Demand uncertainty forces firms to a pro-cyclical behavior. However, particularly in the innovation literature, an alternative approach is discussed that leads to an anti-cyclical investment behavior. According to the opportunity costs approach, in a booming economy it is expected that costs for labor and other input factors for R&D activities are high, while in recessions these costs are low (Rafferty and Funk 2004). Hence, opportunity costs are lower in recessions and firms would benefit if they could shift resources to R&D activities. It is then an empirical issue which situation for which investment type prevails.

So it is interesting and useful to investigate factors explaining firms' crisis behavior with respect to ICT investment and operational expenditures, i.e. their crisis vulnerability of ICT expenditures as shown by the extent of reduction of ICT investment and operational expenditures during the crisis period 2009–2014. This research can contribute to a better understanding of this negative phenomenon, which constitutes one of the most negative consequences of such crises, and also provide a basis for the design of appropriate interventions at firm level, in order to reduce the negative impact of such economic crises on firms' investment and expenditure for these highly important technologies. To this end, we distinguish six groups of factors that might affect ICT expenditure behavior during the crisis 2009–2014: three groups of internal factors, namely ICT-related resource endowment, ICT-related capabilities, and factors indicating overall internal problems such as over-investment in equipment and insufficient cost control, etc.; and also three groups of external factors: competition conditions in a firm's production market, conditions in a firm's broader economic environment, and macroeconomic conditions. We focus our analysis on the internal ICT-related factors. We need all other factors in order to be able to appropriately specify two econometric models, one for ICT investment expenditures and a second one for ICT operational expenditures, and to avoid omitted variable bias. The analysis of the factors that may influence the likelihood of a reduction of ICT investment and operating expenditures as a consequence of the crisis is primarily explorative, thus driven by available data and economic intuition.

Our study is based on Greek firm data from the manufacturing, construction and services sector that have been collected in 2015/2016. We find that all six groups of variables contribute significantly to the explanation of both ICT investment and ICT operational expenditures during the crisis period 2009–2014, even if not to the same extent and not for each of the two dependent variables. To our knowledge, there is no other study investigating these topics, so our paper has also the character of an explorative study in a new and highly important for management practice research field[1].

The paper is structured as follows: Sect. 2 presents the conceptual background and related literature. Section 3 discusses the data. In Sect. 4 presents the specification of the models and the research hypotheses. In Sect. 5 econometric issues and the results are presented and discussed. Section 6 concludes the paper.

2 Conceptual Background

The theoretical expectation for the impact on ICT investment is qualitatively the same as for all other kinds of investment. The main idea is that independent of the source of financing the general investment propensity decreases in periods of economic recession. Firms are confronted with demand uncertainty that makes investment more risky than in 'normal' or boom periods. Decreasing demand limits also internal financing of investment by past revenues. Uncertain economic perspectives reduce also the willingness of banks and other financial intermediaries to finance firms' investment projects. Of course, not all kinds of investment bear the same risk, with innovation projects being considered as quite risky and buildings being seen as much less risky than other investment categories (see, e.g., Kahle and Stulz 2012; Gerner and Stegmaier 2013; Geroski and Gregg 1997). Further, not all types of firms bear the same risk, with small firms being confronted with more difficulties to finance investments in recession than large firms, due to credit rationing, i.e. limited access to external funding by financial intermediates (for the theoretical background see, e.g., Stiglitz and Weiss 1981 for investment in general; Goodacre and Tonks 1995 for investment in innovation). So in general, we expect that economic crisis negatively affects ICT investment. To our knowledge, there are no studies dealing with the question of the impact of economic crisis on ICT investment and factors that affect it.[2]

As a consequence, it is not a priori clear which components of ICT-related resource endowment, e.g., such as ICT applications (ERP, CRM. SCM, etc.), Cloud Computing, or which of a series of ICT-related capabilities (see Sect. 4) might explain a firm's ICT-related behavior in an economic crisis. The analysis of the ICT-related characteristics (ICT-related resource endowment and ICT-related capabilities) that may influence the likelihood of having reduced ICT investment as a consequence of the crisis is primarily explorative, thus driven by available data and economic intuition.

We can nevertheless deduce from the analogous case of overall investment and particularly R&D investment, which overall external factors, e.g., such as competition pressure at product markets, crisis-caused unfavorable behavior of creditors, suppliers

---

[1] Some hints about ICT characteristics at firm level that are correlated with ICT-related 2008 crisis vulnerability are found in Arvanitis and Loukis (2015) for a sample of firms from the glass/ceramics/cement industry in six European countries.

[2] However, there is a paper which is worth-mentioning: In a case study, Leidner et al. (2003) found based on interviews with 20 CIOs that firms reacted both pro- and anti-cyclically to the crisis of 2000-02 depending on their short-term or long-term time-horizon.

and customers as well as unfavorable macroeconomic conditions, might affect negatively investment in ICT. There is some theoretical consent (see, e.g., Barlevy 2007)
and some empirical evidence (see, e.g., Quyang 2011a and Guellec and Ioannidis 1999)
that R&D investment expenditures of firms, the most important input for innovation,
are pro-cyclical, i.e. they are increasing in the business upswing and they are
decreasing in the business downturn. However, there are also some theoretical arguments as well as some anecdotic evidence that firms show an anti-cyclical R&D
investment behaviour. In order to explain pro- or anti-cyclical R&D behaviour we have
to take into account two diverging forces, the demand aspect (see Filippetti and
Archibugi 2011) and the opportunity costs aspect (Rafferty and Funk 2004). Since
R&D investment and analogously ICT investment are predominantly financed through
the cash-flow of a firm, which is expected to fluctuate pro-cyclically with demand, we
would expect a pro-cyclical R&D – and analogously – ICT investment behaviour as
well. Since empirical evidence supports mostly pro-cyclical behaviour we concentrate
here on the hypothesis of pro-cyclical behaviour with respect to ICT investment (see
hypothesis 4).

3   Data

3.1   Sampling

The 'universe' of Greek firms as conceived in this study is given by the original sample
of ICAP (a well-known large Greek business service enterprise) of 6429 firms. To our
knowledge, there is no other source for firm data in Greece that is publicly available.
Our intermediate sample was constructed based on the composition by industry of the
original sample reduced by reducing by about 50% the total number of firms; the firms
for each industry sub-sample were chosen randomly out of the original sample. The
questionnaire was sent to 3308 firms of the intermediate sample, 363 valid answers
have been received, i.e. the response rate is about 11%.

Already the original sample is not representative of the composition of Greek firms
by industry. The Greek economy contains thousands of small and very small enterprises in trade, particularly retail trade, tourism, particularly in catering, and in construction. The ICAP sample concentrates in manufacturing (30.7% of all firms in
sample) and some modern service industries (computer services, business services and
transport/communication; 21.5% of service firms), still keeping a high percentage of
trade and tourism firms (78.5% of service firms). As a consequence, also the intermediate sample contains similar proportions of firms from different industries. For the
response sample we (further) concentrate in manufacturing (40.2% of all firms in
sample) and modern services (27.4%). This structure corresponds to the technologically most developed part of the Greek economy to which we focus in this study. Our
particular interest refers to the ICT-related crisis vulnerability of this part of the Greek
economy, which is also most promising with respect to a recovery from the crisis.

3.2   ICT-Related Crisis Vulnerability

Table 1 shows how frequent each of the six possible values of our two dependent variables, the change of ICT investment expenditures and the change of ICT operational expenditure, have been reported by the firms of our sample: 58.4% of them reported 'small decrease' up to 'very large decrease' of ICT investment, while 62.8% 'small decrease' up to 'very large decrease' of ICT operational expenditures. More than one fifth reported large or very large decrease in both expenditure categories. These figures reflect clearly the impact of the crisis (pro-cyclical behaviour), but it is remarkable that still 41.6% (for ICT investment) and 37.7% (for ICT operational expenditures) reported 'no impact' or even increase. This could be interpreted as a hint that a considerable portion of firms in the sample showed significant robustness of behaviour and refrained from reducing their ICT budgets. An increase of expenditures is found only for 1.6% (investment) and 8.2% (operational expenditures). Only a small minority of firms could afford anti-cyclical behaviour during such a long-enduring crisis.

Table 1. Impact of crisis 2009–2014 on ICT investment and operational expenditures; percentage of all firms

Impact	Investment expenditures	Operational expenditures
Increase	11.6	8.2
No impact	30.0	29.5
Small decrease	15.5	21.3
Medium decrease	20.7	18.8
Large decrease	15.5	16.1
Very large decrease	6.7	6.1

4   Model Specification and Research Hypotheses

4.1   Model Specification

As dependent variable we use a six-level ordinal variable that measures the extent of change of ICT investment (for model 1) and the extent of change of ICT operational expenditures (for model 2) during the long crisis period 2009–2014. This variable is considered to measure crisis vulnerability: the stronger the decrease of ICT investment and/or ICT operational expenditures due to crisis, the higher is a firm's ICT-related crisis vulnerability.

We distinguish six groups of factors that might affect ICT investment and operating expenditure behavior during the crisis 2009–2014: three groups of *internal* factors: ICT-related *resource endowment* (six variables), ICT-related *capabilities* (six variables), and factors indicating overall internal problems such as over-investment in equipment and insufficient cost control, etc. (one composite variable); and also three groups of *external factors*: one referring to the *competition conditions* in a firm's production market (three variables), a second one covering conditions in a firm's *broader economic environment* such as such as *behavior of banks, providers, competitors and customers* (one composite variable) and a third one related to *macroeconomic conditions* (overall development of domestic and foreign demand, price reduction, etc.; one composite variable).

ICT-related endowment. Besides the use of a series of ICT applications (ERP, CRM, SCM, Business Intelligence/Business Analytics Systems, and Collaboration Support Systems) and the share of ICT personnel belong to ICT-related resource endowment, even if indirectly, also the overall employee qualification level (as measured by the share of employees with tertiary-level education), the existence of R&D (as measure of innovation capability), which is closely positively associated to ICT use (see, e.g., Arvanitis et al. 2016), and new forms of workplace organization, particularly decentralization of decision-making, which correlates strongly with the existence of high-qualified personnel (see, e.g., Arvanitis 2005).

ICT-related capabilities. In accordance to relevant information systems literature firms in order to exploit ICT for supporting their activities develop not only their ICT resources endowment, but also relevant ICT capabilities, enabling them to fully exploit their ICT resources (Ravichandran and Lertwongsatien 2005; Gu and Jung 2013). So we also examine the effects of six important and widely cited in relevant literature ICT capabilities on firms' ICT investment and ICT operating expenses vulnerability: for rapid implementation of changes of existing applications or information systems to cover specific firm needs; rapid development of new ICT applications to cover specific firm needs; rapid realization of interconnection and integration of existing ICT applications inside the firm; good cooperation and information exchange between ICT personnel and ICT users inside the firm; good cooperation and information exchange with ICT providers of hardware, software and networks; development of ICT plans that are connected with overall firm strategy. We expect that they might decrease ICT investment and ICT operating expenses vulnerability.

Overall internal problems. Insufficient control of costs, over-investment in equipment, buildings and/or storage capacity as well as over-expansion due to takeovers and mergers (before the observed crisis period) might increase a firm's overall crisis vulnerability and as a consequence also its vulnerability as to ICT investment and ICT operational expenditures.

Competition conditions. Depending on the specific firm behaviour the relationship between ICT investment and competition pressure would be positive during a crisis, if a firm reacts anti-cyclical to crisis, which is mostly the case, or negative, if the firm reacts pro-cyclical (see Arvanitis and Woerter 2014). Thus, for the assumed pro-cyclical behaviour we expect that increased (price and non-price) competition pressure would increase crisis vulnerability with respect to ICT investment and ICT operational expenditures.

Broad economic environment. Decrease of credit limits by banks and suppliers as well as decrease of paying willingness of customers and increased competition pressure at the product market are typical crisis phenomena that are supposed to affect negatively also ICT investment and ICT operational expenditures.

Macroeconomic conditions. Decrease of overall domestic private or public demand and/or foreign demand is constitutive to the notion of economic crisis. Also decrease of prices is often result of decreasing overall demand. We expect decrease of demand to affect negatively also ICT investment and ICT operational expenditures.

We estimated Model 1 (for ICT investment expenditures) and Model 2 (for ICT operational expenditures), which are identically specified and are formally expressed as follows – in the Appendix we can see all variables definitions:

$$ICT\_CRISIS_i = \alpha_0 + \alpha_1 R\&D_i + \alpha_2 HQUAL_i + \alpha_3 ICT\_PERS_i + \alpha_4 ICT\_TECHN_i + \alpha_5 \quad CLOUD_i + \alpha_6 \quad ORG_i + \alpha_7 \quad ICT\_CAP\_NEW_i + \alpha_8 \quad ICT\_DEVELOP_i + \alpha_9 ICT\_CAP\_INTERCON_i + \alpha_{10} ICT\_CAP\_COOP\_INT_i + \alpha_{11} ICT\_CAP\_COOP\_EXT_i + \alpha_{12} ICT\_CAP\_ICT\_PLANS_i + \alpha_{13} INTERNAL_i + \alpha_{14} P\_COMPET_i + \alpha_{15} NP\_COMPET_i + \alpha_{16} OBSOLESCENCE_i + \alpha_{17} MARKET_i + \alpha_{18} MACRO_i + \alpha_{19} LAGE_i + \alpha_{20} Medium\text{-}sized_i + \alpha_{21} Large_i + industry\ controls + e_i$$

4.2 Research Hypotheses

Based on the discussion of literature in Sect. 2 and in this section, we postulate a series of hypotheses:

Hypothesis 1: The six components of ICT-related resource endowment as specified for both models 1 and 2 are jointly negatively correlated with ICT-related crisis vulnerability.

Hypothesis 2: The six components of ICT-related capabilities as specified for both models 1 and 2 are jointly negatively correlated with ICT-related crisis vulnerability.

Hypothesis 3: The composite variable for overall internal factors as specified for both models 1 and 2 is positively correlated with ICT-related crisis vulnerability.

Hypothesis 4: The variables for competition conditions as specified for both models 1 and 2 are jointly positively correlated with ICT-related crisis vulnerability, given pro-cyclical investment behavior.

Hypothesis 5: The composite variable for conditions of a firm's broad economic environment as specified for both models 1 and 2 is positively correlated with ICT-related crisis vulnerability.

Hypothesis 6: The composite variable for macroeconomic conditions as specified for both models 1 and 2 is positively correlated with ICT-related crisis vulnerability.

5 Results

5.1 Econometric Issues

The dependent variable is a six-level ordinal variable. The dependent variable refers to the extent of the change of ICT investment and ICT operational expenditures for the long period 2009–2014. Given the nature of the dependent variable, the appropriate estimation method is ordered probit regression ('oprobit' procedure of STATA).

The independent variables that refer to internal factors are measured either for 2014 (metric variables) or for the period 2012–2014 (ordinal variables), with the exception of overall internal problems that are explicitly related to the time before 2009 (see Appendix). Thus, they reflect a firm's condition at the end and not at the beginning of the observed crisis period. Thus, they could have been affected by the crisis and could reflect a firm's adaptation to the crisis. In this sense they are endogenous. Nevertheless, we have good reasons to consider them as structural factors that would have not changed considerably during the crisis, just because they are factors that could be expected to reduce crisis vulnerability (e.g., ICT capabilities, ICT and human capital endowment, existence of R&D activities).

We also have good reasons to assume that competition conditions at the product market are also of structural nature. We cannot exclude that the overall competition pressure became stronger during the crisis period, but with only small shifts as to the relative strength of competition pressure at different markets.[3]

The endogeneity issue is less a problem in the case of the external factors, which are explicitly reported in the survey as factors that could have affected a firm's economic activities before or during the observed crisis period (see Appendix), thus reflecting factors that could have directly affected crisis vulnerability with respect to ICT investment and ICT operational expenditures.

The problem of possible observed heterogeneity still remains, even if we control extensively for many possible explaining factors as well as for 10 digit industries and 3 firm size classes. For these reasons no claims are made for causality effects but only for conditional correlation effects that might yield useful insights for possible causality effects in accordance with our research hypotheses.

5.2   Estimates for ICT Investment Expenditures

The estimates for the change of ICT investment expenditures (model 1) are presented in Table 2. The six estimated equations show values of Pseudo R^2 between 0.127 and 0.133 that are rather low but still satisfactory for cross-section micro data analysis. Moreover, the high significance of Wald chi2 statistics demonstrates the overall statistical validity of the estimates.

Resource endowment. The existence of R&D activities, the (overall or ICT specific) personnel qualification, and the use of standard ICT applications such as ERP, SCM, CRM, Business Analytics, and Collaboration Support Systems do not seem to be significantly correlated with crisis vulnerability. Negatively correlated with crisis vulnerability appear to be two further components of resource endowment, namely the use of new forms of workplace organization (such as teamwork and decentralization) and the use of Cloud Computing. Obviously these two resources increase a firm's flexibility to react to crisis, given the level of personnel qualification and of use of standard ICT applications, reducing the negative impacts of the crisis on it.

---

[3] There is no information about significant structural changes of the Greek economy as a whole. For single markets, e.g., retail trade and construction, the high number of bankruptcies in the last years indicates a concentration process that rather enhances competition pressure.

Table 2. Factors explaining crisis behavior with respect to ICT investment expenditures

	(1)	(2)	(3)	(4)	(5)	(6)
R&D	0.032	0.031	0.044	0.066	0.033	0.042
	(0.141)	(0.141)	(0.141)	(0.140)	(0.142)	(0.143)
HQUAL	0.455	0.446	0.459	0.495*	0.451	0.494*
	(0.297)	(0.299)	(0.294)	(0.290)	(0.297)	(0.297)
ICT_PERS	−0.114	−0.159	−0.044	−0.057	−0.155	−0.104
	(0.434)	(0.444)	(0.438)	(0.435)	(0.440)	(0.443)
ORG	−0.269**	−0.274**	−0.281**	−0.287**	−0.283**	−0.253*
	(0.137)	(0.138)	(0.135)	(0.135)	(0.136)	(0.136)
ICT_TECHN	−0.058	−0.075	−0.050	−0.038	−0.069	−0.028
	(0.067)	(0.069)	(0.067)	(0.067)	(0.069)	(0.073)
CLOUD	−0.339**	−0.346**	−0.335**	−0.311**	−0.337**	−0.348**
	(0.156)	(0.158)	(0.156)	(0.157)	(0.157)	(0.156)
ICT_CAP_NEW	−0.073					
	(0.061)					
ICT_CAP_DEVELOP		−0.029				
		(0.060)				
ICT_CAP_INTERCON			−0.099*			
			(0.060)			
ICT_CAP_COOP_INT				−0.157**		
				(0.064)		
ICT_CAP_COOP_EXT					−0.042	
					(0.062)	
ICT_CAP_ICT_PLANS						−0.117*
						(0.052)
P_COMPET	−0.040	−0.040	−0.039	−0.047	−0.042	−0.060
	(0.070)	(0.070)	(0.070)	(0.070)	(0.070)	(0.069)
NP_COMPET	0.030	0.035	0.028	0.020	0.035	0.042
	(0.075)	(0.074)	(0.074)	(0.076)	(0.075)	(0.075)
OBSOLESCENCE	0.150**	0.153**	0.156**	0.138**	0.149**	0.141**
	(0.067)	(0.067)	(0.068)	(0.068)	(0.068)	(0.068)
INTERNAL	0.049	0.049	0.057	0.045	0.040	0.040
	(0.082)	(0.082)	(0.083)	(0.083)	(0.082)	(0.082)
MARKET	0.317***	0.316***	0.314***	0.326***	0.318***	0.308***
	(0.091)	(0.092)	(0.090)	(0.091)	(0.092)	(0.091)
MACRO	0.488***	0.488***	0.481***	0.471***	0.487***	0.497***
	(0.093)	(0.092)	(0.092)	(0.092)	(0.093)	(0.093)
LAGE	−3.483	−3.064	−3.431	−3.339	−3.345	−3.012
	(5.447)	(5.363)	(5.458)	(5.311)	(5.317)	(5.327)
Medium-sized	0.132	0.101	0.142	0.182	0.104	0.157
	(0.145)	(0.145)	(0.147)	(0.148)	(0.147)	(0.145)

(continued)

Table 2. (*continued*)

	(1)	(2)	(3)	(4)	(5)	(6)
Large	0.482*	0.432*	0.480*	0.568**	0.447*	0.531**
	(0.265)	(0.261)	(0.261)	(0.269)	(0.267)	(0.260)
Industry dummies (9)	Yes	Yes	Yes	Yes	Yes	Yes
N	292	292	292	292	292	292
Pseudo R^2	0.128	0.127	0.130	0.133	0.127	0.130
Wald Chi2	175.8	179.0	176.4	184.6	174.0	173.3
Prob > chi2	0.000	0.000	0.000	0.000	0.000	0.000
Log pseudolikelihood	−431.9	−432.5	−431.1	−429.4	−432.5	−431.0

Note: Ordered Probit estimates; five constants are not shown; heteroscedasticity-robust standard errors in brackets; *, ** and *** denote statistical significance at the 10%-, 5% and 1%-test level, respectively.

Furthermore, these new forms of workplace organization enable the generation of more value from firm's ICT investment; the same holds for the use of Cloud Computing, which enables some standardized and commoditized ICT components to be accessed through external cloud computing services, so that ICT investment can focus on some highly valuable firm-specific as well as operation critical components. This decreases a firm's propensity to reduce ICT investment as a response to the crisis. Thus, the introduction of new forms of workplace organization and Cloud Computing contribute to a weaker ICT-related impact of crisis, i.e. to a reduction of ICT-related crisis vulnerability. The joint effect of all components of resource endowment is significantly negative, even if this effect is traced back to only two single factors. Thus, *hypothesis 1* is confirmed.

Capabilities: Weakening of the crisis effect is achieved through capabilities for high interconnection/integration of the used ICT-systems, intensive cooperation internally, and existence of a comprehensive ICT strategy (ICT plans). These capabilities contribute to a higher flexibility of firm activities, which is particularly relevant in order to be able to react adequately to crisis, and reduce its negative impact on the firm. Furthermore, the above ICT capabilities enable the generation of more value from firm's ICT investment, so they decrease firm's propensity to reduce ICT investment as a response to the crisis. Also in this case the joint effect of all capabilities is significantly negative, thus *hypothesis 2* receives empirical support.

Overall internal problems. Insufficient cost controls, over-investment in equipment, buildings or storage capacity or over-expansion by takeovers or mergers are not significantly correlated with ICT-related crisis vulnerability. *Hypothesis 3* is not confirmed.

Competition conditions: No effect of price or non-price pressure is found. Competition pressure is in general low in most sectors of the Greek economy (see, e.g., Arvanitis and Loukis 2009). There is a weakening effect of crisis in case of high obsolescence rate of products/services and/or their technologies: if firm's products, services and/or their technologies become quickly obsolete, the firm has to maintain some level of ICT investment for supporting their renewal. Once more the joint effect shows in the expected direction. *Hypothesis 4* is also confirmed.

As expected, macroeconomic effects, but also effects of other market actors (behavior due to crisis of suppliers, financing agencies, competitors, customers, etc.), enhance crisis vulnerability. Overall unfavorable economic conditions and unfavorable behavior of market environment are factors that affect negatively investment behavior of firms in general, even if not all firms to the same extent. Thus, *hypothesis 5* and *hypothesis 6* are confirmed. Finally, large firms seem to be more crisis-vulnerable than medium-sized and small firms, presumably due to higher operation flexibility of smaller firms.

5.3   Estimates for ICT Operational Expenditures

The estimates for the change of ICT operational expenditures (model 2) are presented in Table 3. The six estimated equations show values of Pseudo R^2 between 0.115 and 0.121 are somewhat lower than in the estimates in Table 2, but still satisfactory for cross-section micro data analysis. Moreover, the high significance of Wald chi2 statistics demonstrates the overall statistical validity of the estimates.

Table 3. Factors explaining crisis behavior with respect ICT operational expenditures

	(1)	(2)	(3)	(4)	(5)	(6)
R&D	0.006	0.008	0.018	0.039	0.011	0.015
	(0.138)	(0.138)	(0.138)	(0.137)	(0.140)	(0.142)
HQUAL	0.406	0.383	0.404	0.432	0.392	0.434
	(0.280)	(0.281)	(0.279)	(0.277)	(0.281)	(0.283)
ICT_PERS	−0.081	−0.159	−0.095	−0.106	−0.159	−0.163
	(0.419)	(0.425)	(0.426)	(0.435)	(0.429)	(0.434)
ORG	−0.287**	−0.291**	−0.311**	−0.318**	−0.317**	−0.283**
	(0.134)	(0.135)	(0.132)	(0.131)	(0.133)	(0.133)
ICT_TECHN	−0.030	−0.063	−0.046	−0.036	−0.049	−0.028
	(0.064)	(0.064)	(0.064)	(0.064)	(0.066)	(0.071)
CLOUD	−0.326**	−0.337**	−0.332**	−0.308*	−0.314**	−0.345**
	(0.157)	(0.159)	(0.157)	(0.159)	(0.159)	(0.157)
ICT_CAP_NEW	−0.157***					
	(0.061)					
ICT_CAP_DEVELOP		−0.082				
		(0.057)				
ICT_CAP_INTERCON			−0.106*			
			(0.060)			
ICT_CAP_COOP_INT				−0.162***		
				(0.061)		
ICT_CAP_COOP_EXT					−0.106	
					(0.067)	

(continued)

Table 3. (*continued*)

	(1)	(2)	(3)	(4)	(5)	(6)
ICT_CAP_ICT_PLANS						−0.112*
						(0.067)
INTERNAL	0.266***	0.266***	0.268***	0.255***	0.243***	0.250***
	(0.083)	(0.084)	(0.085)	(0.084)	(0.083)	(0.084)
P_COMPET	−0.120*	−0.121*	−0.119*	−0.128*	−0.126*	−0.139**
	(0.069)	(0.070)	(0.070)	(0.070)	(0.069)	(0.068)
NP_COMPET	0.005	0.005	−0.001	−0.010	0.004	0.013
	(0.073)	(0.072)	(0.073)	(0.075)	(0.075)	(0.073)
OBSOLESCENCE	0.082	0.090	0.070	0.072	0.079	0.074
	(0.071)	(0.070)	(0.090)	(0.069)	(0.069)	(0.070)
MARKET	0.056	0.052	0.056	0.068	0.060	0.051
	(0.089)	(0.092)	(0.089)	(0.091)	(0.091)	(0.090)
MACRO	0.540***	0.536***	0.526***	0.516***	0.534***	0.542***
	(0.094)	(0.093)	(0.093)	(0.093)	(0.095)	(0.095)
LAGE	−3.399	−4.140	−4.076	−4.262	-3.511	-4.502
	(5.881)	(5.729)	(5.821)	(5.607)	(5.705)	(5.662)
Medium-sized	0.038	−0.014	−0.002	0.036	−0.013	0.001
	(0.148)	(0.146)	(0.149)	(0.148)	(0.147)	(0.146)
Large	0.415*	0.321	0.336	0.420*	0.355	0.378*
	(0.225)	(0.220)	(0.221)	(0.226)	(0.228)	(0.217)
Industry dummies (9)	Yes	Yes	Yes	Yes	Yes	Yes
N	292	292	292	292	292	292
Pseudo R^2	0.121	0.115	0.117	0.120	0.116	0.116
Wald Chi2	143.5	142.4	141.6	152.2	133.3	133.4
Prob > chi2	0.000	0.000	0.000	0.000	0.000	0.000
Log pseudolikelihood	−429.7	−432.4	−431.7	−429.9	−432.0	−431.9

Note: Ordered Probit estimates; five constants are not shown; heteroscedasticity-robust standard errors in brackets; *, ** and *** denote statistical significance at the 10%-, 5% and 1%-test level, respectively.

We concentrate here on the differences as compared with the results presented in 5.2:

Resources: There are no differences from these results for the change of ICT investment expenditure. *Hypothesis 1* is confirmed.

Capabilities. In addition to the ability for interconnection/integration of ICT-systems, for internal cooperation and for a comprehensive ICT strategy, also the capability for development of new ICT-applications contributes to a smoothening of crisis **vulnerability** with respect to ICT operational expenditures. *Hypothesis 2* is also confirmed.

Overall internal problems. Insufficient cost controls, over-investment in equipment, buildings or storage capacity and/or over-expansion by takeovers or mergers are positively correlated **with** ICT-related crisis vulnerability. This means that over-investment, over-expansion and/or insufficient cost control increase crisis vulnerability with respect to operational ICT expenditures. *Hypothesis 3* is confirmed in this case.

Competition conditions: Price competition matters, the more price competition a firm is exposed, the **lower** is its ICT crisis vulnerability, which is contrary to our theoretical expectation (see hypothesis 4); a possible explanation is that price competition puts a pressure for reducing overall operating costs, and this does not allow reductions in ICT operating costs that contribute significantly to this (e.g., through automation or support of important activities or business processes). Obsolescence does not matter for operational costs. *Hypothesis 4* is not confirmed in this case.

The behavior of other market partners is – contrary to the results for ICT investment – not relevant for operational costs. Unfavorable behavior of other market actors do not affect crisis vulnerability with respect to operational ICT costs. Thus, *hypothesis 5* is not confirmed. Macroeconomic conditions are also for operational costs relevant, i.e. they increase crisis vulnerability. As a consequence only *hypothesis 6* is confirmed.

Large firms seem to be more crisis-vulnerable than smaller firms also with respect to ICT operational expenditures, but to a smaller extent than investment expenditures.

All in all, for both ICT investment and operational expenditures resource endowment seems to be less important with respect to crisis vulnerability than ICT capabilities and general environment factors.

6   Summary and Conclusions

It is interesting and useful to investigate factors explaining crisis behavior with respect to ICT investment and operational expenditures, i.e. crisis vulnerability of ICT expenditures as shown by the extent of reduction of ICT investment and operational expenditures during the crisis period 2009–2014. To this end, we distinguish six groups of factors that might affect ICT expenditure behavior during the crisis 2009–2014: three groups of *internal* factors, namely ICT-related *resource endowment*, ICT-related *capabilities*, and factors indicating overall internal problems, such as over-investment in equipment and insufficient cost control, etc.; and three groups of *external factors: competition conditions* in a firm's production market, conditions in a firm's *broader economic environment*, and *macroeconomic conditions*. We focus our analysis on the internal ICT-related factors. We need all other factors in order to be able to appropriately specify two econometric models, one for ICT investment expenditures and a second one for ICT operational expenditures, and avoid omitted variable bias.

We have found for ICT investment expenditures that the use of new forms of workplace organization and the use of Cloud Computing as ICT-related *resources* contribute to a weaker impact of crisis, i.e. to a reduction of ICT-related crisis vulnerability by increasing a firm's flexibility to react to crisis, given the level of personnel qualification and of use of standard ICT applications, reducing the negative impacts of the crisis on the firm. The joint effect of all components of resource endowment is significantly negative, even if this effect is traced back to only two single factors. Thus, *hypothesis 1* is confirmed. This hypothesis is also confirmed for ICT operational expenditures.

Further, weakening of the crisis effect is achieved through a firm's high capabilities for interconnection/integration of the used ICT-systems, intensive cooperation and information exchange internally, and the existence of a comprehensive ICT strategy (ICT plans). These capabilities also contribute to a higher flexibility of firm activities, which is particularly relevant in order to be able to react adequately to crisis, and reduce the negative impact of it. Furthermore, these ICT capabilities enable the generation of more value from firm's ICT investment, so they decrease firm's propensity to reduce it as a response to the crisis. For ICT operational expenditures an additional effect is found for the capability to develop new ICT-applications. Also in this case the joint effect of all capabilities is significantly negative, thus *hypothesis 2* receives empirical support also for ICT operational expenditures. *Hypothesis 3* referring to insufficient cost control, over-investment and/or over-expansion before 2009 is not confirmed for ICT investment expenditures, but confirmed for ICT operational expenditures.

The effect of competition conditions is ambiguous. Obsolescence of products and services is positively correlated with crisis vulnerability with respect to ICT investment but not with respect to ICT operational expenditures. Price competition pressure is negatively correlated with vulnerability for ICT operational expenditures but not for ICT investment. Thus, *hypothesis 4* is only partly confirmed.

Hypothesis 5 is confirmed for ICT investment but not for operational expenditures; *hypothesis 6* is confirmed for both expenditure categories.

On the whole, our analysis yields some new insights, first, about the firm characteristics, particularly ICT-related characteristics, and, second, about the characteristics of a firm's economic environment that contribute to a weakening or enhancing of a firm's crisis vulnerability concerning ICT expenditures. Given that ICT constitute a growth-determining factor of increasing importance and that economic crises are an inevitable trait of market-based economies, it is not only for Greek firms relevant to know which factors could enable them to become more resistant to crisis, when the next crisis comes.

Appendix. Definition of Variables

Variable	Definition
Dependent variables	
Impact of crisis 2009–2014 on ICT *investment* expenditures	Six-level ordinal variable; 1: 'increase'; 6: 'very large decrease'; see also Table 2
Impact of crisis 2009–2014 on ICT *operational* expenditures	Six-level ordinal variable; 1: 'increase'; 6: 'very large decrease'; see also Table 2
Independent variables	
ICT-related resource endowment	
R&D	R&D activities in the period 2012-2014: yes/no; binary variable
HQUAL	Share of employees with tertiary-level education 2014

(continued)

(*continued*)

Variable	Definition
ICT_PERS	Share of ICT-specialized personnel 2014
ORG	Use of new forms of workplace organization such as teams, job rotation, decentralization of decision making, etc.
ICT_TECHN	Average use intensity of the following ICT applications: ERP, CRM, SCM, Business Intelligence/Business Analytics System, Collaboration Support system; intensity use is measured on a five-point Likert scale (1: 'no use'; 5: 'very intensive use')
CLOUD	Use of cloud computing: yes/no; binary variable
ICT-related capabilities	
ICT_CAP_NEW	Rapid implementation of changes of the applications of existing information systems to cover specific firm needs
ICT_CAP_DEVELOP	Rapid development of new ICT applications to cover specific firm needs
ICT_CAP_INTERCON	Rapid realization of interconnection and integration of existing ICT applications inside the firm
ICT_CAP_COOP_INT	Good cooperation and information exchange between ICT personnel and ICT users inside the firm
ICT_CAP_COOP_EXT	Good cooperation and information exchange with ICT providers of hardware, software and networks)
ICT_CAP_ICT_PLANS	Existence of ICT plans that are connected with overall firm strategy (ICT business alignment)
Overall internal problems	
INTERNAL	Average of the scores on a five-point Likert scale of the following three single factors that could be considered as sources/causes of firm problems in the period 2009–2014: insufficient cost control; over-investment in equipment, buildings and storage capacity; over-expansion by takeovers, mergers, etc.
Competition conditions	
P_COMPET	Intensity of price competition at the product market; five-level ordinal variable: 1 'very small'; 5; 'very strong'
NP_COMPET	Intensity of non-price competition at the product market; five-level ordinal variable: 1 'very small'; 5; 'very strong'
OBSOLESCENCE	Average of the scores on a five-point Likert scale of the two single factors concerning the extent to which firm's products and services quickly become obsolete/outdated, and also their technologies change quickly

(*continued*)

(continued)

Variable	Definition
Broad economic environment	
MARKET	Average of the scores on a five-point Likert scale for the following four single factors that could be considered as sources/causes of firm problems in the period 2009–2014: decrease of credit limits by banks; by providers; decrease of paying willingness of customers; increase of competition pressure at the product market (1: 'not relevant; 5: 'very relevant')
Macroeconomic conditions	
MACRO	Average of the scores on a five-point Likert scale for the following four single factors that could be considered as sources/causes of firm problems in the period 2009–2014: decrease of domestic private demand, demand of the state; of foreign demand; decrease of product and service prices (1: 'not relevant; 5: 'very relevant')
LAGE	Natural logarithm of firm age (2015 minus foundation year)
Medium-sized	50 to 149 employees; binary variable
Large	250 and more variables

Note: The capability variables ICT_CAP_NEW to ICT_CAP_ICT_PLANS are ordinal variables measured on five-point Likert scale (1: '(available) to a very small extent/not at all'; 5: '(available) to a very large extent').

References

Arvanitis, S.: Modes of labour flexibility at firm level: are there any implications for performance and innovation? evidence for the swiss economy. Ind. Corp. Change **14**(6), 1–24 (2005)

Arvanitis, S., Loukis, E.: Information and communication technologies, human capital, workplace organization and labour productivity in Greece and switzerland: a comparative study based on firm-level data. Inf. Econ. Policy **21**(1), 43–61 (2009)

Arvanitis, S., Loukis, E.: Did the reduction of ICT Investment Due to the 2008 Economic Crisis Affect the Innovation Performance of Firms? An Exploratory Analysis Based on Firm Data for the European Glass, Ceramics, and Cement Industry. KOF Working Papers No. 391, Zurich (2015)

Arvanitis, S., Loukis, E., Diamantopoulou, V.: Are ICT, workplace organization and human capital relevant for innovation? a comparative Swiss/Greek study. Int. J. Econ. Bus. **23**(3), 319–349 (2016)

Arvanitis, S., Woerter, M.: Firm characteristics and the cyclicality of R&D investments. Ind. Corp. Change **23**(5), 1141–1169 (2014)

Barlevy, G.: On the cyclicality of research and development. Am. Econ. Rev. **97**(4), 1131–1164 (2007)

Filippetti, A., Archibugi, D.: Innovation in times of crisis: national systems of innovation, structure, and demand. Res. Policy **40**, 179–192 (2011)

Gerner, H.D., Stegmaier, J.: Investitionen in der Krise? Eine empirische Analyse zum Einfluss der Finanz- und Wirtschaftskrise 2008/2009 auf Investitionsanpassungen. Schmollers Jahrbuch **133**, 67–96 (2013)

Geroski, P.A., Gregg, P.: Coping with Recession – UK Company Performance in Adversity. Cambridge University Press, Cambridge (1997)

Goodacre, A., Tonks, I.: Finance and Technological Change. In: Stoneman, P. (ed.) Handbook of the Economics of Innovation and Technological Change. Harvester, New York (1995)

Gu, J.W., Jung, H.W.: The effects of IS resources, capabilities, and qualities on organizational performance: an integrated approach. Inf. Manag. **50**(2–3), 87–97 (2013)

Guellec, D., Ioannidis, E.: Causes of Fluctuations in R&D Expenditures: A Quantitative Analysis. OECD Business Studies No. 29, (1999)

Kahle, K.M., Stulz, R.M.: Access to Capital, Investment, and the Financial Crisis. Fisher College of Business Working Paper No. 2012-2 (2012)

Keeley, B., Love, P.: From Crisis to Recovery – The Causes, Course and Consequences of the Great Recession. OECD, Paris (2010)

Leidner, D.E., Beatry, R.C., Mackay, J.M.: How CIOS manage IT during economic decline: surviving and thriving amid uncertainty. MIS Q. Executive **2**(1), 1–14 (2003)

OECD: The Impact of the Crisis on ICTs and Their Role in the Recovery. OECD Publishing, Paris (2009)

OECD: Recent Developments and Outlook. In: OECD Information Technology Outlook 2010, OECD Publishing, Paris (2010)

Ouyang, M.: On the cyclicality of R&D. Rev. Econ. Stat. **93**(2), 542–553 (2011)

Rafferty, M., Funk, M.: The effect of demand shocks on firm-financed R&D. Res. Economics **58**, 187–203 (2004)

Ravichandran, T., Lertwongsatien, C.: Effect of information system resources and capabilities on firm performance: a resource-based perspective. J. Manag. Inform. Syst. **21**(4), 237–276 (2005)

Rojko, K., Lesjak, D., Vehovar, V.: Information Communication Technology Spending in (2008-) Economic Crisis. Ind. Manag. Data Syst. **111**(3), 391–409 (2011)

Stiglitz, J.E., Weiss, A.: Credit rationing in markets with imperfect information. Am. Econ. Rev. **71**, 393–410 (1981)

Author Index

Printed in the United States
By Bookmasters